CRITICAL CINEMA

CRITICAL CINEMA

BEYOND THE THEORY OF PRACTICE

edited by Clive Myer

with a foreword by Bill Nichols

 WALLFLOWER PRESS
LONDON & NEW YORK

FOR LYNDA

Above the sea
a rainbow, erased by
a flock of swallows

TAKARAI KIKAKU (1661–1707)

A Wallflower Book
Published by
Columbia University Press
Publishers Since 1893
New York • Chichester, West Sussex
cup.columbia.edu

A complete CIP record is available from the Library of Congress

ISBN 978-1-906660-37-6 (cloth. : alk. paper)
ISBN 978-1-906660-36-9 (pbk. : alk. paper)
ISBN 978-0-231-50456-0 (e-book)

Book design by Elsa Mathern

∞

Columbia University Press books are printed on permanent
and durable acid-free paper.
This book is printed on paper with recycled content.
Printed in the United States of America

c 10 9 8 7 6 5 4 3 2 1
p 10 9 8 7 6 5 4 3 2 1

CONTENTS

PART TWO: CONVERSATIONS

ACKNOWLEDGEMENTS

This book is indebted to all those filmmakers, film tutors and film students who care about the relationship between theory and practice and who have an inkling that the way, what, where, how and why we make films interlinks with the way we live our lives and the values we bring to them.

I would like to thank colleagues who gave papers and presentations at the inaugural conference of the Film Academy in Cardiff in 2003 *BEYOND the Theory of Practice* and who inspired this book: John Adams, Joan Ashworth, Desmond Bell, Dave Berry, Noel Burch, Richard Butt, Michael Chanan, Mary M. Dalton, Patrick Fuery, Coral Houtman, Brett Ingram, Igor Koršič, Ian Macdonald, Laura Mulvey, Suzanne Regan, Angus Reid, Chris Rodrigues, Michele Ryan, Aparna Sharma, Michael Stewart, Rod Stoneman, David Surnam, Zuzana Gindi Tatárová, Ernie Tee, Clive Walley, Brian Winston, Peter Wollen, Jan Worth and Peter Wyeth, as well as those who attended the event over the three days. Special thanks to the Project Manager of the Film Academy Rebecca Davies.

My thanks also go to the conference sponsors CILECT (with special thanks to Igor Koršič), NAHEMI (with special thanks to Yossi Bal), the British Academy, Berwyn Rowlands and his former colleagues at Sgrîn (now the Film Agency for Wales) and the University of Glamorgan.

Chapter 1 of this book began as component of a part-time PhD at the Royal College of Art between 2000 and 2008 and I would like to thank my supervisors A. L. Rees and Professor Jorem Ten Brink for their guidance as well as my external examiners Professors Michael Chanan and Desmond Bell for their perceptive comments. In particular I would like to thank my family; Lynda, Lucy, Mike, Barney, Dorothea and George who tolerated my absence while simultaneously making films, setting up film schools, writing a PhD and editing a book!

Special thanks to Martin O'Shaughnessy for the translation of Noel Burch's chapter 'Cinema, Theory, Women' and to Éditions l'Harmattan in Paris for their permission to translate and publish the chapter. Special thanks also to Laura Mulvey and Aparna Sharma for their additional attention and supplementary referencing to Peter Wollen's keynote speech chapter 'Theory and Practice' which was first published by Intellect in the Journal of Media Practice 6:2 in 2005.

Finally, I would like to add that the notion of a Film Academy, doctoral research through film practice, is not a notion bound by one institution but one that can cross boundaries, geographically and conceptually. The idea that a film student may have two supervisors from two schools, one relating to the representation of the subject in film and one relating to the place of the subject in the social world, remains valid and indeed imperative and I look forward to a wealth of work to be developed at film schools and universities across the world.

NOTES ON CONTRIBUTORS

Clive Myer is a filmmaker, producer and academic. He was founder director of three film schools: the International Film School Wales at the University of Wales Newport; the Film Academy at the University of Glamorgan; and the Skillset Screen Academy Wales (co-founder). He was Senior Lecturer in Communication Studies with special reference to film and television at the University of London Goldsmiths' College. He initiated Ffresh, the student moving image festival of Wales and is a director of the Wales One World film festival. He graduated in film practice with an MA and PhD from the Royal College of Art.

Noël Burch is a filmmaker and theoretician. He was born in California and has lived and worked in Paris for over half a century. He taught film in the UK at the Royal College of Art and the Slade in the 1970s and after some years teaching film in universities in Paris and Lille has returned to writing and filmmaking. His books include *Theory of Film Practice* (1973), *Life to Those Shadows* (1990), *La Drôle de Guerre des Sexes* (with Geneviève Sellier, 1996) and *De la Beauté des Latrines* (2007). He is currently preparing a book on French TV movies with Geneviève Sellier, and another on the libretti of eighteenth- and nineteenth-century French lyric theatre and has directed, with Allan Sekula, a feature-length documentary about the political economy of the sea *The Forgotten Space* (Special Orizzonte Jury Prize at The Venice Mostra, 2010).

Peter Wollen is Professor Emeritus, Film Studies at the University of California, Los Angeles and has previously taught at the University of Essex; at New York University; Columbia University, NY; Northwestern University, Illinois; and at the San Francisco State University, San Francisco. He is the author of *Signs and Meaning in the Cinema* (1972),

Singin' in the Rain (1992) and *Paris Hollywood* (2002), and has edited or contributed to several other books about film and film studies. He has also made a number of films with Laura Mulvey including *Riddles of the Sphinx* (1978) and *Crystal Gazing* (1982), as well as making documentaries for television. He also co-wrote with Mark Peploe, Antonioni's film *The Passenger* (1975).

Laura Mulvey is Professor of Film and Media Studies at Birkbeck College, University of London. She is the author of: *Visual and Other Pleasures* (1989: expanded 2nd edn in 2009), *Fetishism and Curiosity* (1996), *Citizen Kane* (1996) and *Death Twenty-four Times a Second: Stillness and the Moving Image* (2006). She has made six films in collaboration with Peter Wollen including *Riddles of the Sphinx* (1978) and *Frida Kahlo and Tina Modotti* (1980).

Patrick Fuery is Professor and Chair of the Department of English at Chapman University, California. He was previously Professor of Film, Media and Cultural Studies at the University of Newcastle in Australia and Director of the ArtsHealth Research Centre as well as the Research Centre for Creativity, Technology and Culture. He is the author of eight books including: *Madness and Cinema: Psychoanalysis, Culture and the Spectator* (2004); *Visual Cultures and Critical Theory* (2003); *New Developments in Film Theory* (2000) and *Cultural Studies and the New Humanities* (1997). His forthcoming books are *Medicine and the Arts: History and Contemporary Practices* and *Towards an Ethics of Disturbance*.

Nico Baumbach is Assistant Professor of Film Studies at Columbia University, USA. He completed his PhD in Literature on the subject of cinema and pedagogy at Duke University in 2009 under the direction of Fredric Jameson and Jane Gaines. His recent work focuses on the relation between politics and aesthetics in documentary cinema and he is completing a book on the film theory of Badiou, Rancière, Agamben and Žižek.

Ian Macdonald is Director of the Louis Le Prince Centre for Cinema, Photography and Television at the Institute of Communication Studies, University of Leeds. He received a doctorate for his work on the 'Screen Idea' in 2005. He has worked in broadcasting, was formerly Head of the Northern Film School at Leeds Metropolitan University and has taught screenwriting since 1993. He is Co-Editor of the *Journal of Screenwriting* and organiser of the Screenwriting Research Network.

Aparna Sharma is a filmmaker and academic. She earned her doctorate from the Film Academy, University of Glamorgan. Publications include 'The Square Circle – Problematising the National/ Masculine Body in Indian Cinema' in *The Male Body in Global Cinema* (2009) and 'My Brother, My Enemy – the Indo-Pak border through a documentary lens' in *Filming the Line of Control* (2008). She is presently Assistant Professor at the Department of World Arts and Cultures, UCLA, California.

Coral Houtman is a film theorist and filmmaker and is a Senior Lecturer at the Newport Film School, University of Wales, Newport. She is a graduate of the National Film and Television School and gained her PhD at the University of Kent in 2003 on 'Female Voice and Agency in Film Adaptations'. Her *Augustine* – a 40-minute costume drama – was awarded Best Film at the 1995 Houston International Film Festival. Currently undertaking a multi-screen interactive film research project based on the myth of Echo and Narcissus.

Peter Greenaway is a filmmaker. His films include: *The Draughtsman's Contract* (1982); *A Zed & Two Noughts* (1985); *The Belly of an Architect* (1987); *Drowning by Numbers* (1988); *The Cook, the Thief, His Wife & Her Lover* (1989); *Prospero's Books* (1991); *The Baby of Mâcon* (1993); *The Pillow Book* (1996); *8½ Women* (1999); *The Tulse Luper Suitcases Trilogy* (2003); *Nightwatching* (2007) and *Goltzius and the Pelican Company* (2012). He was awarded the Legion d'Honeur in France and a CBE in Britain for services to cinema.

Brian Winston is the Lincoln Professor of Communications at the University of Lincoln. He has taught at the UK National Film and Television School and the New York University film school. In 1985 he won a US prime-time Emmy for documentary scriptwriting (for WNET). His seminal double volumes of *Dangling Conversations* were published in 1974 and 1975. *Messages: Free Expression, Media & the West,* his twelfth book, was published in 2005, followed by an updated second edition of his 1995 history of the documentary, *Claiming the Real,* in 2008. In 2010, he scripted a film on Robert Flaherty, *A Boatload of Wild Irishmen.*

Mike Figgis is an Academy Award-nominated filmmaker. His films include: *Internal Affairs* (1990); *Mr. Jones* (1993); *The Browning Version* (1994); *Leaving Las Vegas* (1995); *Flamenco Women* (1997); *One Night Stand* (1997); *The Loss of Sexual Innocence* (1999); *Miss Julie* (1999); *Timecode* (2000); *Hotel* (2001); *The Battle of Orgreave* (2001) *Co/Ma* (2004); *Love Live Long* (2008) and *The Co(te)lette Film* (2010).

FOREWORD
Bill Nichols

The very mention of the words 'theory' and 'practice' in close proximity tends to produce an ossification of the mind, at least for those who have seen the terms bandied about for a few decades. Their dyadic invocation implies that they belong together in some way and yet our teaching institutions, from which this invocation most commonly comes, seldom integrate the two terms in any meaningful way. Those who believe there is a necessary linkage between theory and practice have only occasionally devised an institutional frame within which this idea can take root. What replaces it most often is what we might call 'doxa', received wisdom, opinion, or, in the type of phraseology that actual occurs, 'This is how we do things here.' The 'doing' may be that of critical analysis and conceptual framing or of actual film production, but within these domains there is a customary form and for these two practices that form remains, to this day, strongly segregated.

Why then does the idea of an integration of theory and practice retain its aura? Is it that of a utopian ideal, a moral compass, a specific way of doing theory and making films; is it the Ideal Form most fitting to the university or college setting? The latter seemed to fuel the initial integrative impulse as film studies gained a foothold in the academy as a humanities rather than social science or art studio subject. Just as a novelist, whose formation included the study of literature, would be expected to know the tradition within which she works and be able to locate her own work within it, so the filmmaker, whose training included a range of humanities-based courses in history, criticism and theory, would be expected to possess knowledge of the cinematic tradition within which she works. This ability to describe a conceptual location for one's work, and, in the best of all possible worlds, apply some aspects of what film studies imparted to the actual making of individual films, would distinguish the university graduate from those who rise through the ranks along the path of the craftsman or artisan apprentice. The graduates' awareness if not their practice would be informed by a conscious, critical familiarity with their chosen medium. They would be aware of critical methodologies and theoretical debates; they would know how to contextualise and theorise, whether these skills entered into their work directly or not. They would be well-rounded in a classic sense and we would all be better for it.

However noble or even correct this argument might be, the simple fact is that it has not prevailed. Most film students do gain knowledge of film history and criticism, if not theory, but those who aim themselves at a career as filmmakers generally see this as a background field against which their filmmaking practice stands out, with a fairly high degree of separation. Unlike deep focus cinematography as a narrative principle, where foreground and background action interrelate, it is more as if film study and film production occupy very distinct conceptual planes that share a certain contiguity but also maintain a sharp separation.

In many ways, given the tendency toward specialisation and division of labour that informs the university as much as the rest of society, this is not entirely surprising. Introductory level courses lead to more advanced courses in more specialised areas of the general field. From a basic intro a student might go on to a course in a genre or national cinema, in studies, and to a course in lighting or post-production sound, in production. Rare is the introduction to film that couples screenwriting and film editing assignments with critical essays and rarer still advanced courses that expressly dwell on the practice of theory or the theory of practice. From square one assumptions operate that foster separation. Attempts to integrate theory and practice then become a catch up game, or a heroic attempt to rescue a jeopardised ideal.

Critical Cinema: Beyond the Theory of Practice both describes, in essay and interview, the current state of the field in relation to this question and suggests ways in which the prevailing assumptions and institutional structures might be altered. Some chapters propose new forms of pedagogical thinking for instructors, some address issues that readily cross the theory/practice divide, some are utopian and some nearly dystopic in their view of the state of the field. Collectively, they invite pause, they encourage reflection, they ask their reader to rethink doxa and question received wisdom. There is no map or blueprint here for how to redesign the university, restructure the curriculum, or reorient the industry, but there is ample ammunition for those who wish to take up these challenges to do so with fresh vigour.

For example, the discussion of practice commonly revolves around the production and post-production phases of filmmaking. Where to put the camera in relation to the implications of the camera's gaze for male and female subjects? How to edit in relation to the theory of suture, and so on. It has often struck me as a closing the barn door after the horse has gone approach. Production and post-production involve massive investments of time and energy in the making of concrete sounds and images and in their assembly. Once a shot is completed (and paid for), intense discussion of why is was done one way and not another, what the camera's gaze implies ideologically, whether the intended colour symbolism succeeds or not all becomes in a basic sense of the word, academic, which, as one dictionary defines it, entails discussion that is 'theoretical and not of any practical relevance' (*OneLook*, an on-line dictionary). It is, in short, too late.

As some of the chapters here suggest and as I have found in my own teaching practice, the ideal time to attempt an integration of theory and practice is in pre-production. This is when everything is up for grabs, when the very topic and approach, theme and tone, structure and effect of a film is the precise subject of discussion. Shooting a film without a carefully thought out idea, without some form of script, or as Ian Macdonald suggests in his chapter here, a mutually comprehensible and commonly shared 'screen idea', is, more often than not, folly. This is when a student can dredge back through examples and counter-examples, learn from the best, avoid the worst, and articulate a framework within which their own conception fits comfortably and intelligibly. This is true whether the intended film is an avant-garde exploration of vision, a polemical documentary about health care, or a narrative fiction about a doppelgänger. Precedents always exist. All of the various ways of seeing and showing that have characterised the cinema can come into play, if teacher and student are willing to step back from the practical production issues a given film proposal raises and begin by locating and contextualising it within the conceptual frames to which it belongs. This is a dialogue in which studies students and production students can contribute meaningfully, and in which that very distinction begins, in fact, to blur. This has, in any case, been my own experience, even though my institutional setting and the compartmentalisation that goes along with academic specialisation make it rarer than I would like.

As a student moves into the actual production of a film the time for reflection and revision rapidly begins to fade. That is not to say that theory and practice have parted company, far from it, but the pressures and tensions that limited time and money produce, as aptly described by Coral Houtman here, take on a reality of their own. As she points out, this calls for a distinct pedagogical model if some sense of integration is to persist; her chapter is a provocative model for one such mode of integration.

Ideas for films 'come up'. How and from where exactly is one question but how to cultivate and refine them once they do come up is quite another. Developing film ideas in a university setting is where they can be nurtured free from immediate economic implications, where they can be set apart from assumptions and expectations that have formed the doxa as it exists at any given moment, where an exuberant sense of the possible can join hands with a rich awareness of already accomplished. This is a space of exploration and discovery, one that is neither in an idea nor in its surrounding context exclusively but in the dialogical space of encounter between thought and action, idea and form. Never as ideal as we would like to imagine it, it is nonetheless more ideal than we often dare to think possible. It is where the image becomes flesh. Its ancestry and descendants now join with their relatives, both near and far, in theory and practice, to continue the long line of film as a living medium.

INTRODUCTION

Clive Myer

This book is derived from and influenced by the Film Academy[1] conference *BEYOND the Theory of Practice* which I convened over three days during the Cardiff Screen Festival in Wales in the UK in November 2003. However, the chapters here are either extensions of a small selection of the papers, pieces that make connections with the theme, or, interviews with filmmakers that contribute towards that connection.

The conference was the third in a CILECT[2] series called to consider what aspects of theory might be imperative for filmmaking students today to consider as integral to their film practice. It was supported by the UK's association of film schools NAHEMI,[3] the British Academy, Sgrîn (the Film Agency for Wales) and the University of Glamorgan. The title of the conference was a reference to the work of my former tutor Noel Burch's seminal 1973 book *Theory of Film Practice*, first published in Paris in 1969 as *Praxis du Cinema*. This conference, more so than its two predecessors, was oriented towards the history and future of reflexive and critical practice and as such approached perhaps somewhat apprehensively by some of its benefactors. But the questions to be raised would not be held down and some thirty papers were presented in total. What had happened, since the last thirty years, to the relationship between film theory and film practice that was emblazoned by the Nouvelle Vague and championed by new academia?

What sort of films and practices are filmmaking students engaging with today? Are they challenging audiences, extending the language of practice and raising issues both social and aesthetic? These questions, doubtlessly of interest to lecturers and students alike, often not only do not get answered, they seldom actually get asked. With an increasing number of film schools and film courses evolving worldwide, what new questions are being raised for and by our graduating students? Are we providing the relevant insight for raising complex issues on the relation of theory to practice or are we simply, inadvertently, or in some institutional cases even purposely, stretching the divide?

The theory of film practice and its discursive relationship with filmmaking can too easily be mistaken for cinema studies or cinema history and many film schools today still separate theory from practice, knowledge from craft, and art from skill. Both inherent and explicit theoretical practices of the moving image have been prevalent from early cinema to postmodern film, television, video, art gallery and internet screenings. Each medium has, in turn, impacted upon, changed and developed its own parameters and in effect crossed the barriers of their sister media. Consequently the cinematic image has produced a very distinctive yet eclectic and embracing relationship with its audience, evolving an attitude of innovation. But, globalisation and postmodern commercial aesthetics have devoured these innovations and now we must ask what are these innovations for? We are told by industry professionals and academic pragmatists alike, that the films and media practices we make and teach, whether fiction or nonfiction, are primarily forms of entertainment and make (and they say we should make) little demand on their audience. On the contrary, I would suggest, the seemingly little demands already made are omnipotent, subliminal, tacit and spurious.

This book is addressed to those daring to reopen the fundamental question of the relation between theory and practice for moving image students and independent film practitioners interested in the language of cinema that shapes the production of knowledge through the now broad categories of the cinematic apparatus. In so doing it aims to contribute towards an investigation of the moribund status of both the independent feature film in the West and its subsequent mirroring in the production of the narrative-based short film culture (both fiction and nonfiction) emanating particularly, but not solely, from film schools across the world. Why are the majority of these film school films so unchallenging and unconcerned to recognise the acquiescent role they play in uncritically supporting the status quo of both the film and educational industries? When such an important relationship surely exists between the imaginary potential of the filmic discourse and the social imaginary of the viewer, why are the majority of filmmakers and film students still locked in to the production of representational fantasy unknown in its powers since the advent of the Hollywood star system and its diversionary role during the Great Depression?

Why, in perusing reading lists on so many films school programmes, courses and modules are there so few books which would help students in film schools around the world with the inspiration that practice itself can be equal to theory and that theory itself can also be practice. This book is trying to reassemble and project into the future the related question of how we might still find a relevant critical practice for film students and independent filmmakers. It has often been said that filmmakers need their own theoretical language. This may be true or else a veiled humility or a disguised avoidance strategy and a preference for the desire to make rather than to think. Industry practitioners have been known to query the relevance and very existence of film schools and in particular media schools, whose graduates, they fear, will be intent to enter a brittle industry without any experience of what the industry refers to as 'the real world'. Well, the education 'industry' is a real world too and probably employs more film industry practitioners in part-time lecturing than the film industry employs graduates. Film schools can also be the largest resource bases of equipment, facilities and short film production. If we are not to fall foul of the film industry's prejudices then what kind of education and training should film schools provide? This book is not, I am afraid, a matrix for a series of course structures or programmes. That is the work for the individual schools and colleges and hopefully there will not be a national or international curriculum. Rather, it is unabashed at situating where these questions come from, how they may be redefined within the theory of practice and where they may go from here.

The first half of the book opens issues of reframing – a term derived from both the theory and the practice of cinema. In my opening chapter 'Diegesis is Not a Code of Practice' I suggest that this terminology, once at the critical edge of radical film practice, has now become static and the very language used to explore the imaginary realm of the ideological impact of film is either ignored or used like some form of political correctness. I re-examine the notion of *diegesis* which I consider to be a key to understanding the pathway between representation and the social world. This leads to the opening of questions on the role of the nonfictional diegetic and I advocate optimism for the continued value of discursive practice in reference in particular to the recent practical work of Jean-Luc Godard and theoretical work of Jacques Rancière.

Noel Burch's chapter 'Cinema, Theory, Women' is from his most recent book, a critique of Modernism, published in France, *De la Beauté des Latrines : Pour Réhabiliter le Sens au Cinéma et Ailleurs* (*On the Beauty of Latrines* (author's translation), 2007). The chapter is the first work of his to be published in English for some time. The title of his book is taken from Théophile Gautier (1811–72), the French poet and writer who impressed Charles Baudelaire and Oscar Wilde and has been claimed by Romanticism, Symbolism and the Decadent movement as well as Modernism. In the Preface to his novel *Mademoiselle de Maupin* (1835), Gautier deliberates on art for art's sake 'Nothing is really beautiful unless it is useless; everything useful is ugly, for it expresses a need, and the needs of man are ignoble and disgusting, like his poor weak nature. The most useful place in a house is the lavatory.' Burch's chapter outlines his respect for feminist theory, his distaste for the male-centrism of cinephilia and, perhaps startlingly for readers of his earlier work, his now strongly formed distrust of the politics of aesthetics. The most important thing, he says, is about the coherent way films speak to us of social, moral and political issues.

Peter Wollen's chapter 'Theory and Practice' was a keynote speech at the conference. He discusses the perceived separation of film theory and practice but through a return to the ideas of Lev Kuleshov reminds us that many celebrated filmmakers have been engaged in exploring the conceptual and therefore theoretical and practical implications of perhaps the most important aspect of cinema: montage. What may have begun as a Soviet methodology and aesthetic was championed by Jean-Luc Godard, Alfred Hitchcock, Sam Fuller, Stanley Kubrick and Ridley Scott. The theoretical aspects of their varied practices, he contends, are connected with a Tense–Mode–Aspect model of narrative drawn from linguistics.

Laura Mulvey examines the politics of change in the context and materiality of cinema in the third chapter in this book, 'Passing time: reflections on the old and the new'. The old technology of cinema at 24 frames a second transforms, she contests, not dies off (as suggested by Peter Greenaway in a later chapter), as it becomes the container of its own history. New technology becomes an intermediate between the old, the present and that which has not yet become. Cinema participates in its own slowing of time to enable the release of the new.

In the next chapter Patrick Fuery observes the resistances between theory and practice in 'Sublime Acts: The Fate of Resistance Between Film Theory and Practice'. Theory and practice engage in the unknown, reinvent themselves and meet in the sublime. They mirror each other as do the Marx Brothers in *Duck Soup* (McCarey 1933) until the third brother or in theory a third term of resistance appears – and the entrancement is broken.

Nico Baumbach in 'Rancière and the Persistence of Film Theory' questions the dissolution of the relation between theory and practice and discusses the work of Louis Althusser's student and later critic Jacques Rancière. What is at stake, he argues, is the relationship between aesthetics, politics and theory. This chapter is based on a paper he presented at a Rancière symposium at Roehampton University in London in May 2008 at which Rancière was present.

In the chapter 'Behind the Mask of the Screenplay: the Screen Idea' Ian Macdonald interrogates the screenplay as a transitional, partial and allusive document. Like Burch he makes reference to Roland Barthes notion of the 'readerly' text and like Fuery calls upon resistance as a creative act as described by filmmaker and theorist Pier Paolo Pasolini who in 1966 described the screenplay as a 'structure designed to become another structure'. The transformative nature of the screenplay makes it a difficult object to study and an unknowable object made known in the hands of the professional script reader. In invoking the work of Andrei Tarkovsky he differentiates between standard commercial practice and that of the author/filmmaker to show that the screenplay is not a fixed, final or unambiguous object.

In her chapter 'The Theory-Practice Interface in Film Education: Observational Documentary in India' Aparna Sharma moves beyond the context of Western centrism to investigate the potential for a revision of praxis. She reminds us that formalism and the decoding of cinema invoked as a mode of self-reflexivity in its own right within modernist avant-garde film work, including documentaries, was and remains an inadequate mode of intervention within the context of maker/viewer interaction. In citing two filmmakers working in the Indian subcontinent, avant-garde artist Kumar Shahani and ethnographic filmmaker David MacDougall, she highlights the relationship between cultural context and theoretical practice. Consequently she regards the potential for student filmmakers to consider their own context in the process of the development of a thoughtful and interventionist practice.

Leading on from this perspective, Coral Houtman asks what are the ways in which we might enable voice and agency in filmmaking? In her chapter entitled 'The Student Author, Lacanian Discourse Theory and *La Nuit Américaine*' she uses François Truffaut's film, *Day for Night* (1973) to illustrate the dilemma of the working process and the instability of discourse. She suggests the potential of the conceptual nature of teaching, rather than the prescriptive – epistemologising the teaching of film crafts leading to the discursive interrogation of students' own and refreshed work.

In June 2008 Peter Greenaway wrote an article for *La Republica* newspaper in Italy and it is published here for the first time in the UK, with a new short preface. 'Just Because You Have Eyes Does Not Mean That You Can See' reminds us that seeing might be natural but understanding what we see is another matter entirely. Painters have been our professional seers for eight thousand years. He appeals to us to take stock of post-filmic technology and use it to transform ourselves from text-masters to image-masters and for a new millennium of visual literacy.

Brian Winston has written 'Theory for Practice: Ceci n'est pas l' Épistémologie' to address the issue of theory's often hostile reception by practitioners through the fear of what might be (mis)understood as abstraction and outside the realm of practice. He argues that the conventional wisdom of the pragmatic approach to filmmaking includes in its denial the very essence of theory itself. He throws down the gauntlet on the grounds of the Academy and the educational institutions and challenges them to remove the theory/practice divide and prejudices that disable rather than enable student intelligence, talent and creative endeavour.

In the second part of the book I converse with three interesting and radical filmmakers (Mike Figgis, Peter Greenaway and Noel Burch) whose work varies from Hollywood mainstream films to art gallery installations and television documentaries. These conversations were videotaped in the hope that they can be screened to film classes and provide a debating point for some of the issues in this book. Please contact me at clive@eclecticfilms. co.uk if you or your library would like to acquire a DVD copy. I have attempted to reflect the conversational nature of these interviews, rather than try to transform them into academic texts, though I have removed some of the more obvious verbal repetitions. I am aware of an ongoing debate concerning the readability of such interviews, their transcription as apparent immediate and spoken text as different to discursive written text and I trust that the reader will accept these chapters in the spirit of verbal discourse (reflecting perhaps the notion of film school masterclass and seminar) in which they are intended.

Mike Figgis came out of alternative community theatre in the 1970s to become one of the UK's most interesting filmmakers. He weaves between his own interests in sound and image and the freedom of spontaneity gleamed from Godard's early to middle period work to big American films where he now gets the freedom to imbricate these films with his own methodologies. His interest in experimental music and his experimental theatre background meld in the live VJ-ing (shared unknowingly with a similar interest by Peter Greenaway) with four-screen film work such as *Time Code* (2000).

Peter Greenaway continues in conversation where his article left off. His commitment to painting and the still image echoes the thoughts of Laura Mulvey as a debate ensues regarding the relative importance of the moving image to the still. Crossing between questions of education and questions of philosophy and aesthetics, uncompromisingly he calls for the primacy of visual communication over text-based communication. He moves from an initially pessimistic view on the death of cinema to an optimistic vision for the use of new technology and the internet. Ultimately, the contradictions and paradoxes involved in auteur filmmaking set the artist filmmakers aside as lone voices, in a predicament for the place of the individual, if not the elite.

When I visited Noel Burch in his Paris apartment in 2003 I had not seen or spoken with him for many years. What transpired was a great difference to what I had expected from his perspective on the politics of representation. He was now diametrically opposed to his earlier formalist approach in favour of what one might ironically call 'contentism' as his position appeared to be a reversal of his earlier stance on film form as a potentially radical ideological tool for the production of a conflictual knowledge-based cinematic and social dialectic. In the early years we were all concerned about what Raymond Williams had referred to as 'incorporation' and what Burch had signalled as 'recuperation'. But in the interceding years (as Laura Mulvey suggests in her chapter) we had all but lost the fight, everything had become a part of the dominant ideology. In fact it was no longer a question of a dominant ideology, in the West there was only one. In order to continue the political struggle in any way Burch had turned to Feminist and Green politics – though his Marxism was showing on his sleeve after three and a half hours of videotaped conversation. A 17-minute version of that recording was edited and screened as the video keynote speech at the Cardiff conference and published in a dedicated issue of the *Journal of Media Practice* (5: 2 – 2004) along with a small selection of other papers. Here the conversation is printed more-or-less in full.

Cynics may ponder on the relevance of the issues raised in this book for filmmaking students, suggesting that students might better occupy their time training for a career. I do not take issue with them training for a career – I take issue with what a self perpetuating industry considers the nature of the form and content of the mainstay of that career, the film itself. In a world where the notion of careerism has also dramatically changed, where jobs are not for life and security of income and position belong to a time passed by, we should consider moving beyond its entrapment within an educational system that in plain language has often been referred to in general as a 'sausage factory' or more recently as producing 'oven ready' graduates for the film industry. At a time when the internet allows and encourages a new physical and intellectual space for the development and procreation of work and thought, it may be useful for us all and in particular those in doubt of the importance and indeed function of critical knowledge to reconsider the notion of studentship and move towards the idea of 'scholars of film practice'. If these 'scholars' do not inquire then who will? When the most basic question of 'why make films at all' has now been boldly asked by Noel Burch, film schools and universities must rise to the challenge and offer a discourse that illuminates a pathway for film practices that this and future generations can embrace and interrogate.

NOTES

1   The Film Academy at the University of Glamorgan, 2003–2007.
2   Centre International de Liaison des Ecoles de Cinéma et de Télévision. Kalos K'Agathos – theory for practice project Chaired by Igor Koršič.
3   National Association for Higher Education in the Moving Image.

PART ONE

REFRAMING

CHAPTER 1
THEORETICAL PRACTICE: DIEGESIS IS NOT A CODE OF CINEMA

Clive Myer

In considering the space between imaginary action and social action, I intend to push the boundaries of the filmic notion of *diegesis* as 'the viewer's mental referent' beyond that which Noel Burch in the early 1970s in his address to film students at the Royal College of Art defined as the mental referent that connects the viewer to that which is viewed. At that particular historical moment the term could be said to have contained a certain dialectic which connected theory to practice, an opening to an understanding of the production of knowledge that engendered possibilities for a counter cinema, now lost in the institutional framework of education and, some would say, devoured by the television zapper and music clip.[1] I take as given the existence of a certain contemporary conjuncture: a mental and corporeal ever-changing and sophisticated relationship between screen action and social action (and beg the question of cinematic intention and indeed intervention) and a social and cultural progression whereby postmodernism and indeed the social fabric of society are undergoing quite radical forms of transition. There would seem to be an urgent need to re-assess a number of definitions that have become part of media folklore and my intention here is to re-evaluate the notion of the diegetic space of cinema as a 'place between' and a 'place beyond' the binary concept of a representational world and a social world. In the struggle for the teaching of a cinema of knowledge (involving the pleasure of knowledge, the pleasure of critical thinking and the pleasure of critical practice), I aim to recuperate the term *diegesis* from its now institutionally bound usage as particularly seen within the frameworks of Cultural Studies and Film Studies as well as a now fairly common mode of description within film schools and independent film practice in general.

I

Let us look at the term diegesis. Etymologically, the word suffers from differing French and English linguistic translations from the Greek διήγησις (De Grève 2007). It was first used by Plato in *The Republic* to describe direct narration, the telling of a theatrical story or poem through the presence of the narrator, so the term did not refer to the narrative content per se but the 'telling' of the narrative. It was then revised by Plato's pupil Aristotle as a 'mode of mimesis' (Taylor 2007), the 'enactment' of the narrative. *Mimesis* translates from the Greek as 'imitation' bringing it closer to the problematic description of the reflection of reality as corroborated by Paul Ricoeur (1984: 180) who reminds us that Plato did not separate mimesis from diegesis but recounted two forms of diegesis, the one 'plain' diegesis which is direct narration (the voice of the narrator) and the other 'by imitation' whereby the narrator imitates the voice of the character. Aristotle, in separating the two, recognised mimesis as the term most descriptive of the development of narrative form. Consequently, decontextualised adaptations of the term diegesis for cinematic usage have slid between the French distinctions of the Platonic form of the 'pure' (Biancorosso 2001) or 'plain' (Ricoeur 1984: 180) delivery of a narrative by the narrator in contrast to the mimetic function of the narrative demonstrated by illusory third parties, by now in the form of actors rather than the narrating poet. Ricoeur warns that we have to be constantly on guard against the superimposition of the two. In the context of cinema, the term was first used by Etienne and Anne Souriau and a group of French intellectuals in the 1950s as part of a series of descriptive technical terms (such as profilmic and afilmic)[2] but spelt *diégèse* differing from Plato's 'pure' narrative (or 'narration' in the sense of the absence of 'impure' dialogue) spelt *diégésis*. The Souriaus' intervention defining diegesis as the world within the narrative resulted in the use of the term as narrative content. However, it was Gérard Gennette in 1972 who, in returning to the Souriau definition, reinforced the term as a potentially radical post-Aristotelian space, contextually innovated by the conscious action of the viewer in recognising the *diégèse* as 'the universe where the *histoire* (story/history)[3] takes place' (Genette 1988: 17–18). In keeping with the French double meaning of histoire this universe may be considered as not just the story or narrative bracketing but as a social structure that also contains the history of its meaning and the context of its future regeneration within the diégèse. The diegetic now becomes an ideological black hole that sucks into the nature of its existence not only the formal articulations that bracket the signification of the narrative but also the history that gave birth to the ideas and articulations and the social, ideological and economic contexts that engendered the history in the first place. Burch's recent postformal perspective,[4] might read Genette's holistic approach to the diegetic as dystopic, commenting, as Burch does, on what he now considers to be an irreversible victory of the dominant system of representation and ideology contaminating 'all there is I see' (see chapter 14). This includes profilmic, filmic and postfilmic[5] referents wherein is contained not just the history but also the desires (imaginary future) of the audience. Earlier Formalist and Structuralist notions from Burch (1973) and Christian Metz (1973) however, would have had more in common with Souriau's separation of profilmic reality and filmic reality in his reference to 'all that I see on the screen' (Lowry 1985: 73–97; emphasis added), imbuing the diegetic with a representational framework which depicts the filmic reality operating through the relatively autonomous self-contained reality that each individual film brings with it – 'everything which concerns the film to the extent that it represents something' (ibid.; emphasis added). This definition, tending to separate representation from reality, contains the kernel of certain structuralist and deconstructive approaches to cinema from the 1970s which emphasise the signifier over the signified whereby the interpretation of representation privileges the form over meaning and distances the subject from the means of expression. Burch attributes his own use of the term to Metz (see chapter 14) but Metz re-attributes it back around to Etienne Souriau (Metz 1982: 145). Metz argued that modern-day use had distorted its Greek origins particularly with the two different spellings in French, and I argue now that the English translation as 'narrative or plot' (Concise Oxford Dictionary 1999) disappointingly avoids the potential of the philosophical aspect of the French meaning altogether (which I would call 'contextual imaginary') which, although still operating on the plane of the illusory, at the level of ideas maintains a perspective for a polemical imaginary. In contradistinction to this complex interpretation of the diegesis, the English usage conflates the Greek origin with a literal French rendition didactically neutralising the reading of the word from its representational, worldly and Other dialectical possibilities. The English definition depoliticises the essence of the French translation rendering it harmless to the dominant cinematic system compared to the Burchian more radical expectations of a diegesis invoking active, dynamic and potentially disruptive relationships between the viewer and the viewed. Since that time it has been assimilated (incorrectly, I believe) within film theory and practice at best as 'on-screen fictional reality' (Hayward 2006: 101). But what does that mean and what are its implications for practice? Sound theorist and practitioner Michel Chion has described the use of onscreen and offscreen music as diegetic and nondiegetic – descriptions that have since been used regularly in film teaching and reflected in student essays and journals. Chion brings the concept of the nondiegetic to the fore, suggesting that, for instance, background music is nondiegetic and synch dialogue is diegetic (Chion 1994: 67). Although he quite amply describes sounds that 'dispose themselves in relation to the frame and its content' (68) as onscreen and those that 'wander at the surface and on the edges' (ibid.) as offscreen he still distinguishes others that 'position themselves clearly outside the diegesis' (ibid.) such as voice-overs that belong on the balcony or orchestral music that belongs in the pit. But does this empirical use of the term serve to simplify and transform a motivating philosophical concept to one that becomes a predetermined code of cinema? From my own perspective, which I discuss later as operating within the postdiegetic social world, the notion of the 'nondiegetic' is a historically relevant but now redundant term useful only to the period of the poststructuralist discourse and a red herring for those working with the non-binary poetics of theory for practice. Chion admits that his definitions and diagrammatic explanations of the concepts of onscreen, offscreen and nondiegetic space, which derived from his earlier work *La Voix au Cinéma* (1982), have become problematic and have been 'denounced as obsolete and reductive' (Chion 1994:74). Notions of the diegetic and nondiegetic manifest as codes of cinema may be the consequence of the confusion over the term diegesis, after all Metz and Burch wrote avidly on the codes of cinema. As an example of diegesis Burch alighted upon the ten-gallon hat as a sign of the 'cowboy film'[6] which legitimatised the viewer to enter that space from their own, socially implanted, imaginary set of relations with the world of the film. Burch was an avowed Althusserian. Louis Althusser promoted a philosophical and politically analytical approach to the study of culture, emanating from a late Marxist examination of the State Apparatus and its implications for ideology. At this time, the concept of the sign, imbricated with semiotic activity and embraced by optimism for cultural counter insurgency, was a theory steeped in potential for political and cultural empowerment in the wake of 1968 power relations in France and elsewhere in mainland Europe. In the UK, through the pages of *Screen* in particular, the Ideological State Apparatus became a blackboard for the development of film theories and practices that responded to and attempted to displace dominant ideology. The world of mental referents heralded a battlefield for a war on ideology where Roland Barthes' analysis of

Figure 1 The world of mental referents heralded a battlefield for a war on ideology. Cover of *Paris Match* 25 June –2 July 1955

.the front cover of an edition of *Paris Match*, the image of the young black soldier saluting the French flag, was, to some, as much a romantic anti-narratological call to arms as it was contradictory heroism within the narrative of the photograph itself (Fig. 1).

The telling of the story of the photograph became as iconic as the notion of black youth/French flag. Postmodernism absorbed this image until it became the equivalent of a new French flag, bringing to mind John Berger's well known reference to the Mona Lisa as an example of acquiescent entrapment within the perspective of Walter Benjamin's notion of mechanical reproduction as demonstrated in *Ways of Seeing* (1972). The expressive awareness and observations of Modernism were shifting from creative acts of discovery to ironic reactions to consumerism. The apparent innocence of the signification of social mass consumption and built-in obsolescence in a Warhol silkscreen contained its own sense of contradiction and the potential for the postmodern irony of the next two to three decades. Structuralism, in representing the critical voice of late Modernism, had laid the path for the elision of Capitalism with cultural radicalism. After the failure of the left in France in 1968 and the failure yet again in the UK in 1984 no longer could aesthetic exploration be seen as a struggle in consciousness but rather as 'the expression of a new social conservatism', as Fredric Jameson remarks in the introduction to Jean-François Lyotard's *The Postmodern Condition: A Report on Knowledge*, (1984: xvii). Terry Eagleton indicates in *After Theory* (2003) that the shift from the philosophy of philosophy (for example, the study of the floating signifier) to the application of the result (for example, the study of Hindu nationalism, or the study of the shopping mall) could be welcomed on the one hand but was 'not entirely positive' on the other. It had become 'typical of a society which believed only in what it could touch, taste and sell' (Eagleton 2003: 53).

The notion of the diegetic had by this time, observed through my own teaching practice, become part of the vocabulary of the relatively new Humanities disciplines of Film Studies, Media Studies and Cultural Studies and by default part and parcel of a consuming and growing industry of education. It had lost its meditative force in favour of the descriptive and had been drawn into pragmatic academia. I say this by no means as an attack on the good intentions of the academics and committed university lecturers but about its very exploitation by the institutions in which they are contained. There, the fervour of a supply and demand approach to education saw the multiple expansions of student numbers and off-shoot related courses, leading to often weakened programmes and a most definitely alienated film and media industry. Within this revisionist historicism, discussed by David Bordwell as a result of the professionalisation of film research (Bordwell 1997: 139–40), the diegesis became another term for the narrative, not simply as storytelling but as a framework for the containment of narrative. D.N. Rodowick describes diegesis as the 'denoted elements of story' (1994: 113) and defers to Metz's suggestion that the aim of narrative in film is 'to efface film's material conditions as a discourse in order to better present itself as story; in sum, the diegesis or fictional world is given as the expression of a signified without a signifier' (Rodowick 1994: 134).

As an extension and an oversimplification of this conceptual proposition, not only could institutional academia now speak of the world contained within the film's diegesis but also of the world outside the diegesis. The often misused notions in film studies of diegesis as 'the main narrative' (Tredell 2002: 158) or that which stands outside the story as 'extra-diegetic' (159), or that which is present but does not exist within the narrative as 'nondiegetic',[7] belies the philosophical complexity of diegesis and its special place within the triangulated modernity of form, content and context. It generates a reductive description of onscreen or offscreen space as the place of the diegesis as it relates to the Platonic truth of the narrative. Offscreen space is referred to often in Burch's writings. This is not so-called nondiegetic space, but is exactly what it says on the label – the space of the world not framed. It is not the nondiegetic space that

Chion separates from onscreen and offscreen, but it most certainly plays a role in the diegetic nature of the viewing experience– after all, the diegesis as I will now define it, is present in the total experience of the viewing subject, whether in the realm of what we see and think or in its opposite state of absence in the world of the unobtainable Other (born from language and operating on the symbolic level of the unconscious).[8] You see, the diegetic is not a 'thing' it is a process, it is not sustainable as the diegesis or the absence of the diegesis in its own right. If the imaginary presence of the diegetic is experienced when engaged in the act of viewing a film and it is the mental referent embedded in myth and locked between the subject-being in (permanent) transition and the object of desire (which is both the filmed image and the image-in-the-world) then its self-perpetuating culture expands from the frame and the mind simul-taneously. Intangible as it is fleeting, diegesis occupies the place of the Other and is as enabling (desire) as it is disabling (fantasy). Its real home is in the rep-resented world but its breathing apparatus exists in the lived-in world. We are the subjects of its gaze; we are *its* Other. The diegetic of any subject or moment does not only produce a meaning for us – we are also the meaning produced by it as it weaves within our post-viewing consciousness, both individual and collective. Its function within the social sphere of the cinematic apparatus ap-pears to be in its overriding powers of connectivity and in particular, belief. The viewer is situated as being phenomenologically locked in a binary duality of both belief and disbelief. Burch alludes to this in *Life to those Shadows*:

> As Christian Metz reminded us some years ago (1982: 101), 'belief' in the cinematic image as an analogue of real phenomena, if it were ever a hal-lucination (such as might be induced by drugs or psychosis, for example) has long ceased to be one: it is indeed a 'willing suspension of disbelief', in Coleridge's words, an emotional involvement which may certainly attain great depths of anguish or compassion, but which is always grounded in the awareness that the subject is 'only watching a film'. (1990: 243–4)

Jacques Aumont goes further into this duality in referring to David Bordwell's cognitive descriptions of the assumed knowledge of the film spectator:

> On the one hand, he or she activates general cognitive and perceptual processes which enable him or her to understand the image; on the other hand, he or she uses forms of knowledge that, to some extent inhere within the text itself … The seemingly irreconcilable difference between theories of knowledge and belief demonstrates that the psychology of the image-spectator is an inextricable mixture of knowledge and belief. (1997: 80–1)

17

Burch's early desire to return to the codes of primitive cinema was not born of nostalgia but was an epistemological enquiry based in historical material-ism which demanded a re-opening of the question of affect on the viewer's sensibility, where the interaction of seeing, hearing and believing empowers, or otherwise awakens, their place in the diegetic process. This process was present during and before (in theatre) silent cinema, but the advent of sound broadened and heightened its perspective. The beginning of the 'full diegetic effect' (Burch 1990: 244), which, according to Burch came with the advent of sound on film was witnessed by Maxim Gorky, whose review of the films of Lumière seen at the Nizhny-Novgorod Fair and printed on 4 July 1896 in the *Nizhegorodsky Listok* newspaper expressed feigned hallucination (Burch 1990: 23), differentiated from complete illusion by its absence of synchro-nised sound. It was not until 1929 that this 'full' effect became a parasite on the back of the sound film. It is helpful to my hypothesis – that 'diegesis' is not a code of practice – and in the endeavour to clarify the misuse of the term and indeed in redefining it beyond postmodernism,[9] in particular ref-erence to its use in relation to narrative, that Burch takes the Gorky example as an indicator of the modern viewer's difficulty with the codes of silent film: 'I take this as a preliminary indication of the relative autonomy of the narrative and diegetic principles' (Burch 1990: 245). This duality of polarity and harmony, image and sound, however, enabled a binary approach to the deconstruction of the codes of cinema as they mirrored everyday life. There was now a direct and formal relationship between representational sound and image - turn off the sound and there was no longer (as there had been during the era of silent cinema) a coherent narrative. Consequently, as a way of deconstructing cinema, sound was now being addressed, in particular by the newly developing discipline of Media Studies, as either a part of the nar-rative's diegesis or extra to it. So-called nondiegetic sound was referenced, typically in Media Studies handbooks, as sound which does or does not live in the fictional world of the narrative. Branston and Stafford produce a con-densed definition:

> non-diegetic' sound – sound which doesn't come from the fictional world
> of the narrative. The clearest example is theme music. Music playing on a
> jukebox in the scene is diegetic. (2003: 329)

Stephen Deutch, composer of film scores and Professor of Music Design, takes this further in elaborating five kinds of 'non-diegetic' uses of music in film, here summarised as:

1. non-diegetic narrative support – music composed to the linearity of the film
2. non-diegetic ironic – music and images tell different stories
3. non-diegetic iconic or referential – music stands for the film (e.g. *2001, A Space Odyssey*)
4. non-diegetic irrelevant – music takes the place of the atmos track (e.g. in Jaques Tati films)
5. combination of 1. and 3. the non-diegetic iconic narrative support where every action has a musical sound (e.g. Tom & Jerry cartoons).[10] (Deutch 2003: 31–3)

Carter Burwell, composer of scores for the Coen Brothers, describes a scene from *Miller's Crossing* (1990) noting certain transitions from one mode to the other as 'diegetic music becoming non-diegetic' (Burwell 2003: 203) within the continuity of the same piece of music.[11] In the scene the character, played by Albert Finney, is seen putting a record on his record player. Finney is a mobster boss and his choice of the Irish tune 'Londonderry Air' ('Danny Boy'), is, for Burwell, significant in understanding the use of music to show the personality of the character. The music we hear is chosen (in these terms diegetically) by this character, not by the film composer nor playing on the radio. As the character leaves the room to walk through the scene of mayhem and murder he has orchestrated, the music comes with him and becomes 'non-diegetic' (Burwell 2003: 204). This literal interpretation of diegesis as the world of the narrative, so often used within Media, Cinema and Film Studies, reinforces Aumont's argument that the viewer is caught in a blend of knowledge and belief without being offered the means necessary for that belief system to be challenged, at least not by narrative deconstructive awareness alone.

A Burchian perspective (both earlier and of late) might tentatively consider that it is diegesis, that imaginary conveyor of the belief system, not narrative, that made cinema (and subsequently television) the most powerful medium of the twentieth century. My reading of Genette's consideration of the diegetic containing its own history (even if one takes the translation of 'histoire' to mean story, for me the notion of 'story' would contain its own history), enables an exploration of dialectical and historical materialism and posits the diegetic as much in the lived world as the represented world. Within the context of late Capitalism, Burch's caveat on the diegesis of 'all there is I see' (see chapter 14) is also *all there is I know or could know*. His concern that everything is tainted pre-empts not just the filmic diegetic but a diegetic society. As such my contribution to the knowledge of the diegetic is on the one hand to cut away the elements of the definition that are impinging on the awareness of its involvedness – diegesis is not only not the narrative, there can also be no such thing as nondiegetic space in film nor extra-diegetic. All elements of form, content and context cinematically contribute to the diegetic space of prefilmic and postfilmic consciousness.

For Burch, the cinematic diegetic was the space of the mental referent that enabled a collective consciousness of identification for the viewing subject, which from his Marxist perspective was a false consciousness. Deconstructing the codes of cinema, for him and for Metz, potentially encouraged the viewer to transform that world through the awareness of its construction. This suggests however that there may be a truth beneath the surface of artificial structure. This idealism would lead in part to Burch's current volteface regarding the uselessness of form as a vehicle for consciousness raising, leaving only accessibility to radical *content* as a method of intervention in Western culture. Whereas Burch has renounced his association with the formal qualities of cinema (see Myer 2004) in favour of accessibility, my own view is that the diegetic problem is not contained in the codes of cinema, in form, and certainly not contained on the level of content. Rather, I would argue, the diegesis resides primarily in the notion of context. My advance from Burch's definition of diegesis is that I remove it with more certainty from its confinement in narrativity, suggesting that its idealised doppelganger exists in the lived world, rather than any view that the lived world is reproduced or reflected on the screen. Accordingly, I consider a new framework for the workings of diegesis today within the evolution of the 'postfilmic subject'. In so doing I refer to Genette's comment on the notion of *metalepsis* (the transition from one narrative level to another), as he cites Luigi Pirandello's *Six Characters in Search of an Author* (1921) and the works of Jean Genet and Alain Robbe-Grillet, invoking the diegetic boundaries of the two worlds they cross: the world *in* which one tells and the world *of* which one tells. Genette quotes Jorge Luis Borges from *Other Inquisitions* (1964: 46): 'Such inversions suggest that if the characters in a story can be readers or spectators, then we, their readers or spectators, can be fictitious.' 'The most troubling thing' wrote Genette 'lies in this unacceptable and insistent hypothesis, that the extradiegetic is perhaps always diegetic, and that the narrator and his narratees – you and I – perhaps belong to some narrative' (1980: 236). The question now becomes a consideration of how we 'belong' and it is here that I beg to free the diegetic from the confines of the illusory world of the so-called fictional cinema to examine its impact on another realm of the moving image that it has so impinged upon since the inception of cinema: the nonfiction film.

II

Here I suggest the transition from Burch's notion of the 'full diegetic effect' to that of a more socially bound concept of the 'full diegetic affect' in an attempt to release diegesis from the confines of narrative form and place it in the imaginary of the social world. This begs the question of the possibility and validity of a special place for diegesis within nonfictional cinema, the cinema that I would suggest is most directly associated through the afilmic with the social world. Proposing the amendment of Burch's definition of the full diegetic effect to the full diegetic affect or 'a'-ffect reverses the signification of a model of communication between reality and representation that, before the reversal, could be formulated as:

lived world ↔ *represented world*

The switched perspective endeavours in its reversal to signify that which lies beyond the first model taking the diegetic with it into the post-representational theoretical arena of socialised action which, by default of collective consciousness could be formulated as:

represented world ↔ *lived world*

The significance of a single phoneme, particularly the use of the letter 'a' has been demonstrated by both Jacques Lacan in his use of the term 'petit a', the small unconscious struggles of the subject during the process of socialisation and Jacques Derrida in his use of the term 'differance' combining the meanings of difference and deferral. For Lacan the 'objet petit a' is by definition an object that has come into being in being lost 'it leaves the subject in ignorance as to what there is beyond the appearance' (Lacan 1994: 77). This is a basic fantasy for Lacan who illustrates the proposition with:

$ ◊ a (Lacan 1994: 209)

The 'barred' or alienated subject '$' is divided through attraction to and repulsion from the object of its unconscious desire . It is correlative to ('◊'),[12] the fantasised lost object, the object petit a or petit autre ('a') being the object cause of desire. This is similar to Sigmund Freud's fort-da game where a toy dropped by a baby elicits pleasure on its return, which Freud maintained was a metaphor for the absence and presence of the mother (Freud 1920: 14–15).

The debarred subject stabilises its position by constructing a fantasy about how the subject is held in the Other, evident only in partial objects, the gaze or voice of his/her love objects, a hair style, or perhaps a filmic representation that can be enjoyed as compensation for its primordial loss of the maternal object. These partial objects, one must assume, can exist representationally within the diegetic space of the viewing subject and can in part account for the fascination, the drive of the viewer in his/her acquiescent relationship with what is seen on the screen. Even more so for Derrida whose notion of the deferral of the drive's fantasies is also represented by the letter 'a'. Differance is the concealed way of seeing something that is deferred out of (collective) consciousness through our diversion with the imagery that captures our notice. 'Differance is the ... formation of form' (Derrida 1967: 63). It is the 'historical and epochal 'unfolding' of Being' (Derrida 1972: 22). The linguistic significance and cyclic possibility/impossibility of the metonymic use of the letter 'a' reveals a playfully serious dialectic with the representational and post-representational inversion in my reference to the 'diegetic affect'. The use of Lacan's 'petit a' within Derrida's 'difference' may be read as 'differ-petit a-nce' and is not insignificant in the complexity of readability within the post-representational cinematic apparatus of nonfictional collective consciousness. This signifies a diegetic rebound that is perhaps more evidently present in nonfiction film than it is in fiction film, in part due to the perception of 'the unshakable reality of the documentary film' as stated by Peter Brook (2005). It is an iconic and graphic expression of the imaginary, enabling a theoretical model for the full diegetic affect. It demonstrates the conceptual remodelling of the social imperative as one which is, at the very least, coloured by the stains of representation and operating as an ideologically determined permeable membrane between the lived world, its reception, construction and reconstruction, present for example in some of the nonfictional film work of the artist Jeremy Deller (2004).[13] The socially constructed, individually apperceived diegetic rebound, then, is fundamental to the proposition that collective consciousness (see below) is an important agency in the delivery of the belief system of nonfictional film awareness.

The diegesis of nonfictional film resides in space and time in correlation to fictional film. The spatial-temporal dimensions and attributes that comprise the moving image can appear more apparent in the fictional context and tend towards opacity in the case of nonfiction. Bill Nichols questions whether

> ...our emphasis on people, places, and things, facts and figures has obscured our understanding of the degree to which the indexical film image, as utilised by nonfiction, has as its referent a temporal dimension. And

is this temporal direction not the domain of lived experience rather than strict chronology? Is it not, in other words, history ... historical consciousness? (1994: xii)

The distinction between fictional and nonfictional, contextualised within the concept of historical and indeed, collective consciousness, lies in the claim of nonfictional film to have a direct relationship with and, beyond the relative, to actually represent reality. Fictional film has never successfully staked that claim – it may make reference to being based on a true story, it may even use the real characters from an event but it can claim nothing more than reconstruction. Conversely, documentary dramas may use the illusory techniques of documentary film, the handheld camera or the attempt at natural characterisation by actors assuming to act naturally, such as in the early films of Peter Watkins and Ken Loach, but ultimately they fall within the diegeses of dramatisation and narrativity. The space between the fictional diegetic and the nonfictional diegetic has become an increasingly prevalent concern for academic discourse concurrent with the development of acceptable modes of production that extend beyond traditional forms of film and television practice. Nichols recognises that:

> Inevitably, the distinction between fact and fiction blurs when claims about reality get cast as narratives. We enter a zone where the world put before us lies between one not our own and one that very well might be, between a world we may recognise as a fragment of our own and one that may seem fabricated from such fragments, between indexical (authentic)[14] signs of reality and cinematic (invented) interpretations of this reality'. (1994: ix)

The question, then, is more complex than simply the difference between factual and fictional moving image making and may indeed reside as difference in both forms in the explicit viewing assumptions of the audience and as differance in the implicit readings of the audience. The 'zone...between' to which Nichols alludes may be heightened and accentuated within the realm of nonfiction film as implicit differance and equally heightened in the realm of fiction film as explicit difference in the knowing of the watching of a film, the consciousness of the spectatorship and the viewers' knowledge of themselves as subjects of the world represented. In her book on the politics of documentary, Paula Rabinowitz (1994) raises questions of the appeal of the documentary form to both the Left and to the establishment based on its duality of place between subject and object, asking whether the invocation of reality reinforces realism or destabilises it. This most interesting place between is also the site for exchange, she continues to argue, where the audience of documentary, like the listener of a joke, participates in the degradation of the third, the object of scrutiny, the butt of the joke – but it also degrades the documentarian as an outsider. This, she establishes, is crucial to the rhetoric of documentary, the knowing outrage, the joke is on everyone (Rabinowitz 1994: 7). Thus, the role of the gaze in Lacan's '$ ◊ a' is a knowing gaze, which could be construed as that which lies inside (Nichols' 'space between') the duality of the contradictory cinematic gazes of the pleasure of looking, as depicted by Mulvey:

> (There are) two contradictory aspects of the pleasurable structures of looking in the conventional cinematic situation. The first, scopophilic, arises from pleasure in using another person as an object of sexual stimulation through sight. The second, developed through narcissism and the constitution of the ego, comes from identification with the image seen. Thus, in film terms, one implies a separation of the erotic identity of the subject from the object on the screen (active scopophilia), the other demands identification of the ego with the object on the screen through the spectator's fascination with and recognition of his like ... the tension between instinctual drives and self-preservation continues to be a dramatic polarisation in terms of pleasure ... they have to be attached to an idealisation. Both pursue aims in indifference to perceptual reality, creating the imagised, eroticised concept of the world that forms the perception of the subject and makes a mockery of empirical objectivity. (1990: 32)[15]

The knowing gaze is that which is simultaneously used by the viewer to see while at the same time the viewer is looked back upon by the screen. Both become imbricated as object/subject in a Sadean struggle for dominance.

Sexuality may indeed be the driving force of this relationship, but in a post-representational society this pervasion embraces more than the notion of pleasure as a mechanism, the penetration residing, I will argue, in the realm of 'collective consciousness', a term coined by Emile Durkheim in 1893. Durkheim recognised the dilemma of the relationship between the individual and society, between what we think we are and what we are formed to be, though debates continue today between the supporters of Durkheim's theories and those of his contemporary Gabriel Tarde who argued that society is comprised of both individual consciousness and their compound, the sum of the consciousness in individuals.[16] Durkheim contested that 'social life is made up of representations' (2002: 276), collective representations through religion as a system of symbols that enables society to becomes conscious of itself. The content of this collective consciousness, iconically religious in Durkheim's time, has

transformed, I would suggest, to a post-biological content ideologically embracing representation itself, whereby religion is disempowered in favour of
the diegetic relationship with representation as the new social construct. In
the overlap between Durkheim's instigations in 1893, two years prior to the
'birth' of cinema, and Freudian and post-Freudian analyses of self, we can make
connections with the primary cinematic illusion of selves (collective recognition rather than individual consciousness) and the illusory intangibility of the
Other, as Lacan questions and signifies in the fifth chapter of *The Four Fundamental Concepts of Psycho-analysis*:

> ...the reality system, however far it is developed, leaves us an essential part
> of what belongs to the real a prisoner in the toils of the pleasure principle.
> ... The primary process ... the unconscious ... apprehended in its expe-
> rience of rupture, between perception and consciousness, in that non-
> temporal locus ... what Freud calls ... the idea of another locality, another
> space, another scene, the between perception and consciousness. (1994:
> 56; my emphasis)

Here I will raise the question of the relationship between the nonfictional notion of reality, perceived to exist outside the realm of the film, half of
the equation of the full diegetic affect, and Lacan's notion of the Real – the
third order in the psychoanalytic field of the Imaginary, the Symbolic and the
Real[17] – the place where that which is not trapped in the unconscious (naturally)
can be traumatised psychotically. This is quite different to the filmmakers'
nonfictional reality but, I would suggest, imbricated within the lozenge of
the full diegetic affect equation as, indeed, the space between perception and
consciousness. The nonfictional real of representation shields the kernel of
Lacan's Real, a persecutory image that cannot be mastered through verbal (or
visual) symbolisation. According to Alan Sheridan, in his translator's endnote
of *The Four Fundamental Concepts of Psycho-analysis*, Lacan's work on the
Real began:

> ...by presenting, in relation to symbolic substitutions and imaginary varia-
> tions, a function of constancy: ' the real is that which always returns to
> the same place'. It then became that before which the imaginary faltered,
> that over which the symbolic stumbles, that which is refractory, resistant.
> 'The real is the impossible', that which is lacking in the symbolic order,
> the ineliminable residue of all articulation, the foreclosed element, which
> may be approached, but never grasped: the umbilical cord of the symbolic.
> (1994: 280)

There is, in a sense, a state of collective trauma brought about by the relationship between the non-assimilatory nature of the Real and transference through the constancy of repetition, and that which is left behind and embedded in the viewing subject through the residue of the mirror phase, the inculcation of the ego on the infant at the moment it recognises itself as 'other' to its mother:

> The relation to the real that is to be found in the transference was expressed by Freud when he declared that nothing can be apprehended *in effigie, in absentia* – and yet is not the transference given to us as effigy and as relation to absence? We can succeed in unravelling this ambiguity of the reality involved in the transference only on the basis of the function of the real in repetition...
>
> We are now at the heart of what may enable us to understand the radical character of the conflictual notion introduced by the opposition of the pleasure principle and the reality principle – which is why we cannot conceive the reality principle as having, by virtue of its ascendancy, the last word? (Lacan 1994: 54–5)

Central to my concern, in this respect, is the reliability of diegesis in nonfictional film. As, according to Freud, both the reality principle and the pleasure principle have a tendency to dominate the psyche (1920: 6–8) and henceforth simultaneously the diegetic space of the film subject (whether fictional or nonfictional), the deferred superior gratification offered by the reality principle in exchange for the constant search for pure pleasure (the constancy of the pleasure principle) can be seen as a potential subliminal arbitrator in the relationship between the diegetic space of fact and the diegetic space of fiction. The referent in any form of nonfiction film plays a vital part in the intertextual role between the space of the reality consciousness of the viewer and the readability of the image. Susan Scheibler examines the bridge between the Freudian/Lacanian Imaginary and its operability in nonfiction film:

> In the documentary form, [knowledge] establishes itself within the conventions associated with the constative dimension of verifiability and facticity ... The imaginary of the documentary, the imagined real, joins with the documentary's symbolic in its concern with language, culture, history, and the other to produce a subject within the promise of the constative ...The spectator is invited into this space of authenticity through the ontological and epistemological promise of a constative that relies on its spectacular

effects to suture the subject into a presumed imaginary relationship to his or her own relation to the symbolic order, to culture and language. (1993: 143–4)

She defines the difference between the constative and the performative by the constative's:

dependence on a belief in the possibility of a knowledge that is able to guarantee the actuality and presence, the facticity, of its observations and remarks. The performative, on the other hand, is unconcerned with its relation to facticity, to truth or falsity, performing its enunciative function apart from and outside of issues of verifiability and authenticity. (1993: 139)

The explication and the foregrounding of the diegetic in this context relies on an epistemological progression between the disembodied knowledge[18] of the classical documentary and the embodiment of 'process' in more radical films that takes on the mantle of ascription to which Nichols, in referring to avant-garde films in the 1990s that have confounded fact and fiction, has given the title 'performative documentary' (1994: 93–106). This nomenclature is fashioned particularly to those films that have sustained a 'sense of historical consciousness in the face of a postmodern tendency to forget the past' (Nichols 1994: xi). History presents itself only in the temporal act of viewing and meaning construction – that is, not reconstruction of a priori events but the subaltern of accumulated readings within collective consciousness, fractured to include temporal disassociation and differentiation. As in any mise-en-scène, the particularity of the diegetic exists not in the objects as such but in the filmmakers' choice and arrangement of iconographic and indexical representations with their discursive interplay of fracture, whether normative (such as classical codes of editing) or non-normative (such as avant-garde film). A problematic superficiality of certainty exists in the binary opposition generally posed between definitions of documentary and fiction. All film work is philosophically both – in documenting that which is placed before the camera, and in so doing fictionalising that space. The problematic does not lie centrally in the question of whether there is a difference between fiction and nonfiction (clearly there are strategic, linguistic and cinematically receptive differences of form and perception held by the producing and viewing subject), rather it lies within the question of specificity in cultural meaning production and reception within film pertaining to deal directly with the social iconic and the social metaphoric. Of course, the metaphoric also exists within the iconic and vice versa and are both linked to the social.

Nichols treats 'fiction and nonfiction as blurred or fuzzy boundaries' (1994: 109). He takes the position that the boundaries in film between documentary and reality, fact and fiction, 'defy simple definition and static identity' (1994: xiii), that they are subject to change and development and though perhaps beyond control are shapable. Nonfiction film serves as fiction '(un)like any other' (1993: 189) stabilised by the belief systems maintained by the spectator. It adds another layer of complexity of narrative to procure the image as evidence assumed to speak for itself, an assumption, in my view, closely linked to the insecurity of the diegetic. This is compounded by the effect of the institutionalisation of postmodernism at the cutting edge of media form. In the absence of any positive philosophical direction everything is important and nothing is important. In containing, and by so doing, disarming the debates, postmodernism became more than the sum of its parts. In the reflexive critiques of the institutions of power and the plurality of theory, it became, instead of a counter-theory, a practice-based theoretical institution of its own – one quite at home inside the dominant ethos that its constituent elements attempted to fracture. This illuminates Burch's switch away from the formal. There was no longer an aesthetic that was dangerous. There was no longer history, not even a history of history. As the past became contained within its own representation it quickly became a commodity. As Vivian Sobchack notes, the self proclaimed mission of the television History Channel, was to offer the viewer: 'All of History. All in One Place™ – if you couldn't be there the first time, here's your second chance' (1996: 4). Nichols takes this further by suggesting that one of the outcomes of this meta-institutionalism resides within the actions of the social subject reflecting the displacement of lack in social interaction. The problematic contrivance of the way nonfictional events are narrativised within the interlocking codes of fictional representation are designed to appeal to a sense of emotion rather than a sense of action and leads primarily to the consuming of a *sense* of event, a *sense* of experience, interiorised within the space of the habitat of the viewing subject. What ensues is a false sense of satisfaction, a need that is constantly nurtured in the adage of 'giving the audience what it wants'. Occasionally, the consumption of emotion may lead to misplaced action. The viewing subject is caught in an illusive self motivated action of an imaginary relationship misrecognised as an actual relationship to a social situation. Whereas fictional forms direct our attention to events and things, nonfictional forms open up a given awareness of the space between representation and that which is represented. We already know, have knowledge of, the nonfictional represented world, after all we (believe we) live it every day. The satisfaction of the reconfirmation is of a different order to that of the intrigue of the fictional world. Real danger, which is shown on the news as war, hurricane, famine does not seem as dangerous as fictional danger which plays with desire, unspoken misplacement and romanticised heroism.

What we end up consuming, in a sense articulated by the work of Jean Baudrillard, is an incongruity, digesting simulacrum and (mis)knowing the historical world. An acquiescent deferment whereby we mean no harm and are not harmed, a fort da of production (of misknowledge) and consumption of a carved up representational carcass of the world we believe we live in. There appears to be a logical pessimism through Burch's contemporary volte-face regarding the now impossible task (in the West) of any radical film form existing as a counter-dominant ideological strategy (Myer 2004: 73). Despite this seemingly defeatist outlook there is, I believe, a new perspective – one that considers epistemological filmmaking to be highly discursive. Paradoxically Burch's position frees us from the tyranny of film form whilst Nichols invokes the performative documentary as a way of understanding the world *in the manner of* [my emphasis] Bertolt Brecht's notion of alienation, despite Burch's perceptive insistence that the new alienation within postmodernism is by no means Brechtian. What it potentially does is to give precedence to the experiential quality of the subject's relation to the sign, to make sense of the world rather than be encapsulated by its logic (Nichols 1994). In Baudrillard's critical philosophical approach we see representation dissolve into simulation and a critique of the object of desire of the intellectuals (2001). The end result is, for him, documentary's loss of force which must lead by default to the false expectations of reality television. He dismisses theories whereby the gaze is external to its object as Burch dismisses Mulvey's understanding of the male gaze and Brecht's notion of alienation as having any use today as filmic modes of distancing or strategies for radical counter-cinematic action (Myer 2004: 77). For both Burch and Baudrillard, reality effects become inextricable from experience of the real. Social order generates simulation, a hyperreal. No longer bound by representability, the implication for nonfictional film is the absolution of responsibility for the transposition of reality to representation. However, this absolution, in my terms, recognises the role of both collective consciousness and the filmic and postfilmic diegesis as residues of the social imaginary and considers the ideologising of representation as a primary necessity. It allows entry back into the filmed system and signals that which comes after postmodernism to be quite reusable. The thought that everything is permissible within the representational perspective of postmodernism leads, not to defeatism, but towards a conscious perspective of posthumanist film practice, a repositioning of the relationship between history and the present, the replacing of metaphorical inverted commas to re-enable comment by including both representational history and the process by which that particular version of history representationally materialised.

Here I look to the later film work of Jean-Luc Godard and the theoretical work of Jacques Rancière. In Godard's eight-part film *Histoire(s) du Cinéma* (1988–98) he reworks historical cinematic representation to produce new meaning. This is by no means a return to the 1960s and 1970s American and British experimental and structuralist work of the Film-makers' Co-ops, rather it is a nonfictional work of diegetical consciousness that demonstrates that all representation is capable of a constructive reallocation of meaning. In 'The Place of Desire in Documentary Film Theory', Michael Renov quotes Paul Ricoeur's statement that 'consciousness is such as it appears to itself' (2004: 98) invoking Freud's challenge of the supremacy of consciousness in Western thought. As he points to Freud's statement, that everything conscious has an unconscious preliminary stage (1965: 651), that which is conscious is but a small part of that which is not, then for the viewer, unknowing is greater than knowing in the presence of the cinematic representation yet is intimately linked to the collective diegetic space – the space between seeing and understanding in cinematic consciousness. Here too is a link between Durkheim's observation of the role of religiosity and the post-religious dominance of the representational that can be seen in my own film work in *Dorothy Carrington, Woman of two Worlds* (2006) and *Song of the Falklands* (2008) as an example of contemporary ideological residue of the totemistic. It is what Godard refers to in *Histoire(s) du Cinéma* (Part 1: 1988) when he sharply combines religious iconography in the form of a detail of a Renaissance painting of the Resurrection superimposed with a clip of the young Elizabeth Taylor rising from the sea. The voice-over proclaims 'The martyrdom and resurrection of the documentary. Oh, the wonder of watching what we cannot see. Oh, sweet miracle of our blind eyes.' With nonfiction film we watch with the desire to know, as Elizabeth Cowie elucidates in her essay on Reality and Documentary, 'it is an epistemological project, requiring that we not only see but are also brought to *know*' (1997). However, it is desire itself which intervenes in the knowing process as Renov quotes Julia Kristeva: 'The knowing subject is also a *desiring* subject, and the paths of desire ensnarl the paths of knowledge' (2004: 100). The attempted resolution of desire in the thinking subject brings with it a conflicting paradox between recognition of representation and the recognition of self. In cinematic terms this leads ultimately to representation as stereotype as the subject struggles to connect with an estranged image of the world it thinks it understands. An amalgamation of tacit knowledge, acquired social values and a constant need for the reaffirmation of self provides the individual with the necessary stability through a sense of collective consciousness.

Daniel Frampton in *Filmosophy* quotes Walter Benjamin on cinema: 'an un-consciously penetrated space is substituted for a space consciously explored by man' (2006: 6). But in the context of my concern that the diegetic space of collective consciousness has engendered a post-representational ideology, a space of confusion between the 'represented' world and the 'lived' world (which automatically contains the represented world), this quote takes on more meaning than just the difference between the 'real' world and the filmed world. The space penetrated (by the nonfiction camera) transforms here to a space of collective consciousness even with Benjamin's professed 'conscious' intervention of man. The representational image created by this intervention does not provide us with a complete knowledge about the world it assimilates, but creates a further complexity within the brackets of the specificity of form and content. It provides us with further knowledges which are themselves subject to the paths of desire. These elements of knowledge are then arranged and potentially rearranged to initiate and excavate complex readings of the relationship between the represented world and the believed experience of the conscious subject. This dichotomy between the represented world and the conscious subject is at the heart of the construction of Godard's film. The fracturing of this seemingly homogenous and ideologically unproblematic status, developed and honed by language-like cinematic conventions in general and the nonfictional documentary apparatus, that which the audience perceives as a truth of the world, is strategically embedded in the creation of the film. The intervention is not determined by a set of rules as such but rather through a focusing and refocusing of the subject film and subject viewer being placed and then re-placed, pushing and pulling the diegetic space within its own parameters. In other words, a de-figuration process of the 'subject' takes place between the subject/form/content of the film and the subject/viewer to evolve as a re-figuration within the bricolage of the filmmaking practice. According to Rancière, a work of de-figuration[19] is the process of reinterpolation of cinematic meaning, to add meaning onto meaning, serving to contradict expectations or to review, reread and rearrange (2006: 8) and refers as such to *Histoire(s) du Cinéma*:

> Godard takes the films these filmmakers made and makes with them the films they didn't make. This calls for a two step process: the first recaptures the images from their subjection to the stories they were used to tell, and the second rearranges them into other stories'. (2001: 171)

Godard in my view fulfils the expectations of a methodology previously stated in his much earlier film *Le Gai Savoir* (1968). In the film the main character

Emile Rousseau (great-great-grandson of J.-J. Rousseau),[20] played by Jean-Pierre Léaud, explains the methodology to Patricia Lumumba (Juliet Berto):

> The first year we collect images and sounds and experiment. The second year we criticize all that: decompose, recompose. The third year we attempt some small models of reborn film.[21]

De-figuration as strategy suggests not just a fracturing of the diegetic space and mental referent in nonfiction cinema but questions the relationship between the perception of the image-in-the-world and that of its representational cinematic avatar.[22] The dialectical possibilities of filmic de-figuration are exemplified by Rancière in his invocation of the work of Godard and similarly with that of Chris Marker, with specific reference to Godard's *Histoire(s) du Cinéma* and Marker's *Le Tombeau d'Alexandre* (*The Last Bolshevik*, 1992). Both auteurs and both oeuvres recognise and depend upon the relationship between history, memory and representation and in their creative de-figuration of existing ideas and representations invoke a crisis of confidence in collective consciousness and diegetic construction. If the diegetic space of the nonfiction subject/viewer is the ideological habitat of the subject/viewer then the poetic conflict produced through the intellectual montage of these films illuminates this entrapment. Rancière extols the power of documentary to rise above classical poetics[23] in its ability not to be 'bound to the "real" sought after by the classical norms of affinities and verisimilitude' (2001: 161) of fiction cinema. He considers the ability of nonfiction film to entwine signs, voices and time, to 'combine meanings freely, to re-view images, to arrange them differently, and to diminish or increase their capacity for expression and for generating meaning' (2001: 161).

III

Within the shifting terrain of nonfiction film the viewing subject becomes more complex, less formally structured in their relationship to knowledge and exponentially more complex in the light of the unknowable Other. Bill Nichols' notion of blurred boundaries attests to this as does Paula Rabinowitz's implication of the knowing subject's paradox of the knowledge of realism. The dominance of the relationship between television and the internet's viewing-subject and their viewed-object has shifted the balance away from the anterior domination of fiction as genre and we are witnessing a rebirth of new forms of documentary film in the guise of nonfiction in television, the internet and consequently, cinema. This is the new context of the post-filmic representational subject, the imaginary world implicitly formed on the internal screen of the viewing subject. The notion of the viewing subject suggests that there can no longer be, in the West, a subject separated from viewing, a subject removed from the desire to see and to know. Representation embalms the viewing subject in diegetic knowledge, outside of real space and time creating a space beyond lived experience. Nonfictional film theorists and filmmakers have approached this problem in different ways. The notion of the performative documentary has been an important field for the progression of an understanding of the problematic as well as a method for understanding the nature of a potential for a discursive film practice. It may well be the case that representational performativity in the guise of experimental and reflexive documentary work can fracture the norm of the dominance of documentary form, momentarily, but my conclusion is in agreement with Burch when he refers to the world of music videos having incorporated the radical and ending up as postmodern empty viewing and bad cinema (see chapter 14). To confirm this I return to Burch's association with Genette's holistic approach to the diegetic containing the universe where history occurs and the dictum that 'all that I see on the screen' becomes the normative. At a conjuncture when cinema is reinventing genre in order that it might commodify audiences and re-classify their interests, documentary feature films serve to extend the range of available choice and are developing further as a popular and award winning form. Within the debate between fiction and nonfiction, the feature documentary appears to be settling down as an acceptable genre alongside other new forms engaged in the use of new technology, such as the computer game film adaptation and even subtitled foreign films are becoming a part of the expanded normative. However, standing to one side of Burch's fully pessimistic view, I infer that in recognising the significance of the inevitable role of collective consciousness in driving the social imperative, a praxis can operate and remain in a state of alienation with recuperation by working within the diegetic at the intensity that Barthes has indicated, as second-level myth at a second or even third level of diegetic interchange – the place where the first level of myth, the sign, can be engaged and re-mythified. For Barthes, the social subject exists within myth, within language itself as a structured subtext of society (1957). Representation, a metadiscourse of language, then exists as a second level purveyor of myth, operating through differently structured codes depending on the particular form of representation. To counteract the illusory nature of being-in-the-world that representation invokes, it was necessary for Barthes to engage with myth itself, to create other levels of myth rather than draw back from representation to any semblance of a real world. The problem of demystification, common to the aims of structuralist and experimental films that attempted to deconstruct meaning, such as those of Wollen and Mulvey, Film Work Group and Noel Burch's early film practice, is that the attempt to operate outside conventional film codes is cyclical. Simultaneous to breaching a filmic code a new code is established. Barthes acknowledged the impossibility of working outside myth. Rather, he suggests, it is possible to create another level of myth in order to play myth at its own game. It is possible to mythify myth and in so doing work on the level of the imaginary that is neither false consciousness nor true consciousness. The first level of myth, the sign, is taken forward, recontextualised and recoded to become another signifier - the second level of myth - and a chain of signification is established between the piece of work and the reading/viewing subject. Myth, according to Barthes, has a double function: 'it makes us understand something and it imposes it on us' (1957: 117). I accept and extend Barthes' original concept in the knowledge of its limitations – that it, too, is contained within the very ideological system that is under review. That which is filmed is delivered to the conscious subject as natural and in order for both the filmmaker and the viewer to engage, rather than passively transmit and receive, it is necessary to enter the myth and work within myth itself, to produce 'an artificial myth' (Barthes 1957: 135) and acknowledge that one can only work within representation, not outside it. This is what has driven Burch back to transparency – the ultimate frustration of not being able to be radical with form without immediate recuperation.

At the time of Brecht in Germany in the 1930s and even earlier, at the time of Sergei Eisenstein in Russia in the 1920s, the social contexts enabled this to be an altogether more direct process of estrangement. Social democracy, according to Burch (Myer 2004: 72), has turned this on its head and alienation is now used as an institutional form of social distancing as difference has itself joined the ranks of commodification. This is not to suggest that the original tenets of alienation and distancing in striving to produce a dialectical relationship with an audience are of no value. They are, however, in need of more complex consideration as part of the process of post-representational incorporation and the necessity to work within myth rather than fruitlessly attempting to operate outside ideology. Rancière's definition of the process of de-figuration, to facilitate contradiction of expectation, or to review, reread or rearrange (2006: 8), needs to be understood as operating at both the source of production and at the place of consumption. The strategy of enterism as a way of dealing with myth empowers the filmmaker and the viewer to reconstruct new meaning, to begin to take back control of the image and sound as exemplified by Godard whose work brings Eisenstein's conception of intellectual montage[24] to a contemporary discursive engagement with collective consciousness whereby the notion of intellectual montage running parallel to the notion of the diegetic and through contemporary critical practice can remain current as praxis. The filmic relationship between Eisenstein and Godard is clear. For Godard, montage is the essence of cinema, the one aspect that if stripped bare would remain intact. In a filmed conversation between Godard and Serge Daney in 1988, Godard stated that 'montage is what made cinema unique ... Eisenstein naturally thought he had found montage ... But by montage I mean something much more vast' (in Temple & Williams 2000: 17). Frampton concurs that Godard's use of editing and superimpositions, sharp shifts and sounds cut short take up where Eisenstein left off: 'Iconographic montage-thinkings such as *Histoire(s) du Cinéma* ... are exercises of thought, using a souped-up version of Eisenstein's intellectual montage ' (2006: 69). The next step for intellectual montage and intellectual cinema then will be to go beyond the notion of the exercise towards the contextualised fulfilment that Eisenstein predicted and Rancière suggests: a renewal of the dialectic that is not anchored to binarism, occupying the discursive spaces of the diegetic between form/content/context, fiction/nonfiction and the gaze of the spectator/gaze of the screen.

BIBLIOGRAPHY

Althusser, L. (1971) *Lenin and Philosophy and Other Essays*. London: NLB.

Aumont, J. (1997) *The Image*. London: BFI.

Barthes, R. (1957) *Mythologies*. Paris: Éditions du Seuil. Reprint, St Albans: Paladin, 1973.

Baudrillard, J. (2001) *Selected Writings*. 2nd edn. Oxford: Polity.

Berger, J. (1972) *Ways of Seeing*. London: Penguin Books.

Biancorosso, G. (2001) 'Beginning credits and beyond: music in the cinematic imagination', *Echo*, 3, 1, Spring [Online]. Available at: http://www.humnet.ucla.edu/echo/volume3-issue1/biancorosso/biancorosso1.html (accessed 11 April 2007).

Bordwell, D. (1997) *On the History of Film Style*. Cambridge: Harvard University Press.

Borges, J.L. (1964) *Other Inquisitions, 1937–1952*. Austin: University of Texas Press.

Branston, G and R. Stafford (2003) *The Media Student's Book*. 3rd edn. London: Routledge.

Brook, P. (2005) Peter Brook in conversation with Michael Kustow. [Symposium at Hay-on-Wye Literature Festival]. 29 May.

Burch, N. (1973) *Theory of Film Practice*. London: Secker & Warburg.

_____ (1990) *Life to Those Shadows*. Los Angeles: University of California Press.

Burwell, C. (2003) 'Composing for the Coen brothers', in Sider, L., Freeman, D. and Sider, J. (eds) *Soundscape: the School of Sound Lectures 1998–2001*.London: Wallflower Press, 195–208.

Chanan, M. (1998) *On Documentary: The Zapruder Quotient*, Filmwaves, 4, pp. 22-23.

Chion, M. (1982) *La Voix au Cinéma*. Paris: Editions de l'Etoile.

_____ (1994) *Audio-vision: Sound on Screen*. New York: Columbia University Press.

Concise Oxford Dictionary (1999) Oxford: Oxford University Press.

Cowie, E. (1997) 'The spectacle of reality and documentary film', *DocBox*, 10, [Online]. Available at: http://www.yidff.jp/docbox/10/box10-1-e.html#n7#n7 (accessed 17 April 2007).

Debray, R. (2000) *Transmitting Culture*. New York: Columbia University Press.

De Grève, M. *International Dictionary of Literary Terms*. Vita Nova. [Online]. Available at: http://www.ditl.info/arttest/art823.php (accessed 11 April 2007).

Derrida, J. (1967) *Of Grammatology*. Les Éditions de Minuit. Reprint, Baltimore: Johns Hopkins University Press, 1976.

_____ (1972) *Margins of Philosophy*. Paris: Les Éditions de Minuit. Reprint, Chicago: University of Chicago Press, 1982.

Deutch, S. (2003) 'Music for interactive moving pictures', in Sider, L., Freeman, D. and Sider, J. (eds) *Soundscape, the School of Sound Lectures 1998–2001*. London: Wallflower Press, 28–34.

Durkheim, E. (2002) *Suicide*. Abingdon: Routledge.

Eagleton, T. (2003) *After Theory*. London: Allen Lane Penguin.

Frampton, D. (2006) *Filmosophy*. London: Wallflower Press.

Freud, S. (1920) *Beyond the Pleasure Principle*. Translated by James Strachey. Reprint, London: Vintage, 2001.

Lyotard, J.-F. (1984) *The Postmodern Condition: A Report on Knowledge*. Manchester: Manchester University Press.

Genette, G. (1980) *Narrative Discourse*. Ithaca: Cornell University Press.

_____ (1988) *Narrative Discourse Revisited*. Ithaca: Cornell University Press.

Hayward, S. (2006) *Cinema Studies: The Key Concepts*. 3rd edn. London: Routledge.

Lacan, J. (1994) *The Four Fundamental Concepts of Psycho-Analysis*. London: Penguin.

Lowry, E. (1985) 'The filmology movement and film study in France', in D. Kirkpatrick (ed.) *Studies in Cinema No. 33*. Ann Arbor: UMI Research Press, 73–97, 184–9.

Metz, C. (1973) 'Current problems of film theory: Jean Mitry's l'esthetique et psychologie du cinema, vol. II', *Screen*, 14 (1/2 Spring/Summer), 40–87.

_____ (1982) *The Imaginary Signifier: Psychoanalysis and the Cinema*. Bloomington: Indiana University Press.

Mulvey, L. (1990) 'Visual pleasure and narrative cinema', in P. Erens (ed.) *Issues in Feminist Film Criticism*. Bloomington: Indiana University Press, 28–40.

Myer, C. (2004) 'Playing with toys by the wayside: an interview with Noel Burch', *Journal of Media Practice*, 5, 2, 71–80.

Nichols, B. (1993) 'Getting to know you ... knowledge, power, and the body', in M. Renov (ed.) *Theorizing Documentary*. London: Routledge, 174–92.

_____ (1994) *Blurred Boundaries: Questions of Meaning in Contemporary Culture*. Indiana: Indiana University Press.

Rabinowitz, P. (1994) *They Must Be Represented: The Politics of Documentary*. London and New York: Verso.

Rancière, J. (2001) *Film Fables*. Paris: Éditions du Seuil. Reprint, Oxford: Berg, 2006.

Renov, M. (2004) *The Subject of Documentary*. Minneapolis: University of Minnesota Press.

Ricoeur, P. (1984–88) *Time and Narrative, 1–3*. Chicago: University of Chicago Press.

Rodowick, D. N. (1994) *The Crisis of Political Modernism: Criticism and Ideology in Contemporary Film Theory*. Urbana: University of Illinois Press.

Scheibler, S. (1993) 'Constantly performing the documentary: the seductive promise of lightning over water', in M. Renov (ed.) *Theorizing Documentary*. London: Routledge, 135–50.

Sobchack, V. (1996) *The Persistence of History: Cinema, Television and the Modern Event*. London: Routledge.

Souriau, E. (1953) *L'univers Filmique*. Paris: Flammarion.

Taylor, H. M. 'Discourses on diegesis: the success story of a misnomer', *Offscreen*, 11. [Online]. Available at: http://www.offscreen.com/Sound_Issue/taylor_diegesis.pdf (accessed 6 February 2008).

Temple, M., J. S. Williams and M. Witt (eds) (2004) *For Ever Godard*. London: Black Dog Publishing.

Tredell, N. (2002) *Cinemas of the Mind: a Critical History of Film Theory*. Cambridge: Icon Books.

Prince, G. (2003) *A Dictionary of Narratology, Revised Edition*. Nebraska: University of Nebraska Press.

FILMOGRAPHY

2001, A Space Odyssey (1968) Directed by Stanley Kubrick [DVD]. USA: Metro-Goldwyn-Mayer Inc.

Miller's Crossing (1990) Directed by Joel Coen [DVD]. USA: Twentieth Century-Fox Film Corporation.

Histoire(s) du Cinéma (1988-98) Directed by Jean-Luc Godard [DVD]. Spain: Prodimag.

Dorothy Carrington: Woman of two Worlds (2006) Directed by Clive Myer [DVD]. Wales: Eclectic Films Ltd.

Song of the Falklands (2008) Directed by Clive Myer [DVD]. Wales: Eclectic Films Ltd.

Le Gai Savoir (1969) Directed by Jean-Luc Godard [DVD]. USA: Koch Lorber Films.

Le Tombeau d'Alexandre (*The Last Bolshevik*, 1992) Directed by Chris Marker [DVD]. USA: Icarus Films.

NOTES

1   See Peter Greenaway, chapter 13, and Noel Burch, chapter 14, in this volume.

2   See Michael Chanan's 1998 article *On Documentary: The Zapruder Quotient*. Profilmic refers to the selected elements of reality put before the lens and afilmic to the unselected elements as may appear in a location shot or indeed a documentary.

3   It is worth noting that 'histoire' in French translates as both 'history' and 'story' and I refer the reader to Godard's filmic work *Histoire(s) du Cinéma* (1988–98).

4   See chapters 2 and 14 of this book. One might perceive Burch's own inaugural doubts about his earlier formalist perspective in the last two pages of his chapter 'Narrative, Diegesis: Thresholds, Limits' in *Life to Those Shadows* (1990).

5   Michael Chanan (1998) refers to the filmic as 'style', in other words the subjective intervention of human agency (camera, direction, editing, and so forth). By post-filmic I refer here to the place of the diegetic as a mental referent and subjective interlocutor beyond the screen and as part of the continuum of the viewer in the social world.

6   When I requested, in a personal discussion in 1972, that he explain the notion of diegesis.

7   Narratology, the theory and study of narrative (proposed by Tzvetan Todorov and developed by Genette), depicts ten diegetic modes: *isodiegetic*, the ability of an actor or prop to exist in more than one diegesis; *extradiegetic*, external to the diegesis; *intradiegetic*, the diegesis of a primary narrative by an extradiegetic narrator; *metadiegetic* or *hypodiegetic*, a secondary narrative embedded within the primary diegesis; *homodiegetic*, the narrator who is also a character; *autodiegetic*, where the character is the protagonist; *heterodiegetic*, a narrator who is not part of the diegesis; *pseudo-diegetic* or *reduced metadiegetic*, when a metadiegetic functions as if it were the primary diegesis (Prince 2003: 20). You will notice that none of these terms refer to the nondiegetic, which I consider to be an unsustainable term. These extensions of the diegetic may be useful in structuralist analysis but they still presume the notion of diegesis as limited to the interior narrative world of story. In my terms, where the diegetic exists in the representational and postrepresentational world simultaneously, the extradiegetic, for example is simply a part of the diegetic.

8   'The Other is the locus in which is situated the chain of the signifier that governs whatever may be made present of the subject – it is the field of that living being in which the subject has to appear' (Lacan 1994: 203). Here we must differentiate between Lacan's concepts of the other and the Other (but distinct from the Post-colonial definition of other as difference). Lacan's other extends from the misrecognition of self at the mirror phase of the infants development and is ego related. Capital 'O' Other, however is born from language and operates on the symbolic level of the unconscious 'the unconscious is the discourse of the Other' (Lacan 1973: 39–72).

9   I would consider today that the notion of the fictional world of the diegesis is totally inadequate. Its dominant historical and indeed contemporary usage situates diegesis as only a part of the narrative despite its claim to the whole of the representational world within it. If the concept of the diégèse is to be developed in the English language then not only is the diegetic not a constituent part of the narrative, it is no longer even the whole narrative (including voice-over). It is rather 'beyond' the narrative at the same time as bracketing it within.

10 I presume this last definition also applies to the modern transmission of silent films on television or on DVDs, especially the comedy films of Chaplin, Keaton, and so forth.

11 Invoking yet another variant of the diegetic – the *transdiegetic*, 'referring to sound's propensities to cross the border of the diegetic to the non-diegetic' (Taylor 2007).

12 In 'The Four Fundamental Concepts of Psycho-Analysis' Lacan refers to this shape as a lozenge (1994: 209), a rim with a left-to-right (reading) direction signifying the relation of a circular process. Not to be confused with the standard mathematical

meaning of <> 'is greater than'.

13 Winner of the December 2004 Turner Prize which includes his nonfiction film *Memory Bucket*.

14 A fingerprint, X ray, photograph, and so forth.

15 Originally published in *Screen*, 16, 3, Autumn 1975, 6–18.

16 Issues between the theories of Durkheim and Tarde were recently revived in a Cambridge University symposium in March 2008. See http://www.tarde-dur-kheim.net/Conference.htm [accessed 15 June 2008].

17 The 'Imaginary' according to Lacan is 'one of the three essential orders of the psy-cho-analytic field, namely the Real, the Symbolic and the Imaginary. The imaginary order is characterised by the prevalence of the relation to the image of the counter-part ... (i.e. another who is me) ... all imaginary behaviour is irremediably decep-tive ... The Symbolic covers those phenomena with which psycho-analysis deals in so far as they are structured like a language' (Laplanche & Pontalis 1973: 210, 439).

> 'The Real is the impossible ... that which is lacking in the symbolic order, the ineliminable residue of all articulation, the foreclosed element, which may be approached, but never grasped: the umbilical chord of the Symbolic' (Lacan 1994: 280).

18 Embodied knowledge here equates to (a potentially dialectical) materialism – dis-embodied knowledge is the prerogative of so-called 'objective' classical documen-tarism.

19 Rancière's definition of 'de-figuration' travels ideologically and politically beyond the term 'defiguration' used in art history, which 'implies a certain willingness by the artist and observer to suspend conclusions in exchange for participation with the un(der)folding of new possibilities and becomings' http://neithernor.com/wonderful/defiguration.htm (accessed 01 January 2007). This art history usage, though interesting in its own right, articulates the space between figurative and abstract works exemplified in this quote by the work of de Silva and Klee. A better term for that aspect of the definition of defiguration might be 'defigurement'.

20 The film was originally commissioned by French Television to be a modern ver-sion of Jean-Jacques Rousseau's treatise on education, the title itself taken from Nietzsche's 1882 treatise on the re-education of a nineteenth-century sensibility. Rousseau was the author of the world's first written democratic constitution – for Corsica in 1765.

21 Text and translation verified in J. Monaco (1975) *Jump Cut*, 7, 15–17. This quote has been an influence on my own film practice and my teaching methodology for many years.

22 An avatar in religiosity is an incarnation of a myth in human form, now used popu-larly in computer terms as a virtual embodiment (as in virtual reality) or as a per-sonified icon in computer games (see Peter Greenaway's comment on *Second Life* in chapter 13 of this book). Here I use the term to imply the representational image of the social world. Godard uses the term in the sense of video being one of the avatars of cinema (Temple & Williams 2000: 21).

23 Rancière alludes to two differing histories of Poetics, the classical Aristotelian

approach regarding the 'representation of men in action', whereby the progression of the action depends on the characters' changes of fortune and knowledge and Romantic Poetics which abandoned action for the signifying power of signs involving expression, correspondence of resonant or dissonant signs, metamorphosis and reflection (2006: 160).

24 Jacques Aumont, writing about Eisenstein's theory of intellectual montage quotes the Hungarian writer and friend of Eisenstein, Béla Balázs: 'images ought not to *signify* ideas, but rather to *construct and motivate them*' (1987: 147) and Eisenstein himself referred to 'a language of cinedialectics' (Aumont 1987: 159).

CHAPTER 2
CINEMA, THEORY, WOMEN

Noel Burch

The outline of a problematic that we are going to discuss here concerning the male centrism of Modernism in general and of educated cinephilia in particular allows us an insight into why it is especially English-speaking feminists who, in the context of a 'post-modern' critique of Modernism, have been able, over the last thirty years, to force open doors that even today remain more or less hermetically sealed in France, notably in the area of theory, criticism and cinema history. And in the process, they have been more broadly able to reconfigure entire fields of research (in history, art history, literature, media and so forth) by bringing to light networks of meaning, in representations and in discourses, that were once so taken for granted as to be invisible.[1]

Even if, out of prudence or delicacy, few women theoreticians have gone that far, one can deduce from their work as a whole that these networks of meaning concerning power relations between the 'sexes', between the 'masculine' and the 'feminine', *fundamentally structure any narrative* – literary, theatrical, filmic – and that, at least as much as other more abstract, metaphorical or 'materialist' networks, they deserve to found their own narratology. The Italian-American semiotician Teresa de Lauretis seems, I think, to confirm this hypothesis when she endeavours to demonstrate that any narrative is essentially oedipal:

In this mythical-textual mechanics, then, the hero must be male, regardless of the gender of the text-image, because the obstacle, whatever its personification, is morphologically female and indeed, simply, the womb. The implication here is not inconsequential. For if the work of the mythical structuration is to establish distinctions, the primary distinction on which all others depend is not, say, life and death, but rather sexual difference ... (T)he hero, the mythical subject, is constructed as human being and as male; he is the active principle of culture, the establisher of distinction, the creator of differences. Female is what is not susceptible to transformation, to life or death; she (it) is an element of plot-space, a topos, a resistance, matrix or matter ... Therefore, to say that narrative is the production of Oedipus is to say that each reader – male or female – is constrained and defined within the two positions of a sexual difference thus conceived: male-hero-human, on the side of the subject; and female-obstacle-boundary-space, on the other. (1984: 118–21)

We should stress that the re-reading of Vladimir Propp carried out by de Lauretis in no way leads her to argue in favour of the making of anti-oedipal, that is anti-narrative, films, as was especially the case in the 1970s, under the impetus of the first important feminist theoreticians.

For the fact is that feminist theorisation initially developed according to the pattern set by the contemporary leftist rejection of 'readable' representation that I call 'revolutionary formalism'. In the manner of a Vertov (or of a Vertovian Godard) and casting anathema on bourgeois representation that was linear, transparent, illusionary and unconscious of its 'process of production', Laura Mulvey in England and later Mary Ann Doane in the United States condemn the 'patriarchal language' of the dominant, narrative, representational cinema. This revolutionary formalism that was initially supported in France by *Tel Quel*, *Cinéthique* and a little later by *Les Cahiers du Cinéma*, would develop in Great Britain in the pages of *Screen*, published by the very official British Film Institute. These female scholars and others would become the advocates and sometimes the practitioners of a feminist avant-gardism whose necessarily limited public appeal would be tacitly accepted as the price to pay for ideological purity. Summing up her exemplary critique of such vaticination, Jennifer Hammett writes:

Feminist film theory has too long equated representation with alienation and error, causing it to become embroiled unnecessarily in questions of epistemology. The struggle should not be over representation, but over representations; what is needed to challenge patriarchy is not an altered epistemological relation to the real, but altered representations. (1997: 85)

Hammett doesn't spell it out in her text, but her target is in fact a modernist reorientation of feminist thought that stresses the 'political scope' of forms, downplays that of contents and scorns the 'immediately accessible' codes of mass culture. Doane citing Hammett writes:

> Sometimes, when I am subject to a strong desire to laugh and hence 'belong' to an audience, or when I am tired, watching late night television, and off my guard, I will find myself laughing at a sexist joke. I 'find myself', I am beside myself, I am other. (1997: 88)

And Hammett comments:

> In this narrative of the split subject, Doane represents herself as vulnerable to the power of the mass media, as yearning to merge with a mass audience which is, almost by definition, uncritical. In a scenario reminiscent of *The Invasion of the Body Snatchers*, her vulnerability is physical (she is 'tired'; the pod people can complete the replication process only after their human hosts have fallen asleep). And yet, finally, as in the movie, it is her mind that is subject to the alien force. (1997: 88)

Now, for women to defend themselves against the pernicious powers of the patriarchal ideology of mass culture, the critical distance that Doane preaches is none other than that of Modernism.[2]

The tendency that Hammett denounces will be abandoned during the 1980s by the leading feminist scholars who want above all to bring new light to bear on real world relationships of alienation and oppression between the sexes. Feminist critics, as Tania Modleski's book firmly reminds us, use Hitchcock's works to elucidate the issues and the problems that specifically affected women under Patriarchy (2002).

Such a resolutely political approach to cinema (but also to figurative painting or the novel) goes against the taboos in force in France and the Latin countries where this type of research, on the few times it surfaces, is pejoratively labelled 'vulgar sociology', 'thematic analysis' or 'contents analysis' by 'cinema studies', that noble discipline. In contrast, such research has routinely been carried out in England and the US, for the last twenty years, under the labels of *cultural* and *gender studies*, where, moreover, it can be linked to textual, auteurist and other approaches. It is essentially a question of relocating the films in their production and reception contexts to bring out a widened form of textuality, notions of the absolute autonomy of art being considered irrelevant. Applied to the history of Hollywood cinema from the end of the 1970s, these approaches represented the first concerted attempt to loosen the grasp of Louis Delluc and the *politique des auteurs* whose grip had recently become strong in English-speaking countries as well.

However, it is necessary to note that if, since Delluc, formalist Modernism had always dominated the way cinema was understood in France, the situation was not the same in the United States. American cinema criticism, which begins to operate as early as 1908, initially only seeks to encourage the industry to make technical and artistic progress. During the classical period, a certain Anglo-Saxon empiricism leads the best critics (Mannie Farber, Parker Tyler, James Agee) to concentrate on the substance of the popular films that they review because they are aware of what their reader-spectators are interested in. And the *auteur* policy, which was imported into the United States by Andrew Sarris in the 1960s, only enjoyed a relative success there for a short decade before being seriously challenged. Today, one might say that it has to 'keep its head down'.[3]

Cultural studies, whose founding father was the great sociologist Raymond Williams, was initially developed by Marxist researchers at the University of Birmingham. For them, it was a question of engaging with mass produced products and the associated cultural practices in order to draw out from them, often in a very subtle way, the 'work of ideology'. Beyond the unqualified scorn of an Adorno, beyond a 'reflection of infrastructures' approach that would echo Lukács, it was a question of studying representations aimed at the masses – in particular social formations and at specific periods – in their relative autonomy. Practiced since then in France by a tiny minority of scholars of communications or of media sociology, this approach seems a precious one to me.[4] But not because of its tendency to want to rescue mass cultural production as a site of 'popular resistance':[5] rather, because of the light it throws on the ideological stakes and strategies with which the products of the cultural industries take real contradictions into account even as they make every effort to obstruct a real understanding of them.

Here we should draw attention to the work of Janet Staiger, who aspires to go beyond cultural studies with an approach that draws on the aesthetic of reception of the Constance School (see for example the work of Hans-Robert Jauss) to establish a materialist and dialectic approach to the interpretation of films. Staiger recommends that we should only read films from earlier periods through the material traces of their 'real' reception at the time, arguing that modern research methods allow us to identify better the 'real' intertext of the works. If Staiger rightly rejects the postmodern relativism that considers that the public of the media is 'primarily an assemblage of individual producers of meaning' (Schiller 1991: 148), and if she accords the greatest weight to class identity, her mistrust of any 'text-activated reading' must inevitably give rise to some reservations. For she seems to rule out any exegesis that explores hypothetical readings that are historically credible despite the lack of printed proof that such readings 'really' existed. How can one assume, for example, that the masochist fantasy that Gaylyn Studlar has brought to light in the work of Dietrich/von Sternberg but that no critic has ever acknowledged, did not affect the spectators of the period at one level or another of their psyche, if only by keeping them away from cinemas, these films having most often been box-office failures ... which is certainly as material a trace as any other (Studlar 1986)! Or again, how can we suppose that the French cinema public of the Occupation years was not affected by the fundamental and spectacular changes that occurred in the screen representation of relationships between the sexes after the resumption of production in November 1940, even if no observer of the period seems to have noted it in writing? (Burch & Sellier 1996)

Textual analysis allows us to know explicitly the class and gender interests of the limited social groups (white, male, petit-bourgeois in general) that are directly responsible for the production of cinematic representations that can usually be read, from the point of view of the producer, as exorcisms of socio-historical traumas: military defeats, workers' revolts, a feminist resurgence, and so forth.[6] Such ideological figures circulate ceaselessly in films and in society but the immense majority of critics and spectators do not consciously make sense of them at the time and can therefore leave no trace of their reception at a deep level.

Even though they suggest very valuable alternatives to sterile formalism, all these approaches systematically avoid the one question formalism has ever deigned to put to a film: the why and the how either of its beauty, the pleasure it generates, or of its ugliness, the displeasure it produces.[7] Now, from our point of view here, avoiding this question is a tacit admission that only a 'science of aesthetics' is able to answer it. No materialist approach now seems to want to even try to take on the question of the 'masterpiece': Anglo-American feminists have gone so far as to banish 'masterpiece' from their vocabulary, the concept seeming as phallocentric as the etymology of the word; and the most politically correct postmodernists judge that it is an irrelevant concept in the era of the abolition of the subject and of the generalised relativity of values, and other fashionable twaddle. Finally, if cultural studies specialists do take an interest in the pleasures felt by consumers of mass culture, they are definitely not interested in those dimensions of mass culture that the different species of auteurists have been able to identify

– and, looking back, this is their principal virtue –where artistic work has taken place that effectively escapes from dominant schemata. But, I would add, perhaps not only at the level of form.

So the question remains, as we look forward to a challenge to cinephilic orthodoxy, even it remains a purely hypothetical possibility in France at the moment: how is it that certain mass cultural works – for example, certain products of classical Hollywood cinema – are more or less universally recognised today for their 'beauty'? Could it simply be because the stylistic mastery of the director of genius carries a worldview made up of a certain number of more or less metaphysical commonplaces that are supposedly identifiable in any film that he has signed? Or is it because of that 'soul' that the authorial genius supposedly communicates to us almost despite himself by his directorial choices[8] – as used to be solemnly explained to us with respect to certain of Fritz Lang's Hollywood films where 'the mise-en-scene effaces even the characters' (Mourlet 1959), and as almost all cinema students in French universities 'spontaneously' still believe?

I am aware that my desire to re-examine this outdated question (that many still wonder about nonetheless), as well as some of the replies that I suggest and the reservations that I express regarding French modernist criticism, might well be seen as regressive or conservative. Which, from a certain point of view is not false, for I have a feeling, and I'm not the only one, that with the passing decades we have lost track of some important things that we will sooner or later have to go back to.

In the favourable review that he devotes to *La Drôle de guerre des sexes du cinéma français* (Burch & Sellier 1996) in the *Cahiers du Cinéma*, Joël Magny observes that, 'Their (Burch and Sellier's) refusal to restrict themselves to masterpieces and to 'auteurs' leads to some curious observations: great films like *La Règle du Jeu* (*The Rules of the Game*, 1939) show the capacity to escape from the common mould of a period even as they deal with its problematic in their own way'. Magny goes on to ask; 'Could it be aesthetic hierarchy is therefore not simply a matter of form?' (Magny 1997 p. 12). A question worth its weight in gold, coming as it does in the pages of the *Cahiers du Cinéma*.

Certainly, if one accepts the definition, put forward in quite a casual way by Gérard Genette (1997: 15), according to which 'aesthetics' only concerns the surface appearance of works, Magny's question is a pointless one. But if the aim of the expression 'aesthetic hierarchy' is to take in both the 'artistic value' of a cinematic work and the 'naïve' pleasure that it can arouse in the 'average spectator' which we all are (at least for films that are addressed to us, within the context of our culture, and whose representations we can link to social life as we know it), we cannot limit ourselves to surfaces.

The work of Jan Mukarovsky comes in useful here. A member, alongside Roman Jakobson and Nicolaï Troubetzkoy, of the Prague Circle, he is much less well known in France, judging by the total lack of translations of his work into French. But his most important work, *Aesthetic Function: Norm and Value as Social Facts* inaugurates, in 1936, an approach to the question of aesthetics that locates itself beyond formalist descriptivism as well as the poetics of Jakobson, founded on a dialectics of observance or non-observance of linguistic codes. Mukarovsky posits that any cultural artefact simultaneously presents sets of aesthetic and *non-aesthetic* values and that these two heterogenous sets will determine its *artistic value* in the society where and the period when its value is assessed.

Art in general and individual works in particular adjust in different ways to the 'naturally' hegemonic ambitions of the aesthetic norm. In the manner of the abstract paintings and sculptures of the era of Mukarovsky, some artefacts tend to exclude any non-aesthetic function.[9] That is the dominant tendency that leads to high Modernism. But despite the attempts of the *Nouveau Roman* or American Underground cinema, any narrative art, including of course 'the talkies', manifests a *resistance*, offers up composite objects, within which aesthetic and non-aesthetic (moral, political, libidinal etc.) values overlap permanently. Paul Sharits and other avant-garde film makers of his generation used habitually to equate representation itself with the narrativity that they scorned (an outlook which resembles the hunting down of 'tonal reminiscences' by the purists of serial music). From their point of view, they were right. A cinema which even shows recognisable fragments of the world cannot avoid producing meanings beyond aesthetics: spectacular evidence of this is provided by the three films where Stan Brakhage strives to aestheticise urban reality (in the *Pittsburgh Trilogy* (1971), filmed in a hospital, accompanying policemen on patrol and at the forensic medicine institute of the city). By breaking these scenes down into fragments whose meaning is weakened or obliterated, these films inadvertently document the modernist avoidance of the reality of suffering social classes.

One imagines that for Mukarovsky the high Modernism that would prevail in Europe and the US after World War Two would be the final outcome of a logic that was inherent in the very principle of the aesthetic norm and in its 'totalitarian' disposition to submit everything to itself.

Clement Greenberg ... demanded not only a renunciation of representational images (and even of the suggestion of images) but also an end to depth, framing, drawing and value contrast. Every feature of painting was to be tested for indispensability in the interest of a radical simplification, excluding and divesting until only the the optically irreducible was left. (Wollen 1993: 15)

Even more than in the abstract shapes we have seen since Wassily Kandinsky or Constantin Brancusi, this imperialism of the aesthetic norm reaches its high point in post-Webernian music with its purist refusal of any code accessible to those who aren't professional musicians – with the outlawing of 'tonal reminiscences', the triumph of 'irrational rhythmics', and so forth. In the 1950s the Domaine Musical concerts in the Petit Théâtre Marigny on the Champs Elysées represented one of the most exclusive artistic circles of the capital.

The triumph of aestheticism was complete in the plastic arts and music, which have always been elite arts. But because fiction cinema was largely a 'prisoner' in the domain of mass culture, quite simply because of economic imperatives, it has always been a model of the hybridity of which Mukarovsky speaks.

The period 1930–60 would see not only the progressive socio-political enthronement of high Modernism but also the high-point of 'classical cinema'. If one takes it as a reference point, one can confidently state that, when they attribute value to this or that film, the vast majority of that cinema's spectators do so because of non-aesthetic, referential and communicational functions that are encrusted, as it were, in any narrative work no matter how aestheticised it may be. That recognition of value depends on how we become attached to characters, their words and their look upon things; it depends upon their story, upon the interplay of their class, gender and possibly racial or ethnic identities; it depends finally on the particular charisma of this or that actor – not on the 'how it's told' but on *what it tells and what it means*. Of course, it is the cinematography and the *mise-en-scène* and their associated aesthetics which hold all those other things together by giving them a form and style. But for the 'average spectator' – someone who is inside each of us since we have been going to darkened theatres or sitting in front of televisions – the primary value of a film is dependent on the relationship to that 'real' from which, in the eyes of Christa Wolf, the function of aesthetic theory is to 'protect' the masculine intellect; it depends, all in all, on what Jean-Jacques Rousseau already calls 'imitation'. When it denigrates this 'naïve' relationship to the screen, the *politique des auteurs* makes the quintessential modernist gesture. Like the formalisms that preceded its invention (Louis Delluc, Lucien Rebatet, André Bazin...) or which followed it (let us cite practices as distinct as those of Raymond Bellour and of ... *Theory of Film Practice* (Burch 1973), it enshrines the superiority of the cultivated enthusiast, venturing onto mass culture's home ground – 'placing its head in the lion's mouth' so to speak – but knowing how to avoid the 'facile' and vulgar readings of the populace.[10]

As it happens, the current text intends to locate itself firmly on the side of the 'naïve' perception of films to show that in the final analysis, it is the mode of reading – when pushed further, of course, than the paying spectator habitually does – which can configure them in the richest way, whether they are or not, moreover, 'great films' by 'great *auteurs*', universally recognised as such. For me, it is a question not only of imagining how a film may have been understood by its intended public, but also of how the film continues to speak to 'us', in a coherent, illuminating way of social, moral and political issues that will always concern us.

For a large part, I will base my approach on writings in English carried out in the areas of *gender studies* and *cultural studies*. But my efforts, and this is maybe what will justify them, will set themselves a different 'goal' that is more presumptuous if not more ambitious than most of that work: I am trying to develop a materialist 'grid' of both ethical and artistic *values* able to contribute to the development, for 'readerly' cinema (with the meaning that Barthes gives to the word, but reversing his hierarchy, as the 'unreaderly' does not interest me), of an *impure poetics*. Impure in that it would associate the aesthetic and the non-aesthetic and would value the discourse as much as its form.

I should specify that I am not seeking here to promote films committed to the left of the sort that Robin Wood rightly qualifies with the noble word agit-prop (Wood 1998), which is a rare bird in Europe nowadays and one always rare in the United States. Films like *Salt of the Earth* (Biberman 1954), *Northern Lights* (Nilsson and Hanson 1978) or *Bob Roberts* (Robbins 1992), to limit oneself to a few fine American works made far from Hollywood, have the virtue of an exemplary and gratifying commitment. But these films are characterised by their refusal of the very ambiguity that gives life to so many Hollywood productions, some of which even manage to give authentically dialectical representations of social tensions.[11] For when a Hitchcock, a Lang, a Vidor or indeed other more inconsistent or less famous directors, manage to construct, in the fertile context of Hollywood's ambiguity, a complex discourse about fundamental social contradictions, something that many would call a masterpiece can suddenly appear.

The French, Spanish, Italian, Belgian, Quebecois, Argentinian ... or Cuban reader will have understood that the aim here is to go against the grain of a set of ideas that are still taken for granted among the intellectuals of our countries, where the traditional level of political consciousness (happily!) remains relatively high compared to the United States, for example, but where feminism is still weak and beleaguered. That is doubtlessly why, when they are denouncing American economic and cultural imperialism, people in our countries so habitually bundle together the ideas that are those of the left of all English-speaking countries, casually dismissing them under the catch-all label of 'political correctness'. We should remind ourselves that, in the United States, this label, which was originally a self-mocking joke uttered by the post-1968 left, has become a reductive formula that is very useful to the very conservative American right: as Gerard Graff notes, citing Michael Berubé, what enrages American conservatives is that they have not managed to exert the same domination over American Universities as they have over most other areas of life in the US (1992: 157). It is a question of avoiding discussions for which a lot of men and women in our Latin countries are not yet 'ready', to put it mildly.[12] But it is especially because of this conflation of ideas that modernist doctrine continues to reign unchallenged among university cinema researchers, most critics and a cinephile public that is more extensive in France than anywhere else in the world. It is important for this public that it experience, when watching 'commercial' films, a pleasure that is qualitatively different to that felt by the films' intended audience (who pay for the films, moreover, by buying their seats). Apparently independent of the cult of stars and the infinite repetition of certain primary 'myths' or certain universal reflexes like suspense or fear, things associated with the diet of only the 'ordinary spectator', the superior pleasure of the cultivated cinephile notably works to camouflage the embarrassing fact that the sophisticated spectator feels the same emotions as his or her social inferior.

Nowadays, the cultivated public is concerned above all with distinction, and satisfies itself with choosing films to see according to their critical status. At the same time as he invented cinephilia, Louis Delluc was already giving birth to some of the strategies of distinction associated with it. On the one hand by projecting his own formalism onto 'the people':

> In a ghastly little cinema in Clermont-Ferrand, I saw popular sensibility. The charm of the screen makes the taste of the crowds, who are so reluctant to allow themselves to be cultivated by any other art, burst violently into blossom. A few hundred workers and humble women were raptly absorbed by a delicate little Japanese film, without action, made up of gestures, flowers and decorated paper. After which came an episode of *Coeur d'héroine* with Irene and Vernon Castle. Do you think that this crowd was moved above all by the drama or its serial-like twists and turns? They barely noticed it. They experienced an hour of pure pleasure simply because of Irene Castle's dresses, the harmony of the furnishings and the remarkable elegance of the various props. (1985: 73)

And on the other hand, by distancing himself from those of his own class who dared mock this popular good taste through a practice which anticipates postmodern *jouissance* before 'trash' or 'kitsch'.

> Why can't the *faithful and elegant clientele* of the most exclusive of the Paris film theatres do without watching popular films? ... [T]he worst fictions ('ciné-romans') are regularly listed on the programme and of course bring the house down with laughter ... [T]hat is why we'll see, for a long time, in this pleasant theatre so-called popular films which allow people of refined taste to publicly demonstrate their superiority. (1985: 71)

The opposite of this idealised vision of a tamed popular crowd, in Delluc's mind, is a socially rebellious 'people' of whom he is rather afraid. His vision is reminiscent of that which Maurice Barrès had had a few years earlier of the crowd before Victor Hugo's coffin and that, in his eyes, anticipated the coming together of the social classes and the imaginary abolition of their differences that his proto-fascism dreamed of:

> This prodigious mixture of the enthusiastic and the debauched, of the stupid, the simple and the sensible, organises itself into one tremendous being ... Its face, which it turns towards the coffin and which is lit by the funeral torches, is made up of one hundred thousand faces, some revolting, others ecstatic, but none unmoved. Its breathing is like the sound of the sea. (1988: 466)

In the eyes of the rather internationalist Delluc, what (cinematic) culture would cement together was not the French nation but the 'peoples of the world'. However, the idealised unity that he wished for them is the same as that desired by Barrès watching the funeral of the great man, a Republican anticipation of the national-fascist spectacle.

I myself spent years resisting meaning as I viewed films of every period under the aegis of that great modernist Henri Langlois. But I think that if just about everyone must be sensitive to the beauty of a film like, for example, King Vidor's *Beyond the Forest* (1949), it is because of the tension generated by its simultaneous and co-extensive representation of two opposing visions – one repressive, the other subversive – of the dilemma of a petit-bourgeois American wife in 1947, locked into domesticity with consumption as her only distraction. And, of course, it is also, but only *also*, because of the talent of the script-writers, the actors and the director who were able to bring this dialectical struggle to life with such rigour and emotional intensity.

I think that this is always the way with *our cinematic pleasure*. Catch-all notions like 'the beauty of the mise-en-scène' are often naïve substitutes for a vocabulary that the critic simply does not possess. But sometimes aesthetic appeal is an alibi. If that other Vidor film, the vile *The Fountainhead* (1949), was able to move some of the leading (left-wing) lights of French cinephilia (Bertrand Tavernier, Luc Moullet) so deeply, it is perhaps because of the homage it pays to the modernist tradition through a heavy-handed directing style that can just as well pass for expressionist or 'camp'. But it is certainly also because of the ideology that underpins this story of the heroic determination of a virile genius of modern architecture. The film's powerful fascistic echoes certainly disturb those who sing its praises, but the cult of the solitary genius always fascinates the modernist critic, as does the spectacle of a haughty blue stocking who lets herself go in the arms of the Nietzschean phallus: so one draws a veil over these disturbing issues. Moullet, for example, prefers to speak of 'a courageous tract with diverse meanings', of a film where 'one's fascination ... comes from the aesthetic value of motifs that, for Vidor, are either metaphysical or ethical' (1962: 30). But not political of course. As may be demonstrated by reference to the auteurist reception of the films of Howard Hawkes in France, the modernist '*détournement*'[13] (hijacking) functions like a watertight and sterile protective suit for the person who wants to get close to a popular art that of necessity deals with 'ignoble human doings' (Théophile Gautier 1834). Just as it works to hide, in this particularly regressive sector of the French elite, an increasingly unjustifiable fascination for Hawksian masculinism. Nonetheless, delivering an apologia for films like *The Fountainhead* (Vidor1949) or *The Big Sky* (Hawks1952) is surely made easier by an intellectual milieu where the Mademoiselles de Maupin of this world must still become soldiers for the causes of men to escape the abjection that they supposedly bear.

We are tempted, in the end, to amend Jacques Rivette's famous statement: if aesthetics is a form of morality – and why not? – the hegemony of aesthetics is decidedly immoral, as is the scorn cast by the supporters of this hegemony on uncultured people, who, in their minds, merge with the feminine.[14] Many today admire a film like the Coen brothers' *Fargo* (1996) (always given 'four stars' for its television re-runs). This is a film that fits well into the modernist canon: a distant inheritor of Flaubertian impassivity, it manages, through its ironic treatment of a particularly absurd and macabre crime, to silence all the signs that might lead one to fundamental social determinations – for example, to those which make money the sole real value of US 'democracy' – and to limit itself to tongue-in-cheek satire at the expense of the petite- and middle-bourgeoisie of North Dakota ('Will you dare laugh at it?', the posters challenge).

What is the root of these evil deeds? Why, the stupidity of 'ordinary people', of course. How do we know? All of them, crooks, businessmen, housewives or police officers, remain democratically glued to their television screen, like Madame Bovary absorbed by her sentimental novels in her convent.

These pernicious new 'prophets', the Tim Burtons, Coen brothers, David Lynches, Quentin Tarantinos and the like, are admittedly valued more highly by French cinema criticism and its cinephile public than by their equivalents over the Atlantic. But, helped by fashionable anti-Americanism, this rejection by an audience judged to be slightly barbaric can only serve to confirm the Parisian perception of the quality of works in which, moreover, people are happy to recognize a gratifying echo of the New Wave and its *auteur* policy. And in which our journalists find the reflection of their own social renunciation, which goes back to what some have called the 'new betrayal of the intellectuals' of the early 1980s.[15] The struggle against the modernist hijacking – and its 'postmodernist' disguises – is decidedly not a mere issue of university hypothesising.

My students, who had been taught to admire these false prophets, would justify their tastes with a catch all cliché: these films are meant to 'criticize American society'. Big deal. The films assuredly reflect the resentment that many American intellectuals feel towards an American heartlands prey to the cultures of death (racism, the cult of the revolver, consumerism, religious fundamentalism, and so forth). Alas, their own fathomless lack of understanding of power relations under a productivist and patriarchal 'free enterprise' system means that they invariably scapegoat the mass of poor whites for their own air-conditioned nightmare, a group manipulated, conditioned and misinformed for decades by a servile media (only the vulgarity of which these refined film-makers seem to notice). This cinema of chic scorn, which draws its justification from European culture (Surrealism, Nouveau Roman ...) and its forms from popular American culture – which it satirizes at the same time as it 'transcends' it, to impress cinephiles (Tarantino's *Pulp Fiction* (1994), Rodriguez's *From Dusk till Dawn* (1996), Lynch's *Twin Peaks* (1990)) – is assuredly a product of our 'postmodern' times, one of those against which this work is attempting to react ...

Translation by Martin O'Shaughnessy

BIBLIOGRAPHY

Barres, M. (1988) *Les Déracinés*. Gallimard: Folio [1897]

Baudelot C. and M. Cartier (1998) 'Lire au Collège et au Lycée: de la Foi du Charbonnier à une Pratique Sans Croyance', *Genèse de la Croyance Littéraire*. Actes de la Recherche en Sciences Sociales, 123, pp. 25–44.

Benda, J. (1980) *The Treason of Intellectuals*. London: W. W. Norton & Co.

Burch, N. (1972) *Theory of Film Practice*. London: Secker and Warburg.

Burch, N. and G. Sellier (1997) *La Drôle de Guerre des Sexes du Cinéma Français, 1930–1956* (new, revised edition). Paris: Nathan-Fac.

De Lauretis, T. (1984) *Alice Doesn't: Feminism, Semiotics, Cinema*. Bloomington: Indiana University Press.

Delluc, L. (1985) *Les Cinéastes, Ecrits Cinématographiques*. Paris: L' Éditions Cinémathèque Française.

Frank, T. (2002) 'New Consensus for Old: Cultural Studies from Left to Right'. Chicago: Prickly Paradigm Press.

Genette, G. (1997) *L'Oeuvre de L'Art. 2, La Relation Esthétique*. Paris: Seuil.

Graff, G. (1992) *Beyond the Culture Wars: How Teaching the Conflicts Can Revitalize American Education*. New York: W.W. Norton.

Hammett, J. (1997) 'The Ideological Impediment: Feminism and Film Theory', *Cinema Journal*, 36, 2, pp. 85–99.

Huyssen, A. (1986) *After the Great Divide, Modernism, Mass Culture, Postmodernism*. Bloomington and Indianapolis: Indiana University Press.

Julliard, J. (1997) 'L'Oncle Sam et L'Amour', *Nouvel Observateur*, 2–8, January, p. 25.

Magny, J. (1997) 'Le Cinéma Français Fait la Guerre des Sexes', *Cahiers du Cinéma*, 510, February, p. 12.

Modleski, T. (2002) *Les Femmes Qui en Savaient Trop: Hitchcock et la Théorie Féministe*. Paris: Éditions L'Harmattan [1986].

Moullet, L. (1962), 'Rétrospective King Vidor', *Cahiers du Cinéma*, 136, October, pp. 26–33

Mourlet, M. (1959) 'Trajectoire de Fritz Lang', *Cahiers du Cinéma*, 99, September. pp. 19–24.

Mukarovsky, J. (1970) *Aesthetic Function, Norm and Value as Social Facts* [1936]. Translated from Czech, with notes and afterword by Mark E. Suino. Ann Arbor: University of Michigan.

Sartre, J.-P. (1988) *"What is Literature?" and Other Essays*. Cambridge, Massachusetts: Harvard University Press. Pp. 21–239.

Schiller, H. I. (1989) *Culture, Inc: The Corporate Takeover of Public Expression*. New York and Oxford: Oxford University Press.

Silverman, K. (1992) *Male Subjectivity at the Margins*. London: Routledge.

Staiger, J. (1992) *Interpreting Films, Studies in the Historical Reception of American Cinema*. Princeton: Princeton University Press.

Studlar, G. (1986) *In the Realm of Pleasure: Von Sternberg, Dietrich and the Masochistic Aesthetic*. New York: Columbia University Press.

Williams, L. (1994) 'Autre Chose qu'une Mère', in N. Burch (ed.) *Revoir Hollywood: la Nouvelle Critique Anglo-Américaine*. Paris: L'Harmattan, 2007, pp. 78–93.

Wollen, P. (1993) *Raiding the Icebox: Reflexions on Twentieth Century Culture*. Bloomington: University of Indiana Press.

Wood, R. (1998) *Sexual Politics and Narrative film: Hollywood and Beyond*. New York: Columbia University Press.

NOTES

1   It was especially the art, writing, filmmaking and criticism of women and minority artists with their recuperation of buried and mutilated traditions, their emphasis on exploring forms of gender and race-based subjectivity in aesthetic production and experiences, and their refusal to be limited to standard canonisations, which added a whole new dimension to the critique of high Modernism and to the emergence of alternative forms of culture (Huyssen 1986: 198).

2   For an alternative feminist critique of this theoretical avant-gardism see Williams 1994.

3   But faced with the mindless excesses of Postmodernism and the different forms of intellectual laziness favoured by its 'academically correct' attitudes, some notable figures have started to look back at it nostalgically (see Wood 1998: xi).

4   The journal *Communications* was a pioneer in this area as early as 1960. To it can be added today three other journals: *Actes de la recherche en sciences sociales*, *Réseaux* and *Champs visuels* (which became *Champs audio-visuels* in 2001).

5   See Frank (2000) for a caustic critique of the drift of cultural studies in this direction, a drift that has taken on massive proportions in work on film and television, judging from the conference I attended at Washington, DC in 2001.

6   As Silverman (1992) shows using some mainstream Hollywood films of the immediate post-war period. Drawing on the Marxist current within cultural studies and British-American feminism, Geneviève Sellier and I derive a similar thesis from a large corpus of French films made before, during and after World War Two (Burch & Sellier 1996).

7   The so-called 'cognitivist school', whose principal practitioner in cinema studies is the very influential David Bordwell and whose approach originates in phenomenology, is not included in my discussion here. Rightly or wrongly, and notably because of the way it postulates a universal spectator, this approach seems to me to be a psychologised variant of formalist Modernism and of art for art's sake.

8   Borrowed from modernist literary criticism, this magical mode of creation was taken apart by Sartre (1947) in *What is Literature?* four years before the birth of *Cahiers du Cinéma* and the first statements of the *politique des auteurs*. Reading him today, one can better understand why Sartre so rapidly became the number one enemy in the eyes of an intelligentsia among whom modernist ideology had reigned for so long. The break-up of the alliance, that had coincided with the period of the French Resistance (Sapiro 1996), between the few (mainly communist) proponents of a committed literature and the defenders of a Modernism that was not yet so labelled in France, echoed in the hostility most auteurists showed to Sartre.

Bazin's Sartrean ideas, the generous humanism that competes with his formalism, make him a survivor of this alliance as well as the precursor of the 'auteurism' that was to come.

9   In his rereading of Benjamin he expresses doubt about whether it is possible to distinguish between the totalising demands of aesthetics and those of politics (Hewitt 1993: 165).

10   Two sociologists of culture have shown at length how the typical school career of a secondary pupil in France includes a decisive threshold (the transition from the secondary school to the *lycée*), where he or she is initiated into the cultural obligation to prefer high literature to Stephen King and *to read the former for its style*:

> Encouraged in secondary school, the positions and dispositions required by the principle of ordinary reading will be disqualified in the *lycée* through the imposition of new norms which require a mental conversion from the pupils for which many today are not prepared ... Here, the adjective 'ordinary' means that the book and how it is used are fully grounded in the immediate concerns of everyday life (to enjoy oneself, to inform oneself) ... The concept of a 'literary reading' gathers in a broad sweep all the ways of reading that, from aesthetic contemplation to structural analysis, and including the straightforward reading for literary references, make the text itself ... the focus and the goal of the reading ... The formalist reading is not concerned with the world represented by the book but with the machinery of representation. (Baudelot & Cartier 1998: 25–44)

11   The principal theme of the second half of *On the Beauty of Latrines* (author's translation).

12   See Jacques Julliard's hilarious column from 1997 where he attributes the upsurge in aggression of Yankee imperialism to the need for (psychological) compensation felt on the other side of the Atlantic by men trapped 'between the feminist party which is considering castrating them and the marriage party which wants to put them in a cage'. Julliard in fact makes a classic misogynist gesture here: noticing, during a stay at a university, this widespread disorder in American masculinity (something that resurfaced in the person of 'Dubya' and his foreign policy), he lays the blame at women's door (Julliard 1997).

13   A term invented by the avant-gardist Situationist International to describe the subversive reworking of elements taken from an existing form of expression in a new context.

14   A French film aimed at the general public, and which was a success right around the World, rigorously developed this problematic associating elitism and misogyny. In *Le Goût des autres* (The Taste of Others, 2000) a middle-class boor, fascinated by a left-bank actress, manages to sensitize himself to high art, but his wife is irredeemable because of her feminine nature and remains bogged down in petit-bourgeois kitsch. The fact that this film was made by a woman – the scriptwriter-director, Agnès Jaoui tells us a lot about Parisian blind spots.

15   The reference here is to the book *La Trahison des clercs* (*The Betrayal of the Intellectuals*) published by Julien Benda in 1927 (translator's note).

CHAPTER 3
THEORY AND PRACTICE

Peter Wollen

We tend to think of 'theory' as something far removed from the professional task of filmmaking – or film 'practice' as it is sometimes called. It is as if they were two separate worlds – one of which is entirely concerned with the theoretical study of film, the other with the actual making of films. In fact, the two enterprises have consistently been very closely connected. Filmmakers have developed their own film theories and film theorists have been involved in making films. Indeed this was my own experience. After all, before I became a film theorist, I was already a screenwriter and during the 1960s, I lived partly by selling film scripts. But this was the decade in which certain books and essays, that would influence my work with film theory were being published. Roland Barthes' first essay on Structuralism, *Elements of Semiology*, was published in 1964 as was Levi Strauss' *The Structural Study of Myths*. Noam Chomsky's *Current Issues in Linguistic Theory* came out in 1964, Jacques Lacan's *Ecrits* in 1966. 1967 saw the beginnings of modern film theory: Umberto Eco talked about *Ideology and Language in the Cinema* at the Pesaro Film Festival and Christian Metz's *Essais sur la Signification au Cinéma* was published. My own *Signs and Meaning in the Cinema*, was completed in May 1968 and published the following year. It was then republished in 1972 with a new 'conclusion', in which I particularly noted Jean-Luc Godard's insistence on the 'continual examination and re-examination of the premises of filmmaking accepted by filmmaker and spectator' – theorists, directors and, of course, cinema-goers (Wollen 1998: 113) .

Working as co-director with Laura Mulvey, I made a series of films during the 1970s. This was also the decade *Screen* magazine began to publish theoretical texts, in which we read Christian Metz's *Film Language: A Semiotics of Cinema* (1974) and Raymond Bellour's *The Analysis of Film* (1979). *Signs and Meaning* was reissued once again in 1998, with an interview added, in the course of which the interviewer, Lee Russell, asks me a pointed question: 'So the theoretical aspects of your book are directly relevant to your filmmaking as well as to film study?' To which I replied: 'Absolutely!' (Wollen 1998: 166). During the 1960s, I still had not done any filmmaking, but I was writing scripts and it was definitely there on the agenda. And then the arrival of the 'new' Godard and structural film and experimental narrative all set me thinking about filmmaking in terms of the avant-garde rather than the industry – a project related to Godard's own interest in theory.

With the completion of the script of *The Passenger* in the early 1970s (released 1975) I had achieved all I wanted to as a screenwriter. So I then turned to filmmaking myself, but as an experimental filmmaker, working with Laura Mulvey. Our work as co-directors was closely connected to our work as theorists. And for me, of course, Eisenstein was a distant model for this. I went on to praise those filmmakers who, while working in the industry, had still retained their ongoing commitment to experimentation – I was thinking of films like *Citizen Kane* (1941) or Hitchcock's *Rope* (1948), Sam Fuller's *Shock Corridor* (1963), Kubrick's *2001* (1968), even Ridley Scott's *Blade Runner* (1982). All these films had an experimental dimension. Lee Russell asked me bluntly: 'Do you think theory and practice can be combined even in a film school?' Perhaps my reply has some relevance to the issues at stake in this book ... theory, experiment, film directing. I responded as follows:

> Eisenstein taught directing in a way which included teaching theory. But that's very rare. In my experience, even the best film schools keep the two well apart. They might argue that filmmaking simply does not leave enough time for serious study of film theory and vice versa, but I think that's just a lazy way of avoiding the issue. In an ideal world, production students would have a solid grounding in history and theory, just as academic students should have a grounding in production. But will it ever happen? The divide between the two curriculums seems to get wider each year. (Wollen 1998: 167)

Hopefully one outcome of this book will be a further strengthening of the ties between theory and practice. 'Does that matter?' I was asked. 'Yes, it does, very much so. It really troubles me that, in the University where I teach, students doing academic degrees – PhDs – never get a serious chance to make a film – and vice versa, production students don't have the time or mind-set or the opportunity to think seriously about film theory' (ibid.). Theory should ask questions of practice and vice versa. I was struck by an interesting question I was once asked – 'You were saying that *Signs and Meaning* should be read in conjunction with viewing your films, weren't you?' I responded as follows, '*Signs and Meaning* asks the question, "What kind of films should we make?" which *Riddles* answers. And then *Riddles* asks "So what kind of theory do we need?"'

In 1974 Christian Metz's *Essais Sur La Signification au Cinéma* was translated into English and published as *Film Language: A Semiotics of the Cinema*. Metz raised a very important issue when he shifts aesthetic emphasis away from the script to the director: 'A filmmakers cinema? What about the concept of a "filmmakers cinema", as distinct from the old "scriptwriters cinema"?' After all, 'today's cinema is often a "cinema cinema", while the old cinema was often the secondary illustration of an already worked-out story'(1974: 201). It is at this point that Metz, quite naturally, turned to the example of Jean-Luc Godard. Godard's films bore witness to his own narrative inventiveness. He was a director whose 'inspiration can only be fired', as Metz puts it, 'during the actual shooting'(1974: 202), when he is able to draw upon his own constant reflection on the subject of the cinema, 'what it is and what it could be...'. Godard was, of course, a dedicated cinephile, steeped in the cinema of the past while, at the same time, determined to break new ground and create a cinema of the present. He was a living example of the filmmaker who was also a film scholar and historian. His practical attitude to film theory was expressed in an ad hoc and paradoxical manner. For instance he once observed:

> I like to say that there are two kinds of cinema: there is a Flaherty and there is an Eisenstein. That is to say that there is documentary realism and there is theatre, but ultimately, at the highest level, they are one and the same. Through documentary realism one arrives at the structure of theatre, and through theatrical imagination and fiction one arrives at the reality of life. To confirm this, look at the work of the great directors, how they pass from realism to theatre and then back again. (Sterritt 1998: 180)

For Godard Renoir was the model example as he represents a fusion of naturalism and theatricality. For instance, he points out that Renoir embraced a proto neorealism in *Toni* (1935), moved towards the theatrical with *Le Carosse d'Or* (1953) in the 1950s and then turned to television, in search of the utmost simplicity. Godard himself then commented on the linkage between realism and theatricality in his own film, *Vivre Sa Vie* (1962), 'a realistic film and at the same time extremely unrealistic. It is very schematic: a few bold lines, a few fundamental principles' (Sterritt 1998: 6). It is these 'fundamental principles' of course which are the material of film theory. After all, as Godard himself once put it: 'Motion pictures were invented to look, tell and study things. They are mainly a scientific tool for seeing life in a different way.' (Sterritt 1998: 176) Godard also discussed Eisenstein, observing that:

> Eisenstein was on the way to montage but he didn't reach it. He wasn't an editor, he was a taker of angles. And because he was so good at tak-ing angles, there was an idea of montage. The three lions in *October* are actually the same lion but taken from three different angles, so that the lion looks as if he's moving – in fact it was the association of angles that brought montage. (Sterritt 1998: 190)

As for Godard's own approach to filmmaking, he is quite clear about the pro-cess: 'For me there are three equally important moments in making a film – before, during and after the actual filming. With somebody like Hitchcock everything is calculated down to the last second and so the editing is less important' (Sterritt 1998: 172).

Yet Godard's own *A Bout de Souffle* (*Breathless*, 1960) owes a great deal to montage. He himself admitted as much, noting that 'it is a film in three movements, the first half-hour fast, the second *moderato*, and the third *alle-gro vivace* again' (Sterritt 1998: 6). Clearly he is describing his film as if it were analogous to music, suggesting that the rhythm and timing were pre-emi-nently crucial to him. In an interview with David Sterritt, Godard described himself 'half a novelist and half an essayist' (1998: 176) yet he could also be described as half a documentarist. Godard also noted that he wrote the actors' lines, but at the very last moment – a few bold lines and a few basic principles. Godard's theory of cinema was clearly determined by the urge to combine theatre with reality.

At this point it might be as well to look at Alfred Hitchcock's attitude to film theory. A film depended on its plot and the plot depended on the cre-ation of gripping situations which arose from within it. Suspense was of cru-cial importance – the spectators should always be asking, 'What will happen next?' Hitchcock put forward the idea that the film script was comparable to a blueprint, describing the film shot by shot, image by image. He also noted that spectators should be given information that characters lacked, in order to increase suspense. It was the filmmakers job 'to put things together visually, to embody the action and the juxtaposition of images that have their own specific language and emotional impact – *that* is cinema!' (Gottlieb 1995: 214). He also insisted that a film should never rely on dialogue, which pulled the film towards theatre rather than pure cinema.

It was the director's job, Hitchcock noted, 'to move his action forward with the camera, whether the action is set on the prairie or confined to the telephone booth' (Gottlieb 1995: 216). Hitchcock was also critical of Hollywood films, observing that 'the plushy architecture of Hollywood militates against a pure atmosphere and destroys realism' (Gottlieb 1995: 218). His own menu of ingredients will have considered that lighting creates mood, the camera dramatic impact, music would stir the emotions, colour would have an aesthetic effect and widescreen provide showmanship and spectacle - all of the elements needed for the machinery of the production. He was very clear about the process of filmmaking. First came the story synopsis, laid out on a single sheet of foolscap. Out of this synopsis he started to build the treatment – including characterizations, narrative and visual detail. The narrative itself should combine two different rhythms – the rhythm and pace of the action together with the rhythm and pace of the dialogue.

A necessary feature, of course, was suspense, which fell into two categories: the chase – 'objective suspense' – and suffering, as felt by the spectator – which Hitchcock referred to as 'subjective suspense'. Particularly interesting, however, is his endorsement of Russian montage, as the key element of film, along with an analogy between film and music. In his exact words: 'To me, pure film, pure cinema is pieces of film assembled. Any individual piece is nothing. But a combination of them creates an idea – montage, you can call it that. But there are many kinds of montage' (Gottlieb 1995: 288). And, as just one example, he then cites *Rear Window*:

> He observes. We register his observations on his face. We are using the visual image now. This is what I mean by pure cinema. Creative imagery. Every piece of film that you put in the picture should have a purpose. You cannot put it together indiscriminately. It's like the notes of music. They must make their point. (Gottlieb 1995: 289)

Hitchcock, like Houston later, was also fascinated by Freud. Tippi Hedren (as Marnie) was given notes mentioning her 'psychological complex', her 'childhood trauma', her early 'oedipal situation', her 'fantasy concerning her real-life father' and her sense of guilt.

Eisenstein was, *par excellence*, a director who was interested in the theory of filmmaking. In his early texts Eisenstein mainly discussed the issue of montage, which he described as fundamental to cinema. He immediately stressed the importance of 'angles', just as Godard described, emphasising that 'the work of the film director requires – in addition to a mastery of production, a repertoire of montage – calculated angles for the camera to capture' (Eisenstein 2004: 106). He goes on to note that 'these directorial considerations play a decisive role in both the selection of camera angles and the arrangement of the lights. No plot "justification" for the selection of the angle of vision of the light is necessary' (ibid.). Subsequently Eisenstein established his own 'Teaching and Research Workshop' in which he was able to experiment and to develop his ideas, both theoretical and practical.

Eisenstein was interested in the relation between montage and language. For him, montage approach was the essential, meaningful and sole possible language of cinema and, furthermore, analogous to the role of the word in spoken material. This analogy between the film shot and the written or spoken word was ultimately to become almost a commonplace. However, as a result of joining a linguistics programme at the University of Essex, where film was readily accepted as a parallel form of language, with its own lexicon, its own syntax and its own semantics, I became interested in certain links between language and film. Film developed as a medium for storytelling. We might expect, therefore, that it would develop devices for making more complex narrative forms easier for spectators to follow and understand. These devices would speed up our pragmatic understanding of stories by coding certain features so they could work automatically, just as we interpret the features of verbal languages. For example, all known languages have a system that assigns tense, mode and aspect to verbs. Scholars argue that all known 'Tense–Mode–Aspect' (TMA) in systems can best be explained by looking at the structure of narrative, which consists of a series of actions in chronological order. To follow a complicated story, we need to know (1) whether an action is ongoing (sequence-shot); (2) whether it is real or imaginary (a dream sequence perhaps); and (3) whether it is in the past (flashback). Of course Hitchcock, in *Stage Fright* (1950), made use of a 'lying flashback'.

Thus images can function as *tenses*, placing a situation in time, in the present or in a flashback or in a flashforward. Or images can function like *modes*, presenting different degrees of truth or likelihood or untruth – not only dream sequences, but fantasy sequences, as in Robbe-Grillet and Resnais' *Last Year In Marienbad* (1961) or as brazen falsehoods, as in Robbe-Grillet's own *The Man Who Lies* (1968). *Aspect*, however, relates to editing – whether the imagery is ongoing or complete. In all these various ways film functions as a practical language whose output is based on the intersection of time, image and plot. Using the concept of 'action categories', we can define situations as 'stative', 'durative' or 'punctual', as different verb forms are described in linguistics. The purpose of these categories is to define the different temporal characteristics of happenings or events. We know that reading is a durative action, that it continues over a period of time – not unlike watching a film. And we distinguish between the intransitive form of the verb 'to watch', which refers to an action which ends simply when the viewer has stopped watching and, on the other hand, the transitive form, 'to watch a film', where the action ends only when the viewer has finally watched the very last image on the very last reel. A film is structured to make sense of the various time-bound events or images which are the basic elements of a film. Actions might develop, and they change state – for example from running to walking to standing still. They also change action – as in giving a lecture and then answering questions.

Now I would like to return to the question of montage through the theories of Lev Kuleshov. Although he is best known for his intervention of the 'Kuleshov effect', he believed strongly that the shot was the basic unit of film. Filmmakers needed to think in terms of shots, to-be-photographed objects and actions which could be edited and arranged to create a story. Shots were, to so speak, 'word equivalents' or idea-phrases which could convey meaning through gestures of facial expressions, and could be edited into a 'dramatic chain', laid out like bricks. Kuleshov discussed the way a poet places one word after another, in a definite rhythm and the same was true of shots. Shots, Kuleshov believed, were like the ideograms in Chinese writing, images which produced meanings. He recommended that scriptwriters should create the content of the film by determining the character of the shot-material and that the director express the scriptwriter's conception by creating a montage of shot-signs. In other words, writing should come first, then the shot breakdown (which would be storyboarded) followed by the actual filming and, crucially, the editing.

Kuleshov's ideas about montage lead to questions of narrative through his close friendship with Russian linguistic scholar and folklorist, Victor Shklovsky who was specifically interested in the subject of the plot, its structure and its effect. Indeed they collaborated on Kuleshov's first film *By The Law* (1926). Shklovsky was particularly interested in the way that 'plot' dominates in the cinema, emerging, for instance, as melodrama, adventure or farce. He distinguishes between the properties of story, which may be borrowed from any literary source, for instance, a novel, a drama, a poem or a folktale and, then, how a story is subsequently transformed, through segmentation, for film. This involves two processes. First of all the film is prefigured in a skeleton scenario, which takes into account the relation between individual shots and the overall ensemble. Secondly the shots, once photographed, are composed through montage, into sequences. As the plot is reconstituted through the selection and arrangement of shots, the film ultimately emerges out of its double raw material. Thus Shklovsky recommended that scriptwriters should create the content of the film and translate it into the shot-material. The director then expresses the scriptwriter's conception by his montage of 'shot-signs'. In other words, writing should come first, then the shot breakdown (which would be storyboarded) followed by the actual filming and, crucially, the editing.

In this context, it is interesting to compare the 'montage'-based cinema preferred by Kuleshov or Eisenstein to George Wilson's description of the 'Classic Hollywood Film', as described in his book, *Narration in Light*. Wilson begins by discussing a montage sequence from Orson Welles' Hollywood classic, *The Lady From Shanghai* (1947). Welles' montage appears to break with logical sequence. Thus, a three-shot sequence, begins (1) with a shot from a car revealing that a truck has unexpectedly pulled out onto the road ahead of it, is followed (2) by a second shot of a woman pressing an unidentified button, followed in turn (3) by a third shot of the car, which contains two men, as it collides violently with a truck. Wilson notes that we are left with a sense of uncertainty as to how these images relate and their role in the ongoing story. There are a number of ways in which this shot sequence might be interpreted. Among them, for instance, he suggests that the sequence might function like Eisenstein's sequence of the three lions. On the other hand, we might recall Jennifer Selway's comment that in *The Lady from Shanghai* 'Welles simply doesn't care enough to make the narrative seamless' (2008). Welles, I think, wanted to disturb his viewers.

On the other hand, Wilson also hypothesises that the sequence might suggest a memory image or perhaps an hallucination, experienced by one of the car's occupants immediately before the crash. Luis Buñuel's use of montage in *Un Chien Andalou* (*An Andalusian Dog*, 1929), a film with 300 shots lasting for 15 minutes (that is to say, an average of one shot every three seconds), exploits this kind of use of discontinuous or hallucinatory montage. For instance, Buñuel makes striking use of visual simile or metaphor – a woman's underarm hair is matched with a sea urchin, a cloud crossing the full moon is matched with the notorious shot of a razor slitting an eye. Buñuel used montage to create effects of contrast or similitude and to provoke shock or even horror. In his fascinating book, *The Secret Language of Film*, Buñuel's long-term screenwriter, Jean-Claude Carrière describes a sequence in *Un Chien Andalou* in which:

a character approaches a door and reaches for the handle. In the next shot, which links up with it perfectly, his hand, in close-up, opens the door. Between these two shots, which precisely succeed one another, Buñuel has inserted a fade-in. The two successive images melt into one another in a curious disequilibrium, as if to smuggle a slice of time into an apparent continuity. (1994: 119)

In Elia Suleiman's film *Divine Intervention* (2002) a young Palestinian throws an apricot pit out of the window of his car, for no particular reason. As it happens the apricot hits a tank that is rumbling past and which instantly explodes. This introduces an element of discontinuity in narrative cause and effect: there is no reasonable 'logic' to these sequences of events, but there is certainly a meaning. In fact a set of meanings, which derive both from the editing and the story situation. In Suleiman's film, the images only acquire meaning from narrative context.

Both Pier-Paolo Pasolini and Raul Ruiz (both of whom attacked the Hollywood cliché of 'Central Conflict Theory') were interested in 'inconsequential' montage in narrative. In his *Poetics of Cinema*, Ruiz argues the case for action scenes:

which follow in sequence without ever knitting into the same flow. For instance, two men are fighting in the street. Not far away a child eats an ice cream and is poisoned. Throughout it all, a man in a window sprays passers-by with bullets and nobody raises an eyebrow. In one corner, a painter paints the scene, while a pickpocket steals his wallet and a dog in the shade of a burning building devours the brain of a comatose drunk. In the distance multiple explosions crown a blood-red sunset. This scene is not interesting from the viewpoint of Central Conflict Theory unless we call it Holiday in Sarajevo and divide the characters into two opposing camps. (Ruiz 1995: 11)

These images also suggest the way in which film so easily incorporates, or slides into, dream. Dreams bring an irrationality, or inconsequentiality of their own which provides one way in which film theory has been so encroached upon psychoanalysis. Perhaps the most lucid exposition comes from the surrealists, quick to take note of the complex relationship of film and dream, brought to their attention, of course, by the films of Luis Buñuel, also present in a few Hollywood films, such as Hathaway's *Peter Ibbetson* (1935), a film whose seamless transitions between reality and dream greatly endeared it to André Breton. Nor should we forget Hitchcock's *Spellbound* (1945) and Pabst's *Secrets of a Soul* (1926), masterpieces from the dream factory. Of course, Freud himself had little to say about films and I have discussed this in relation to John Huston's film, *Freud* (1962), elsewhere (in my book *Paris Hollywood*, 2002).

Finally, 12 quotations:

1. In the *New Oxford Dictionary*, the editors define 'theory' as: 'An idea or set of ideas that is intended to explain something.' Or else 'a set of principles on which activity is based, as in "a theory of education", – or presumably 'a theory of film.'

2. The French artist Daniel Buren observed that 'art works [as well as films] signal the existence of certain problems ... Exact knowledge of these problems will be called theory. It is this knowledge or theory which is now indispensable.' (1969: 155)

3. Gregory Ulmer has described the role of contemporary theory as follows: 'It will not be hermeneutics, the science of interpretation, but will look to photography, the cinema, television and the computer as the sources of ideas about invention.' (Ray 2001: 13)

4. Victor Shklovsky: 'History exerts its influence on the work of art – the film – through style and ideology in contrary directions.' (Wollen 1976: 492)

5. Hitchcock: 'I don't care about subject matter. I don't care about acting, but I do care about the pieces of film and the photography and the sound track and all the technical ingredients that make the audience scream.' (Pomerance 2004: 66)

6. Jean-Luc Godard: 'Sternberg cut every sequence in his head before shooting it and never hesitated while editing.' (Wollen 1972: 137)

7. Antonin Artaud: 'In the scenario which follows I have tried to realize my conception of a purely visual cinema, where action bursts out of psychology.' ([1927] 1976: 150)

8. From Buñuel's scriptwriter, Jean-Claude Carrière, who once noted, 'we all live with disconcerting rhythms – cosmic, seasonal, respiratory, cardiac, as well as cinematic.' (1994: 119)

9. Alfred Hitchcock: 'Sometimes I select a dozen different events and shape them into a plot.' (Hitchcock 1939)

10. Franz Kafka: 'Was at the movies. Wept. Lolotte. The good pastor. The little bicycle. The reconciliation of the parents. Boundless entertainment. Before that sad film.' (Nervi 2004)

11. Noel Burch: 'Antonioni creates a relationship between his characters as they speak and his camera as it records them speaking, which can best be described as a ballet.' (1973: 76)

12. Robert Bresson: 'Hide the ideas but so that people find them. The most important will be the most hidden.' (Bresson 1975: 44)

But I nearly forgot! *A last-minute postscript*: In November 1928, the psychoanalyst Hanns Sachs observed that: 'The film can be effective only insofar as it is able to externalise and make perceptible – if possible in movement – invisible inward events. (Walton 2001: 47)

BIBLIOGRAPHY

Artaud, A. (1976 [1927]) 'Cinema and Reality', in S. Sontag (ed.) *Antonin Artaud: Selected Writings*. Berkeley and Los Angeles: University of California Press, 150–4.

Barthes, R. (1967) *Elements of Semiology*. Second edition. London: Jonathan Cape.

Bellour, R. (1979) *The Analysis of Film*. Bloomington: Indiana University Press.

Bresson, R. (1975) *Notes sur le cinématographe*. Paris: Gallimard.

Burch, N. (1973) *Theory of Film Practice*. London: Secker and Warburg.

Burren, D. (2000 [1969]) 'Beware', in A. Alberro and B. Stimson (eds) *Conceptual Art: a Critical Antholog*. Cambridge, MA: MIT Press, 144–57.

Carriere, J. C. (1994) *The Secret Language of Film*. New York: Pantheon Books.

Chomsky, N. (1964) *Current Issues in Linguistic Theory*. The Hague: Mouton and Co.

Eisenstein, S. (2004) 'The Montage of Attractions', in P. Simpson, A. Utterson and K. J. Sheperdson (eds) *Film Theory: Critical Concepts in Media and Cultural Studies, vol. 1*. London: Routledge, 99–110.

Gottlieb, S. (ed.) (1995) *Hitchcock on Hitchcock: Selected Writings and Interviews*. London: Faber and Faber.

Hitchcock, A. (1939) *Melodrama and Suspense*. [Lecture: Radio City Hall, New York City]. 30 March. Online. Available at: http://www.hitchcockwiki.com/wiki/Lecture:_Radio_City_Music_Hall,_New_York_City_(30/Mar/1939) (accessed 13 November 2008).

Lacan, J. (1966) *Ecrits*. London: Tavistock Publications.

Metz, C. (1968) *Essais sur la signification au cinéma*. Paris: Éditions Klincksieck.

_____ (1974) *Film Language: A Semiotics of the Cinema*. Oxford: Oxford University Press.

Nervi, M. (2004) *The Kafka Project*. Online. Available at: http://www.kafka.org/index.php (accessed 13 November 2008).

Pomerance, M. (2004) *An Eye for Hitchcock*. Piscataway, NJ and London: Rutgers University Press.

Ray, R. B. (2001) *How a Film Theory Got Lost and Other Mysteries in Cultural Studies*. Bloomington: Indiana University Press.

Ruiz, R. (1995) *The Poetics of Cinema*. Paris: Editions Dis Voir.

Selway, J. & Auty, M. (2008) 'The Lady from Shanghai', *Time Out Film Reviews*. Online. Available at: http://www.timeout.com/film/reviews/80011/The_Lady_from_Shanghai.html (Accessed: 9 April 2010).

Shepherdson, K. J. (2004) *Film Theory: Critical Concepts in Media and Cultural Studies*. London: Routledge.

Sterritt, D. (ed.) (1998) *Jean-Luc Godard: Interviews*. Jackson: University Press of Mississippi.

Strauss, C. L. (1968) 'The Structural Study of Myth', in *Structural Anthropology*. London: Allen Lane, 206–31.

Walton, J. (2001) *Fair Sex, Savage Dreams*. Durham: Duke University Press.

Wilson, G. (1988) *Narration in Light: Studies in Cinematic Point of View*. Baltimore: The Johns Hopkins University Press.

Wollen, P. (1972) *Signs and Meanings in the Cinema*. Bloomington: Indiana University Press/BFI.

_____ (1976) 'Cinema and Semiology: Some Points of Contact', in B. Nichols, *Movies and Methods: Vol. I*. Berkeley: University of California Press, pp. 481-492.

_____ (1998) *Signs and Meanings in the Cinema*. 2nd edn. London: BFI Press

_____ (2002) *Paris Hollywood: Writing on Film*. London: Verso.

Wilson, G. M. (1986) *Narration in Light: Studies in Cinematic Point of View*. Baltimore: John Hopkins University Press.

FILMOGRAPHY

2001: A Space Odyssey (1968) Directed by Stanley Kubrick [DVD]. Amazon: MGM Distribution Company.

A Bout de Souffle (*Breathless*) (1959) Directed by Jean-Luc Godard [DVD]. Amazon: Sony.

Blade Runner (1982) Directed by Ridley Scott [DVD]. Amazon: Warner Brothers.

By the Law (1926) Directed by Lev Kuleshov [Film]. Brooklyn, NY: New York Film Annex.

Le Carosse d'Or (1953) Directed by Jean Renoir [DVD]. Amazon: Criterion Collection.

Un Chien Andalou (1929) Directed by Luis Bunuel and Salvador Dali [DVD]. Amazon: Transflux Films.

Citizen Kane (1941) Directed by Orson Welles [DVD]. Amazon: Turner Home Entertainment.

Divine Intervention (2002) Directed by Elia Suleiman [DVD]. Amazon: Koch Lober Films.

Freud (1962) Directed by John Huston [DVD]. Amazon: Universal Pictures.

Lady from Shanghai, The (1948) Directed by Orson Welles [DVD]. Amazon: Medusa Pictures.

Last Year in Marienbad (1961) Directed by Alain Resnais [DVD]. Amazon: Rialto Pictures.

Man Who Lies, The (1968) Directed by Alain Robbe-Grillet. [Film]. New York: Grove Press.

October 1917 (1927) Directed by Sergei M. Eisenstein [DVD] Amazon: Tartan Video.

Passenger, The (1975) Directed by: Michelangelo Antonioni [DVD]. Amazon: Sony Pictures.

Peter Ibbetson (1935) Directed by Henry Hathaway [DVD]. Amazon: Universal Pictures.

Rear Window (1954) Directed by Alfred Hitchcock [DVD]. Amazon: Universal Studios.

Riddles of the Sphinx (1977) Directed by Laura Mulvey and Peter Wollen [DVD]. London: Mulvey.

Rope (1948) Directed by Alfred Hitchcock [DVD]. Amazon: Warner Brothers.

Secrets of a Soul (1926) Directed by G. W. Pabst [DVD]. Amazon: Transit.

Shock Corridor (1963) Directed by Sam Fuller [DVD]. Amazon: Criterion.

Spellbound (1945) Directed by Alfred Hitchcock [DVD]. Amazon: MGM (Video & DVD).

Stage Fright (1950) Directed by Alfred Hitchcock [DVD]. Amazon: Warner Home Video.

Toni (1935) Directed by Jean Renoir [DVD]. Amazon: Eureka Video.

Vivre sa Vie (1962) Directed by Jean-Luc Godard [DVD]. Amazon: Madman Entertainment.

CHAPTER 4
PASSING TIME:
REFLECTIONS ON THE OLD AND THE NEW

Laura Mulvey

This chapter revolves around ways in which the cinema, over the last decade or so, has been overtaken by change. The old celluloid medium has given way to the new, to the digital, so that many of the aesthetic and theoretical assumptions that characterise my thought, and presumably that of many of my generation, seem to have been displaced or lost their relevance. My long-standing involvement with cinema has, by and large, had two strands: that of specificity, invested in celluloid as a medium, within the tradition of Modernism and as a key concern of avant-garde film; secondly that of spectacle, within the tradition of modernity, invested in the cinema of industry, particularly Hollywood and the star system. Recently, especially in my 2006 book *Death Twenty-four times a Second: Stillness and the Moving Image*, I have been reflecting on ways in particular that new forms of moving image consumption have necessitated re-thinking my 1970s theories of spectacle and spectatorship. Here I want to focus more on the attributes traditionally associated with film as a medium and their paradoxical relationship with the new.

Furthermore, changes affecting the cinema have taken place within a wider context: another sense of an 'end of an era' that followed the decline of Modernism and the collapse of Socialism. It was during the watershed period, marked aesthetically by Postmodernism and politically/economically by neo-liberalism, that cinema fell back into a 'then' of a past based on celluloid recording and projection, in opposition to the 'now' of a present media prolif-eration into complex relations with other technologies. It is this division that has led certain theorists to pronounce the cinema 'dead'. To my mind there is a political significance to these divisions between the 'old' and the 'new' that emerges out of the strange moment in which conservative politics embrace the 'new' and the 'old' left has to try to keep the utopian aspirations of the past alive. We see here a reversal: the conservative has become radical and the radical now, I am suggesting, struggles to hold on to the past. Of course, there is a certain absurdity to this role reversal – but it is also logical. Those who hold onto dreams of progress now want to delay the forward movement of history and stretch out, horizontally as it were, the process of change for a dialogue between the old and the new – that might change both. If the figura-tion is re-worked, if the figure of opposition is woven into a more dialectical relationship rather than separated along binary lines, another picture might begin to emerge.

These two apparently separate and unrelated issues, the cinematic and the political, have come together in my mind and raised further questions about the representation of time. That is, the ways in which the human mind struggles to grasp this elusive concept and reorganise it into a comprehensible pattern or order. Moving from factors outside the cinema, that are influen-tial, even determinate, on its history, to factors inside the cinema, specific to the properties of film as celluloid and their meeting with the properties of new technologies, in order to consider ways in which the cinema itself might enable thinking about time.

I. 'THE END OF AN ERA': CINEMA AND THE WIDER HISTORICAL CONJUNCTURE

The history of cinema has had close ties with the history of modernity and the utopian teleology that is associated with the left both aesthetically and politi-cally. During the last years of the twentieth century a gap or gulf came to break up the continuities of both histories. The cinema has been profoundly affected by electronic and digital technologies, more than it had been either by the coming of synchronised sound or by television. At the same time, right-wing neo-liberalism and the collapse of Communism contributed to a perceived breakdown in continuity, however mythical it might have been, of modernity and, however fraught or fractured, of left aspiration. How is it possible to chal-lenge this abrupt 'end of an era'? Should those still committed to a progres-sive politics attempt to do so? How does the visualisation of time and history contribute to the process?

On a cultural level, left politics and cinephilia have had a close relation to modernity. Looking back to the avant-garde of the 1920s, Annette Michelson has pointed out:

> The excitement, the exhilaration of artists and intellectuals not directly involved with [the cinema] was enormous. Indeed, a certain euphoria enveloped early film making and theory. For there was, ultimately, a very real sense in which the revolutionary aspirations of the modernist movement in literature and the arts, on the one hand, and of Marxist or Utopian tradition, on the other, could converge in the hopes and promises, yet undefined, of the new medium. (1979: 407)

In the second half of the twentieth century, the terms and context in which it was articulated shifted but the aspiration continued. The cinema came to be an important cultural site for liberation struggle and left politics during the de-colonisation period and its aftermath in the 60s. Furthermore, the great, radical cinemas emerging in Latin America during the same period clearly associated the politics of a film with its conceptual and aesthetic principles. In Europe, political cinema could mediate between modernity's proliferation of imagery, the prevalence of the society of the spectacle, and Modernism's commitment to questioning the transparency and authenticity of these images. Fluctuating across cinema's history, varying from period to period, it is possible to find belief in cinema merging with belief in radical political change.

The decline of this 'radical aspiration' lies across the 1980s, confused and disorientated by economic and political changes on national and international scale. The 1980s mark out a gap between the fluctuating continuities of culture and politics that crossed the twentieth century and late twentieth century developments such as globalisation, post-Communism, post-Fordism, the export of industrialised production to parts of the developing world, the rise of religious fundamentalism and so on. These gaps or fissures have found a pattern in the image of historical time creating a 'then' and a 'now', a binary opposition that stagnates time into a quasi-spatial relationship. The changes are, of course, real and profound. But, as they harden into a pattern and image that divides history in 'eras', the problem of challenging the new and finding the means to articulate the aesthetic and political within a changing configuration becomes harder.

On the one hand, from the perspective of the cinema, new technologies are a key element in creating the 'then' and 'now', 'before' and 'after', effect. On the other, as they open up new forms of film consumption so that digital and electronic formats give new life to the old cinema of celluloid. In negotiating a relationship between the different media, some negotiation across the 'great divide' is also necessarily set in motion. While this attempt to break down the opposition between the 'old' and the 'new' may only be figurative in the first instance, it also brings the aesthetics of cinematic temporality into visibility. Furthermore, without necessarily entailing its death, the cinema itself becomes history as a medium of celluloid with its privileged relation to the reality of the image recorded. As Jean-Luc Godard has definitively and characteristically illustrated in *Histoire(s) du Cinema* (1988–98), with the passing of time, the cinema's own history becomes increasingly entwined with history as such.

II. 'THE END OF AN ERA':
A NEW INTER-MEDIA CONJUNCTURE

In the first instance, the arrival of digital technologies brought to an end the longstanding aesthetic relation between celluloid and reality. Although easily subject to special effects and alteration, the image in front of the camera had been inscribed by light onto film. Digital technologies, with their capacity to create an illusory image of reality, broke that assumption forever, ending the short history of celluloid as a dominant medium soon before it celebrated its centenary. Might it be possible, however, to forge a new, critical or theoretical relationship between the celluloid cinema of the past and the new technologies of the present? Might this fusion of the old and the new create a means of avoiding the terminal nature of 'the end of the era' to forge new metaphors and ways of understanding time?

New technologies enable the spectator to vary the temporality of a film. Moments may be repeated or even slowed, the image may be stilled. These simple developments, that anyone may now easily employ, immediately affect the conventions and aesthetics of the cinema and bring to the fore questions about its relationship to narrative on the one hand and its own materiality on the other. To still the cinema's movement is to question the effect for which it was invented, the illusion of movement, but also reiterates the challenge to its dominance that echoes down the whole history of the cinema. Avant-garde film looked on narrative film, generally, but not necessarily rightly, as having a phobic or paranoid attitude to cinema's stillness and thus its materiality. For a cinematic story to be credible in its own terms, it had to assert the power of its own story time over the simple photographic time when it was actually filmed. Now, by stilling or slowing movie images, the time of the film's original moment of registration suddenly bursts through its artificial, narrative, surface. Another moment of time, behind the fictional time of the story, emerges through this kind of fragmentation. Even in a Hollywood movie, beyond the story is the reality of the image: the set, the stars, the extras take on the immediacy and presence of a document and the fascination of time fossilised can overwhelm and halt the fascination of narrative progression. The now-ness of story time gives way to the then-ness of the movie's own moment in history.

Although the avant-garde has had widely varying aesthetic preoccupations, making visible the cinema's dependence on the still frame not only made visible its materiality but also, negatively, worked against the alliance between the illusion of movement and the mass of narrative film. Now, this old opposition can be broken down by any video tape or DVD, so that movies that have always been seen at a certain speed can be opened up to new temporality and unexpected detail. Stopping a film seems, at first glance, to disrupt narrative, breaking its continuity and the flow of movement that has closely linked cinema to story telling. But a pause, or a stop, in the flow of a story may also enable a return to narrative within a different perceptual framework and awareness of its formal structures and aesthetic properties. A movie's linearity, its apparent dependence on a horizontal narrative structure, can mutate. As sequences are skipped or repeated different hierarchies of privilege are brought into being. In a digression from the story line, detail can become as, or more, significant, than the chain of meaning invested in cause and effect. Details, as they break loose from the whole, may also trigger the special affinity with reality that seems to belong to the accidental, the intrusion of chance into an overall design. Or, the changed pace, the slow motion, can transform one moving image object into another as happens, for instance, in Douglas Gordon's *24 Hour Psycho* (1993). And in W.G. Sebald's novel *Austerlitz* (2001) the hero describes his search for any trace of his mother lost in the SS run ghetto Theresienstadt and his attempt to find her image in the fragments of a Nazi propaganda film:

> In the end the impossibility of seeing anything more closely in those pictures, which seemed to dissolve even as they appeared, said Austerlitz, gave me the idea of having a slow motion copy of this fragment from Theresienstadt made, one which would last a whole hour, and indeed once the fragment was extended to four times its original length, it did reveal previously hidden objects and people, creating, by default as it were, a different sort of film altogether, which I have since watched over and over again. (2001: 345)

An illustration across two pages shows how the damaged bits of the tape break up into illegible pixelation; a smaller 'still' shows:

...at the left-hand side, set a little way back and close to the upper edge of the frame, the face of a young woman appears, barely emerging from the black shadows around it, which is why I did not notice it at all at first. (Ibid.)

The process of slowing down, repeating or stilling the image allows hidden details to emerge within a film sequence or previously insignificant moment, once frozen, can generate the emotional impact of a still photograph. Out of the interaction between celluloid and new technologies, as the concealing mask of narrative falls away, the presence of the past inscribed onto film is enhanced. Not only does the dialectical relationship across old and new media challenge the 'great divide', creating an interweaving out of an opposition, but the 'then-ness' that appears within the old celluloid image brings the history that belongs to it palpably into the present, translated onto an easily accessible form. Once on video or DVD, film of the past can become the subject for reverie. Questions about time emerge both from the image, located in the past, and from the properties of film itself, able to contain movement and stillness within its formal structure.

III. BRINGING THE PAST INTO THE PRESENT: THE CINEMA'S IMAGING AND IMAGINING OF TIME

The transfer of film originally shot on celluloid onto electronic or digital carriers allows some properties of film to find greater visibility. The temporal has always had an extremely complex aesthetic and conceptual presence in any kind of cinema, fiction, avant-garde, documentary but often these different genres have been understood in terms of antagonism and incompatibility. Might the new forms of consumption of old film not only break down generic barriers but also bring cinema's temporalities into new visibility? Does the present moment, both within the history of cinema and history more generally, invest particular interest and importance in the way the cinematic past is used and understood?

I began, in the first section, with the 'great divide' that separates the old from the new creating a binary opposition, an 'old' and a 'new' across technological and economic change. In the second section, I tried to suggest that the way that new technologies have given new life to old cinema could be seen figuratively as working against the old/new opposition in a mutually enhancing alliance. Even on an immediate level, as carriers, video and DVD keep the old cinema alive. More and more people, beyond the earlier world of buffs and cinephiles, are taken into its history, perhaps most especially in the case of DVD, as commentaries, interviews and documentation expand the consumption of film out of its traditional format into a new context of knowledge and critical self-awareness. But for the film historian and theorist, artist, and, in this context, those historians interested in reflecting on the representation of time, different kinds of temporality and relations between times become more clearly apparent as the indexicality of celluloid is translated onto and manipulated through new media.

However, the way that my argument has been formulated raises problems of its own. Having founded this paper on a critque of binary systems of thought, I seem to have built another aesthetic binary into my assumptions. The material and the indexical are found in opposition to narrative and illusion. This opposition resurrects the old opposition between avant-garde materialism and the illusion of fiction, with an implicit validation of avant-garde practice, stripping away the mask of narrative to reveal the material presence of celluloid and the cinematic apparatus. This approach was one that influenced my thinking about film during the 1970s. I would argue now that the relation between new and old technology offers, on the contrary, the opportunity to break down the opposition, most particularly through an investigation of the complex temporalities of film that are now becoming visible and available to theory.

Important for my thinking has been Raymond Bellour's observation on the affect the appearance of a still image has on the moving image. His example is taken from Max Ophuls' *Letter from an Unknown Woman* (1948) at the point when the narrative introduces a series of photographs:

> As soon as you stop the film, you begin to find time to add to the image. You start to reflect differently on film, on cinema. You are led towards the photogram – which is itself a step further in the direction of the photograph. In the frozen film (or photogram), the presence of the photograph bursts forth, while other means exploited by the mise-en-scene to work against time tend to vanish. The photo thus becomes a stop within a stop, a freeze frame within a freeze frame; between it and the film from which it emerges, two kinds of time blend together, always inextricable but without becoming confused. In this the photograph enjoys a privilege over all other effects that make the spectator, this hurried spectator, a pensive one as well. (1987: 6–7)

Bellour is taking stillness within the moving image as the point at which the pensive spectator emerges into consciousness. This was indeed the case during the long history of film projected at 24 frames per second through a projector in the darkened auditorium. Now, not only is stillness available to the electronic spectator at the touch of a button but with its prolongation further effects can emerge for reflection. Bellour points to this greater complexity with the phrase: 'between it [the photograph] and the film from which it emerges two kinds of time blend together, always inextricable but without being confused' (ibid). Here, there is an opening towards rethinking the opposition between a concrete past of stillness and the illusion of narrative time associated with the illusion of movement itself. The two kinds of time are 'entwined' and the division between them simplifies the complexity of film. Although a film is a series of celluloid stills, it is only through a relationship with the continuities of movement, of sequence and serial that cinema comes into being. The cinematic representation of time cannot be pinned down exactly or stabilised. Even when I stop a favourite movie on a favourite moment, to think about the presence of the past inscribed there, it is also a moment to 'reflect differently on film' rather than to reduce it to the photograph.

This temporal 'entwining' has always been an aesthetic advantage for film and many of its greatest exponents, whether in Hollywood or in the avant-garde, have exploited it across cinema history. Now a further dimension of complexity emerges simply, perhaps, through the greater availability of its effects and more and more does the spectator confront the difficulty of conceptualising time preserved and its illusiveness. The time of movement and of narrative itself adds to this dimension as an essential part of the relationship rather than as mask or disguise. The index as a signifier of a fixed 'then' begins to float as it is detached from the still and attached to the moving image. Roland Barthes' term 'this was now'[1] as applied to the still photograph evokes the difficulty of translating photographic temporality into ordinary language, giving rise to a feeling of giddiness, as though confronted with a trompe l'oeil effect. Out of this, the content of a specific image begins to recede and it's replaced by the heavy weight of temporality itself materialised in all its uncertainty. This is, to my mind, a glimmering awareness that human consciousness creates history in order, not only to understand events that are in themselves important and determining of their successors, but to organise the unspeakable and intractable nature of time itself. This sensation is aggravated in film's relation between stillness and movement, the interaction between fiction and the illusive reality of the past, between the present of spectatorship and consciousness of time passing and, ultimately, of death. The sequence essential to cinematic time stretches out into an irreversible duration that can be stilled or even reversed but, without that dimension cannot be cinema. Time persists, its forward movement becomes palpable and even harder to pin down than that of the still photograph.

I have tried to suggest that the cinema has always been a medium in which time plays a complex part, inextricably asserting the indexical presence of a single, preserved, moment alongside its inexorable materialisation of temporal duration. By a strange paradox, this essential quality of film becomes more readily visible when the medium is transferred onto its new carriers, more tractable and more easily manipulated by the viewer. The question of time itself can become the subject of imagination and reverie and, if only as a figuration or metaphor, leads to the question of historical time and its relation to the human imagination.

There is another, more substantial side to the cinema as its history is retrieved more and more thoroughly in the early twenty-first century. This is the period of the archive. New technologies both make the appearance of film's history more practical but also represent the break with its indexical relation to the actuality it recorded. In this sense, the cinema has had a short history, one that is co-terminate with the aspirations of the twentieth century, particularly its radicalism. From this perspective, it is an essential means for thinking through the problems of the late twentieth century, the vanishing legacy of modernism and the 'radical aspiration'. Perhaps, from this perspective it can help to establish some continuity from that past into the present and challenge the apparent inevitabilities represented by the 'great divide'.

CODA: BEYOND THE OLD AND THE NEW.

I want to end by suggesting that, rather than seeing the present moment as one of an irreconcilable gap between eras, it is possible to reconfigure the visual imagery that lies behind it and shift the metaphor from one of opposition to one of flux. We are in the midst of a complicated period of change and it is the persistence of eras and their intermingling that gives this present period a particular interest. Although we are all aware of the impact of the new - politics or technologies - they are still in process, still mutating not yet indicating a future certainty. This threshold, a space of liminality (as anthropologists and narratologists might say), offers an opportunity for the old and the new to co-exist and mediate in relationship or dialogue between the past and the present. The perception of change shifts away from an imaginary pattern derived primarily from the register of time, a foreclosing of the past, a hastening towards the end of an era, into an imaginary pattern derived from space, of threshold, of holding past and future suspended in an uncertain present. Into this space, an aesthetic of delay can emerge.

A dialectical relationship between the old and new media can be summoned into existence creating an aesthetic of delay. In the first instance, the image itself is frozen or subjected to repetition or return. But as the new stillness is enhanced by the weight that the past acquires during such 'threshold' periods, its significance goes beyond the image itself towards the problem of time, its passing, and how it is represented or preserved. To stop and to reflect on the cinema and its history opens into a wider question: how time might be understood within wider, contested, patterns of history and mythology. Out of this pause, a delayed cinema gains a political dimension, potentially able to challenge patterns of time that are neatly ordered around the end of an era, its 'old' and its 'new'.

In this context, the cinema, rather than simply reaching the end of its era, can come to embody a new urgency to look backwards, to pause and to delay the combined forces of politics, economics and technology. The cinema's recent slide backward into history can, indeed, enable this backward look at the twentieth century. In opposition to a simple determinism inherent in the image of a void between the 'old' and the 'new' of an era that had suddenly ended, the cinema provides material for holding on to and reflecting on the last century's achievements as well as learning from its catastrophes. To turn to the past through the detour of cinema has a political purpose. While the coincidence between the cinema's centenary and the arrival of digital technology created an opposition between the old and the new, the convergence of the two media translated their literal chronological relation into a more complex dialectic. The dialectic between old and new produces innovative ways of thinking about the complex temporality of cinema and its significance for the present moment in history. As the flow of cinema is displaced by the process of delay, spectatorship is affected, re-configured and transformed so that old films can be seen with new eyes and digital technology, rather than killing the cinema, brings it new life and new dimensions. I have argued across a variety of attributes of the cinema to suggest that it has a privileged relation to time and also to the history of the twentieth century. If the cinema may now be turned back on itself, into means of looking backwards at history, at the cultures of modernity, the new life offered to old cinema by new technologies paradoxically maintains its presence within this threshold period of transition and uncertainty.

BIBLIOGRAPHY

Banfield, A. (1990) 'L'imparfait de l'objectif: The Imperfect of the Objective Glass', *Camera Obscura: A Journal of Feminism and Film Theory*, 24, 65–87.

Barthes, R. (1981) *Camera Lucida. Reflections on Photography*. New York: Hill and Wang.

Bellour, R. (1987) 'The Pensive Spectator', *Wide Angle*, 9, 1, 6–10.

Michelson, A. (1970) 'Film and the radical aspiration', in Sitney, P. A. (ed.) *Film Culture Reader*. New York: Praeger, pp. 404-42.

Mulvey, L. (2006) *Death Twenty-four times a Second: Stillness and the Moving Image*. London: Reaktion Books.

Sebald, W. G. (2001) *Austerlitz*. New York: Random House.

FILMOGRAPHY

Histoire(s) du Cinema (1988–98) Directed by Jean-Luc Godard [DVD]. London: Artificial Eye.

24 Hour Psycho (1993) Directed by Douglas Gordon [Video]. Glasgow/New York: Douglas Gordon

Letter from an Unknown Woman (1948) Directed by Max Ophuls [DVD]. Amazon. com: Dawoori Entertainment.

NOTES

1   Roland Barthes' French term for the photograph's moment is 'ça a été', which has been translated in different ways, including 'that-has-been' in Richard Howard's translation of R. Barthes (1981) *Camera Lucida: Reflections on Photography*. New York: Farrar, Strauss and Ginoux, 77, and 'this was now' in Ann Banfield's proposed interpretation in 'L'imparfait de l'objectif: The Imperfect of the Objective Glass' (1990).

CHAPTER 5
SUBLIME ACTS:
THE FATE OF RESISTANCE BETWEEN
FILM THEORY AND PRACTICE

Patrick Fuery

I. RESISTANCE AND THE THIRD TERM

It would seem that one of the unspoken, perhaps unrecognised, structural relationships between theory and practice[1] in film is that it is mirrored in the basic configuration of the sign. The difficulty, once we recognise this, is determining the ways in which to reconfigure the sign. In one sense this is the idea that theory and practice oscillate between the role of signifier (materiality) and signified ('meaning/interpretation', or something that comes to be seen as that). This can be approached in any number of ways, but three can be listed here:

1. Practice is the signifier to theory's signified

Such a configuration is to read issues and processes of film practice as the materiality of the filmic text, through which theory produces interpretation and meaning. If we can speak of a classical model of theory and practice then this would seem to be the closest to it. In such a scenario theory comes 'after' practice and is utilised to produce meaning. This is a type of *a posteriori* approach (with the film itself standing in for the empirical, experiential process) and interpretation is seen as coming out of the materiality of the practice, but only via a theoretical injunction. An atypical example may help to illustrate this; 'atypical' because it relies on a disturbance of how the film example is presented. Watching *Dial M for Murder* (Hitchcock, 1954) now (that is, not in its original 3D format, because this is how it is most often screened today) yields a number of scenes that appear unusual. For example, early in the narrative there is a scene of Tony and Margot Wendice, two of the central characters, having a discussion. In a number of shots we see a row of bottles and glasses in the background. That same row reappears a little later on, only this time the camera position is behind them, that is shooting across and through the objects into the apartment. For this to take place the camera has to be positioned in an impossible location (either 'behind' the wall, which needs to have disappeared, or as part of the wall itself). Of course originally this has a 3D effect, and that is its primary function – a *trompe l'oeil* that exists exclusively to show off the technological effects. Compare this to something like the close-up of the snow-ball globe in the opening scenes of *Citizen Kane* (Welles, 1941), where the foregrounding of the object is cinematically impressive as well as having a narrative meaning. In *Dial M for Murder* the foregrounding of the bottles has no narrative significance (there are no future issues of alcoholism or events caused by drunkenness, no slipping of poisons into a bottle to sedate or murder, that we might suspect to take place – thus is the cause-effect convention of Classic Hollywood cinema). Yet this technological moment (that is, the practice) becomes lost when the film is not seen in 3D; and outside of that format it becomes strangely alienating. (Compare this to the attempted murder scene where the 3D effect is employed to emphasis the terror of the body; here there is a direct narrative consequence to what is being visually portrayed).

If we disregard the 3D intent, this practice of locating the shot outside of the original space, as well as foregrounding objects that have no narrative 'weight', lends itself to interpretation of, for example, alienation (from a Brechtian perspective) or unsettling the domestic scene (the uncanny, from a Freudian perspective). Thus the narrative and textual function becomes something altogether different for the spectator not watching in 3D. The conflict, of course, is that the practice (here read as the signifier) is supposed to operate in a capacity of purely special effects; it is the bringing in of other theories that produces these sorts of readings. In other words, the intent of the shot of the bottles is a practice based phenomenon (that is, the technique of 3D technology), operating entirely within those terms of spectator's pleasure; it has no *message* beyond that within the film's narrative. Once this practice based technique is removed (by watching the film not in 3D) we are seduced in bringing other theories into play to explain the effect.

I suggest this example is atypical because it draws on a number of conditions, not the least the knowledge the spectator (who becomes theorist) has regarding the scene. If we know this was originally produced as a 3D film then the shot through the bottles is easily understood and perhaps dismissed as irrelevant (beyond its dimensions of pleasure and trickery). If this knowledge is not held then the scene looks alienating because the practice of film making has been foregrounded. Under those conditions the spectator may believe they have encountered a sort of Hitchcock version of the jump-cut; a highly stylised piece of filmmaking that draws attention to some of the fundamental (and usually hidden) technical aspects. But what the example really shows us is what happens when a bit of the practice is shown so that we have to do something with it – interpret it, cogitate over it, position it within a sense-making rule. In short, this is when a piece of filmmaking practice appears to demand theorising.

2. Theory is the signifier to practice's signified

In this configuration the relationship is, in effect, inverted and many of the classical assumptions are questioned. Theorising (the materiality of the act) comes before the practice (where all meaning eventually becomes embedded), thus producing an *a priori* model. This may sound enigmatic, for it suggests a theorising of the text before the text exists! However, in one sense this has always been the case. At the most literal level, all spectators and all practitioners come to the film object with interpretations, knowledges, experiences, and modes of comparison. Beyond this level of the individual, there is also a larger order of this process that is embedded in the phenomena of film itself. Both early theories and practices of cinema were mostly derived from pre-existing models, including narrative structures and narratology (literature), theatre (including performance studies), photography (Siegfried Kracauer), as well as systems of ideas as diverse as psychology (Sergei Eisenstein, Rudolf Arnheim with Gestalt theory), formalism (Bela Balázs), political theory (Vsevolod Pudovkin), and so on. Even when specific film theories are developed, they will often draw on concepts and modes of analysis from non-cinematic sources. Theories of montage, for example, were drawn as much from psychology as they were from the unique elements of film itself. Christian Metz's ideas on film are heavily indebted to semiotics (initially), then Louis Althusser's version of Marxism, and then Jacques Lacan's version of psychoanalysis. Read in this way, the relationship between theory and practice is seen as one proceeding as theoretically anticipatory (theory anticipates the practice and in doing so informs it) and practical fulfilment (modes of practice are seen as fulfilling those held theoretical tenants); which is, of course, a perversion of history and progression.

Another version of such a reading is that we come to the practice with pre-conceived and established theoretical *judgements*[2] which inevitably shape the ways in which we see and make sense of the practices. To a certain extent this is true; after all we can hardly watch a film with no theoretical perspective. Even the youngest child will make sense of a simple narrative and quickly establish rules for understanding (much the same as the case with the learning of any language). Furthermore, what is revealed in this is that practice will often function as theory; it is as much about interpretation and sense making as it is about production. So when we speak of theory as the signifier of practice, part of what is being suggested is that the two acts will often cross over and operate in the same manner.

A third corollary of this equation is to do with how theory will reposition the practice 'outside' of its original design (and perhaps even purpose). If there is a battleground between theory and practice then this would be such a conflictual space; for this is the moment when theory attempts to draw practice into an altogether different function. Part of this is a consequence of the fact that a great deal of film theory concerns itself not with practical issues, but with seeing cinema within a diverse range of subjects (film as ideology, or cultural process, for example). One of the key linking points, and one that has been trampled underfoot for some time now, is film as an aesthetic moment. For in such a moment the relationship between theory and practice becomes entwined so one closely mirrors the other.

3. The destabilising of the relations between theory and practice

In either case the relationship between signifier and signified in the cinematic sign becomes one founded on instability and resistance. Central to this is the manner in which theory and practice function in similar ways, and exchange identities, all the while attempting to assert their difference. Rather than see this as a problem it will be argued here that the instability inherent in this allows for a dynamic that is necessary for certain developments in both theory and practice. It will also be argued that this is fundamental to the idea of the sublime – that is, the destabilising of the signifier/signified relationship, the rupturing of any sense of wholeness and finitude in the cinematic sign. It is this cinematic sublime that offers a certain perspective on theory and practice, both in terms of each other, and as a model for exploring how the two deal with a common subject matter. By considering how theory and practice engage in the sublime we might come to understand further their relationship to one another and the formation of the cinematic sign, particularly in terms of the aesthetic moment.

This idea of instability is represented here by the model below:

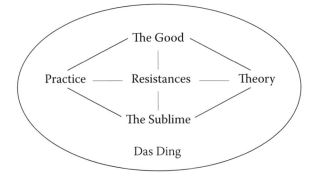

Theory and practice are seen as forming a relationship between two compelling forces, the Good and the sublime.[3] The Good, as we shall note later, is the compulsion towards the beautiful, the ethical, the moral, the socially determined; the sublime is the forceful collapse of such things and a domination of the uncertain, instability, the impassioned, the startled. Between these four positions we find the negotiations of certain vicissitudes; two are nominated but there are clearly many more in operation. These are: the Thing/*Das Ding*; and Resistances. It is this final one, positioned between all of these, which will serve as a point of departure. It is also the substance that infiltrates all the processes nominated, including the relationship of theory and practice. In this sense it separates and connects theory and practice, just as it separates and connects the Good and the sublime.

To understand resistance in this context we can turn to one of Sigmund Freud's footnotes that almost has an air of resignation to it. In *The Interpretation of Dreams* (1899), after so much careful and persuasive analysis, after extraordinary teasing and cajoling of images, words and meanings, Freud admits that there will always be in various instances a core that is impossible to analyse and resolve. This is set up by Freud within a larger context of the wide range of resistances that are brought to the analytic scene by the subject of analysis, including distortion, doubt, interruption, forgetting, hostility, and so on. Beyond these is this other type of resistance – something which is integral to the dream-work – that Freud calls the navel: 'There is at least one spot in every dream at which it is unplumbable – a navel, as it were, that is its point of contact with the unknown' (1985: 186) and elsewhere:

There is often a passage in even the most thoroughly interpreted dream which has to be left obscure; this is because we become aware during the work of interpretation that at that point there is a tangle of dream-thoughts which cannot be unravelled and which moreover adds nothing to the contents of the dream. This is the dream's navel, the spot where it reaches down to the unknown. (Freud 1985: 671)

Within this model the line of resistance between theory and practice finds the navel of each located at their habitus. In other words, film theory's unplumbable navel – that where it reaches down to the unknown – is the site precisely defined as the most abstract in relation to practice; and the same holds for film practice. For in each enterprise the act of production is compelled towards this sense of the unknown, and unknowable. Somewhat curiously, and this is why the dream metaphor holds up so well here, the navels of film theory and practice are necessary qualities within those activities and are not necessarily derived from the relationship between the two. Or, put another way, film theory and film practice have their own depths of the unknown – that is why they continue to be productive – which operate independent of other forms of resistance between the two. Theory and practice constantly engage in this unknown, and in doing so reinvent themselves. A consequence of this is that when theory and practice turn towards these acts of productive engagement in the undiscovered material of their core business, they also set up certain resistances to one another. At the same time, however, they look to the other for possible solutions. The unknowable navel of film practice, for example, will always be just that – unknowable; however theory holds *in potentia* different possibilities for approaching this. Likewise, theory's unknowable elements may be revealed through film practice. It is precisely when the two come together that a unique and often startling cinematic moment takes place. A cautionary note must be added here. This is not to suggest that the function of film theory is to resolve the navel of practice, and vice versa. In many ways the unknowns remain no matter how they are tackled. As with Freud, we need to see these moments as those that reflect upon our analytic and creative practices; these navels reach down to unknown depths because they challenge all forms of analysis. That said, theory and practice do precisely offer the possibility of engaging with these unknowables from a different point of view.

If theory and practice each have their own navels of resistance, providing the compulsion to change, develop, and evolve, then we can see that the *aporia* of all this is the resistances between the two. These resistances, which are seen here as lines of connection rather than repulsion, emerge out of the materiality and specifications of these unknowable navels. So, for example, theory has its unknowable attributes, and in the struggle to engage in these critical issues, resistances are formed. A similar scenario exists for film practice. In this sense such lines of resistance are not about theory and practice resisting one another, but rather the formalised progression of the struggles of each to deal with their unknowables. As such these lines are prone to shifting, subject to invention and alteration – they are premised on fluidity rather than stability.

There is the sense of the need and desire to resist here, the reasons for which will be dealt with later. This necessity results in what can be called the third term of resistance. To illustrate this I would to evoke the perhaps unlikely source of a particular scene from the Marx Brothers film *Duck Soup* (McCarey 1933). It is a famous scene, yet one that surprises even after numerous viewings; this is in part because of its reflexive, almost self-mocking premise. Chico, fleeing from a pursuing Groucho, breaks a large mirror and stands on the other side, adopting a stance in what is normally the impossible space of the other side of the mirror.[4] Dressed as Groucho (in bedclothes, nightcap, and of course glasses atop the unmistakable and eccentric moustache), Chico proceeds to impossibly mimic all the actions of Groucho; creating a mirror where none now exists. The two Marx brothers test one another; they are, in effect, resisting on all sorts of levels, not the least being the logic of the mirror. This logic is that reflexivity will preserve the illusion of mirroring whilst reversing the natural order; when we look into the mirror we resist the fact that the image is reversed. The two Grouchos allow all sorts of collapses in the logic of the mirror, always maintaining the relationship of image and reflection. They can even step through the very apparatus, confounding its fundamental structure. What disintegrates the illusion are not these improbable tests and impossible ontologies; rather it is the introduction of the third Groucho, Harpo. Once this

The (fearful) recognition of the self

The self and the mirror testing boundaries and the sense of reality

third term comes into play everything collapses. Here, then, is the metaphor for some of the issues at hand. Like the two Grouchos, theory and practice mirror each other, and the play has a certain level of productivity within its own parameters (it entertains, sets up relations, tests dimensions and histories, creates narratives, forms rules (as well as breaking them), and frames the whole process as self-contained).

However things only really change when the third term is introduced. This, I would argue, is the introduction of different orders of resistance between the two. It is not simply a matter of reconfiguring relationships – the two Grouchos do that just fine in many, many different ways. It is ultimately about altering the reflexive practices (of both theory and practice) to allow new forms of resistance to operate. Two of these are designated on the model, and once we have considered these it is possible to look to the curious relationship of the Good and the sublime in terms of theory and practice.

The next line of connection in this schema (represented below the line of resistances on the model) is *Das Ding*, the Thing. This can be seen as both a part of resistance as well as a quite distinct relationship. The Thing is Lacan's term, via Freud, to denote the strange, the unknowable, the unrepresentable, the outsidedness, and Otherness. He introduces it to negotiate an interpretation of the opposition between the reality principle and the pleasure principle. The Thing is the absolute Other of the subject (1992: 52) that we continue to search for through our desires, swept along through the manifestations of the pleasure principle. Opposed to this is the reality principle. So in effect the Thing is that which we know nothing of – the eternally strange – and yet at the same time it is the absolutely familiar. In this sense it can be related to Lacan's idea of extimacy. This is the term he coins to deal with the issue of the Real and its presence in the Symbolic; it is that which is more intimate than the most knowable, intimate detail, yet to confront it is to see a fearsome and disturbing thing. It is more real than real, yet is constantly hidden from us; when we confront it we witness the absolutely familiar and at the same time the totally foreign.

I believe this can be worked into the understanding of film theory and practice, and once more the three Grouchos can lead us into this. The mirror game of the two Grouchos does not allow for extimacy or the Thing. This is in spite of the fact that the logic of the mirror, and so reflection, is broken so many times. The game they play is a tempered version of the pleasure principle, located and defined within a controlling discourse of the reality principle. The pleasure is derived from repetition and having a sense that cause and effect remain bonded. It is a comfortable and comforting situation, even if it is built on a certain amount of mistrust (particularly by the original Groucho, who here stands as a sort of universal subject, and well as a metaphor for both film spectator and film maker). Once the third term – the third Groucho – is introduced we see the effect of extimacy and the force of the Thing. Relationships collapse, order disintegrates, meaning is problematised and questioned. What the two Grouchos confront when the third appears is something totally familiar and yet foreign, totally known and yet unknowable. (This of course has resonance of Freud's reading of the uncanny). The two Grouchos move from a sense of the other as a sort of manageable process and relationship, to the idea of the absolute other as something that cannot be contained within the existing order.

To return now to the relationship between film theory and practice. These two can be seen as having a relationship based on extimacy, each being the Thing for the other one. As with all relationships of extimacy, theory and practice recognise the familiar and known contained within the other, but it is so often presented as something almost unrecognisable. What is recognised of course is the common element of 'film', but it is presented to the other one in such a way that it becomes the strange and different. Thus theory makes film strange – presents extimacy in effect – to practice, and practice will do the same for theory. How this defamiliarising takes place (for theory and for practice) is through the rendering of the known (what each approach feels it knows about film, and thus how it locates it) in an altogether different configuration. That is, the essence of film is still recognisable to the other, but how it is positioned evokes a sense of strangeness. It is important to read this strangeness in a particular way; and I hope to illustrate this here with the notion of the sublime, but as with all examples if not a certain failure, at the very least a certain restriction, is ensured.

As with the lines of resistance it is important to see this relationship of extimacy between theory and practice as one that is necessary and fecund, rather than alienating and destructive. Theory and practice should see the other as extimacy for within such a perspective the possibility of change resides. Once more this is the intervention of the third term, which is, it should be noted, not a distinct element, but the Thing of theory and practice in dialogue with each other. By positioning the other one as its other, both theory and practice continually exert the forceful existence of the uncanny. Alterity becomes how theory and practice intervene with, and engage in, one another. Such otherness is produced – that is, it is formed directly out of the economy between theory and practice. As such neither is capable of producing the Thing, this level of extimacy, without the presence of the other one. Clearly this means that we are speaking of a particular type of agency, one that exists in the junction of theory and practice; one that can only be produced when either of these reflects on its relationship with the other. And this is precisely why it is a version of extimacy, for it is the interaction of two systems with the same originary point, and yet has been cast apart. In this sense theory and practice need their difference to one another in order to be productive, and at the same time they constantly reflect on the practice of the other. (To follow the Marx brothers' scene, it is the intervention of the third brother that allows change to take place and to break the illusion.) This is not dissimilar to the story Lacan recounts of the two children on a train; as the train pulls into a station the girl points and says: 'Look, we are at Ladies'; to which the boy responds, looking out of his window: 'No, we are at Gents.' Thus, points out Lacan, we are sent on our different directions. Theory and practice do pull into the same station, but they have more often than not looked out of different windows.

II. THE SUBLIME

The sublime may seem to be a curious concept to introduce into this topic of a beyond to the theory of practice. However I would like to argue that it provides us with some interesting possibilities as a way forward, especially in terms of the issues raised so far. I do not propose to engage in too much detail on a history of the sublime, but will take this next part through what might be seen as five key ideas from such a history. The source of these is necessarily wide ranging – from Longinus, through Edmund Burke, Immanuel Kant and on to Jean-François Lyotard – but this is not to suggest homogeneity between these theorists. That said, there does seem to be a sort of definable agenda in terms of the sublime. The task here will be to suggest some ways in which this agenda might be used to comment on the theory and practice of film.

1. Beyond the Theory of Practice and the Sublime

The history of the sublime is marked by the attempt to do something that resonates in a great many of the discussions between film theory and practice. Put in the crudest way this is the relationship between style and substance. The analysis of the sublime has had to negotiate the difficulty of what constitutes the sublime as such; what, in effect, makes something sublime. In 1674 the French translator and commentator of Longinus, Nicolas Boileau, emphasised the difference between the rhetoric of the sublime and the sublime of content; or the style versus the content. In doing so he set in motion the European (and especially the English) theorising of the sublime in a particular direction. This becomes the idea that we can read the sublime effect either by the ways in which it represents, or by what is represented.

We can adapt this aspect of the history of the sublime here in a number of ways. We could consider how theory and practice can be compared to a rhetoric of film (theory) and the content, or spirit, of the sublime (practice). Or, and this is not in itself excluding this other order, we could consider how theory and practice engage with the sublime. The first of these would use the theories of the sublime to comment on theory and practice, whereas the second would be interested in how the issues of the sublime are dealt with differently through film theory and practice. A third level to all of this would be the idea of producing the sublime in theory and practice – and this project is the one that perhaps is the most appealing, but certainly beyond the limits of this chapter. What follows are some possible points of connection between all this – of how the sublime can be used to inform a discussion of the resistances between theory and practice.

2. Where does the sublime reside?

This was one of the great debates, settled, or at least focussed, perhaps most notably in Kant. Kant dismissed the idea that there can be a sublime object; for him it could only ever exist within the subject. All writers on the sublime seem to agree on one thing – the sublime is all about the effect on the imagination/emotion/mind. And it is the effect that defines the sublime, rather than any particular quality of the object. (Disagreement breaks down with Kant because he is adamant that the sublime cannot exist in the object as such; for Kant the sublime is called a "feeling of the spirit".) The sublime effect, it must be recalled, is not an easy one – in fact the sublime is typified by fear, passion, awe, tumult, sweeping emotion. Indeed the defining points for the sublime, summarised by Boileau, is that its effects elevate, ravish, and transport. Only if something had these effects could it be called the sublime.

How can we locate the relationship of film theory to practice in such a context? The framing notion here has been resistance and reflexivity; what this notion of the sublime gives us is a foregrounding of the duality of these issues once more. In one sense we can rephrase this question to read: how is it possible for theory and practice to create the sublime effect? And from a related perspective it can be asked as: how can theory and practice be brought to bear on the issue of the sublime in order to understand it? By conflating theory and practice in such questions we avoid the easy divide of using theory to explicate the sublime, and practice to create it. In doing so the processes become engaged in a reflexive moment. When theory attempts to create the sublime effect it necessarily questions its own methodologies (or genealogies as Foucault might say) – this is evident in obvious ways in Lacan and Jacques Derrida, but all theorising worthy of consideration should, at some level, attempt to be sublime. And when practice attempts to analyse the sublime it does so by questioning its core components. In both these we witness a breakdown in the theory/practice divide and figuring out which is which can be quite a complicated process. In this way what I am suggesting is that the introduction of the sublime offers one way forward in this notion of a beyond to the theory of practice. The sublime's inherent reflexivity means that both theory and practice move beyond their own restrictive practices. As Lyotard, via Kant, points out:

> The sublime is the child of an unhappy encounter, the encounter of the Idea with form. The encounter is unhappy because the Idea reveals itself to be so unwilling to make concessions, the law (the father) so authoritarian... (1994: 124)

The sublime arrests any easy flow between conceptualisation and form. The third Groucho becomes the sublime intervention, moving the self-placating mirror effect of theory and practice beyond the established processes. This is the promise of the sublime – to ravish theory and practice in order to elevate and transport them to an altogether different order. The sublime relation between theory and practice is born out of certain (historically formed) resistances; yet it is different from these because it offers the possibility of change, of overcoming the circuitous relation of theory and practice mirroring one another.

3. Reflexivity, the Sublime, and the Beautiful

This leads us to the next point, which will involve the introduction of the beautiful. In Kant's schema one of the primary differences between the beautiful and the sublime is marked by a certain arrangement of the internal and external. The judgement of beauty is something that is always external to ourselves (as participants in the sense of the beautiful) and understanding; the sublime, on the other hand, is always internal. The beautiful, like the Good, is located in a position that is essentially antithetical to the sublime. The beautiful is part of the Law, the authoritarian, and as such has a certain sense of placation. For all of the sublime's stormy upheavals, the beautiful offers calm and poise. Note should be made of the concepts occupied in the upper position of the model – that of the Good – to better understand what is proposed here.

Both theory and practice are often drawn to the beautiful; there is a certain seductive quality to the beautiful and culturally we are trained/taught to privilege it in a certain way. The sublime is beauty's other, and we are not exactly with Kant nor against him to position the sublime against the Good in this sense. (Kant saw relationships between the sublime and the Good, but it is not a simple one by any means). The Good is positioned in terms of the Law, and as such is connected to morality, the cultural paradigm, the Superego – in short the domain where ethics are decided and maintained. I'd suggest that the sublime provides a space outside of this – this is part of the reason it is so seeped in awe, fear, and force. And when theory and practice engage with one another they potentially achieve this same space.

This may seem slightly grand and to be fair it is probably more of an abstract idealism rather than a practical aim. What is potentially more tangible, how-ever, is the idea that the reflexivity of theory and practice are capable of pro-ducing something that wrestles their existence out of the Good. In this sense the Good holds the laws of theory and practice, of how their histories conflate and contest, of the economies of discourse and discursive practices that allows them to exist in the relationships they currently occupy. In other words, the notion of the sublime offers the possibilities of a beyond to the theorising of practice because it runs counter to the Good of existing relationships. One of these has been cited here as the relationship of resistances between the two.

A note is necessary on the relationship of the Good to each of theory and practice. It has become somewhat accepted to avoid the sense of good theory and good practice (much along the lines that we avoid the idea of a 'good film'), and yet there are many debates which originate, at the very least covertly, around such notions. It is necessary to put to one side the issue of whether it is appropriate to speak of good practice and good theory, particularly in terms of absolutes. Instead we can concern ourselves with the idea of these versions of goodness in terms of the larger order of the Good. In other words, the issue becomes not one of whether or not there are examples of good practice and theory; rather how such concepts are to be measured and created in the larger sense of the Good (the Law of the good, the socialised good, the correct sense of the good in terms of theory and practice). For example, the good film practices as dictated by Dogma 95 become seen in the good films (we would naturally assume examples by Lars Von Trier would feature) which adhere as closely as possible to such a manifesto. This does not make them good films (that is, perfect and universally acknowledged), but rather good because they are examples which fit into the Dogma beliefs. Similarly, a theoretical inter-pretation of a film using feminism (or psychoanalysis or Marxism) does not make the theoretical approach good, but it may show a good rendering of that theory's tenants. At another level, either in theory or practice, the recogni-tion of the Good in them does not necessarily invest the text with a universal quality of goodness. A film can be a good example of feminist politics, but that does not make it a 'good' film; a film may be innovative and unique in its making, but similarly, that does not make it a 'good' film. What lies at the heart of this is that so much of both theory and practice is invested in notions of a universal good – be it to make such a film or to be able to analyse it.

Invested in this is the idea of judgements, and once more we find that the relations are dense and multi-layered. Both theory and practice set up systems of judgements; and when they reflect on the other, each utilises a version of judgement. Kant sets out what he calls the four reflexive judgements in *The Critique of Judgement* (1790); the agreeable, beautiful, sublime, and good. These judgements are reflexive, argues Kant, because they involve the subject's participation, and contribution, to the process. They are what Kant calls the 'subjective universal' because they are arrived at by the individual subject, but have a sense that they are, or will be, universally acknowledged and understood. Issues of Kant's argument aside, what we can gain from this is the idea of the judgement of theory and practice having this same sense of the subjective universal. What has prevented this in the past is the inability of theory or practice to align the sense of the subject with the universal. Their separation has only allowed one of these attributes, rarely both – and this is the situation that has developed particularly since the 1970s.[5]

The issues of the sublime and the creative resistances that yield a beyond to the theory of practice will always operate outside of such notions of the good film, and in doing so they continually operate at the level of dissatisfaction. This is the force of agitation and restlessness that cajoles a discipline – theoretical or practical – to move beyond its current status quo; it is the internal energy that promotes change, and works through a different form of resistance to what already exists. One of the key ways this dissatisfaction is manifested, both positively and negatively, is through terror. This is a notion of terror that we find embedded in the theorising of the sublime, and central to all sublime practices; and it is to which we must now turn.

4. Terror

Part of the idea here is to suggest that somehow the sublime offers us a way of considering theory and practice from a different perspective; and that such considerations may well operate like the sublime. With the centrality of terror I'd suggest that this is precisely one of the debilitating forces against thinking beyond the limitations of theory and practice. In other words it is the terror that makes us retreat to established patterns and ideas – to the preservation of the good and the conformity of beauty. Burke's treatise on the sublime focussed on terror; the famous passage on this reads: 'Whatever is fitted in any sort to excite the ideas of pain, and danger, that is to say, whatever is in any sort terrible, or is conversant about terrible objects, or operates in a manner analogous to terror, it is a source of the sublime; that is, it is productive of the strongest emotion which the mind is capable of feeling' (Burke 1990: 39). Significant to the discussion at hand, Burke mentions both the ideas which cause terror (theory) as well as the objects (practice); which is quite in keeping with the sublime as both internal and external (in the observer, creator, as well as text). Terror thus becomes associated with a type of fear and conservatism of both ideas and practices. The liberation that terror potentially provides is to rework the discursive practices between the two.

Herein we witness a further distinction between the Good and the sublime. The Good is presented as outside of terror, for in its placations resides the comfort of the known and the socially sanctioned. Of course often the Good of one social order is precisely the terrifying of another – witness the consequences of colonialisation, slavery, apartheid, patriarchy, to see the disguising of fear and terror by an assertion of the 'Good'. The Good will also utilise terror for its own sake, evoking a defence against all that comes against it by arguing the negativity of terror. At one level this is the separation that has taken place between theory and practice as they have come to mistrust the other. In the sublime, however, there is no space for such a (political) use of terror, because this is what the sublime must always produce.

The final 'word' (and the irony of course is that this scene is performed entirely in silence) on all this goes to the three Grouchos. Why does not the third Groucho instil terror in the other two? After all he disrupts the perfectly tuned relationship between them; he collapses the system that seems to be working so well as it tests the fabric and process of action and counter action. The simple answer is that this is comedy, and the history of the sublime has tended to be invested in tragedy. But, and this may well be labouring the point too much, is that the terror is subsumed into the new order – the breaking away from the frame (the mirroring process); an order that will, in time, create its own versions of mirroring and repetition. The mirroring and repetition of theory and practice can be disrupted in many ways – the cinematic sublime is just one of many possibilities. The trick is to subsume the terror of the new, be that the new of theory or the new of practice, or indeed the new merging of theory and practice as an enterprise still to be born.

BIBLIOGRAPHY

Bordwell, D. (2008). *Poetics of Cinema*. Berkeley: University of California Press.

Burke, E. (1990 [1757]) *A Philosophical Enquiry into the Origin of our Ideas of the Sublime and Beautiful*. Ed. Adam Phillips. (World's Classics). Oxford: Oxford University Press.

Freud, S. (1985 [1899]) *Interpretation of Dreams*, trans. J. Strachey, Middlesex: Penguin.

Kant, I. (1987 [1790]) *Critique of Judgment*, Trans. Werner S. Pluhar, New York: Hackett.

Lacan, J. (1988) *Freud's Papers on Technique*. Cambridge: Cambridge University Press.

Lacan, J. (1992) *The Ethics of Psychoanalysis*, trans. D. Porter. Ed. J-A Miller, London: Routledge,

Lyotard, J-F. (1994) *Lessons on the Analytic of the Sublime: Kant's Critique of Judgment*. Stanford: Stanford University Press, pp. 23–9.

Myer, C. (2004) 'Playing with Toys by the Wayside: an Interview with Noel Burch', *The Journal of Media Practice*, 5 (2) pp. 71–80.

FILMOGRAPHY

Duck Soup (1933) Directed by Leo McCarey [DVD]. USA: Image Entertainment.

Dial M for Murder (1954) Directed by Alfred Hitchcock [DVD]. USA: Warner Home Video.

Citizen Kane (1941) Directed by Orson Welles [DVD]. USA: Warner Home Video.

NOTES

1   'Theory' and 'practice' are used here as overarching terms, yet clearly they are not homogenous within themselves. In reality we should speak of 'theories' and 'practices', acknowledging that there are conflicting models even within each category. Lacan (1988) and Bordwell (2008) both use the term theory, but both mean quite different things by it. Similarly, practice can be seen as constituted of a myriad of activities, some connected, others removed, from one another. To speak of the relationship between the two should always hold these heterogeneities in mind.

2   This notion of judgement will be of great significance in the following pages. It is used here in anticipation to the notion of aesthetic judgements, particularly within a Kantian sense.

3   The 'Good' is capitalised here to distinguish it from the good. 'Good' stands for the larger order, of a repository or even system; 'good' denotes the specific manifestations and examples. In one sense this is something like: the Good = moral order and ethical interdictions; and the good = a specific act or deed that comes to reflect such an order.

4   A space, it can be noted, which operates in terms of theory and practice in a very similar manner to the impossible space that the camera occupies in the scene from *Dial M for Murder* mentioned above.

5   This is an idea that comes from Clive Myer's succinct articulation of the central issue of theory and practice: '... why has film practice gone in one direction, towards a mini-industrial process while theory has gone in a different direction, which is more-or-less to avoid practice altogether' (Myer 2004: 71)

CHAPTER 6

RANCIÈRE AND THE PERSISTENCE OF FILM THEORY

Nico Baumbach

In an essay entitled 'An Elegy For Theory' by D. N. Rodowick in the Fall 2007 issue of *October*, Rodowick begins by revealing that when he says 'Theory' he means 'a certain idea of theory' and the narrative he draws is a familiar one. 'From the late 1960s and throughout the 1970s, the institutionalisation of cinema studies in North America and Europe became identified with this idea of theory' (2007: 91) now in decline which he describes as 'an interdisciplinary commitment to concepts and methods derived from literary semiology, Lacanian psychoanalysis, and Althusserian Marxism' (ibid.). For twenty years we have been told that this 'certain idea of theory' is in crisis and in need of revision if not simply obfuscating, poisonous and in need of disposing with in its entirety.

The current interest in Jacques Rancière, the former student of and collaborator with Louis Althusser who became one of his most stringent critics, might be seen as part of this tide – another name to signify our suspicion of the hermeneutics of suspicion. But rather than offering another condemnation, apologia or elegy for 'Theory', I would like to suggest that Rancière's work may provide a way to start rethinking the very problems and questions about this legacy that still persist in contemporary cinema studies. Rancière's thinking about the relation of art, theory and politics in relation to Althusser's own thinking about that relation makes it possible to reconsider and rearrange the terms that dominate the current retreat from an Althusserian film theory which all too often amounts to a retreat from politics.

Introductions to Rancière usually begin with the story of his parting of ways with his Althusserian past over what he detected as the position of mastery in the mode of reading attributed to Marxist science. What is interesting about this story, however, is how its consequences have unfolded over the course of Rancière's writing. It is not just a simple narrative in which the king is revealed as naked—the radical politics of the intellectual master shown to be enhancing his own power while excluding the excluded he claimed to be speaking for. This gesture of unveiling is no more emancipatory than the discourse that absolves itself of vulgarity through a theoretical edifice designed to ensure the rigorous separation from bourgeois ideology. Rather, politics defined as axiomatic equality must, as Rancière's recent work has shown, be conceived of in relation to aesthetics. His disagreement with Althusser over science and politics was from the very beginning a disagreement over aesthetics. More broadly, what is at stake is thinking the separation and entwinement of aesthetics, politics and theory.

I

Althusser wrote little about art and aesthetics, but he did have in interest in Brecht, which has informed much of the uptake of Althusser in film and literary theory. The link between Brechtian political modernism and Althusserian symptomatic reading is found both in Jean-Luc Godard's *La Chinoise* (1967) and in much *Screen* theory of the 1970s. In a piece from 1968, Althusser draws an analogy between Brecht and Marx. This analogy is established on the basis that they both generate within their respective domains, philosophy and theatre, a new kind of practice based on a knowledge of the repression of politics that founds both their practices. Althusser makes clear that for both Brecht and Marx this not a new philosophy or new theatre but a de-mystification of philosophy and theatre within their respective places. Politics, which according to Althusser determines both theatre and philosophy, is repressed in favour of enjoyment – aesthetic enjoyment or enjoyment of speculation. One must put philosophy and theatre in their true places but to do this one has to carry out a 'displacement' within philosophy and within theatre (Althusser 2003: 141). Through the displacement of the point of view of philosophy and theatre we can in Althusser's words, 'yield the floor to politics (ibid). But we can only do this by showing that philosophy or theatre are not politics and that they are only philosophy or theatre. Politics in both cases is conceived as the ground of these practices, but it speaks only when its silence is revealed.

But this analogy between Brecht and Marx, Althusser suggests, can only go so far because not only is philosophy not politics and theatre not politics, but the theatre is not philosophy. Here Althusser makes clear that he is unsatisfied with Brecht's explanation because it turns out that the specificity of theatre, its difference from philosophy, politics, science and life is that it shows and entertains, and yet showing and entertaining are the very things that *disguise* theatre's difference from philosophy, politics, science and life. To show what theatre is, we have to betray what it is but it must remain theatre and only theatre in the process without generating a new mystification. Althusser asks rhetorically, how is it that theatre can still provide entertainment through mere showing while also thwarting this logic at the same time? Althusser excuses Brecht for not solving the problem, because he is finally a man of the theatre and not a philosopher, and insists that the importance of Brecht is not his theory but his theatrical practice that takes ideology for its raw material.

II

The essay remained unfinished, but its twisted logic can be found smoothed over using Althusser's Lacan-inspired definition of ideology throughout film theory. Christian Metz provides us with the formula: The role of film theory, according to Metz, is 'to disengage the cinema-object from the imaginary and win it for the symbolic' (1982: 3). Cinema, we are told, is a machine of the imaginary and theory by imposing questions of representation and the subject into a phenomenological experience that effaced those questions is a political intervention. As Pier Paolo Pasolini claimed, the work of theory was to add something to our knowledge of its object and hence to separate itself from 'the obscure ontological background' that arises from 'explaining cinema with cinema' (1988: 197). As the example of Pasolini should remind us, this period was not anti-cinema, but was firmly committed to a cinema of the symbolic, whether in the camera-stylo of Nicholas Ray or John Ford in which the mise-en-scene functions as écriture to reveal the contradictions of the film's official narrative or in the more overtly oppositional cinema of a Godard or Pasolini in which the cinematic-imaginary is perpetually under erasure. The concern, according to Godard, was not with the representation of reality, but the reality of representation; that is, not with the imaginary, but the symbolic.[1]

Peter Wollen linked this logic explicitly back to Brecht to advocate for a materialist cinema that countered ideology in contrast to the apolitical Greenbergian Modernism that he detected in the American avant-garde. According to Wollen, 'Brecht wanted to find a concept of representation

which would account for a passage from perception/recognition to knowl-
edge/understanding, from the imaginary to the symbolic' (1976: 18–19).[2]
Here we see how the Althusserian-Lacanian language is used to account
for the logic of separation, both as problem and then through the Brechtian
V-effect[3] as solution. Whether conceived of as an immanent break within the
artwork itself or through the intervention of theory, the goal is conceived as a
passage or break out of appearance or sensory experience and into knowledge.
In film, like theatre, distance is perceived as immediacy, but once we become
aware of the distance through distancing we are restored to real immediacy in
the form of cognition. To offer another example from this era of film theory,
this is what Jean-Louis Baudry called, in a reference to Vertov, 'the return of
the apparatus in flesh and blood' (1986: 296). Mediation made present breaks
us out of the illusions of mediation. But as Althusser himself recognised in the
case of Brecht, this linking of art and theory in a common project of political
modernism reaches an impasse unless we rethink the very relation between
the imaginary and symbolic, art and philosophy.

III

This logic may be out of favour but its repudiation is not. Indeed, what is striking today is how often the repudiation takes the form of a strict obversion of
this logic. Sometimes anchored in an historical argument about the decline
of the narrative feature film and more fluid, dispersive images in the age of
the information and networks, the current emphasis in much film theory on
'the body', affect, sensation tends to take its cues from one of two sources:
Gilles Deleuze and Henri Bergson or a return to phenomenology to assert an
immanent theory of film no longer conceived of as representation. With some
significant exceptions, much of this work amounts to a simple reversal of the
Metzian dogma—theory becomes an attempt to disengage cinema from the
symbolic and win it for the imaginary, returning us to that obscure ontological
background that Pasolini declared it was theory's role to cut through.

Phenomenological and Deleuzian writings would likely wish to separate
themselves from what David Bordwell and Noël Carroll have termed 'Post-
Theory'. Bordwell and Carroll hoped to usher in a new era by dethroning
'Grand Theory' in favour of a more modest 'piecemeal' approach turning to
the natural sciences for methodological support for new 'theories' (in the plural) not marred by Marxist or psychoanalytic jargon or extrinsic concerns such
as class, race and sexuality. If cognitivism, offered as the most promising new
avenue of investigation, does not seem to have had the traction within film
studies departments the authors may have hoped, the polemical dimension of

their book seems less and less like the contrarian position it was announced as at the time. A stated polemical distance from 'Theory' should be familiar to anyone who has read the introductions to books on film put out by academic presses in the last twenty or so years. All too often anti-Grand Theory might rather be called Grand Anti-Theory in that it turns Theory into such a monolithic project that once a little common sense is offered to undermine some the most provocative claims that have been influential, then suddenly a vast range of philosophical inquiry and scholarly research can be swept under the rug.[4] If the cognitivists' interest in 'biological propensities' and 'cognitive universals' would strike the Deleuzian as too normative and not properly nomadic, let's identify what they have in common: a refusal to see media in terms of either the subject or representation and an unqualified dismissal of the utility of concepts such as identification, ideology or any terminology derived from psychoanalysis or Saussaurian linguistics.

A serious examination of Deleuze's relation to both phenomenology and Althusserian film theory is beyond the scope of this essay, but it is worth looking at a typical example of the Deleuzian turn. Deleuze's remarkable *Cinema* books sit uneasily alongside a tradition of French theory that they are often indirectly commenting upon. Turning our attention to effaced mechanisms – be it through breaking down the illusion of movement, the return of sprocket holes or the return of the gaze – in order to pass from identification to knowledge is of no interest to Deleuze, because for Deleuze nothing has been effaced. Deleuze announces in the introduction to *Cinema 1: The Movement Image* that 'cinema is always as perfect as it can be' (1991: x). The identification of matter and image is also an identification of matter and its movement and temporality, being and becoming. As Giorgio Agamben suggests, Deleuze grasps that the movement-image undoes the distinction between psychical and physical reality (2007: 153). There are no components of the movement-image that can be isolated to reveal how cinema works because, 'cinema begins with the movement-image – not with any 'relation' between image and movement; cinema creates a self-moving image' (1995: 65). Deleuze takes the famous maxim of Edmund Husserl's phenomenology that 'consciousness is always consciousness of something' and argues that Bergson goes farther by proposing that 'consciousness is something' (1991: 56). Hence an image, as a form of consciousness, has an autonomy and materiality that is only obscured by bringing in questions about a subject of enunciation.

To say, as I have, that cinema for Deleuze actualises the identity of matter and image may seem paradoxical since the identity of matter and image is not an identity and not actual in Deleuze's terms. The image is rather virtual in Deleuze's sense – an immanent plane of potentiating fields that create signs out of blocks and movement and time. It is a grin without a cat, an event-sensation without body or object (1997: 168). To preserve the creative power of the new sign grasped as image, Deleuze rejects the Saussurian distinction between signifier and signified, which means he also rejects the distinction between imaginary and the symbolic.

If we remove all elements of dissensus and pedagogy, then Deleuze's claim that cinema is always as perfect as it can be readily adapted to something called *Filmosophy*, as a 2006 book by Daniel Frampton has it. This book is of interest to the extent that it demonstrates an impasse when grasping film theory/philosophy's role once it has shaken off the shackles of any form of hermeneutics, historicisation or ideology critique. The concept of filmosophy (which the book's cover informs us is trademarked and the use of it is subject to copyright laws) is meant to be a way of writing about film as a purely imma-nent thinking and feeling. No source, no outside, no recourse to a 'language of representation', to filmmaker or spectator needs to be appealed to speak of the cinema-effect. Each film is its own perfect cybernetic machine. Cinema for Frampton cannot be thought of as reflexive or in terms of excess, supple-ment, void or lack because all these concepts betray the film's own immanent expression. The language of production and technology adopted by film stud-ies is therefore taking what a film does or is and recoding it in a language of representation that refers only to how it was made. 'We should not be taught to see zooms and tracking shots but led to understand intensities and movements of feeling and thinking' (Frampton 2006: 169). This may sound Deleuzian (or Lyotardian), but what does it mean to be 'led to understand' something that Frampton will have to claim that we already understand? In Frampton's words, 'we do not need instruction in how to read film, we only need a better language of those moving-image sounds—we are already well suited to understanding film' (2006: 175). Ultimately, Frampton's argument can only affirm a kind of transparency of images in the pure self-sufficiency of what he calls the 'filmind'. But then why do we need a language for these images at all if language applies a representational over-coding to images that are always already their own 'filmosophy'?

To get out of this tautology that would seem to negate the need for his own project, Frampton affirms a poetics of interpretation: 'The film … might be said to be crying in empathy, sweating out loud, feeling pain for the char-acter. The concept of the filmind should provoke these kinds of interpreta-tions' (2006: 174). What Deleuze attempts to create is a semiotics of moving images that presupposes an importance for philosophy as a creative practice separate from cinema; Frampton's Deleuzian reading anchored in a new age of information and fluid digital images is finally interested only in a descriptive language (generously termed poetic) that is still analogical and vague. Before we start 'sweating out loud', this 'better language' can be deferred in favour of a back and forth between speculative utopian claims that consciously echo writings of the 1920s about film's equivalence to mind and a repetitive insistence on the way academic 'film theory' reterritorialises the immanent singularities or intensities of film's own creative power.

IV

It should be mentioned that a fidelity to the older model of film theory remains visible in the Lacanian cultural criticism associated primarily with Slavoj Žižek. Here, too, there is a shift away from the symbolic, but it is toward the failure of symbolisation – not a turn to body and affect, but rather the way that films and generally filmic narratives reach an impasse in the third prong of the Lacanian triad – the traumatic void of the Real. While Žižek insists on preserving the political project of film theory against the post-theory turn, there's little trace of the political Modernism of his predecessors. Like them he privileges the symbolic over the imaginary, theory over aesthetics, but the logic of exposing mediation through mediation is now on the side only of theory and not of art. The relation between film and theory is viewed as just that: a relation, and not a non-relation in the Lacanian sense. In regard to his use of Krzysztof Kieslowski, Žižek says that his aim is

> ...not to talk about his work, but to refer to his work in order to accomplish the work of Theory. In its very ruthless use of its artistic pretext, such a procedure is much more faithful to the interpreted work than any superficial respect for the work's unfathomable autonomy. (2001: 9)

For Žižek, the tendency is for film to have only an instrumental function in the illustration of Lacanian concepts. It is part of his charm to have made this so explicit. These are not then the concepts cinema gives rise to, as they are for Deleuze, but mere repetitions of the same. For Žižek, the effect of the work of art is imaginary. And this is what leaves him with the false choice of prostrating ourselves before the work of art as autonomous entity or relegating it to a pretext for theory.

In this adventure, the unsymbolisable real must be found everywhere in an endless process of generating meaning out of inconsistent common sense by attributing a lesson to its rhetorical inversion. For all the canny insights and love of the game, the mixture of discourses and taste for paradox, the self-cannibalising and proliferation across media, Žižek's machine works too well.

In Žižekian fashion it might be asked whether this discourse isn't precisely Lacan's discourse of the university, in which everything must be counted and in which 'objet petit a' is continually brought into the fold of the big Other?[5]

V

Rancière's work, on the other hand, suggests that we need not side with the symbolic over the imaginary or vice versa. The thwarting logic that Althusser found in Brecht's theory is only a theoretical impasse if we also wish to ensure that the work of theory or art accomplishes the passage from identification to knowledge. As Rancière has proposed, constitutive of art and the thinking of art over the last two centuries is this very thwarting logic, an identification of the unity of contraries. And the images of cinema and art, are not defined by their destiny in either the symbolic or the imaginary, studium or punctum, actual or virtual, but rather they invent new possibilities out of their capacity to play with these contradictory functions.

Rancière has proposed that the realm of appearance and broadly of aesthetics is a contested terrain not to be grasped in its truth only by identifying its symbolic constitution. On the contrary, for Rancière, the symbolic constitution of the social is what he calls the police (1998: 28). The social is symbolically constituted through the various mechanisms by which sensible or sensual experience is both shared and divided, distributed and recognised. Police is a term for when the imaginary and symbolic coincide without remainder or on the other hand, when one falsifies the other. It is any sensorial or conceptual orientation that offers no room for supplement or lack. Metz's call for winning the imaginary for the symbolic and the reversal that claims that the affective dimension must be liberated from its interpretive territorialisation are but two modes of policing the uses and meanings of images. Politics is not then on the side of the imaginary, but it is an inscription of supplement or lack that rearranges what constitutes the distinction between imaginary and symbolic.

Rancière retains the critique of the Feuerbachian 'humanism' of the early Marx and its uptake in twentieth-century Western Marxism, initiated by the Althusser-led *Reading Capital* project of which he was a part. The difference between police and politics, whatever may appear to be the connotations, is not the difference between alienation and self-consciousness. According to Althusser, the production of the Marxist theorist is not outside ideology but rather it is the only standpoint from which to properly say 'I am in ideology'. But in Ranciere's reading, this is merely another twist on the discourse on alienation by drawing a distinction between good and bad forms of knowledge.

For Althusser, the good Marxist no longer says, 'I am outside ideology but the masses are not'; instead, he says, in effect, 'We are all in ideology. The difference is I *know* it, but the masses (and the bad Marxists) do not.' Knowledge as production, the symbolic, is posed against knowledge as sight, the imaginary.

This privileging of the symbolic over the imaginary can be accomplished only through a strict separation between theory and art. In Althusser's open letter to André Daspre published in English as *A Letter on Art*, Althusser states that 'the real difference between art and science lies in the specific form in which they give us the same object in quite different ways: art in the form of 'seeing', 'feeling', 'perceiving', science in the form of knowledge (in the strict sense, by concepts)' (1971: 223). He continues, 'Art makes us "see" "conclusions without premises", whereas knowledge makes us penetrate into the mechanism which produces the "conclusions" out of the "premises"' (1971: 224). In other words, for Althusser, art offers objective appearance, but is silent about its own conditions of possibility. Science is what gives us knowledge of causality, the mechanism that generates the logic of cause and effect. Even as Althusser's notion of structural causality attempts to break from bourgeois conceptions of scientific method, his conception of the distinction between science and art remains resolutely classical.

But the impasse that Althusser recognised in Brecht is the same impasse Rancière recognises in Althusser. Philosophy, art and politics must all maintain their places to ensure the passage from ideology to knowledge-effect. And yet this very passage is impossible if these places remain unmoved. For Rancière, aesthetics is a name for the blurring of these places.

VI

To return to where we started, while Rodowick's elegy does not wish to salvage this idea of Althusserian-Lacanian theory, he does wish to critique the critique of it that in the name of Cognitivism or analytic philosophy attempts to restore film theory to a model based on the natural sciences. Using Wittgenstein Rodowick proposes that theories of culture are not properly analysed empirically, but can only ever be matters of soliciting agreement about sense and meaning. Therefore he poses a third way, a philosophical turn, in which Deleuze is recruited for an ordinary language philosophy that is separated from empirical investigation in favour of an approach defined by an 'ethical' commitment to 'epistemological self-examination'(Rodowick 2007: 100).

In the same issue, Rodowick's essay is followed by a dissenting response from Malcolm Turvey. Turvey also appeals to Wittgenstein's work to suggest that these ethical and epistemological commitments are just as extrinsic to the theory of film as psychoanalysis, Marxism and cognitivism. Theories, according to Turvey, should stick to explanatory 'generalizations about film' that proceed within a community with shared standards toward progressive knowledge of how film functions (2007: 120).[6]

In this debate over methodology, hinging finally on a conflict over what the late Wittgenstein does or does not authorise we can say about film, we find only brief mentions of Marxism, feminism, or political analysis, reduced to examples of so many *ethical* commitments that we should, depending on who you believe, Rodowick or Turvey, either be responsible to through self-examination if and only if they happen to inform our approach or should dismiss because they underdetermine workable explanatory hypotheses about what cinema is and does. That this debate should take place on these terms in a journal that still bears the name *October* should impress us with its irony.

If I offer Rancière's writing to signal the persistence of film theory, it is not in the name of returning wholesale to this certain idea of theory that Rodowick highlights so much as to one aspect of it: the thinking of the relation between film theory and politics. The persistence of film theory does not mean shoring up a disciplinary practice by determining the contours of the object and delimiting the shared criteria for generating knowledge and debate. On the contrary, it means a break from this very logic of consensus. Yet Rancière avoids the tedious language of the 'break' or 'rupture'. In Rancière, there is no muscular assertion of deep temporality or emphatic will. Possibilities for thought are found in a montage of associations and disassociations not in the signalling of commitment. An investigation into the conditions of possibility of thinking about cinema in cinema and in film theory is no longer in the service of resting on knowledge of the system, but of dissociating the very logic of cause and effect that gives theory and cinema their specifiable places.

BIBLIOGRAPHY

Agamben, G. (2007) *Infancy and History: On the Destruction of Experience*. London: Verso.

Althusser, L. (1971) 'A Letter on Art' in *Lenin and Philosophy*. London: NLB, 221-228

_____ (2003) 'On Brecht and Marx', in W. Montag, *Louis Althusser*. New York: Palgrave Macmillan, 136–49.

_____ and E. Balibar (1970) *Reading Capital*. London: NLB.

Baudry, J-L. (1986) 'Ideological Effects of the Basic Cinematographic Apparatus', in P. Rosen (ed.) *Narrative, Apparatus, Ideology*. New York: Columbia University Press,

286–98.

Bordwell, D. and N. Carroll (eds) (1996) *Post-Theory: Reconstructing Film Studies*. Madison: The University of Wisconsin Press.

Deleuze, G. (1991) *Cinema 1: The Movement Image*. Minneapolis: University of Minnesota Press.

_____ (1995) *Negotiations 1972–1990*. New York: Columbia University Press.

_____ (1997) *Essays Critical and Clinical*. Minneapolis: University of Minnesota Press.

Frampton, D. (2006) *Filmosophy: A Manifesto for a Radically New Way of Understanding Cinema*. London: Wallflower Press.

Lacan, J. (2007) *The Seminar of Jacques Lacan Book XVII: The Other Side of Psychoanalysis*. New York: Norton.

Metz, C. (1982) *The Imaginary Signifier: Psychoanalysis and the Cinema*. Bloomington: Indiana University Press.

Mulvey, L. (1990) 'Visual pleasure and narrative cinema', in P. Erens (ed.) *Issues in Feminist Film Criticism*. Bloomington: Indiana University Press, pp. 28-40.

Pasolini, P. P. (1988) *Heretical Empiricism*. Bloomington: Indiana University Press.

Rancière, J. (1998) *Disagreement: Politics and Philosophy*. Minneapolis: University of Minnesota Press.

Rodowick, D. N. (2007) 'An Elegy For Theory', *October*, 122, Fall, 91–109.

Turvey, M. (2007) 'Theory, Philosophy and Film Studies: A Response to D. N. Rodowick's "An Elegy for Theory"', *October*, 122, Fall, 110–20.

Wollen, P. (1976) 'Ontology and Materialism in Film', *Screen*, 17, 1, Spring, 7–23.

Žižek, S. (2001) *The Fright of Real Tears: Krzysztof Kieślowski between Theory and Post-Theory*. London: British Film Institute.

FILMOGRAPHY

La Chinoise (1967) Directed by Jean-Luc Godard [DVD]. London: Optimum.

NOTES

1   The symbolic for Lacan is realm of signifiers and language. It is also the locus of the law and the superego. The imaginary, on the other hand, is the pre-reflective mode of understanding that involves a méconnaissance or misrecognition. It is more complicated than this however, as the imaginary and symbolic are never truly extricable and can be arranged in more complex permutations. To take one important example, Laura Mulvey's famous essay *Visual Pleasure and Narrative Cinema* (1990 pp. 28–40) may seem at odds with Metz's dictum since she criticises the way that the realm of the law and the symbolic is codified as masculine in typical Hollywood narrative films, but she is, in effect, talking here about an 'imaginary symbolic'. When she proposes that theory be used to destroy the pleasure generated by the ease and plenitude of narrative cinema, she is, like Metz, valorising the symbolic dimension of theory over the imaginary experience of conventional

spectatorship informed by historically determined inequality.

2   Clement Greenberg was associated with a Modernism that retreated from the critique of ideology to an over-emphasis on medium specificity that Wollen thought limited the politics of the American 'structural-materialist' avant-garde. For the latter, 'materialism' meant exploring the material substrate of the film strip rather than the narrative codes and conventions of mainstream cinema.

3   The Verfremdungseffekt or V-effekt, a term coined by Brecht, is often translated as alienation-effect or defamiliarisation-effect.

4   See Bordwell and Carroll (eds) 1996. Here they refer to 'the Theory' as 'top-down', 'homogeneous', 'univocal', and so forth. If I use Metz's statement to unite '70s film theory', it is not to support these characterisations. Rather, I wish to isolate a tendency that I believe connects a complex range of material that had its own internal divisions and debates.

5   'Objet petit a' in Lacan is the 'object cause of desire' and is always defined in terms of excess or lack. It is what cannot be incorporated into the big Other or the symbolic constitution of the social though this is what 'the discourse of the university' (which for Lacan might be a synonym for bureaucracy) tries to do. For the discourse of the university, everything must be counted. See Lacan 2007.

6   Despite his resistance to cognitivism, in this respect, Turvey defends the terms of Bordwell and Carroll's 'Post-theory' turn.

CHAPTER 7
BEHIND THE MASK OF THE SCREENPLAY: THE SCREEN IDEA

Ian W. Macdonald

In the multiplicity of writing, everything is to be *disentangled*, nothing *deciphered*...

Roland Barthes (1977: 147; original emphases)

INTRODUCTION.

The screenplay is the common starting point for almost all fiction films. How though can we study it, and the intention within it to become a film? Over the past century there have been many attempts to discuss effective ways of telling stories via this form, usually in the form of manuals (Stannard 1920; Margrave 1936; Vale 1998; Parker 1998; McKee 1999 and so forth), as well as attempts to consider the screenplay less as an industrial planning document and more as a literary form with artistic merit (Malkin 1980; Viswanathan 1986 and so forth). The former approach is restricted to working within parameters set by the norms of our film and wider cultures; screenwriting craft manuals overwhelmingly talk of being creative in relation to classic and normative patterns.[1] The impression they give is that while there is certainly artistic licence to break rules, the screenplay itself is some form of sacred text – imperfect and partial perhaps but the basis to which the makers of the film always return.

The latter approach is less concerned with using the screenplay as a creative tool than it is with attempting to read the text as closely and accurately as possible. The goal is essentially to gain acceptance of this form of text as an object as worthy of major study as, say, the novel. On the back of this ride various concerns; about the lack of critical attention paid to work that must surely have merit, the desire to understand better how the script form is used, and about the position of the author – the screenwriter – who is perceived as being doubly neglected by commentators in both film and literary fields.

Both these approaches are valuable, but their common reliance on the screenplay as the tangible text privileges that text as the major – sometimes only – focus of study. Of course, 'the scene text is the major carrier of screenplay information', as Claudia Sternberg puts it (1997: 231), and it is certainly the most accessible form of the film in the pre-production stage but, as commentators like the director Pier Paolo Pasolini (1977) have pointed out, it is only a document on the way to becoming another document. This chapter examines the implications of the screenplay as something partial referring to a whole, a synecdoche, and the value of the concept of the screen idea as something residing between the players in the production process.

THE SCREENPLAY AND THE SCREEN IDEA

The screenplay itself is the record of an idea for a screenwork, written in a highly stylised form. It is constrained by the rules of its form on the page, and it is the subject of industrial norms and conventions. In what it can show and do in relation to the screenwork, it is partial; for example, the dialogue is quite clear to the untrained eye, but with other aural components (such as music) there are common industrial injunctions against specification.[2] The visual is only approximated, not completely specified. The architecture of the page is important in identifying key visual elements, and how the visual interacts with time. Clearly this is a form that requires training and experience to use. It has been described as a 'blueprint';[3] as 'less than a blueprint and more than a libretto' (Corliss 1975: xv), a 'hint fixed on paper' (Eisenstein in Mehring 1990: 7), and 'a reverse pyramid … a platform you wear on your shoulders that a talented director can stand on and perform' (Stern in Mehring 1990: 7). However, the screenplay is not the whole story, as writer-director Ingmar Bergman found :

> Bergman finds that the screenplay is an inadequate medium for clearly indicating the visual qualities of his films, especially the way in which they are to be edited and the relationship between shots; in short it is impossible

for Bergman to indicate in the screenplay how a film will breathe and pulsate. (Winston 1973: 115)

The sophistication that Bergman desired could result in a more detailed or unwieldy document, however. It is its general nature, in outlining the narrative in a dramatic structure and common dramatic form, which makes the screenplay an approximation, a sketch. This generality is nevertheless its strength, and is the reason for its centrality in the process of production.

There are some things the screenplay is not: it is not a finished piece of work (in relation to the screenwork – the finished film). It is not normally, by the start of shooting, the work of only one person, despite what it says on the cover. It is not complete, as a description of all the aspects of the screenwork. It is not image-based (surprisingly), and despite being text-based it does not appear literary in a traditional sense, except possibly in parts. There is never a definitive version of the screenplay of a film; by definition it must relate to the screenwork but also by definition it cannot, as more work must precede the final outcome and make the screenplay itself redundant. 'The scenario dies in the film' said writer-director Andrei Tarkovsky (1986: 134). At no point in its development can the screenplay be said to truly reflect the final screenwork. As a discarded piece of work, can it be considered except in relation to what it *might* have become? Given that the screenwork does not exist during pre-production, can we say that the *potential* screenwork exists? And does it exist in the text of the screenplay, or in the minds of those involved in production, or both?

Within the mind of a screenwriter there surely is, possibly only half-formed or ill defined, a potential screenwork which he or she must try to convey to those that will produce it. Before pen is set to paper, this idea has some form or basis. A professional screenwriter will identify its suitability and give it shape, based on the norms of the screen industries, and it becomes a 'screen idea'. I use the term here to refer to the core idea of anything intended to become a screenwork, that is 'any notion of a potential screenwork held by one or more people, whether or not it is possible to describe it on paper or by other means'. I use it therefore as a theoretical term, meaning a singular concept (however complex), which may have conventional shape or not, intended to become a screenwork. The value of this term is that it allows us to refer to an essence, the idea that (in all probability) the writer has had from the start and which is discussed within, and outside, the screenplay document.[4] The screenplay is intended to convey (or at least record) the screen idea, but the idea itself is formed in the minds of all those involved in its production. Therefore, this essence is an idea shared with others during, the readers of the screenplay (script editor, producer, director, and others) particularly during what Sternberg has called the 'blueprint stage' (1997: 50–2) including script development, where the shared idea is discussed, made clear and changed. The screenplay itself is a record of the shared screen idea, redrafted in stages as the collaboration proceeds.

Conventionally in film it progresses from a very short synopsis and then treatment to five or six different variations of script form throughout and beyond production (Macdonald 2004: 50–1).[5] Each version may contain several drafts. The written record of the screen idea may therefore occur in many tens of drafts, in highly different levels of detail, and in two main forms; synoptic and script. Any one document presents the screen idea, in essence, as a framework within which others will work. But the screenplay is not the screen idea *in toto*; that exists both within and around the screenplay, shared amongst its readers.

To study the screenplay alone as the source for the screenwork therefore seems unsatisfactory. A clearer focus might be on the shared screen idea itself, if we could see it. This is impossible directly, but we can observe the process of development of the screen idea. Development is, on one level, a formal planning process involving rights acquisition, financial terms and production scheduling (Bancroft & Davies 1989: 18). It follows, therefore, that all involved must share a similar cultural vision of the screenwork, even if only partly. Those involved in developing a particular screenwork form a specific group similar to Helen Blair's notion (2001; 2003) of a semi-permanent work group (SPWG), in which she applies Norbert Elias' theoretical framework of power relationships in terms of figurations and networked agency. In other words, the loose grouping of those involved in screenwork development – a Screen Idea Work Group (SIWG) – operate as any work group might in relation to both internal and external positions of power and status. Negotiations over the screen idea involve these as well as individual notions of habitus and personal disposition, as outlined by Pierre Bourdieu (1996). With only a few exceptions for individually produced work, the SIWG formation applies however the screenwork is produced, whether for commercial or non-commercial reasons, or whether it involves conventional or unconventional work practices. Essentially, there is always a screen idea with a congregation of people working on it. Film production defined as a 'community of practitioners' has been raised before by Bill Nichols, for example, who provided one definition of documentary practice as an institutional formation, a community of filmmakers with a shared sense of common purpose and a particular discourse (1991: 14-15; 2001: 25–6). The notion of the screen idea applies that to the unique grouping of individuals working on a specific production, and the question then is about their interaction and its effect on developing that idea.

On a basic – or ideal – level, collaboration involves reading and rereading, notes, discussion and redrafting, creating and recreating something that represents a common understanding. The reader(s) of the screenplay and other documents – who include the writer at that point – inevitably construct a version of the screen idea in their heads which (unlike readers of novels) they then have to contribute to. There is an imperative towards consensus, otherwise the screenwork will not get made. It also helps if everyone has a similar conception of what they are working towards.[6]

In seeking the source of the visualisation of the screen idea, Pasolini claimed that the 'technique of the scenario' is founded on the collaboration of the reader, a particular collaboration that 'consists of endowing the text with a 'visual' completion which is absent but to which it alludes' (1977: 42). He refers to the role of the reader in constructing the full 'cinematic' meaning of the text using cues from the screenplay, and claims that this operation involves a different 'language' from that involved in reading written text, a language based on a 'system of 'cinemas' or of 'im-signs' (im-segni, images, imagination signs) (1977: 42–3):

> The principal characteristic of the "sign" of the technique of the scenario is that which *alludes to the meaning through two diverse paths concomitant (concurrent) and confluent*. That is, the sign of the scenario alludes to the meaning according to normal path of all written languages and, specifically, literary jargon; *but at the same time, it alludes to this same meaning, leading the viewer* [sic] *to another sign, that of the film in the making*. Each time our brain, when confronted by a sign of the scenario, scans the two paths simultaneously – the former rapidly and normally and the latter specially and at length – to clean the meaning from them. (1977: 42; emphasis in original)

In asking what this fundamental im-sign is, Pasolini is unsure; he does not immediately assume the frame or a shot or a particular sequence of shots. He also rejects as arbitrary the notion that an im-sign might be part of a structure similar to a linguistic structure, like a 'slice in the movement of images, of undetermined, shapeless, magmatic duration' (1977: 44). The im-sign therefore appears to be Pasolini's way of assigning a term to something as yet undefined; an attempt at using a quasi-scientific linguistic approach to describe what he is aware (as a filmmaker) must be considered when reading a screenplay and for which literary textual analysis is only partially applicable. The difficulty for Pasolini is that he does not appear able to identify the 'grammar' of im-signs, as the components of the moving image system of language. More than that, it appears to him to be still a developing thing. Film is:

> ...a stylistic system where a linguistic system has not yet been defined, and where the structure is not known or has not yet been described scientifically. A director, let us say, like Godard, shatters the cinematographic "grammar" before one knows what it is. (1977: 46)

Despite the difficulty of describing the moving image in linguistic and grammarian terms, Pasolini is clear about a number of things. Firstly, he acknowledges that the reader is involved in a collaboration with the writer in understanding the implications of the screenplay. Then there is something about these implications which refers to the screenwork that is to be constructed, something more than just prosaic instructions or a clear use of a language that has a grammar. His analogy here is to poetic symbolism, which also requires the collaboration of the reader, but one which must refer to an as yet undefined (unfortunately) cinematographic grammar. A screenplay is therefore a 'metalanguage' which moves from one system to another, a 'process ... from the passage of stage A to stage B' (1977: 45). This concept appears to suggest that the screenplay holds simultaneously a narrative in literary form (stage A), and the moving image structure it is to become (stage B), and that the (trained or experienced) reader should be able to see ('re-live') both points on the passage from one stage to another as well as the passage itself.[8]

So the screenplay is a hybrid form, using both literary and other unknown criteria to describe two forms of the same thing, 'a structure designed to become another structure' (the title of Pasolini's original 1966 article). This is a concept studied further by others such as Viswanathan (1986) and Van Nypelseer (1989), who suggest that the screenplay is not a visual text per se but one which describes principally the 'message of the image' (Van Nypelseer 1989: 59).[9] The reason for such hybridity is easy to assume, in that there is a need for those involved in screenwork production to see in tangible form some record of what they work towards, and that necessarily this must use an appropriate medium (in this case written language) to describe what they will eventually produce using other media. This prosaic need does not help in understanding some of the power of the screenplay as an artwork in its own right; one commentator has argued that Pasolini's un-made film *St. Paul* is powerful precisely because it exists between literature and film, and so 'by an almost internal necessity cannot be turned into a film' (Mariniello 1999: 76–7). The problem, as Pasolini makes clear, is that there is confusion over how to describe the moving image – it seems as if there is one grammar (of film) being described using another (the literary). The difficulty is then that the nature of the 'metalanguage' – the sum of these two parts – will remain un-analysable as long as this second grammar (of film) remains undiscovered or undefined, or even just vague and shifting.

However, the idea of a grammar or language just appears inappropriate. Pasolini was clearly proposing that cinema functions as (or by using) a language-type structure, even if it produces meaning by using other codes, such as gesture, environment, dreams and memories (Keating, 2001: 3), but his references to the terms 'language' and 'meta-language' are sometimes unclear. The assumption that there is a common basis for film analogous to the common structures of language is neither proven nor helpful. So the study of the screenplay as an object remains awkward; we recognise that it refers only partly and sketchily to the screen idea. Its appearance as a solid, literary object is undermined by the fact that it is both transitional and refers to more than what is on the page. The screenplay as text has a different status to that normally ascribed to most written objects.

THE SCREEN-READER

However, by recognising its hybridity as key and by shifting the focus of study more towards the process of which the screenplay forms a part, we might reach a more complete understanding of the narrative being told and understood. The role of the reader – in this case any reader in the professional context – now becomes more important. Professional norms inform and circumscribe what readers seek, such as Terry Rossio's detailed 60-point checklist divided into (a) concept and plot, (b) technical execution and (c) characters (1997). This is used to guide readers in providing their review of a screenplay, or coverage. Jeff Rush and Cynthia Baughman have written about 'the highly inflected screenplay' (1997), as something which requires considerable careful analysis to be understood through inference and nuance. They differentiate between shooting scripts (as denotative documents or instructions) and screenplays (i.e. writers' drafts) which rely on conventions and language, and therefore require more particular reading. Their claim emphasises the reader's role and responsibility.

> Narrative voice – that perspective that shapes and at times comments on the story – can be expressed through the use of screenplay language, which, *properly interpreted*, embodies the nuances of directorial style. (Rush & Bauman 1997: 28; my italics)

Sternberg (1997) takes a similar stance, analysing the 'nature' of the screen-play text through various components such as dialogue, and implying that close analysis by the reader can reveal the 'hidden director' that the screen-writer has become – an idea that has much in common with the notion of the Implied Author.[10] Again it is the text that is the focus of study, along with the assumption that because it is the 'major carrier' of information and the most visible, close analysis will reveal both its unequivocal meaning and its artistic merit. The problem is that the screenplay does not contain everything that the reader needs to read it as a potential screenwork. As Sternberg's work makes clear, there is much in the professional screenplay that is implied.[11] The pro-fessional reader is (probably) experienced in reading material into such impli-cations; the codes used will be familiar.[12] The 'close textual analysis' approach to the script masks a more important observation; that the screen idea does not reside in the screenplay text alone but separately as the sum of all that the writer and reader understand about this and similar ideas. The instant the reader completes reading the screenplay, their vision of the potential screen-work exists and is shared (imperfectly) with the writer. This is a notion already outlined in relation to literary works, by Wolfgang Iser:

> The literary work has two poles, which we might call the artistic and the aesthetic: the artistic refers to the text created by the author, and the aes-thetic to the realisation accomplished by the reader. From this polarity, it follows that the literary work cannot be completely identical with the text or with the realization of the text, but in fact must lie half-way between the two. (1974: 274)

Effectively the narrative idea exists, of course, in the minds of those who share it. Those who have written on reader-response theory (as noted by Schneider 2005: 485) have discussed the strategic encoding of information by the author for the reader (Umberto Eco), the governing of the reader's response by the codes of a cultural community (Jonathan Culler), and membership of an interpretive community (Stanley Fish). Iser's contribution involved 'picturing' the text, anticipation and retrospection and the gaps in the text which allow the use of imagination (1974: 274–94). He refers to the difference between how one 'sees' in the act of reading, and seeing in actuality; and in doing so shows the main problem that writing, sharing and developing the screen idea presents:

> With a literary text we can only picture things which are not there; the written part of the text gives us the knowledge, but it is the unwritten part

that gives us the opportunity to picture things; indeed without the elements of indeterminacy, the gaps in the text, we should not be able to use our imagination. (1974: 283)

Iser was interested in the ability of a written text to stimulate the imagination, but the goal of the conventional screenwriting process is actually the opposite – the ability of the text and imaginary to become a concrete object, the screenwork. A screenwork is developed from the human imaginary to the visually concrete, but when finished the film no longer directly involves the imaginary – it is there on the screen.[13]

The act of reading (or indeed listening) involves imagination – creating our own images – whereas watching a screenwork involves no such imagination. We watch concrete images on screen; the imagination needed when doing so is for what is *not* on screen.[14] What is unlike a novel or other written text (or audio text) is that images are there – shots are presented, as Metz says, more as a statement than a word (1974: 116). On the other hand writing, reading and discussing a screenplay clearly involves the imaginary, in planning for visual and other realisation by describing the imaginary in specific terms. The early British screenwriters occasionally described their work as 'picturising', as in 'picturised for the screen by Kate Gurney' (1923). However, as these are word-pictures the requirement is on the reader to create them. As Pasolini pointed out a screenplay asks for the reader's imagination as any story would, but also requires the reader to contribute towards an imaginary realisation – to read it, and to 'write' it or see it as a screenwork, in more concrete terms than in the conventional literary text.

Screen-readers are therefore both readers in the traditional literary sense, and also readers who are asked to bring their understanding of the current norms of screenworks to their view of the screen idea. The rather abstract notion of the screen idea then makes sense as something the reader comprehends and shares with others within a Screen Idea Work Group, within an unreferenced professional and cultural context where judgements are made according to individual habitus and in relation to (unclear and shifting) power structures. It recognises a process, a focus of activity around which the dialectic of production and reception is situated. It involves those narratological ideas mentioned above – encoding by the author, governing of the reader's response by a cultural community, and membership of an interpretive community. During conventional production the screen idea is never fully defined or outlined – it cannot be until the screenwork is realised – but it is referred to in terms understood in detail by professional screen-readers. This must also be the case in unconventional production – negotiating processes within the SIWG take place in relation to the field and to assumptions of power and status even where the discourse and practices are dissimilar. Analysis of the screen idea itself is, as we have seen, only partially possible through the screenplay alone, and is essentially impossible except through an understanding of the process through which that idea is progressing. How the writer addresses his/her readers via the script is on the basis of who or what the screen idea is intended for; as a children's TV serial, for example. How screen-readers view the idea and understand and contribute to the idea, depends on where they find themselves within the traditional development process and within the wider context.

This problematises the study of the screenplay as a written text. It clearly has value in the study of the work of an individual writer. As a creative work that is *not* intended to be a film, it could be taken on its stand-alone merits.[15] But the study of the written text in relation to its ostensible intention, the screenwork, remains a partial activity, because it misses out other parts of the screen idea. Studying authorship and skills in using the screenplay form are only part of the story, so what else must we look at within and outside the screenplay?

BARTHES, THE SCREENWRITER AND THE SCREEN-READER

Literary and screen theory have for several decades debated the place of author and reader and the production of meaning. However, the location within one person of a particular way of presenting a story is clearly still important. 'Authorship is the principle of specificity in the world of texts' says Burke (1998: 202); retracing the work back to the author equates to working back to its historical, cultural and political embeddedness. In literary theory, Roland Barthes' 'The Death of the Author' (1968)[16] had attempted to remove the idea of the author from textual production, on the basis of a wider view that language creates the work, and the writer writes it rather than 'authors' it. 'Nothing comes out of nothing', as true for literary creation as for organic nature, said Barthes (in Burke 1998: 23); and the source is not the power of a single transcendental imagination to generate ideas from nowhere, but the coming together in the writer of the discourses that arise from language. Despite Burke's view, the convenience of 'one author/one text' does not address the complexity of how meaning is generated in a work of art (in Kohn 2000: 494), particularly in relation to the development of the screen idea into a screenwork. As Kohn points out: 'in Barthes' (1974) terms, screenplays are model "writerly texts" – open to being rewritten – as opposed to closed "readerly texts" which "can be read but not written ... classic text[s]'" (2000: 495).

Barthes' work (in particular *The Death of the Author* and *S/Z*) includes a number of points that are useful to the analysis of screenwriting and the screen idea. Firstly, the notion that the text is a 'tissue of quotations drawn from innumerable centres of culture' (1977: 146), that is, that there is no single theological meaning (the message from an 'Author-God'). If meaning is cultural, and plural, then it resides in the first instance in the reader (including the 'reader' part of the writer), not the writer alone, because it is the reader that creates the meaning of the text from what is written. The surface meaning of a text may be suffused with resonances or nuance (normally described in terms of the author's power of evocation), but it is the reader that finds that resonance from his own cultural experience, from comprehending (even unconsciously) the extent of that resonance from his own point of view. The writer does not figure here, as he/she is not creating or describing a universal essential truth (says Barthes); 'his only power is to mix writings, to counter the ones with the others' (1977: 146). The shock of Barthes' denial of the writer as creator is great, and difficult to accept, but it does place the writer firmly in a context that connects with others.

Barthes is referring to the individual writer (although he also referred with approval to the surrealist practice of collective writing[17]), but in screenwriting the process is multiplied by the collective involvement of many in the process of development, despite screenwriters and others emphasising authorial possession of aspects of 'their' work. Barthes' assertion that the author of a book is plural is demonstrated more clearly with a screenwork, as an overtly collaborative process. This brings us back to the part played by the screen reader (that is, anyone who reads and contributes) in the construction of the screen idea.

Barthes goes on to say that 'once the Author is removed the claim to decipher a text [that is, to find its true meaning] becomes quite futile' (1977: 147). Barthes talks of 'disentangling' rather than deciphering the text, where (in a famous metaphor) the text is like an onion whose layers are peeled away to reveal yet more layers until finally nothing is revealed (ibid.). The idea that the locus of meaning is the text alone becomes problematic if the only place where the multiplicity of meanings is focused is the reader. This would also be true of screenwriting, made more complex because there is no definitive written text, and there is more than one reader involved. Deciphering the screenplay therefore means both establishing a coherent set of meanings by (and for) the individual reader, and agreeing a coherent set of meanings for the group of readers. Rereading a text is a process Barthes referred to in *S/Z*

(1974: 15–16) as important in the disentanglement of the structure, the way of deconstructing the text's unity and 'naturalness', making possible the discovery of the text's plurality (Olsen 1990: 186). However, what Barthes refers to in *S/Z* is the rereading of a fixed text, *Sarrasine*; how much more complex, then, is the process in screenplay development, where readers are also de facto writers, expected to contribute further text for other readers, in a dynamic process of continual 'refinement'? This occurs during 'script development', a process of reconstruction that along the way creates several new contributors to the screen idea and more readers in a collaboration. It is not a process of analysis alone, in an attempt to construct meaning from a (series of) fixed text(s); it is a process where the screen idea is disentangled and collectively reconstructed according to normative practices of screenwork production, within constraints and conventions. The screen idea – the essence of the screenwork – therefore exists properly in the consciousness of the writers and readers who produce the screenwork; the written text is only a (partial) record of it.

Barthes' work in rethinking the place of the reader as other than a passive consumer also has strong parallels in the actual industrial requirements placed on the professional reader of screen ideas. In trying to bring together the notions of reading and writing in *S/Z*, Barthes is describing a silent and unobservable process that occurs (he asserts) between a single writer and a single reader, but in doing so he has also described the same (and more overt) process that occurs between writer(s) and readers who collaborate over the screen idea. Could the screen idea readers be seen collectively, as a 'self' made up of multiples? It is possible, if one were to re-separate the notions of writer and reader, to describe the process of screen idea development and production as a writer and a reader interacting on many different occasions, in different roles. In that way, there could be said to be a collective character to this 'reader' who is constructing the idea. It may be clearer to conceive of this as a second level of readership, a multiple 'collective reader' at a level above the individual one (which is itself composed of multiple and constantly developing elements). This second level of complexity has one main difference from the primary individual level – that its operation is more overt. It may be observed in action during script development, even as it contributes the development of the written text. Unlike Barthes' work on Sarrasine, where the fixed nature of the word on the published page allowed Barthes to identify codes at work, the second level of readership in screen idea development (the 'collective reader') can be observed at work, in the process of de- and reconstructing that screen idea. However, three significant problems remain; that the primary (individual) level is still also operating and is less (or in-)visible, that the observer is also reading and constructing the screen idea, and that when production is complete, the viewer will also construct the text from the screenwork.

According to an article by Sheila Johnston (1985), in *S/Z* Barthes developed his arguments away from his previous attempts to present a single hypothetical model that could be applied to any narrative, towards the idea that each narrative is itself unique, its own model. As Johnston points out, citing Derrida, 'each work of literature *differs*, obviously, from other works; equally, however, it *defers* to them, i.e. relies on them for its distinctive meaning' (1985: 240; original emphases). This notion therefore locates a text (and its structure) within and against other social and cultural discourses. 'A work of art, then, should be seen not mechanistically, as a closed system, a completed, inert object which will always remain the same, but dynamically, as an endless process of rereading and rewriting.' (Johnston 1985: 240). Johnston is referring, of course, to a completed work, where the physical presence is virtually unchanging,[18] and not to the uncompleted work which is the screenplay. How much more complex does this render the development of the screen idea? The awareness of the reader as a focal point in creating meaning within a given context, and the collaborative attempt at a shared system of meanings that operates in development, also creates a dynamic process which functions in a complex way. There is an oscillation between people and between meanings that appears to resemble the endless process of rereading and rewriting a work of art, with the difference that there is also at play a group dynamic (including power struggles) within norms of professional behaviour which involves roles, 'ownership' and leadership.[19] The intertextuality that is fundamental to Barthes' concept of literary meaning is, in this process, influenced (perhaps driven) by cultural concepts of film, TV, genre, the audio-visual industry and the audience. The process of script development of the realist text (the screenwork) is ostensibly to ensure, to confirm, the internal logic or intratextual economy (as Johnston puts it) of that text, but the external relationships that apply to this process (power, status, norms, negotiations and so on) are perhaps less well acknowledged.

Barthes' distinction between 'readerly' and 'writerly' is a useful one for the screenplay form, as a form which presents both a narrative that is intended to be read easily and with pleasure, and an invitation to consider and imagine ways in which this narrative is to be realised. 'The readerly is what we know how to read and thus has a certain transparency; the writerly is self-conscious and resistant to reading' (Culler 2002: 22). This was a distinction that Barthes applied between classic realism and modernist reflexive literature, but can be considered as a distinction between works that claim to depict things as they are, 'naturally', and those that point up or create their own narrative construction, such as hypertexts.[20] In screenwriting the conventional approach outlined by screenwriting manuals appears typically realist, in that it:

> ...pretends to be an innocent representation, a mimesis, a reality ... controlled by the principle of non-contradiction ... with a narrative structure which makes us read horizontally from start to finish, revealing a single unified meaning. It employs rhetorical devices which tie together the writer and reader in the production of meaning. (Olsen 1990: 184)

The goal of most screenwriting manuals is to advise on creating just such 'good' scripts, those which read easily, and which work as 'page-turners' in creating a surface 'unity' (Field 1994: 8-9). That this approach appears often to be taken as 'natural' is something that Barthes fought against, as 'it makes the reader an inert consumer of the author's production, [and] is always assigned an origin (an author, a character, a culture)...' (Olsen 1990: 184).

This could apply to a viewer as a consumer of a mainstream screenwork, but the professional reader is not an inert consumer; s/he is producing meaning from both the written text and other references, as Pasolini suggests the reader does at what he calls Stage B. The writerly text requires the reader to produce meaning from a 'galaxy of signifiers, not a structure of signifieds' (Barthes 1974: 5). This is a more 'difficult' process for the reader, one in which plurality is clearer.[21] The process is more writerly (Kohn 2000: 495 *passim*), even if the screenwork itself is (or is intended to be) readerly. For example, a writerly text

> ...is not a finished product ready for consumption. Such [writerly] texts invite the reader to 'join in', and offer us some kind of 'co-authorship'... Barthes writes 'the networks are many and interact, without any of them being able to surpass the rest ... it has no beginning, it is reversible, we gain access to it by several entrances, none of which can be authoritatively claimed to be the main one (*S/Z*: 5). (Olsen 1990: 185)

While many conventional screenplay texts clearly have beginnings, and follow a realist 'readerly' approach in their narrative, the process of development of that text is indeed reversible, and readers gain access to the text through whatever 'entrance' seems appropriate – as director, producer, actor and so on. It is as if development and production, as a writerly process, has been grafted on to a readerly (or proto-readerly) text. The writerly text is not representational – it is intended to show its plurality rather than be mimetic ('advance pointing to your mask ... this is all Barthes finally asks of any system, any work of art or literature') (Burke 1998: 52). However, the basic intention of the process of development – to produce a screenwork – appears conventionally to move a screen idea towards a screenwork that can be consumed and accessed easily. It is an industrial process of shaping a writerly text into a readerly one, towards a screenwork that presents in some way a (fairly) seamless view of a world, if not the real world. Elsaesser and Buckland's comparison (2002: 146–67) of the readerly film with the logic of the video-game concludes that 'the pre-determined structure of narratives excludes the possibility of interactivity – that is, that interactivity is incompatible with narrative structure. Narratives are inherently readerly – it is narrative that makes a text readerly' (2002: 167). This view therefore supports the notion that the interactive writerly process of development, the results of which are recorded in successive drafts of a screenplay, is necessarily directed towards the creation of the readerly.

Barthes' later ideas about pleasure (*plaisir*) and *jouissance* in the reading of the text – a development of his earlier distinctions of writerly and readerly (Culler 2002: 82) – and his concept of the influence of the body (replacing the mind), helps to understand how those involved in reading and judging the screen idea might react. *Plaisir* is a general pleasure of euphoria, fulfilment and comfort that accompanies the readerly text, 'one we know how to read' (Culler 2002: 83). It is the pleasure of the familiar, a variation of the known that confirms our beliefs and drives further down into our subconscious any awareness of how that text operates. *Plaisir* is what the viewer of mainstream cinema will generally feel.

Opposite this is *jouissance*, the pleasure that 'discomforts … unsettles the reader's historical, cultural, psychological assumptions, the consistency of his tastes, values, memories, brings to a crisis his relation with language' (Barthes 1975: 14). It is closer to what the reader of the writerly text feels, in having to work at the meaning. One might also propose that the professional screen-reader's stated search for 'originality' (Macdonald 2003: 32) is a search for *jouissance*. It is recognition of the 'edgy', the challenging of norms which nevertheless relate sufficiently to those norms to allow the reader to hang on to, or create new meaning. If *plaisir* comes from a direct or clear meaning, *jouissance* comes from a lack of clarity, from an estrangement or shock value; the 'corporeal "grain of the voice"' (Culler 2002: 79).

The professional screen-reader may take a position as a proxy for the later viewer, making arguments for the production green light on the basis that an audience can be reached, and on maximising that audience. Any such argument is based on beliefs about known behaviour, which will incline judgements towards the readerly. The suspicion is then that professional screen-readers, in a less adventurous market,[22] will tend towards the readerly when developing conventional screenworks and move away from the writerly, and *jouissance*. And if (as Sheila Johnston suggests, 1985) readerly and writerly are to be viewed as opposite extremes of a spectrum, it becomes problematic for a screen-reader to seek a screen idea that is both. It could explain why the complaint has been heard for almost the whole of cinematic history that there are no 'good' screenplays around.[23] Writers are also aware of this requirement, and if the end result of the industrial process is intended to be *plaisir* for the viewer, is it surprising that what screenwriters propose will tend towards the familiar, the seamless and the comfortable? An 'original voice' is different. The industry appears to seek what they regard as originality (Macdonald, 2003: 37), and one could argue that this is what provides *jouissance* for the reader. One might then also consider that the industrial process begins to shape and absorb it into that which produces *plaisir*. A screen idea which retains something of this originality while having been put through the process may well be regarded as critical success. This brings us to looking more closely at the process of shaping the screen idea, of development.

THE PROCESS OF DEVELOPMENT AND THE SCREEN IDEA

If the individual level of reading is not observable, the 'second level' of collective reading and rewriting practice is. Semi-structured interviews with professionals involved in the development process have suggested a belief in four common goals; realisability, an appropriate structure, a clear thesis and some aspect of originality (Macdonald 2004: 244). Their experiences and actions were in line with personal strategies 'guided by their interests linked to their position in the structure of the field' (Bourdieu 1996: 199), which invokes a shared belief in the nature of the field and a shared process of shaping the screen idea in relation to that belief. This would apply whether it was a mainstream development process or another, oppositional or alternative, one; although in the latter case practice might be different.

Unfortunately direct evidence of a particular development process is not available. It has however been staged as role-play for educational purposes; notably at the CILECT conference 'Triangle 2', held at Terni, Italy in 1998, which had as its purpose the demonstration, analysis and strengthening of the creative relationship between writer, director and producer, seen as key participants in any screenwork production (Ross 2001). Although the participants for each project comprise students and experienced professionals, and the tone is therefore instructional (in places at least), the transnational nature of the project groups and the serious intention to develop a professional proposal for each film provides an insight into the normative processes of screenplay development.[24]

The transcripts of two projects[25] were analysed for common signs of method and progression. The process within each firstly took the form of question and answer, of establishing understanding of the proposal and of the 'world' it presented. Secondly (and shortly after the start of the process), the questioning referred to dramatic conventions and genre, so clearly placing the proposal into a framework that was taken as a given. Knowledge of this framework was assumed or explained (but not questioned) during the session. The process here was one of probing and testing, similar to defending a thesis, which then opened out into a shared discussion involving raising problems and solutions to those problems. The assessment criteria became overt during the conversation; the internal structure and argument (story) were being tested for consistency and internal logic, as well as against other criteria (dramatic, logistic, aesthetic, genre, market, examples of successful films).

Discussion left the written text (shared before the session) behind, so that the only location for the screen idea was within the discussion, or (with subsequent sessions) in the initial introduction at the start of discussion. The general discourse was (in both cases) around the creation of a classic text, and on occasion it became clear what the professionals felt were the conventions, as professional screenwriter Neville Smith confirmed.

> In movies, why do heroes find love and why do they end up doing the job? It's always because they don't want to do it. Sometimes a man's gotta do what a man's gotta do! ... [in movies] people are made to do things because that's drama! (Smith in Ross 2001: 36)

All participants made suggestions, with the professionals affirming or rejecting. The process, described by a student as 'being forced to constantly talk about the ideas, having to explain precisely what had actually changed in the last 24 hours' (Ross 2001: 76), was one which encouraged verbal encapsulation (such as a high-concept description), and using other films as shorthand for ideas (such as 'going down the *Marnie* route'). The students' reaction to this process was initially shock at the 'violence' shown to their ideas (Ross 2001: 37), then appreciation (that they were being given suggestions) and wistfulness, when they realised that they were being led away from their original ideas – 'the most difficult thing to understand was when our tutors' tips were taking us further away from the idea we had of our own film' (Ross 2001: 37); 'this is not the film I wanted to make' (Ross 2001: 73). The process was one in which the screen idea was being shaped, altered and drawn towards what the professionals thought of as right, based on internalised experience and expressed as craft or lore.

Despite different roles, all participants contributed. The screen idea was 'rewritten', overtly and sometimes in the face of resistance from some, by the participants. Readers here were active participants, making meaning not just from a written text but from verbal discussion, sometimes in complex and even confusing ways as understanding and contribution oscillates between the participants. It is not possible to decide who was the 'author' of this screen idea, other than the collective character of the group and the norms and conventions that inform it. The underlying drive is towards making the shared idea 'readerly'; what was unacknowledged were the underlying criteria for this. The process, which appears to be writerly (in that it is essentially one in which writer and readers deconstruct and reconstruct the screen idea together), has a purpose that aims towards the readerly.

The conclusion from analysing this exercise is that in a conventional context the focus is the screen idea rather than on text on a page. Control and negotiation over that idea determines the screenwork. Andrei Tarkovsky, the director and co-writer of *Solyaris* (*Solaris*, 1972) and *Zerkalo* (*The Mirror*, 1974) and an avowed 'author' of his own films expressed the struggle behind 'highly commercialised productions'.

> The director's task is merely to co-ordinate the professional functions of the various members of the team. In a word it is terribly difficult to insist on an *author's* film, when all your efforts are concentrated on not letting the idea be 'spilt' until nothing is left of it as you contend with the normal working conditions of filmmaking. (Tarkovsky 1986: 126)

Tarkovsky's own working method as 'author' director also relied on the conceptualisation of a screen idea which was then developed with others, even while it was closely retained by Tarkovsky himself. In his description of the development of *The Mirror*, Tarkovsky talks of working in close collaboration 'with his literary colleagues' (1986: 127)[26] but of leaving a great deal to be finally thought out during shooting, as a deliberate point of principle (1986: 131). Earlier films were, he says, more clearly structured (ibid.), but on *The Mirror* there were no prescriptive plans for scenes or episodes as complete visual entities; 'what we worked on was a clear sense of atmosphere and empathy with the characters' (1986: 132). His focus was on the inner state, 'the distinctive inner tension of the scenes to be filmed, and the psychology of the characters' and not 'the precise mould in which it will be cast' (ibid.). This is clearly a personal working method, but one which had concluded that the screenplay was not a fixed, final or unambiguous document:

> This account of the making of *The Mirror* illustrates that for me scenario is a fragile, living, ever-changing structure, and that a film is only made at the moment when work on it is finally completed. The script is the base from which one starts to explore... (Tarkovsky 1986: 131)

Tarkovsky is essentially stating the same case as those working in the 'Triangle 2' script development exercise, though from a different perspective. Whatever the extent of collaboration, from a major commercial production with many screen-readers to a much tighter production centred around a single *auteur*, all those involved work on a concept of a screen idea informed by their own involvement in its development. For them the screenplay or other script is an *aide-memoire*. In his popular account of his own practice *Adventures in the Screen Trade*, Hollywood screenwriter William Goldman includes fascinating interviews with the other creatives on a film, about their personal working methods and their particular understanding of a script. Designer, cinematographer, editor, composer and director have views of the script based in most detail on their professional specialisation, but this common demarcation does not preclude their reading of the script as a general reader and contributor to general development. Editor Dede Allen said 'I think Morris, the father, came off as a much richer character in the story. In the screenplay, I had very little feeling for Morris emotionally. I miss a feeling of loss on Morris' part.' (Goldman 1996: 384). The cinematographer saw the film as 'simple Americana, structurally and visually' (381), and the designer felt the ending was slightly unresolved. Like 'Triangle 2' these interviews are artificial exercises, but they illuminate clearly the approach of non-writers who nevertheless felt they were contributing to the development of the whole screen idea. The collaborative nature of this process is neatly illustrated by Goldman in describing his own acceptance of it – 'if enough people tell you you're drunk, it's not inadvisable for a screenwriter to consider lying down' (Goldman 1996: 398).

ADVANCING FURTHER, POINTING TO THE MASK

My argument has been that in studying screenwriting and the screenplay in relation to the screenwork, the focus needs to be on the screen idea rather than the written text. The screenplay itself is clearly an important document which, during the 'blueprint' stage, represents key narrative elements which are to be realised. We can value the screenplay as a document which can be written skilfully in relation to conventions. It is a strong indicator of what those who develop it believe will make a 'good' film, so it also tells us something about their attitudes towards film itself. But in relation to the screenwork itself the danger in describing a screenplay as a 'blueprint' is that the analogy suggests both a detailed final plan, and an accurate representation of what it is to be. Difference from the screenplay is inevitable, even where the 'plan' is clearly followed. The inestimable Hollywood writer William Goldman refers erroneously to the famous crop-duster scene in *North by Northwest* (1959) as 'filmed exactly as [Ernest Lehman] wrote it' (2000:175 [his italics]). This is not true, even if the narrative structure is the same.

The screenplay form is more of a framework, perhaps even a pro-forma, and each version of a screenplay is a snapshot of a moment in the development of the screenwork. It's not even a complete picture; it's a clue as to how the production was going, and under current conventions it is clearer about dramatic structure and dialogue than it is about the visual look of the film. In practice, it is the screen idea itself which is the actual focus of attention despite the fact that it exists only virtually. The screenplay as *aide-memoire* is defined in relation to the wider field by the Screen Idea Work Group. This has implications for how the SIWG see their screen idea and how they develop it.

Wolfgang Iser's notions of 'picturing' a written text and of understanding anticipation retrospection and the 'gaps' in that text, suggest that they produce, in an ordinary reader, an imaginary that is personal and individual. It is clearly the same for the professional screen-reader, except that development of this imaginary is directed towards the concrete, and that the shape of this development is shared and negotiated with others in the development community that is the Screen Idea Work Group. The individual view of the screen idea is therefore also connected to what lies outside the written text. What becomes more important in conventional development is the influence of industrial and cultural norms and assumptions used within that process that might otherwise be hidden or remain unacknowledged. In this sense I disagree with Kohn's quoting of Deleuze and Guttari (1987) to claim that the screenplay (as literature) has 'nothing to do with ideology' (2000: 504), as it seems clear that development - of which the screenplay is a part – is designed to shape or confirm a screen idea in a particular relationship to the field. Therefore understanding the role of the screen-reader is helpful in understanding the process of screenplay development in several ways outlined by Barthes: in understanding the collaborative process that creates and shapes the screen idea; in locating the screen idea as a shared concept within that process (and regarding the screenplay as a partial record of that); in observing and considering the elements that make up that process of collaborative development; and in understanding that process as dynamic and complex during which meaning is explored, shared and created. Unlike the production and reading of a novel, the process of screenplay development is overt and thus observable.

For the non-professional and academic reader, reading a screenplay may occur often only after seeing the screenwork. The screen idea for this reader is then an amalgam of both the screenwork and a version of the screenplay text. To complicate things further, published versions of screenplays (Sternberg's 'reading material', 1997: 48–9) are often tidied up, obscuring some of their meaning, or shooting scripts are released (via the internet, for example) as being a close simulation of the extant screenwork, rather than the potentially more interesting writer's earlier drafts. In these cases, the reading exercise is clearly as an aid to interrogating that finished screenwork. This is different from the process of development, though it can illuminate it. On the other hand, the study of unproduced screenplays (or those of films we have not seen) starts the process for us of sharing in the development, if only virtually, in the development of a screen idea. We share in the visibility of the idea behind the film, at a point when it was not fully formed. A screenplay poses such questions as 'how would this look?' and we answer them in our imagination much as Iser outlines for the novel-reader. It is unsurprising that our reactions to and conclusions from the written text then concentrate on that text, as in 'have I understood this correctly?' or 'what does the presentation tell me about the idea here?'. It is right to read the written text carefully, but the danger is assuming that this is the complete *ur*-text for the screen idea. When we read any screenplay, we need to accept it as one expression of an ongoing discussion amongst collaborators, and one that in any case privileges some aspects more than others.

Barthes' distinction between 'readerly' and 'writerly' texts is helpful in understanding the conventional process of screenplay development as one in which writerly activity is conventionally directed towards the production of a readerly text. Barthes' later distinctions between *plaisir* and *jouissance* seem also to be helpful in considering the screen reader's search for 'originality', and in understanding the tension between the originality that professional readers commonly seek and the drive towards the familiar that is industrially desirable. Barthes' preference for the writerly, in opposition to the usual public's search for the easy, the readerly, is similar to the preference some of us have for that which makes us work at narrative more – say, for example, in the emerging 'genre' of world cinema. In producing writerly work, we are looking at challenging frameworks, in maintaining the openness of possibilities that we see in a script or which we discuss with others when making a film. In his preface to Barthes' *S/Z*, Richard Howard says (of literature) 'if we were to set out to write a readerly text, we should become no more than hacks in bad faith' (1974: ix), and what some of us find difficult in the classic realist screenwork (and in the screenwriting manuals that serve them) is the require-ment to conceal all, and pretend that this is the best, the only way to do it. The screenplay, however, reveals more and the process of script development is open, at least until it finishes with the completed screenwork.

The plurality of a screenplay text, situated as it is in the middle of an ongo-ing discussion about how it should be developed, is the exciting thing. Classic realist screenplays are designed to become more clothed in readerly comfort eventually, but for the moment they are naked, revealing more of the artifice and structure than the makers wish to see in the final screenwork. The pos-sibilities of the screen idea recorded in the script are (if not endless) open not closed, plural not fixed in the singular. Barthes prized the writerly literary text for making the reader a producer of that text rather than a consumer, thus gaining access to 'the magic of the signifier, to the pleasure of writing' and avoiding the poor freedom of only being able to choose between accepting or rejecting the text (1974: 4). In the process of developing the screen idea the screen-reader is also producer of that text, recognising the plurality inherent in the peculiar document that is the screenplay. The reader actively seeks to create both vision and meaning, to 'see' a film even as they turn the pages regularly in accordance with the conventional 'page-a-minute' convention of master-scene screenplay construction.

What of the screen idea represented in the screenwork itself? It is a suc-cession of concrete images, not word-pictures as in the script. Film images exist unambiguously in the finished work – they are *there*, on screen. If screen idea development by the practitioners is finished the viewer must still con-struct their screen idea, and what remains of the writerly process lies in the opportunity for the viewer to continue to work at the meaning, significance and narrative possibilities of what is on screen. The 'constituency of view-ers' as Bill Nichols has termed them in relation to documentary practice (1991: 24; 2001: 35) constructs a screen idea from what Nichols calls 'recipe knowledge', based on prior knowledge as well as what is demonstrably in the screenwork. At one end of the spectrum the readerly classic realist film usu-ally produced for the commercial markets directs the viewer and closes off possibilities; at the other the writerly film offers the viewer the opportunity to produce meaning(s). Many screenworks will have elements of both. Bergman and Tarkovsky and their collaborators were no strangers to the conventional professional industrial processes for example, but their work also shows an awareness of a screen idea behind the screenwork that allows the viewer a more open-ended involvement. We see the importance of knowing what processes are employed, the people involved in them (the Screen Idea Work Group) and their relationship(s) to the field, in congregating around a singular screen idea.

I have been arguing here that the study of screenwriting and screen-reading benefits from the concept of the screen idea because, instead of focusing on the screenplay as a proto-screenwork in a different form, it allows us to consider it as part of a more complex process. This way it accommodates both the centrality of the screenplay as a core document and its ephemerality as a way-station in the process of production. It is one way of countering an over-reliance on the written text, while not breaking faith with that text. It is a concept that can be understood in relation to narrative and cultural theories, and can be considered with others such as cognitive and framework theory (though I have not addressed this here). It links commercial and artistic practices and offers a way of understanding both. It suggests a way of discussing the potential screenwork creatively in relation to a particular industrial framework, while at the same time making the relationship with that framework clearer. And it allows us to take the study of what film-makers intend for the screenwork further, towards an understanding of what they thought was 'good' in relation to a particular time and culture. Importantly, finding the way into the screen idea behind a film opens up possibilities rather than closing them down. As screen-readers (and 'writers') we might then rely less on the documented 'blueprint' and more on an understanding of what lies behind it, of the potential of the screen idea thus described. This applies whether we make films or study them, or both.

These opinions raise, I hope, many more questions than answers...

BIBLIOGRAPHY

Barthes, R. (1974) *S/Z*. Oxford: Blackwell.

_____ (1977) *Image, Music, Text*. London: Fontana.

Blair, H. (2001) '"You're Only as Good as Your Last Job": the Labour Process and Labour Market in the British Film Industry', *Work, employment and society*, 15, 1, 149–69.

_____ (2003) 'Winning and losing in flexible labour markets: the formation and operation of networks of interdependence in the UK film industry', *Sociology*, 37, 4, 677–94.

Bourdieu, P. (1996) *The Rules of Art: Genesis and Structure of the Literary Field*. Cambridge: Polity Press.

Burke, S. (ed.) (1995) *Authorship: From Plato to Postmodern.* 2nd edn. Edinburgh: Edinburgh University Press.

_____ (1998) *The Death and Return of the Author.* 2nd edn. Edinburgh: Edinburgh University Press.

Cole, H. And J. Haag (1999) *Complete Guide to Standard Script Formats: Part 1, The Screenplay.* North Hollywood, CA: CMC Publishing.

Cook, P. (ed.) (1985) *The Cinema Book.* London: British Film Institute.

Corliss, R. (1975) *Talking Picture: Screenwriters of Hollywood.* Newton Abbot: David and Charles.

Culler, J. (2002) *Barthes: A Very Short Introduction.* Oxford: Oxford University Press.

Dancyger, K. And J. Rush (2002) *Alternative Scriptwriting: Successfully Breaking the Rules.* 3rd edn. Boston: Focal Press.

Elliott, W. J. (1915) 'The Picture Playwright'. *The Bioscope,* 16 September, p.1249.

Elsaesser, T. And W. Buckland (2002) *Studying Contemporary American Film: A Guide to Movie Analysis.* London: Arnold.

Field, S. (1994) *Screenplay: The Foundations of Screenwriting from Concept to Finished Script.* New York: Dell.

Frensham, R. (1996) *Teach Yourself Screenwriting.* London: Hodder Headline.

Friedmann, J. (2003) 'Form Over Content is Damaging the Film Industry'. *ScriptWriter,* 11, July, p.5.

Friedmann, J. (1995) *How to Make Money Scriptwriting.* London: Boxtree Press.

Goldman, W. (1996 [1983]) *Adventures in the Screen Trade: A Personal View of Hollywood and Screenwriting.* London: Abacus.

Gurney, K. (1923) 'A Hunting we will go', *Woolwich plays,* M49, 71938, British Library MS collection, London.

Hauge, M. (1992) *Writing Screenplays that Sell.* London: Elm Tree Books.

Herman, D., Jahn, M. & Ryan, M-L. (2005) *Routledge Encyclopaedia of Narrative Theory.* London: Routledge.

Howard, R. (1974) 'Preface', in R. Barthes, *S/Z.* Oxford: Blackwell, vii–x.

Iser, W. (1974) *The Implied Reader: Patterns of Communication in Prose Fiction from Bunyan to Beckett.* Baltimore: Johns Hopkins.

Johnston, S. (1985) 'Barthes', in P. Cook, *The Cinema Book.* London: British Film Institute, 238–41.

Kohn, N. (2000) 'The Screenplay as Postmodern Literary Exemplar: Authorial Distraction, Disappearance, Dissolution', *Qualitative Inquiry,* 6, 4, 489–510.

MacDonald, I. W. (2003) 'Finding the Needle: How Readers See Screen Ideas', *Journal of Media Practice,* 4, 1, 27–39.

_____ (2004) *The Presentation of The Screen Idea in Narrative Film-Making.* Leeds: Leeds Metropolitan University [unpublished PhD thesis].

McKee, R. (1999) *Story: Substance, Structure, Style and the Principles of Screenwriting.* London: Methuen.

Malkin, Y. (1986) 'The Screenplay as a New Literary Form, Its Affinity to the Theatre Play', *Les Cahiers du Scenario,* 1, Summer, 15.

Margrave, S. (1936) *Successful Film Writing.* London: Methuen.

Mehring, M. (1990) *The Screenplay: A Blend of Film Form and Content*. London: Focal Press.

Meister, J. C. (2005) 'Narrative Units', in D. Herman, M. Jahn and M-L. Ryan (eds) *Routledge Encyclopaedia of Narrative Theory*. London: Routledge, 382–4.

Nichols, B. (1991) *Representing Reality*. Bloomington: Indiana University Press.

_____ (2001) *Introduction to Documentary*. Bloomington: Indiana University Press.

Nunning, A. (2005) 'Implied Author', in D. Herman, M. Jahn and M-L. Ryan, *Routledge Encyclopaedia of Narrative Theory*. London: Routledge, 239–40.

Olsen, B. (1990) 'Roland Barthes: From Sign to Text', in C. Tilley (ed.) *Reading Material Culture*. Oxford: Basil Blackwell, 163–205.

Parker, P. (1998) *The Art and Science of Screenwriting*. Exeter: Intellect Books.

Pasolini, P. P. (1966) 'The Scenario as a Structure Designed to Become Another Structure', *Wide Angle*, 2, 1, 40–7.

Ross, D. (ed.) (2001) 'Triangle 2: Terni, Italy. October 1998: A Conference for Teachers and Students Demonstrating the Principles of Collaboration Between Writers, Directors and Producers in the Development of Feature Screenplays', Terni, Italy: CILECT/GEECT/Centro Multimediale di Terni/Provincia di Terni/MEDIA II.

Rossio, T. (1997) *Death to Readers. Screenwriting Column 05*. On-line. Available at: www.wordplayer.com (accessed 3 October 2001).

Rush, J. And C. Bauman (1997) 'Language as Narrative Voice: the Poetics of the Highly Inflected Screenplay', *Journal of Film and Video*, 49, 3, 28–37.

Russell, D. (2003) 'Narrative Structure: Can Media Studies Deliver?', *ScriptWriter*, 11, July, 36–40.

Schneider, R (2005) 'Reader-response theory' in D. Herman, M. Jahn and M-L. Ryan, *Routledge Encyclopaedia of Narrative Theory*. London: Routledge. 484–6.

Singleton, R. S. And J. A. Conrad (2000) *Film-makers Dictionary*. 2nd edn. Hollywood, CA: Lone Eagle.

Stannard, E. (1920) *Writing Screen Plays*. London: Standard Art Book Co.

Sternberg, C. (1997) *Writing for the Screen: The American Motion-Picture Screenplay as Text*. Tubingen: Stauffenberg.

Thompson, R. J. And G. Burns (eds) (1990) *Making Television: Authorship and the Production Process*. New York: Praeger.

Tilley, C. (ed.) (1990) *Reading Material Culture*. Oxford: Basil Blackwell.

Tobin, R. (2000) *How To Write High Structure, High Concept Movies*. Santa Monica, CA: Xlibris Corporation.

Vale, E. (1998) *Vale's Technique of Screen and Television Writing*. Oxford: Focal Press.

Van Nypelseer, J. (1989) 'Le Scénario, Littérature', *Les Cahiers du scénario*, 6–7, Summer, 49–72.

Viswanathan, J. (1986) 'Lectures de scénarios', *Les Cahiers du scénario*, 1, Summer, 7.

Winston, D. G. (1973) *The Screenplay as Literature*. Rutherford, NJ: Fairleigh Dickinson University Press.

FILMOGRAPHY

Magnolia (1999) Directed by Paul Thomas Anderson [DVD]. Amazon: New Line Home Video.

Marnie (1964) Directed by Alfred Hitchcock [DVD]. Amazon: Universal Studios Home Entertainment.

Memento (2000) Directed by Christopher Nolan [DVD]. Amazon: Columbia Tri-Star.

The Mirror (1975) Directed by Andrei Tarkovsky [DVD]. Amazon: Kino Video.

North by Northwest (1959) (1975) Directed by Alfred Hitchcock [DVD]. Amazon: Warner Brothers.

Pulp Fiction (1994) Directed by Quentin Tarantino [DVD]. Amazon: Miramax.

Solaris (1972) Directed by Andrei Tarkovsky [DVD]. Amazon: Home Vision.

GLOSSARY OF TERMS

Blueprint:
: Sternberg divides reading a screenplay into three types: property, blueprint and reading material. These correspond to the commissioning stage, the production stage and the text as seen by a critical readership, for example when published (1997: 48–59).

Continuity:
: See shooting script

Coverage:
: 'A synopsis of the screenplay, and an analysis of the recommended course of action' (Rossio 1997: 1) produced by a professional script reader. The analysis may be detailed but rarely extends past two pages.

Cutting continuity:
: Shooting script used in editing.

Property:
: See Blueprint

Scenario:
: 'An old term for screenplay; most commonly used today to refer to plot or storyline' (Singleton & Conrad 2000). Quotes used here from Pasolini and Tarkovsky both refer to scenario, meaning screenplay.

Screen Idea:
: The 'screen idea' is a term that Philip Parker has used to describe the start of a screenplay's development (Parker 1998: 57). See also Lucy Scher (2003) on shaping ideas and a story for the screen in 'Finding the Story in Your Idea', *ScriptWriter*, 13, November, 6–10. The term is used here to refer to the core idea of anything intended to become a screenwork, that is 'any notion of a potential screenwork held by one or more people, whether or not it is possible to describe it on paper or by other means'.

Screenplay:
: Usually a term for a film script, often the writer's draft, in Master Scene format. In this essay I mean any draft in any script form, except a published version.

Screenwork:
: The completed film, TV drama, and so forth. A term from Parker 1998: 10.

Script:
: Used here generically to mean any written outline for a screenwork.

Shooting script:	An often very detailed script, possibly as a shot-list rather than in Master Scene format (for example, *Alien III* (1992)) and perhaps with additional notes and drawings in MS.
Synopsis:	In this chapter I use the term 'synopsis' to mean anything written in the present tense of a line or two to a full treatment.
Treatment:	A prose synoptic outline of the narrative, usually in the present tense, and probably from 10 to 30 pages long (Friedmann 1995: 45–6; Parker 1998: 45–7; Frensham 1996: 176–8; McKee 1999: 414–16). This is variously termed a 'treatment', a 'synopsis' (if extracted from a novel), an 'outline', a 'story outline' or 'storyline'. Terms are used inconsistently or vaguely; for example, Parker (1998: 42), Tobin (2000: 66) and Hauge (1991: 246) suggest shorter treatments are sometimes called outlines, Rossio (1998: 5) suggests outlines are longer than treatments, while Field (1994: 166) suggests 'outline' is a term used especially in US television, and may be from 28–60 pages in length. McKee (1999: 415) and Parker (1998: 42–3) refer to inconsistent use. The term 'treatment' is also used to mean a collection of several documents. There appears to be consensus over style and purpose generally, in several components of the basic treatment: it is written in prose, in the present tense, has minimal dialogue (using quotation marks), covers all the points of the story as it will appear on screen, and is intended to elicit emotion or enthusiasm in the reader. It may be analogous to the verbal 'pitch', and its length is designed to provide a quick but substantial introduction to the proposed screenwork. It will include all major scenes and is intended to show dramatic structure as well as story.
Ur-text:	The essential, core text; the one with the original and supposedly fixed meaning.

NOTES

1   This does not mean formulaic writing. As Claudia Sternberg notes, 'formulaic writing is not prompted by the nature of the screenplay, but by fixed expectations of the US mainstream cinema that are determined by economic and cultural conventions and norms' (1997: 59). Some manuals make a point of discussing how rules may be broken, such as Dancyger and Rush (2002).

2   For example, 'Now, don't *you* indicate the musical selection you'd prefer. In fact, don't refer to music at all. That's someone else's job' (Trottier 1998: 119). See also Cole & Haag 1999, Sternberg 1997, among others.

3   See Sternberg 1997: 50–2.

4   During the production process the screen idea will change but there will be a limit, a point where someone (perhaps the writer) may identify (a) change(s) that signifies the limit of that screen idea and the start of a new one. What that limit is may

not be important, only that the change is regarded as profound enough to refer to it as a new 'screen idea'. In narrative theory the difference between what have been described as essential units or nuclei (Barthes) or kernels (Chatman), and non-essential units or satellites may be useful here. See Meister in Herman *et al.* (2005: 383).

5 The six versions are: writer's draft (screenplay), approved screenplay/rehearsal script, shooting script/continuity, cutting continuity, release script/transmission script/legal version, and published version, where this occurs.

6 This is most clearly seen when people vary in their understanding of the goals. For example, at the 'Triangle 2' conference on the creative relationship between writer, director and producer, it was noted that US professionals showed greater concern for the role of the audience in relation to the impact of the narrative than did European professionals (Ross 2001: 5). They were also quicker in their responses to development problems, suggesting a clearer idea of a basic general film narrative framework in the US context (Ross 2001: 76–7).

7 'A magmatic grammar, by definition, is characterised by chapters and paragraphs absent from the grammars of written-spoken language' (Pasolini 1977: 44).

8 This, says Pasolini, contradicts the affirmation of Levi-Strauss, which is that 'One cannot define rigorously together and contemporarily Stage A and Stage B…and empirically relive the passage of one to another' (Pasolini 1977: 47). The structure of the scenario consists 'precisely of that, in this "passage of the literary stage to the cinematographic stage"' (Pasolini 1977: 47).

9 Paper presented to the Colloque Belge de l'Association Internationale de Littérature Comparée (AILC), University of Liege, 1989.

10 The 'implied author' refers to Wayne Booth's notion of an author's 'second self', who 'embodies the text's core of norms and choices' (Nunning in Herman *et al.* 2005: 239). In the context of a particular screenplay, the screenwriter is effectively a proto-director, or someone who wishes to suggest how it might be directed, and who presents it accordingly. Therefore in that text the writer presents him or herself as a voice taking a particular stance. However, as in literary theory, the usefulness of the idea of an Implied Author is debatable. See Sternberg 1997: 230–2.

11 'Possibilities in the staging of the material are offered through the selection of images or the leaving of open spaces and through information about genre, music, length of scenes or the time structure. Dialogue and scene text, in which film technique and narrative are combined, demand a certain degree of cinematic-technical imagination from their readers…' (Sternberg 1997: 231).

12 Fifty per cent of screenplay readers have had over 10 years experience in reading scripts (Macdonald 2003: 31).

13 Iser quotes Roman Ingarden's terms of concretisation or realisation to differentiate what the reader imagines from the text itself (Iser 1974: 274). Here I refer to the 'visually concrete' or realisation of the narrative as a screenwork, an actual object.

14 Imagination is needed to make sense of the image, rather than to see it, conjure it up. This is where anticipation or retrospection come in, such as anticipating the storyline, character action, style and tone as it unfolds and so forth. Gaps in the

narrative require imagination, speculating on answers to unresolved questions, for example. When the film is ended, imagination is required to consider what might have been, which of course informs our view of the value of the work.

15 Sternberg refers to 'reading or closet screenplays' as those which may or may not have been written for production, but which finally have no relation to an actual screenwork. See Sternberg (1997: 2).

16 Burke (1998:211) notes that this essay was first written in 1967 for an American magazine *Aspen* Nos. 5 and 6, and then republished in 1968 as 'Le mort d'auteur' (a title which in French echoes more clearly, and wittily, that of the legendary tale 'Mort d'Arthur') in *Manteia V.* The version quoted here is reprinted in Burke (1995).

17 In 'The Death of the Author' (Burke 1995: 127).

18 Of course, a completed film may actually change (through deterioration of film stock or videotape for example) and it may take different forms (such as 35mm or DVD) that could affect meaning.

19 Even where the work is genuinely collaborative, roles and responsibilities are qualified in practice. Producer Mark Shivas says that a film 'starts off as the producer's film ...[when s/he] has to have a certain amount of arrogance...(Ross 1997:36). Then it becomes the director's film, when the producer 'needs to have a certain amount of humility' (Ross 1997: 37), and 'if the director is able to take everyone else along with him or her, then it will be everybody's film' (Ross 1997: 35).

20 George Landow's work on hypertext, *Hypertext 2.0* (1997) is referred to by Elsaesser and Buckland (2002); Landow is described as the first person who realised that Barthes' work in *S/Z* could be applied to hypertexts: '...Barthes describes an ideal textuality that precisely matches ...hypertext – text composed of blocks of words (or images) linked electronically by multiple paths, chains or trails in an open-ended perpetually unfinished textuality described by the terms *link, node, network, web* and *path*' (Landow 1997: 3 in Elsaesser 2002: 161–62).

21 The difficulty for the reader is not necessarily a guide to 'writerliness', as some screenplays could demonstrate an unfamiliar structure based nevertheless on a complication of classic realism (for example *Pulp Fiction* (1994), *Magnolia* (1999), or *Memento* (2000)). However, we are not concerned here with the final screenwork, but with the screenplay – whether the screenwork constitutes a 'readerly' or a 'writerly' text, does the same apply to the screenplay?

22 Derek Paget quotes Bourdieu as describing the audience for a cultural product as being conservative, and refers to TV executives as being similarly conservative (1998: 126–7).

23 In his 1915 article *The Picture Playwright* William J. Elliott complained about a vast number of 'incompetent amateurs' spoiling the market for the professional, with 'crude, unworkable, inartistic and utterly impossible caricatures of scenarios' (1915: 1249). This was a rallying call for technical competence and standardisation, but close attention to such norms came under fire later; J. J. Murphy quotes a 1959 article by Jonas Mekas complaining that scriptwriters perpetuate standard film constructions and follow closely textbooks of 'good' screenwriting (Murphy

2007: 1). A more recent example is Julian Friedmann in *ScriptWriter*, 11/07/2003: 5.

24 Each project involved a student producer, director and writer, talking with their 'tutors', a professional producer, director and writer. The imbalance in status between tutor and student was noticeable but not always so, and the workshops were intended to 'concentrate on the script/narrative development process' (Ross 2001: 7), as 'an opportunity to study the methodology of top [tutors/professionals] working in the field of story and script development' (Ross 2001: 5).

25 The Italian project and the British project (Ross 2001: 17–50, 51–78 respectively).

26 *Solaris* was written with Friedrich Gorenstein from a novel by Stanislav Lem, and *The Mirror* was written with Aleksandr Misharin.

CHAPTER 8
THE THEORY-PRACTICE INTERFACE IN FILM EDUCATION: OBSERVATIONAL DOCUMENTARY IN INDIA

Aparna Sharma

In recent years the political modernism that emerged following the events of May 1968 has come under review within the academies of Europe and North America. The critical revisitation of political modernist thought and practice has raised reflection upon the theory-practice frameworks and approaches for developing critical and politically interventionist *praxis*. The political modernist discourse in film was not unified or monolithic; its intellectual trajectory spanned Marxism and psychoanalysis, bound with a common concern – the relation of film to ideology (Rodowick 1994: ix). The principle criticism of political modernism has been its simplification of the theory-practice interface in terms of the idealised and simplistic binarisms pertaining to code/ deconstruction, transparency/reflexivity, and illusionism or idealism/materialism. According to D. N. Rodowick the dualisms of political modernism were portrayed as a 'dialectic' that 'obscured the importance of theory in the study and critique of ideology by excluding all but formal relations.' (1994: xvi). Paul Willemen adds to this by pointing out that the counter-cinema theorists such as Peter Wollen and Claire Johnston had never posited that:

> the strategies and characteristics of counter-cinema should be canonised and frozen into a prescriptive aesthetics. They pointed to the importance of cinematic strategies designed to explore what dominant regimes of

signification were unable to deal with. Theirs was a politics of deconstruction, not an aesthetics of deconstruction. (Pines & Willemen 1994: 07)

Noel Burch, a key figure in the political modernist discourse, has himself
attended the problematics of political modernism and its aesthetic strategies
arguing that in the contemporary late-capitalist and post-modernist context,
a confusion has been rendered between market, culture and political struggle.
Strategies deployed in developing a theoretically informed interventionist
praxis in the 1970s have been abstracted from their ideological discourse and
usurped by mass media. He succinctly summarises his concern thus:

> ... particularly because of the way America is, always has been, having no
> tradition of struggle really, at least one which has completely been per-
> verted for so long, that it has become fundamentally confused with indeed
> this objective illusion of capitalism and capitalist societies toward basi-
> cally everything becoming market and the culture itself simply becoming a
> market value. The confusion is such that it is almost impossible to extricate
> the one from the other and this is what has broken down I think any kind
> of serious cultural or political resistance... (Myer 2004: 73)

In the critical revisitation of the political modernist discourse, which was
articulated equally through film scholarship as through cinema practices ranging from the literary to the painterly avant-garde, one shortcoming that has
surfaced is the cultural opacity of film theory and the avant-garde generally.
This sentiment is most clearly articulated by Robert Stam who states that the
discipline of film has for long; 'sustained a remarkable silence on the subject'
of race and ethnicity' (2002: 663). While scholarly interests in issues of cultural
difference have increased in recent years particularly with the ascendance of
fields such as cultural studies and postcolonialism, Stam problematises the
common modality of text analysis focussing on racial and ethnic stereotyp-
ing, particularly within mainstream cinema, such as Hollywood. According
to Stam the stereotype approach necessarily formulates into pre-occupation
with positive and negative images leading to a kind of 'essentialism' and 'ahis-
toricism', '... as less subtle critics reduce a complex variety of portrayals to a
limited set of reified formulae' (2002: 663).

Filmmaking practices from the 'third world' such as South American guer-
rilla and social cause-espousing documentaries from South and South-east
Asia are constantly gaining exposure and interest in the Western academies
and festival circuits. They offer to the Western academic and viewer the possibility of an interventionist praxis standing in for political struggle. While the

ascendance of interest in third and subaltern cinemas, practices and issues of representing ethnic and cultural difference, alongside a closer meditation on post-colonial frameworks and discourses widen the scope of film scholarship and confront the universalism underpinning modernism generally; the sorts of cultural and ethnic issues as well as the strategies for attending those that have developed thus far are fraught with certain risks. Third-world Marxist scholars have consistently alerted that there is a 'certain urgency in the task of the third world inside the first', but they emphasise that it is imperative a third worldist mentality does not get perpetuated by this process (Kapur 2000: 281). Art historian Geeta Kapur asserts that the representations of radical issues in the third world should not inadvertently get overdetermined by the first world (2000: 281). Further, any gesture towards cultural, ethnic or racial subjects in Euro-American liberal contexts need to be disentangled from the wider public discourses of cultural diversity that overlook cultural specificity and social historicity in their celebratorily inclusive modes. Lastly, and most importantly in the study of cinemas outside Europe and North America it is pertinent to work with theoretical criteria with extreme caution so that concepts developed in one cultural context do not get summarily deployed in reading texts from distinct cultural contexts. This does not mean that theories and discussions developed in Euro-American academies cannot be applied in studying third and subaltern cinemas. What is necessitated is the careful application of different theoretical criteria with an understanding of their limits and strengths while in application in differing contexts.

In this chapter, I aim to examine the documentary oeuvres of two prominent filmmakers working in the Indian subcontinent to unpack the theory–practice interface in their works in order to highlight how cultural specificity and socio-historical disparities impact the interrogations and strategies practitioners develop. Avant-garde artist Kumar Shahani and acclaimed ethnographic filmmaker David MacDougall, through a complex oeuvre bring forth for us the possibility of a phenomenological engagement in documentary that serves in contextualising and problematising post-coloniality generally and its impacts on the body specifically. The documentaries of Shahani and MacDougall present us with a complex matrix of considerations and practices that facilitate working through the issues and concerns pertaining to a radical and interventionist practice that have arisen in light of the critique of political modernism.

The key question pertaining to the theory–practice interface in film education spans issues of how students critically engage with their creative impulses, the histories and philosophies linked to the media they work with and the wider exhibition and distribution networks they explore and within which they situate their practice. These are not merely pragmatic or practical concerns. In inhabiting these questions, it is aimed a student, prospective film practitioner, can critique and contextualise his/her work as an intervention in thought. Shahani and MacDougall work within very distinct disciplines — the former a radical and independent avant-garde filmmaker from the subcontinent who has questioned the terms of reference for an interventionist practice both within and outside the Indian subcontinent developing practice that boldly inaugurates the interface of Indian classical, folk and philosophical traditions with documentary. MacDougall is an ethnographic filmmaker whose films in India make for students and aspiring documentarists a rich resource of deeply thought discursive and aesthetic modalities pertaining to observational cinema. The discussion in this chapter is divided into three sections. In the first, I contextualise Shahani's documentaries surrounding Indian arts and cultural practices, to explicate how his films first formulate as a radical critique of mainstream Indian nationalist ideology, and second, how his aesthetics, particularly the use of the long-shot extend conventional film theory discussions. In the second section, I examine MacDougall's school films in India to exposit how they attend the shaping of the body in a postcolonial context. Alongside this critical perspective, I share MacDougall's development of a phenomenologically-informed haptic visual regime that links with early cinema modes of representation to argue how his documentaries stress viewership into perceptually complex realms. The conclusion to this chapter summarises how the specific strategies of both filmmakers emphasise the formulating discourse between filmmaker and subjects and how that is articulated subjectively and expressively into a historically critical and aesthetically complex formulation that presents to the student of film the convergence of socio-cultural and historical imperatives on the body – of both subject and filmmaker, thus lending sociality and historicity to issues and techniques such as self-reflexivity in practice. This is a necessary move for student-practitioners so that the techniques they work with get contextualised socio-historically rather than deployed as essentially laden with specific meanings only, extracted and abstracted from their historical contexts.

CLAIMING CLASSICISM

Within the context of the Indian subcontinent, documentary film tends, in a summarily reductionist gesture, to often get posited as antithetical to the mainstream fiction film emerging from industries such as from Mumbai or Chennai. As against Bollywood, which is perceived as selling dreams, fantasies and escapist entertainment, documentaries are considered as more serious and 'real'. While not totally invalid in the stated context, the terms of reference for such a polarisation have stressed documentary practice into a largely social-realist modality, identified with a largely mass-communication determined informational and educational function. This perception of documentary reflects an understanding of moving image technologies as a media for recording 'reality', in a sense that lacks the deliberation upon the scope and efficacy of the cinematographic apparatus that has occupied film theory since its inception. The sole identification of documentary's claim with a will to preservation has overdetermined image and sound as largely evidential and socially functional components. This reduction of the scope of documentary to issues of social cause and argumentation based on the equation of film components with truth and veracity has had its critics and has festered a generation of practitioners seeking more innovative and creative approaches to practice.

After India's independence in 1947, the Films Division – a public agency geared towards promoting documentary film production – was set up in 1948. In its first two decades the Films Division extensively supported documentary projects. Implicated closely in the euphoria and celebratory discourses surrounding a newly formed 'nation' documentary practice got linked to goals of information, education and propaganda. Though the division supported masters such as Satyajit Ray and Sukhdev, within successive years a scourge of bureaucracy overruled it and documentary film form got institutionalised. Experimentation and innovation at the level of form were undermined as documentary got increasingly burdened with social realist investments of a peculiarly reductive, functionalist modality bearing closest proximity to television and broadcast documentary films that are made under particular time and budgetary constraints that affect both content and form. Critic Amrit Gangar vociferously and succinctly summarises the impact of the Film's Division on documentary filmmaking in India thus:

> The Films Division's virtual stranglehold has another fall-out besides a definite "distaste" for documentaries that it has been able to create among the minds of people. The more serious fall-out is that the FD has also eventually muffed up the voice of documentary – the voice largely in the sense of stylistic expression, its various possibilities and alternatives. This government outfit makes its films largely by risking aesthetic issues, notwithstanding the fact that it has on its shelf some "award-winning" or really significant films by filmmakers such as Sukhdev, Satyajit Ray and Mani Kaul... (Chanana 1987: 36)

The institutionalised practices of the division came under criticism from film-makers for jeopardising the scope for an ideologically critical and formally experimental documentary practice. This critique was the foundation for independent documentary filmmaking in India and fashioned the discourse underpinning it. The independents developed a critical posture against the hierarchical and hegemonic, institutionalised discourses of the nation. This led to documentaries determined by the investigative and interpretive modalities – documentaries assuming an activist posture for espousing socio-cultural causes alongside historical issues. While such an activist agenda deservingly bears a function within the wider rubric of a democratic and developing society, in terms of filmmaking it tends to overplay content in documentary with an un-reflexive and under-theorised posture towards the implication of film form in practice.

A minority of avant-garde documentary work, steadily getting obscured from the pages of film history in the subcontinent, has however resisted the definition of documentary as content-oriented and a solely activist practice. This small body of practice shares with wider independent documentarists the critical stance against the nation and the institutionalised discourses and practices of documentary filmmaking as perpetuated by public agencies such as the Films Division. Kumar Shahani's cinema including fiction and documentary is grounded in a critique of the nation in terms of the reductionist, affirmative and institutionalised worldview mobilised in the nation-building process. However his critique is enmeshed within a wider project of innovation with film form and experimentation with alternatives of narrative derived from the epic and folk forms from the subcontinent. Kumar Shahani's cinema is characterised by a particular posture in which film form is crucially implicated in the critique of the nationalist discourse, i.e. for Kumar it is not enough to articulate a critical posture explicitly through film content as with the mass communication informed pervasive modes of independent documentary filmmaking in the subcontinent. He, like his esteemed teacher, Ritwik Ghatak, and other master predecessors including Satyajit Ray, has pursued the interrogation of documentary's claims of objectivity, truth and ventriloquist activism through a reflexive and aesthetically variegated register of techniques. Shahani's documentaries make for a body of work that challenges the dominant documentary discourses in the Indian subcontinent and cut into some critical theoretical debate and discourse internationally.

Shahani trained under Ritwik Ghatak at the Film and Television Institute of India, Pune. Ghatak was a contemporary of Satyajit Ray and the two film-makers emulate pronouncedly disparate ideological postures. Both Ray and Ghatak were deeply influenced by the discourse of the modern Indian poet, litterateur, artist and thinker, nobel laureate, Rabindranath Tagore. Central to the Tagorean discourse is the denunciation of the nation as a 'rapacious and illegitimate category' (Nandy 1994: 2). The cinema of Ray and Ghatak emulates a critical posture against the nation through very distinct visual discourses and strategies. Ray derived hugely from neo-realism and formulated it, given his liberal and upwardly mobile background, into an 'orientalist naturalism' through which he mapped the aching transition of a society from rural feudalism towards progressivist modernity. This is best exemplified through the internationally acclaimed *Apu trilogy* (1955–60). Ray's nostalgic take for the rural past being lost at the altar of modernity was the mode and extent of his critique of the post-independence nationalist discourse emphasising modernity in affirmative terms (Kapur 2000: 201–32). Ghatak, on the other hand, was hugely influenced by Sergei Eisenstein. He used Eisenstein's montage principles to critique Bengali Hindu conservatism, particularly its take on gender. This critical posture is rooted in Ghatak's sense of exile having migrated from East Pakistan during the birth of the independent Indian and Pakistani nations. The exilic discourse led to psychologically expressive cinematography and use of critical montage juxtaposition to disassemble the category of Indian traditions being mobilised in a nascent nationalist rhetorical jargon and imagination (Dunne & Quigley 2004).

Shahani derives from Ghatak but extends his approach towards the cultural and aesthetic traditions of India. His approach is more experimental and innovative towards film form. He attempts to claim Indian aesthetic and philosophical discourses but in a historicised and contextualised gesture far distinct from the celebratory, affirmative and reductive assertions of India's past in the wider, more institutionalised and rhetorical discourses of nationhood. In this way Kumar's cinema formulates as a truly independent practice – one that is not determined by, or solely in opposition to the hegemonic national-statist institutions and apparatuses. His cinema is at once critical and poetic – constantly exploring, configuring and reinventing its own terms of construction and aesthetics. His approach is holistic with film form and content being tightly intermeshed.

Shahani's documentaries on the arts in India focus on the idioms of dance and music – both classical and folk. *Bhavantarana* (1991) is a grand documentary of epic scale, an hour-long rendition spanning the life and work of the Odissi dance maestro Guru Kelucharan Mohapatra. Besides *Bhavantarana*, which is internationally acclaimed as one of his finest efforts, *Birah Bharyo Ghar Aangan Kone* (*The Bamboo Flute*, 2000) and *As the Crow Flies* (2004), are other documentaries surrounding the arts in India. The former is a documentary rendition of the flute using as its impulse the Indian spiritual and philosophical discourses surrounding the instrument wherein it is metaphorically equated with all organic life. The latter is an evocation of the painter Akbar P. Adamsee's work.

Bhavantarana is structured around the thinly linked interplay of dance sequences and dramatic reconstructions of key instances from Guru Kelucharan's life. The dance sequences include solo performances by Guru Kelucharan and his dance classes where we see him training dancers. Kumar's selection of Odissi, as indeed the Indian arts generally as the subjects for his documentaries constitutes as a radical political gesture. As indicated above, in its early decades the Films Division had emphasised informational, educational and propaganda films emphasising the cultural heritage of India.

Kumar Shahani's *Bhavantarana* (1991)

A series of travelogues, mapping geographical landscape, aesthetic and cultural practices had been developed to mobilise, among audiences across India, a sense of coherent and cohesive history and unity. Under the aegis of the Films Division such representations had tended to be quite celebratory underpinned by a near rhetoric emphasising the diversity in Indian society as the foundational ethos of a new nation. As filmmakers became critical of the Films Division's propagandist posture, and alert to its usage in masking the nation's normative discourses grounded in the mechanisms of displaying, patronising and excluding ethnic and cultural minorities it became, and continues to be quite problematic for independent filmmakers to engage with any aspect pertaining to India's cultural heritage – the risk always being the appropriation of such representation into a mainstream discourse celebrating nationhood. For many filmmakers this has meant completely deserting India's arts, aesthetic practices and cultural heritage discourses, thus further grounding the understanding of documentary in socially functionalist terms. In this light Kumar's documentaries assume significance for their boldness in claiming and bringing into the cinema India's aesthetic, philosophical and cultural discourses without slipping into ahistoricised or reductive essentialism.

Kumar's documentaries are acclaimed for their elegant choreography of performers and the camera. *Bhavantarana* is structured around two parallel narratives. At an immediate level the narrative pertains to the life of Guru Kelucharan, suggested through minimal dramatisations of key instances from his life such as his decision to pursue Odissi, marriage and dance training. These sequences are interlaced with sequential renditions of the master's body as dancer/ performer. These sequences of dance catapult the film away from a chronological documentation of Guru Kelucharan's life towards an experiential realm. In documentary terms, these sequences formulate as an observation of the dancer's body in performance. This is historically extremely valuable as a visual record and archive of the master's works, given that India's defence budget and aggressive economic growth rates leave little by way of any funding for the arts or cultural heritage preservation and dialogue. In the dance sequences Guru Kelucharan performs a spread of mythical and epic episodes from India's ancient classics. Besides the intricacy and finesse of his expression, one cannot but marvel at the refined and highly perceptive performance that reveals his depth command over the dance. In the highly evolved idiom of Indian classical forms, Kelucharan's performance reflects a unique mix of individual expression melded with a tightly structured dance tradition.

Kelucharan was in his late seventies when *Bhavantarana* was developed. Shahani had researched the project for nearly a decade. The dance sequences in the film bring to life the splendour and grandeur of Kelucharan's body in performance. In ethnographic terms, the camera serves as an observer-participant – a position that favours observation over participation in the processes being documented. This results in a very specific and contained cinematographic design. The camera maintains enough distance from the performer through which his body is largely seen in full, without being fragmented or objectified. Shahani uses long shots that fully accommodate the dancer's body and more importantly, situate it in context, i.e. the natural landscape in which the Odissi dance form is rooted and from which it derives its vocabulary. *Bhavantarana* is shot in the exteriors of rural Orissa, amidst either a thick, lush green backdrop or on the sea-coast. These images are reminiscent of the opening shot from Maya Deren's *Choreography for the Camera* (1945) wherein the dancers' bodies are seen in an exterior location, amidst thick foliage. A fine usage of depth-of-field links the performer and landscape and through this the cinematographic apparatus emulates the ecological worldview informing the dance. In the classical forms, the performer and performance are considered as co-extensive of temporal and spatial coordinates. This understanding is at the heart of the principle of embodiment in performance and derives from the aesthetic discourses of Indian art that bear an ecological approach i.e. art is the instance whereby the artist, the object of perception and the perceiver meld and share in unity.

Landscape is thus not merely a location backdrop in the classical practices, instead artistic expression is tightly linked to and derives from it. The long shot melds the dancer's body with the backdrop and this specificity in terms of site, here involving a regional definition pertaining to India's eastern coast, bears ethnographic relevance in terms of contextualising the dancer as embedded in a culturally inscribed landscape. This coupled with the short dramatisations of Guru Kelucharan's life through which we gather a sense of the meagre resources at his disposal to pursue dance historicise his practice and body as a socialised composite in a post-national context. These devices are crucial as they resist appropriation of the dancer's body within a wider nationalist or propagandist representation that tends to valorise the dancer's body by abstracting it from space thus propelling an ahistorical and essentialist projection. A liberal democratic sentiment in the Indian context is marked by a celebratorily inclusive gesture whereby disparate cultural traditions and practices are all posited as mingling as in a mixed salad. The regional, aesthetic and historical disparities, and also the contemporary conditions surrounding the various arts of India are evaded, and this ossifies these practices, foreclosing the possibility to understand and interrogate them as living traditions. By consistently bringing in the contemporary context in which Guru Kelucharan performed and taught Odissi dance, Shahani provides us with a historicised and ethnographically precise understanding of the dancer's body and this prevents *Bhavantarana* from slipping into what at first might seem like a purely exoticist representation given the film's occupation with a visually clearly oriental subject.

While we see Kelucharan performing through long shots, through single-point, diagonal lighting we experience a sense of nearness with his body whereby the most minute and intricate gestures and movements: facial, hands, feet and even those of the muscles are clearly registered. Camera movement in these sequences is measured and sustained — becoming a kind of responsive choreography. The camera is never hand-held and that complements the flow of fully embodied, conscious and sustained movements performed by Guru Kelucharan in dance. While the camera observes the dancer's body and the will to preservation cannot be separated from the film, the film text extends beyond that imperative to create a newness in which the dance experience is altered through the input of camerawork and editing.

Douglas Rosenberg, founder of the Dziga Vertov Performance Group in the USA in 1991, asserts that: 'There are numerous approaches to the practice of creating dance for the camera', however there are similarities in that all approaches 'place the choreography within the frame of the camera and offer the makers the opportunity to deconstruct the dance and to alter its form and linearity in post-production' (2000: 04). Close examination of *Bhavantarana's* structuring principle reveals a constant use of stark juxtapositions of block frames with continuous action. Sharply juxtaposed locations lead to visual variations in the middle of intense performance sequences. The juxtapositions of landscape have a more stark effect on viewer perception given that the dancer's movements in the foreground maintain a narrative continuity. This is again reminiscent of Deren's *Choreography for the Camera*, where a dancer begins a movement in one shot with a clearly defined background (filmed at a specific camera magnification) and the movement is completed in another shot with a starkly varying background and magnification. Through this continuity of action but juxtaposition in location, the dance performance deconstructs the organisational principles of the dance. This does not destabilise the organic unity of the dance form however the camera's intervention including editing does alter the perceptual experience of the dance. This is a very crucial move as the camera's subtle restructuring of the dance makes the documentary exceed the functions of record and preservation, and in the national context, this interplay with form becomes a critical gesture. An organic dynamic emerges between the dancer and the filmmaker. This stresses the film beyond 're-presentation' of dance, towards a new creative unity embedded in the eliciting discourse between filmmaker and dancer actualised through form. In ethnographic terms this is a modernist take at cultural documentation grounded in poly-vocality if we include voice in the structuring principles of the film text.

With respect to the discussion surrounding the theory–practice nexus in film education, Shahani's corpus – including films such as *Bhavantarana* – presents us with a few interventions that enable in thinking about film praxis as a medium for critiquing dominant and hegemonic ideological systems, without necessarily reducing the question of the critique of ideology to an aesthetic issue or one exclusively surrounding film form at the cost of film content. Shahani's use of the long shot and depth-of-field, discussed above in the stated context is a strategy that counters the appropriation of culture through a summarily reductionist, ahistorical and propagandist gesture on behalf of the institutionalised-statist apparatus. The long shot contextualises as in *Bhavantarana*, the Odissi dance within a regional, cultural landscape. Film theory, as it has developed in the Western academies has consistently critiqued dominant ideology as exemplified through cinematic conventions of mainstream industries such as Hollywood. Critical practice was thus posited as including 'deconstruction' of mainstream cinematic conventions.

In film theory, the long shot and depth-of-field have been conventionally equated with cinematic realism as theorised by André Bazin, who is often, simplistically projected at odds with the modernist theorists and practitioners – namely Sergei Eisenstein and Rudolf Arnheim. Shahani's use of the long shot and depth-of-field serve as critical tools that ethnographically contextualise and historicise the subjects of his films. As argued above this contextualisation serves as a mechanism for countering the hegemonic and institutionalised discourses of the nation state, which in the context of a visual discourse propel ahistoricised and essentialised representations of India's cultural practices. More internationally, Kumar's aesthetics intervene in complicating the neat binarisms upon which the categories of realist and modernist cinema have been founded.

After training with Ghatak, Shahani worked under Robert Bresson in France in the late 1960s. In 1968 he was introduced to Jean-Luc Godard who had invited Shahani to join the Dziga Vertov Group. Kumar engaged with Godard over the question of developing an ideologically critical cinema practice. He, however, disagreed with the equation of ideological critique through cinema as a question of deconstructing dominant codes of representation only. For Kumar it was limiting to think of a radical praxis in terms of reversing codes and conventions associated with the mainstream and dominant cinemas. Shahani summarises his concern thus:

> The theory that there exists a Cartesian polarity between arbitrary (aesthetic) signs and total realism necessarily led to quantitative conclusions and meaningless oppositions: the proliferation of detail against metaphysical truth (where quality cannot be seized), the fluidity of mise-en-scene as against the metre of montage, the existential tension of suspense (Hitchock) as against the tragic release from pity and fear. The terms of reference were purely idealist: the human being unsocialised and nature untransformed. Or when socialised or transformed, superficially so. This attitude necessarily tended either to exclude syntax progressively (realism) or to impose it as totally arbitrary structures. (1986: 72)

Shahani's criticism of the 'realism-modernism' polarity perpetuated by film theory raises issue with the equation of the discourses of realism and modernism with cinematic code i.e. depth-of-field equates with realism and montage with modernism. This, according to Shahani is limiting as it ossifies cinematic codes and techniques as embedded with only one set of meanings, supporting one form of discourse or worldview only. His own work has revealed that while a critical practice cannot be separated from the deconstruction and reworking of dominant cinematic conventions, it calls for the reconfiguration of form and content in terms of context — that within which a filmmaker works and that of the subject he/she documents. This implies the filmmaker and subject as both socialised and historicised bodies. Shahani's emphasis on the subject as a 'socialised' category is not simply in terms of historico-cultural definition, instead it involves interrogation of the terms at which the body, be it the filmmaker or the subject, is represented and appropriated in varied discourses including the normative national. This has led to in his case a departure from one of the key philosophical discourses within India – the *advaita* (the philosophy of the non-dual self).

According to Shahani social contradiction and spirituality are not oppositional or antithetical categories as some of the key philosophical schools such as the *advaita* in the subcontinent as also sections of Marxist thinking in the subcontinent and the west have made them out to be. For Shahani the spiritual imperative underpinning art cannot be abstracted from art's role as a mode of politico-ideological critique. Neither, according to him, does attending social or political conflict through art amount to a reductive commitment to material reality as against the immaterial and contemplative pursuit. He states:

> In our own little environment here for instance, most of the people who speak in the philosophical tradition of *Advaita* make what I think is a very big mistake. It's as if social contradiction doesn't have anything to do with the spiritual — that the two are divorced, polar opposites. They want to exclude social contradiction from spiritualism. These exclusions are really evasions. Those who have taken this or the other position are evasive. They deny that the very being who is stating or taking a position is a material being always seeking spiritual freedom. Within pre-religious thought or paganism, spiritual freedom is recognised as an aspiration. In our own context this is clearly the pursuit of *mukti* or *moksha*. The body is not denied. Society is not denied. Contradiction is not denied. Mahabharata and Krishna's discourse of the Srimad Bhagvad Gita is based on this — how the material conflict is entwined with the spiritual quest. See any of our epics, or for that matter Homer. The first Sanskrit dramas always acknowledge social contradiction and spiritual pursuit. I always hope that Marxists would recognise this, because Marx himself did – the fundamental contradiction of capitalism that it will end up paying the one who binds the book more than the poet. Marx said this so clearly and indisputably. To me there is no contradiction between the spiritual and the political. Art is obviously spiritual. And its impulse you can barely name or say it is out

there. It is not an objective thing. The objective thing is perhaps only the lens. But what it is that makes art cannot be instrumentalised. Any instrumentalised art or mass communication object will eventually boomerang. (Sharma 2007: 206)

Within the context of the theory-practice interface in film education Kumar Shahani's culturally grounded documentaries extend the understanding of radical film practice beyond a socially-functional, ventriloquist agenda as in the context of the Indian subcontinent and the 'third world' generally. More internationally his films present to us an alternative whose occupation for radicalism extends beyond the deconstruction of cinematic codes and conventions. Kumar Shahani's films constitute a critical discourse within the context of institutionalised worldviews and practices in India. Their aesthetic arises from Shahani's consistent engagement and focus upon the eliciting discourse between the subjects of his films and himself representing the wider cinematic apparatus in ideological terms. Shahani's filmic discourse emphasising socio-cultural specificity is the basis for the critical posture he develops through his practice. Through this he constantly raises questions of historicity in documentary practice. If Shahani's cinema is deployed for encouraging students to think about filmmaking as a mode of ideological critique, then through him we are extending the terms of reference for what constitutes as radical film practice beyond an occupation with cinema onotologically in terms of cinema codes and the worldviews they represent. This is merited on two grounds. One, the terms of reference for thinking about cinema vary in disparate socio-cultural and historical contexts – an aspect that the political modernist discourse and how it influenced film education in the Western academies has completely evaded. Two, Shahani's emphasis on cultural specificity enables in a more nuanced and politically sophisticated gesture to understand and reconstitute what constitutes as radical in historically and socio-culturally variegated contexts. Therefore radical practice cannot be determined by one set of objectives alone. Shahani's cinema arises from a position critiquing the dominant national and state apparatus. In doing this, his documentaries do not only attend questions of history and culture, but makes central to the filmmaking the question of how the eliciting discourse between filmmaker and subject effects documentary aesthetics.

OBSERVATIONAL DOCUMENTARY

David MacDougall's ethnographic films and theorisation surrounding them constitute a complex project on the scope and dynamics of observational cinema. His sustained study of post-colonial formations and conditions in India, presents to us not only a richly textured view of the social, cultural and class formations in India, but also furnishes for the student of documentary an intricately fashioned body of work shaped principally through the discourse between subject and filmmaker/ documentarist as observer in phenomeno-logical terms. Conventionally ethnographic research methods are divided into two categories – the participant-observer and observer-participant modali-ties (Seale 1998: 222). As ethnography has critiqued its positivist credentials and reconfigured its scope as a modernist practice, the former has come to be emphasised as a more subjective, indeterminate and reflexive practice. Participant-observation is a conjunctural practice developing the documen-tarist as participant's experiences as the basis for documentation. However, the two positions of the participant-observer and observer-participant are not necessarily antithetical, or in any hierarchical equation, as the empha-sis on participant-observation has inadvertently made them out to be. Both modalities suit variegated field research and filmmaking contexts as critical and creative tools for documentation, and the observer-participant modality itself raises modernist possibilities for subjective, expressive and critical docu-mentation as MacDougall's cinema shows to us. MacDougall's observational documentaries are decisively experiential and dialogic, privileging the sense of being through emphasis on touch and texture in documentation entwined with critical argument and historicisation around the subjects that he focuses upon.

MacDougall's films are grounded in the relationships forged between eth-nographers and the subjects they examine. This is at once reflexive because film content is clearly derived from the interactions — verbal and corporeal in the ethnographic instance between the documentarist and the subject. Observational cinema arose around the time that the 'cinéma vérité' prac-tice of filmmakers such as Jean Rouch was taking shape. Though related to 'cinéma vérité', observational documentary is a distinct practice in that it does not include reconstructions or fictionalisations — approaches seen particu-larly in Jean Rouch's ethnographic films. MacDougall trained at the UCLA Ethnographic Film programme, and his work springs from an interrogation of ethnographic documentary as an objective practice. This understanding at once chimes with modernist and avant-garde film practice and theory wherein the individual shot is broadly understood as 'latently ambiguous', available for meaning through interaction with other shots, as say in Eisenstein's theories (Becker & Hollis 2004: 11). However, unlike the modernists for whom the indeterminacy of the moving image led to a formal occupation with issues of montage and deconstruction, observational cinema being an ethnographic practice privileges human inter-subjectivity in documentary prior to any formal occupations.

> To pretend that the camera is somehow invisible and detached from the situation implies that the filmmaker's presence doesn't become part of the event and that the film records the action from the outside with an objective and omniscient eye. But objectivity is a fabrication. (Sherman 1998: 50–1)

Placing human inter-subjectivity at the centre, MacDougall's observational documentaries hold the image as both a record and as partial, subjective and expressive. This has implications for understanding self-reflexivity in practice. Critiquing realism's 'seamless verisimilitude', modernist cinema, be it the early avant-garde (1920s–1930s) or later, political modernism, developed an occupation with self-reflexivity (Hayward 2000: 232–8). In doing this, it tended to reduce the approaches and scope of self-reflexivity into a question of form and film code. The laying bare of cinematic devices somehow within the image through a suggestion of apparatus or through the processes of editing got and continues to be considered as the established mechanisms to reflect and imply that the film is constructed. While relevant, it is imperative that for the student of documentary the understanding of the apparatus be expanded and widened including the filmmaker as a socialised and historicised subject.

MacDougall's approach emphasises that self-reflexivity in cinema does not comprise a finite inventory of formal codes or techniques. In keeping with the ethnographic position, for MacDougall the 'self' is a contested body implicated in socio-cultural and historical fashionings that are fluidly and contingently evoked in the filmmaking process. Political modernism's emphasis on self-reflexivity through form overlooked this. The body of the filmmaker remained unsocialised if not fully ahistoricised and abstracted from the filmmaking context. MacDougall's emphasis on the self as socialised does not amount to a radical negation of the apparatus. A broad survey of his study of prominent schools in India reflects a steadily evolving practice that makes as its basis the inter-subjective, eliciting discourse between filmmaker and subjects, developed through an expressive visual vocabulary at far remove from mainstream and dominant documentary conventions.

MacDougall's films in India clearly evoke a cross-cultural register. They are not in the order of cultural description or interpretation on behalf of an outsider, but deploy socio-cultural disparities between filmmaker and subject as a mechanism to raise wider historical questions. Most recently MacDougall has examined two philosophically very disparate schools in India - the first is the Doon school, a prestigious boys boarding institution in Dehradun, north India, and the second, the Rishi Valley school founded by the contemplative philosopher and thinker, J Krishnamurthy. Exploring the foundational ethos of both schools becomes for MacDougall the basis for unpacking wider issues of post-coloniality.

Founded in the early decades of the twentieth century the Doon school is tightly implicated in the founding ideology and vision for a developing nation. MacDougall's very selection of a boys' boarding school cuts straight into questions of gender, specifically the male body within a post-colonial framework. MacDougall's approach to the body is clearly social-constructionist and in a broad sense, the films in the *Doon School* series unpack how the male body gets fashioned affirmatively in relation to the post-colonial nation state. The films are structured around the observation of key events in the school calendar, everyday routines, the school's myths and folklore, the textures of its environs and activities, all intermixed with conversations of varied modalities – some structured interactions between filmmaker, staff and students, others including classroom discussions and spontaneously conjured exchanges among students. In this way the Doon School films are clearly polyphonic – including a tapestry of variegated experiences and worldviews. The varied voices in the films are not tantamount to a celebratory or ventriloquist gesture of inclusiveness. The complexities, textures and nuances of verbal exchange between subjects reveal wider socio-cultural discourses and facilitate in accessing the underpinning and performative worldviews of each subject we encounter, thus making the films critical historical texts.

MacDougall's conversations with student subjects in the school films do not elicit information or descriptive experiences. They are more of exchanges sharing close experiences, thoughts and interests. These conversations reveal his subtle equations with the interviewees and their mode serves more to question the efficacy and authority of the spoken word than utilise it as the sole and authoritative source of information. This approach complicates our understanding of the goals and techniques for interviews as data gathering devices. It presents an alternative for questioning how the testimonial of a subject can be interrogated and developed to unpack that which lies further than but informs words. Avant-garde filmmaker Satyajit Ray, in an early writing, had raised this problematic surrounding interviews in documentary thus:

How can we ever be sure that an interviewee is making honest statements and not merely saying what he believes is the right thing to say? To me the really significant things that emerge from spot interviews are the details of people's behaviour and speech under scrutiny of the camera and the microphone. (Jacobs 1979: 382)

MacDougall's films and writing also raise this problematic and he responds, stating:

> Interviews in films not only convey spoken information but also unspoken information about the contexts in which they occur. They allow their speakers to describe their subjective experiences of past events, while simultaneously we interpret the emotions and constraints of the moment. (in Devereaux & Hillman 1995: 245)

The conversations MacDougall conjures in the school films situate the interview as a fluid, impetuous and contingent instance. This exceeds the conventions of interviews as data collection devices and becomes the basis through which a critical dimension for documentation is opened that in MacDougall's work serves in critiquing the dominant Indian state apparatus and the ideological postures it perpetuates. The school films bring forth worldviews mobilised in a post-colonial framework that are inescapably linked to the national category and the individual subject's situation within it. This is achieved through a very subtle cinematographic and editing design of the films.

MacDougall's sustained observation of the students' bodies complements the verbal discourses in the film and serves in a radical unpacking of social history and its transactions with individual subjectivity. The subjects consistently reference the camera and the whole gamut of their gestures and movements reveals how their bodies and its vocabularies are all intimately tied to and shaped by the spaces they occupy and that are socio-historically constructed. In some senses the ground for the school films had already been laid through David and Judith MacDougall's *Photo Wallahs* (1992) a film that through a bricolage of voices explores experiences, memories and desires linked to photography as a practice introduced during the colonial era in the hill town, Mussoorie in north India. The varied voices and experiences in this film introduce the viewer to a vast spectrum of postcolonial class and subject positions ranging from the English-speaking elite on to the lower middle classes.

This project on class takes a distinct, more decisive and in-depth turn in the *Doon School Chronicles* (2000) that clearly gesture towards class contradictions and divides festered in a post-colonial context. The films reveal how the school envisioned and maintained a visionary zeal in the context of nation-building aims to develop an ideal male consciousness through which the imagined aspirations of a developing nation can be performed and realised. MacDougall maps a range of processes including the shaping of the male

David and Judith MacDougall *Photo Wallahs* (1992)

body through physical exercise, social etiquette and discipline, through to the enculturation and cultivation of a mind adept in the specifics of the nation's history and commanding a mobility across cultures and ideas to serve progressively in the development of the nation.

The Doon School films clearly raise for us the contradictions pertaining to the oft-repeated post-colonial binarism between the categories of 'tradition' and 'modernity', and here 'tradition' does not just reference the precolonial medieval or ancient mythic and folkloric, but those traditions that are selectively extracted and encumbered by the ruling elites in the euphoria surrounding new nationhood and the norms deployed in fabricating its definition. The textures of the students' everyday activities, body gestures and fashionings – classroom organisation, the learning processes in and outside class, food eating habits, the hierarchies of organisation and the dynamics in interpersonal contact and relationships, spatial dynamics, students' extracurricular interests and hobbies, their deeper aspirations, all point to the conflict between the school's ideals linked to a Victorian past emphasising the 'nation'

David MacDougall, *Doon School Chronicles* (2000)

in progressivist and affirmative terms and a contemporary popular culture, selectively 'global' and in which the nation is a problematical, if not a fully subdued category. Principally, the films, in the context of India as a social democracy reference how a feudal and colonial past constantly co-mingles first with the residue of institutionalised socialism and the more recent, aggressive capitalism heralded by the economic liberalisation of 1991. This introduces to us a particular identity dynamic whose logic is formulated through the pulls between social-functionalism and consumerist-individualism. Mapping the convergence of these competing socio-cultural imperatives on the bodies of the students serves as a historical commentary and catapults the films from a wilfully preservationist recording towards a more critical and discursive stance in which our engagement pertains to how dominant and ruling ideology shapes and informs subject world-views.

The nationalist project and the implication of youth bodies in it has been a subject of the parallel Indian cinema starting with figures such as Satyajit Ray and Ritwik Ghatak. MacDougall is touching upon similar issues as the Indian avant-garde but his observational approach is distinct in that it does not in any way tap into India's aesthetic discourses. MacDougall's is a phenomenological approach emphasising the sense of *being* evoked in relation to space as socio-historical category. Space is not merely location but is a more ecological and interactive complex. In his words:

> ... the appearance of a people and their surroundings, their technology and physical way of life; their ritual activities and what beliefs they signify; the quality of interpersonal communication, and what it tells of their relationships; the psychology and personalities of individuals in the society; the relation of people to their environment — their knowledge of it, use of it, and movement within it; the means by which the culture is passed on from one generation to another; the rhythms of the society, and its sense of geography and time; the values of the people; their political and social organisation; their contacts with other cultures; and the overall quality of their worldview.' (Nichols 1976: 146)

Tapping into the institutionalised aspects of youth culture, the *Doon School* films enable us to access and contextualise the factors and symptoms linked to the rising apathy among the Indian middle class – a characteristic that has sharply risen since India's economic liberalisation. Pavan Varma links the Indian middle-class attitudes in a post-liberalisation consumerist context to a 'devaluing of idealism, as an aspect of leadership and as a factor in society', coupled with the 'erosion of the legitimacy of the State as an effective economic factor' and the 'legitimisation of corruption as an accepted and even inevitable part of society' (Varma 1998: 82). These trends have, according to him, contributed to a decline in concern towards wider socio-political and economic issues such as poverty and inequality. The Doon school films are dotted with instances and conversations through which we access the conflicts and frustrations that result when such a middle-class background encounters the school's ideals that have not necessarily been revisioned in keeping with the socio-cultural changes percolating Indian society. This is succinctly evident when for example one student suggests how the boarding school is so abstracted from the socio-economic complexities and contours of the 'real' world beyond its boundaries. He suggests, in a rather incoherent manner, how such an abstracted context impedes an individual's relations and interactions with one's environment. The conflicts in student mindsets are furnished more fully when we repeatedly observe them learning, which is clearly an exercise in rote and its incumbent attitudes.

The male body in a postcolonial context is historicised and problematised in terms of the confliction between and the co-mingling of liberal-consumerist attitudes with the Victorian. Art historian Geeta Kapur, who has deliberated on the distinction in the conception of the body through documentary

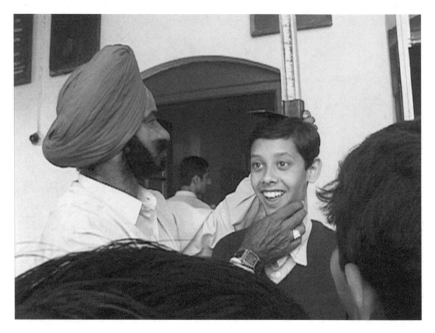

David MacDougall, *Doon School Chronicles* (2000)

in India, argues that the 'contemporary body' is tightly imbricated with the urban cityscapes and topographies as fashioned by India's economic liberalisation. She substitutes, for 'polemical effect', the phraseology of 'body-language' instead of the 'body' to draw the disparity between the socio-historical and cultural determination of the body on the one hand, and its conception in more poetic terms. She states that while one alludes to 'material metonymies that map desire – the fragments ingested, disgorged, relayed to the receptor as a series of signs', the other bears 'the pleasure in beholding repossessed bodies, in decoding allegories that spell mortality' (2005: 107). According to her, 'The mode of cross-referencing [between body and city] is indexical: the body positioned in contiguous relationship with the city, so that we look for mutual trace and imprint in the body-city interface' (ibid.). If we combine this proposition with the deliberation on changing cityscapes of India after economic liberalisation, as discussed by Pavan Varma, we are better positioned to appreciate MacDougall's specific take on the male body that locates in it an urbane and quite aggressive consumerist investment. The intermixing of the Doon school's zealous vision imbued with nationalist vigour – itself a residue of the colonial era, with a contemporary youth culture implicated in globalisation, define a clearly upper-class and elitist overture that is at far remove from India's little, folk, and classical traditions as nativist alternatives.

Since his early films in India, including *Photo Wallahs*, the duration of the shot in MacDougall's films has steadily increased. This is a crucial and critical strategy that facilitates observation – the viewer's relationship to the image is open-ended as the camera deliberates upon and maintains distance from subjects. MacDougall's cinematography is not indexical, instead it invites the viewer to scan the field of vision and engage with his ruminations. His essay-istic style privileges putting subjects and their actions in the context of space as a historical and sensorial construct. The viewer is allowed to engage with aspects of human subjectivity that are not readily or tangibly available through performed and spoken discourse but only suggested through body gestures, postures, conduct and codes of dress. In this process the authorial imperative is not fully determined or authoritarian and neither is it effaced. *Schoolscapes* (2007), the film surrounding J. Krishnamurthy's Rishi Valley school is edited as a compilation of single shot scenarios – entire scenes performed in a sin-gle shot. Here MacDougall takes us back to early cinema and reinvigorating the primitive mode of representation as discussed by Noel Burch (1981). The early cinema aesthetic is evoked at two levels in *Schoolscapes*. The single shot scenario is an explicit reference to single shot early films, prior to the use of editing and intercutting that emerged around 1904. In his lecture accompa-nying the screening of *Schoolscapes* at the Royal Anthropological Institute's Ethnographic Film Festival 2007, MacDougall had stated that *Schoolscapes* is inspired by early cinema techniques particularly the Lumières' single-shot films. MacDougall's single-shot scenarios in *Schoolscapes* are however dis-tinct from early cinema's tightly structured narratives. They do not contain

David MacDougall, *Schoolscapes* (2007)

any explicit or causal narrative – they are principally observational and evocative of spatial constructs and textures and how those link with the bodies. Due to this the viewing experience is of a different order as narrative is thinly constructed and so engagement is largely at the level of discourse.

The sustained shots with sparse camera movement reflect a highly evolved rapport between ethnographer and his subjects. The films are dotted with rich instances where a relationship between MacDougall and different subjects is forged and performed through the film process – a relationship that extends towards a more humane and expressive dimension. Through this MacDougall references key elements of Krishnamurthy's philosophical discourse emphasising relationship as the structuring principle of human experience and contemplation. A more critical and complex approach to documentary emerges that exceeds social-functionalism, which dominates documentary practice in the subcontinent. The element of relationality in MacDougall's work makes documentary as an evocative and creative practice bearing a phenomenological dimension that serves to decentralising the source of meaning and emphasis. This is not only useful in the context of problematising documentary in a post-colonial framework, but more broadly for interrogating the truth and scientific claims underpinning documentary as a discipline. With regard to this, Bill Nichols observes:

> It may be no coincidence that both David MacDougall and Alison Jablonko envision an experiential or perhaps gnosiological, repetitive, poetic form of filmic organisation that would foster 'haptic learning, learning by bodily identification', or would replace subject-centered and linear models with ones 'employing repetition, associative editing and non-narrative structures' ... Efforts such as these would move away from attempts to speak from mind to mind, in the discourse of scientific sobriety, and toward a politics and epistemology of experience spoken from body to body. Hierarchical structures designed for the extraction of knowledge (the interview, the informant, the case study) might yield to more fully personal, participatory encounter that makes an expansion or diffusion of the personal into the social and political inevitable... (1994: 82)

At a further level, MacDougall develops a highly evolved haptic visual regimen, which is also characteristic of early cinema. Sustained images from competing angles disassemble a centralised humanist perspective. The sense of touch and texture emerges as the principle register for visual engagement. MacDougall's films reveal a proximity to Vertov's *kino-eye* with its extensive range of camera angulations. Dramatic foregrounds, with carefully deployed close-ups and depth-of-field enable us a viewing position in which the subject within the frame, animate or inanimate, assumes a corporeal and embodied presence. It is pertinent to qualify here that MacDougall's use of depth-of-field and close-ups exceeds the conventional understandings of these as discussed in film theory – the former contributing to the realism effect in keeping with Bazinian realism and the latter contributing in detail or emotion. For MacDougall the sense of vision is not physical or objective serving a corroboratory or informational function only. It is as he points succinctly in the introduction to *The Corporeal Image*, co-extensive with the experience of being. He says:

> Our consciousness of our own being is not primarily an image, it is a feeling. But our consciousness of the being, the autonomous existence, of nearly everything else in the world involves vision. We assume that the things we see have the properties of being, but our grasp of this depends upon extending our own feeling of being into our seeing. In the process, something quintessential of what we are becomes generalised in the world. Seeing not only makes us alive to the appearance of things but to being itself. (2006: 1)

MacDougall's images serve a sensorial function for the viewer extending the experience of film viewing into experiential realms exceeding visually verifiable narrative or information. Consequently while MacDougall's documentaries deploy the camera's capacity to record, his approach is more complex in that it facilitates in extending engagement with subjects to the realms that exceed words and physical or objective actions. Film viewing is extended into a corporeal direction wherein vision and viewing do not purely serve an evidential function. Instead the haptic visual regime is principally evocative. Here evocation is not of the order of bias, but a sense of nearness and touch both as a tactile encounter as well as a humane gesture that defamiliarises commonsense reality:

> For MacDougall, this evocative potential seemed linked to a potential shift in epistemology, or at least a radical reconceptualisation of the terms and conditions of ethnographic film so that it would no longer be seen simply as a colourful adjunct to written ethnography but offer a distinct way of seeing, and knowing of its own. But MacDougall does not insist on this rupture. There is the lingering sense that the texture of life contributes to an economy and logic that are still fundamentally referential and realist. MacDougall also evokes a generic oneness ('the overall quality of their worldview') which leaves the position, affiliation, and affective dimension

of the filmamker's own engagement to the periphery. Performative documentary seeks to evoke not the quality of a people's worldview but the
specific qualities that surround particular people, discrete events, social
subjectivities, and historically situated encounters between filmmakers
and their subjects. The classic anthropological urge to typify on the basis of
a cultural identity receives severe modification. (MacDougall's own films
exhibit these performative qualities, to a greater extent than this quote,
and may attempt to persuade traditional ethnographers to give greater
attention to film but in a way that leaves traditional assumptions essentially
intact.) (Nichols 1994: 101)

The presence of the camera and the haptic visual regimen registers the students' rapport with MacDougall and in turn references the experience of space
in sensory terms. The verbal conversations and gestural exchanges between
MacDougall and the students extend the filmmaker as socialised being. The
particularity of the observational mode is that it does not privilege a specific
code or set of coda as *the* coherent and normative mechanisms for developing a reflexive or deconstructionist approach. The observational mode is
a critical practice that disrupts received relationships within the social field.
Thus MacDougall's films present the most clear fusion of the modernist and
ethnographic imperatives for self-reflection in terms of inter-subjectivity as
socio-historically constituted and uses that as the basis for inviting the viewer
into deciphering an ideologically critical stance as opposed to a polemical or
didactic posture that idealises or essentialises by abstracting all but formal
codes and issues as the means and level for an interventionist practice.

CONCLUSION

A survey of Shahani and MacDougall's documentaries in India raise for us
two interventions. Firstly, they both emphasise the body – the subject and
filmmaker – as socio-cultural and historical categories. Much modernist
and avant-garde practice overlooks this. Approaching the body as socialised
invests in practice in the distinct edge of historicity and cultural specificity,
crucial in any representation for resisting universalism. Further, both practitioners present to us alternatives for critiquing dominant ideology. Here it is
pertinent to qualify 'dominant ideology' not in terms of mainstream cinema,
but nationalist ideology – that which the filmmakers encounter in the filmmaking process and context. This is useful because the critical imperatives of
both filmmakers extend the notion of a radical and interventionist practice
beyond critique of mainstream cinema codes towards context-specific criteria

that in the case of both filmmakers pertains to the nationalist rhetoric and jargon of the Indian subcontinent. Both filmmakers emphasise the interrelations and eliciting discourse between filmmaker and subjects as the basis for developing film form. In Shahani this takes shape in his specific use of juxtaposition and the long shot; in MacDougall this takes the form of his conversations with subjects and an evocative, haptic visual regimen. Both filmmakers reconstitute film form within the specific context of the film encounter, their formulations exceed and critique dominant and mainstream cinematic conventions. Film form in their practice emerges as context-specific rather than an ossified category that bears fixed meaning and connotations irrespective of film process or cultural context. In the theory-practice debate within film education, this intervenes by stressing that while dominant conventions necessitate critique and deconstruction, that project cannot be conducted in abstraction and isolation from the filmmaking encounter and process. In this process the filmmaker's subjectivity is a crucial player and merits equal unpacking as the subject's socio-historical and cultural context. These aspects cannot be isolated, and are intimately tied to and visible in the formal techniques and processes that filmmakers such as Shahani and MacDougall deploy. Though distinct in disciplinary approaches, both MacDougall and Shahani present to us complex documentary formulations that emulate a critique of nationalist ideology in India and extend through their documentary aesthetics our understanding of film form as implicated with the filmmaking encounter.

BIBLIOGRAPHY

Becker, L. And R. Hollis (2004) *Avant-Garde Graphics 1918–34*. London: Hayward Gallery Publishing.

Burch, N. (1981) *Theory of Film Practice*. Princeton, NJ: Princeton University Press.

Chanana, O. (1987) *Docu-Scene India*. Bombay: Films Division.

Devereaux, L. And R. Hillman (eds) (1995) *Fields of Vision: Essays in Film Studies, Visual Anthropology and Photography*. Berkeley, CA: University of California Press.

Dunne, J. A. And P. Quigley (eds) (2004) *The Montage Principle*. Amsterdam and New York: Rodopi.

Hayward, S. (2000) *Cinema Studies: The Key Concepts*. 2nd edn.. London: Routledge.

Jacobs, L. (eds.) (1979) *The Documentary Tradition*. 2nd edn.. New York and London: W. W. Norton and Company.

Kapur, G. (2000) *When was Modernism?* New Delhi: Tulika Books.

_____ (2004) 'Tracking Images', in M. Nash, *Experiments with Truth*. Philadelphia, PA: The Fabric Workshop and Museum, pp. 105-111.

Lutyens, M. (1987) *The Penguin Krishnamurti Reader.* 11th edn. London: Penguin.

MacDougall, D. (1976) 'Prospects for the pp. 135-150. Ethnographic Film', in B. Nichols, *Movies and Methods – Volume I.* Berkeley, CA: University of California Press, pp. 135-150.

_____ (2006) *The Corporeal Image: Film, Ethnography and the Senses.* Princeton, NJ: Princeton University Press.

Myer, C. (2004) 'Playing with toys by the wayside: an interview with Noel Burch', *Journal of Media Practice,* 5, 2, 71–80.

Nandy, A. (1994) *The Illegitimacy of Nationalism: Rabindranath Tagore and the Politics of Self.* New Delhi: Oxford University Press.

Nichols, B. (1994) *Blurred Boundaries: Questions of Meaning in Contemporary Culture.* Bloomington: Indiana University Press.

Pines, J. and P. Willemen (1994) *Questions of Third Cinema.* 3rd edn. London: BFI.

Rodowick, D. N. (1994) *The Crisis of Political Modernism: Criticism and Ideology in Contemporary Film Theory.* Berkeley, CA and London: University of California Press.

Rosenberg, D. (2000) 'Video Space: a Site for Choreography', *Leonardo,* 33, 4, 275–80.

Shahani, K. (1986) 'Dossier – Kumar Shahani', *Framework,* 30/31, 80–101.

Sharma, A. (2007) *Montage and Ethnicity: Experimental Film Practice and Editing in the Documentation of the Gujarati Indian Community in Wales.* Unpublished PhD thesis, University of Glamorgan.

Seale, C. (1998) (ed.) *Researching Society and Culture.* London: Sage.

Sherman, S. (1998) *Documenting Ourselves: Film, Video and Culture.* Lexington, KY: University Press of Kentucky.

Stam, R. (2002) *Introducing Film Theory.* London: Blackwell Publishing.

Varma, P. K. (1999) *The Great Indian Middle Class.* New Delhi: Penguin.

FILMOGRAPHY

Apu trilogy (1955–60) Directed by Satyajit Ray [DVD]. Amazon: Columbia TriStar Home Entertainment.

As the Crow Flies (2004) Directed by Kumar Shahani [Film]. India: Immanence.

Bamboo Flute, The (2000) Directed by Kumar Shahani [Film]. India: Immanence.

Bhavantaranaa (1991) Directed by Kumar Shahani [Film]. India: Immanence.

Choreography for the Camera (1945) Directed by Maya Deren [DVD]. Amazon: Mystic Fire Video.

Doon School Chronicles (2000) Directed by David MacDougall [DVD]. Berkeley: Berkeley Media LLC.

Photo Wallahs (1992) Directed by David and Judith MacDougall [DVD]. Berkeley: Berkeley Media LLC.

Schoolscapes (2007) Directed by David MacDougall [DVD]. Berkeley: Berkeley Media LLC.

CHAPTER 9
THE STUDENT AUTHOR, LACANIAN DISCOURSE THEORY AND *LA NUIT AMÉRICAINE*

Coral Houtman

> I start off wanting a film to be good. Then problems start and all I can hope
> is that we finish. I take myself to task – 'You could have worked harder: still
> you have some time left.'
>
> – *La Nuit Américaine* (François Truffaut, 1973)

François Truffaut, himself acting the role of a film director in a film about
filmmaking, muses in voice-over whilst fighting to keep his film afloat in *La
Nuit Américaine* (*Day for Night*). The film is amusingly and painfully accurate
about the difficulties of filmmaking and the mountain to be climbed in order
to achieve a creative result. The vicissitudes of chance, of personal life intrud-
ing on the film, of the money men refusing to back the project, have to be
negotiated and Truffaut's solution is finally that of creativity. His response to
the travails of filmmaking is to 'try to make the film come alive more vividly',
and this he does, at the cost of the death of one of his lead actors, Alexandre
(played by Jean-Pierre Aumont). This chapter is about the difficulties, inhibi-
tions and necessities of such creativity, and the ways that this might be understood and taught. In film schools, university departments, and art schools,
students are busy making films, working under very different circumstances
to those of Truffaut in his professional filmmaking. Nevertheless, I will argue

that through the pressures of no-budget, strict-schedule filmmaking students hoping to find their voice and achieve their grades have travails that are in some ways equal to those of Truffaut in *La Nuit Américaine*. I suggest that we, as teachers, understand these pressures and have ways of countering them in order to foster student creativity. In *Augustine* (Houtman 1993), my graduation film from the National Film & Television School, I told the story of a hysterically mute girl committed to the asylum at La Salpêtrière and treated by the famous neurologist, Jean-Martin Charcot, who eventually finds her 'voice' and breaks out of her captivity. This was an expression of experience at film school finding myself traumatised by the demand to 'speak' creatively, to perform the discourse of filmmaking in a context where it seemed that my career (and future life) depended upon critical and popular success. Since teaching, I have found that this specifically creative trauma is far from being unusual or unique to me. The aspiring filmmaker is in a highly competitive environment where it is very easy to be seduced by narcissistic identification with the rewards of the media industries and become devastated by the failure to develop the skills and competencies which enable a 'speakability' within this environment. I shall suggest that it is possible to develop what I shall call 'Authorship skills' – that is critical and reflexive skills which are directed towards the understanding and expression of desire and the finding of 'voice'. Using these skills the student may find the ability to value their own creativity, to find ways of expressing it and thus to develop strategies against trauma.

What are the ways in which we might enable voice and agency in filmmaking? One way would be to take postmodern concepts of authorship seriously and structure our teaching accordingly. This is, happily, partly already happening by default, as we teach larger numbers. We increasingly encourage group work and teams rather than individuals. However, if authorship is no longer seen as an individual act of creation or origination, but as an inevitable and often non-voluntarist performance of the self, spoken by and speaking discourse, then we can both enable a more playful inhabiting of the role of filmmaker and also encourage our students in the study of film and culture generally, in order to foster their intertextual performativity. We can encourage them to find signifiers for their desire and become aware of those barriers which restrict them.

In the beginning of *La Nuit Américaine* the actors are interviewed by paparazzi about their roles in the film, and they all come up with different interpretations of the script. This is the postmodern concept of the instability of discourse, made visible. It is the job of the director, (in this case, Truffaut as a character within the drama and also as director of the actual film) during the filming process, to marry these different interpretations into a satisfying whole without reducing the film to a lifeless schema, and to communicate this consensual writing, to the audience acting as consensual viewers. By the end of the film, by utilising what I would pragmatically call 'the creative use of compromise' or, in other words, by performing the discourses which surround the film making process – the collaboration of crew and cast in the face of events beyond their control, he makes the best of things, and finds the film that incorporates meaning in the most rich way possible. He brings death back to creative life, by shooting a scene in the snow to recreate a dead actor, and even incorporates the real life words of his British lead actress, Julie Baker, played by Jacqueline Bisset, into the dialogue, to explain the motivation of her character. How do we teach such creativity to our students?

I have two main suggestions for helping students to find their filmmaking potential. These are not necessarily new suggestions or even surprising. The first suggestion is very directly about the importance of theory to practice. By offering our students a choice of conceptual frameworks, a lively and iterated sense of cultural history and theory, we free them from the slavish adherence to models of film-making, models of seeing the world which only allow of one perspective, one technology. It is our contextual knowledge, as teachers, which enables us not to fall into binarised or reductive thinking, of trying to make students' ideas fall into our templates, but recognising that original ideas can come from many different traditions and that we know how to weigh one tradition against another and to use whatever technique is productive for the idea. Thus, as teachers we constantly relate the new speech to its intertext and interrogate it to discover its own production of meaning. Students learn from our example as skilful practitioners of theory and of practice, that filmmaking and contextual thinking are intimately related skills and that each broadens the potential of the other. In such a rapidly changing media world, conceptual skills are vital in order to create an energised and inhabited sense of 'craft'. For example, in the world of writing, then having postmodern ideas of the writerly text, as explored by Barthes (1977: 142–9) and of the postmodern authorial subject,[1] enables us to give our students confidence against the rather ubiquitous Hollywood Aristotelian ideas of script, without junking the insights of Robert McKee (1999) *et al.* completely. Instead we may ask 'What does having a character led film mean?' in a world where subjectivity is defined performatively, or psychoanalytically, or 'What does it mean to organise a three-act structure with inciting incident on page 23', and so forth, where meaning is unstable and contains the seeds of its own chaos. Indeed we may look at the instabilities of our students' films and in them find what it is about them that is revealing, meaningful despite itself.

Deconstruction as an act of textual criticism has become regarded in some circles as passé, whereas deconstruction as an act of script development has always been important and should certainly be part of current practice. We may then return to the Aristotelian comforts of character catharsis and closure by appeal to myth and to the functions of identification desire and empathy in fiction, but we will be returning informed and fresh. By interrogating the basic tenets of drama, for example 'What is action? What do people do to each other?' we are then able to rearticulate and reinvigorate basic dramatic questions for our students and enable them to come up with their own answers. Furthermore, finding correspondences, 'this work resembles the plays of Strindberg', or 'this film works with an oblique sense of character and point of view like the films of von Sternberg', or 'this film has a feminine/feminist aesthetic', allows us to help situate our student 'authors' as spoken by discourse and yet inflecting it differently. The students need not be placed in the invidious position of having to produce 'originality' from nothing. The craft skills of writing may, hopefully, engage with the narrativity of our current lives so that they are the skills of the current and the future media industries and arts. Personally, I do not feel it is acceptable any more to populate the academy with expertise in only one kind of writing, or one form of industrial production, however deeply imbricated and skilful this expertise might be, unless a lively critique is also available to situate this work and to suggest alternatives. However, we do, like Truffaut, need to enable our students to pick the version most appropriate to their film and give them the courage to see it through.

The kind of approach to discourse outlined above is illuminated if we see it through the filter of Lacan's Discourse Theory as discussed by Paul Verhaeghe (1995). Lacan has a model of communication of how we are performed by discourse and in particular, how both our conscious and unconscious statements are positioned in regard to the other of our address. Lacan's Four Discourses were designed primarily as tools for understanding the process of the psychoanalytic session. They comprise a model of how analysts and analysands may take up different subject positions in the session and how these positions illuminate both what is being conveyed through the communication between analyst and analysand and also what is being repressed, what fails to be communicated, and what is at stake for the individuals communicating in this particular way. The Four Discourses also enable a political analysis of the act of communication between two people and of the relationship between that and the psychoanalytic condition of a particular individual. They can therefore be applied in all circumstances, not just that of the psychoanalytic session. The discourses comprise the four types of social bond which can and are taken up by all people at some time. They do not indicate pathological conditions, but rather tendencies, particular approaches towards others, towards oneself, and towards knowledge, which may be weighted in particular individuals towards one discourse rather than another. The Four Discourses are the Discourse of the Master, the Discourse of the University, the Discourse of the Hysteric, and the Discourse of the Analyst.[2] One of these, his Discourse of the University, actually accounts for what I have been talking about when I have argued about the necessity for a fluid and pluralist approach to conceptual frameworks and contexts in film work.

The basic model is of the speech act, so in all Four Discourses, on the left, we have the agent or speaker and on the right the other or receiver.

$$
\begin{array}{ccc}
 & \text{impossibility} & \\
\text{The agent} & \rightarrow & \text{The other} \\
\uparrow \quad \text{- - - - - - - - - -} & & \text{- - - - - - - - - - -} \quad \downarrow \\
\text{truth} & // & \text{production} \\
 & \text{inability} &
\end{array}
$$

Underneath the bar on both sides is a repressed element, so that the agent/ speaker on the left is motivated by some truth, under the bar, which when introduced to the other as unconscious communication leads to a production, under the bar on the right. The qualities under the bars cannot communicate directly as they are the unconscious of the communication. In each of the Four Discourses, these basic terms are also filled by other qualities which are super-imposed upon them. Lacan provides terms which he has developed elsewhere in his theories which are superimposed upon the equation always in the same order, but starting from different places in the equation. The terms are:

S_1 = the Master signifier
S_2 = knowledge (savoir)
$ = the subject
a = surplus enjoyment

In each Discourse different terms are placed in the position of repressed truth, and in the place of production, in the place of the agent and the other, and therefore there are different places for impossibility and inability, different aspects of discourse get repressed or fail to be communicated within the dif-ferent Four Discourses.[3]

Thus, in the Discourse of the University, the following equation is super-imposed on the basic model:

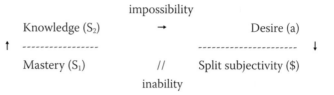

If the student filmmaker is in the position of Agent, and Mastery is below the bar, then this mastery is (a) their knowledge of filmmaking, (b) their reflexivity upon their act of filmmaking which can justify it in historical/contextual/aesthetic terms, or (c) the Academy justifying or contextualising their effort. On the right is their film, the object of their desire, and hidden underneath the bar is what Elizabeth Bronfen calls their 'knotted subjectivity' (1998: 8–12), i.e. all the influences, conscious or unconscious which speaks and misspeaks them. Thus, the successful Discourse of the University produces a film, but also the knowledge of the student that they are fallible, that they are humble in the face of discourse.

In *La Nuit Américaine* Truffaut comments that the director is 'someone who is being asked questions all the time. Sometimes he knows the answer, sometimes not', and the film shows Truffaut and his collaborators finding the answers to any number of questions throughout the film. Here, the Discourse of the University speaks in both directions – the crew as Agent with Truffaut as Desire, and vice-versa. The crew need to know what Truffaut wants, and they interrogate him for the answers, which he produces. This is reversed when he does not know how to do something, for example, deciding on what to reshoot after Alexander's death. Sometimes, the answers come by the process of the Discourse of the University so that, for example, when a cute cat fails to perform properly and lick some milk left in a discarded breakfast tray, the make-up girl remarks to the props man that they should have had a replacement cat, an operation of the Discourse of the University in that it emanates from the make-up girl's superior knowledge and experience. Truffaut as a listener is also operating within the Discourse of the University; his openness to suggestions is the mark of a good and experienced director who is prepared to find answers wherever they appear – although it is probably also a mark of desperation in the face of the seemingly impossible. The Discourse of the University, as I have already outlined, also operates through any directorial interpretation of script which is based on sound methodological basis. The ability to make decisions based on an understanding of relative conceptual frameworks is a skill that the University is ideally suited to teaching, and we are able to give our students an understanding of character interpretation, or understanding of the structural importance of a scene, supported by textual and historical knowledge, is an imperative for their creative work. Enabling our students to have a broad understanding of where their scripts are going and what is important about them will enable them not only to choose what to include, but like Truffaut, to choose what they do not need to shoot, and how contingencies may be met.

However, sometimes Truffaut's directing decisions are made just so that a decision has been taken, for example, when he is choosing props or cars, items that have no structural implications for the script. At these moments, Truffaut is operating through The Discourse of the Master where the positions have all rotated by 90 degrees:

impossibility

Mastery (S_1) $\rightarrow$ Slave (S_2)

$\uparrow$ -------------   ----------------------- $\downarrow$

Desire (a)   //   Split subjectivity ($)

inability

Truffaut has to make a decision, otherwise filming would stop, and therefore any decision is better than none. Lacan's prime example here is of Churchill during the Second World War, who needed to be followed, but whose decisions were made out of seemingly impossible and doomed situations, and in the dark. This is the role of a leader. The paradox here is that experienced directors know this, and know that giving orders or making decisions is actually their job, and this therefore also falls into Discourse of the University, as established practice.

La Nuit Américaine, although a European art film is far from being introspective – Truffaut is a figure of action and we actually have little access to his decision-making processes, indeed we get to know him very little (his occasional voice-over sums up, gnomically, general theses about filmmaking, not his motivations whilst making this particular film) – and therefore it's not easy to see the hidden terms of the discourse lying under the right hand bar of Lacan's equations or what they produce within the film. Yes, we can see that as Truffaut or his filmic family solves each arising problem operating under The Discourse of the University: he is led by desire onto the next (the Desire (a) on the top right of the equation) but we don't see the split subjectivity ($) hidden underneath it. However, we do see the result of these discourses on the crew obeying Truffaut operating The Discourse of the Master. Their love affairs and petty rivalries are the repressed subjectivities returning not in the filmmaking process, but in their personal lives and in the compressed spare time surrounding the film.

The Discourse of the University and the Discourse of Mastery together produces an end product. Nevertheless it is not possible to operate solely within these discourses in order to produce or create a product. This is because the Discourses of the University and the Discourse of the Master as we have seen, hide or repress any unconscious subjectivity and therefore they are the pure iteration of discourse. Iteration without change is an impossibility, language is inherently unstable. Judith Butler, in her work on performativity, suggests that agency is the space between our interpellation and therefore constitution as subjects through language and societal frameworks, and our inability to iterate these frameworks. We are both 'spoken by' and 'speakers' of discourse:

> The speaking subject makes his or her decision only in the context of an already circumscribed field of linguistic possibilities. One decides on the condition of an already decided field of language, but this repetition does not constitute the decision of the speaking subject as a redundancy. The gap between redundancy and repetition is the space of agency. (1997: 129)[4]

In other words, the creative film is the product of the failure of iteration. For this filmmaking has also to operate under Lacan's other two discourses, and will always operate under these, as our subjectivity is always implicated, and this is where my second suggestion for teaching the techniques of 'authorship' becomes important.

As well as offering students conceptual frameworks and skills in mastery and knowledge acquisition, I believe we need to treat their desires and unconscious seriously. Thus, my second suggestion is that we train our students in emotional literacy, so that cognitive and emotional skills go hand in hand. Part of this would just be to create a container[5] for them so that their trauma is not too great so as to inhibit their functioning. This is possible, partly through our operations of The Discourse of Mastery and the University, where we lay out strict ground rules to give them security, but ones based on fairness, and therefore knowledge. Here, the producer in *La Nuit Américaine* fulfils this function; using the Discourse of the Master, he calmly controls the money and tells it 'how it is', forcing Truffaut to make changes to get the film shot. He shows that actions have consequences, yet he nevertheless supports Truffaut.

However, holding our students is not enough. We might have very happy students, but not necessarily very productive ones. Jean Laplanche called trauma 'the enigmatic message' (1998: 265), by which he meant that trauma is that message/signifier which we cannot understand or integrate and which passes from the past to the present and back again, being constantly reinterpreted. The creativity of making something from nothing, of making a film, involves just this engagement with trauma, as Truffaut so exquisitely demonstrates. We have to ask our students at some point to engage with the nothingness of creativity, the blank page, and they have to be supported in their coping strategies. At the University of Wales Newport we always start the first year course with a self-portrait project. We expect them to interrogate their history and make sense of it. This, at some level, aims to promote a helpful engagement with the student's hysteria, and therefore their own personal investment in the knowledge that they learn. This may be achieved in two ways. The first, and perhaps the most creative, is again, part of the holding technique. If we set the students strict boundaries, i.e. production briefs and so forth, we are bound to produce hysteria and rebellion in them. This is where the use of Lacan's Discourse of the Master, where the imposition of our will creates inevitable backlash, repressed under the bar on the right ($). It is different from the Discourse of the University because it actually demands the students to obey, without having to give an explanation. We impose our hidden desire on our students to perform and their knowledge is supported by their split subjectivity, their own hysteria, revealing their own questions and doubts about our authority. They engage with trauma through a symptomatic or rebellious defence against it, often a productive defence.

If the student becomes hystericised through our exercise of the Discourse of Mastery, then they cannot settle on a fixed identity, they cannot fall back on cliché or convention. However, this may provoke another 90 per cent turn so that they become agents in the Discourse of the Hysteric:

$$
\begin{array}{ccc}
& \text{impossibility} & \\
\text{Child (\$)} & \rightarrow & \text{Parent/Master (}S_1\text{)} \\
\uparrow \text{ ----------} & & \text{--------------------} \downarrow \\
\text{Desire (a)} & // & \text{Knowledge (}S_2\text{)} \\
& \text{inability} &
\end{array}
$$

This posits the student filmmaker as a child at the Oedipal stage in the symbolic encounter with society and makes them ask what Lacan called the hysterical questions 'Am I a Man or A Woman?', and 'Am I Alive or Dead?' They are trying to find out from us, as surrogate parents, the secret of our desire, in order to conform to it. Alphonse (played by Jean-Pierre Leaud, Truffaut's long term surrogate from his autobiographical films) is the character most operating under the Discourse of the Hysteric within the film. He is hystericised by not feeling able to act well in the film, then by Julie Baker sleeping with him and subsequently rejecting him, and he then applies the discourse himself, cruelly trying to break up Julie's marriage by revealing her adultery to her new husband. He acts exactly like a child with no parental boundaries in a difficult situation. Whilst it might not be possible to change his behaviour, it is the responsibility of Truffaut to control it, something he fails to do, and this is his failure of responsibility. Film Schools also have their responsibilities; they must often act as arbiters between students, making sure that their students pull their weight in their production teams, and that there is no favouritism or bullying. However, this is harder to achieve with large class sizes and limited resources. Nevertheless, Film Schools often act as primal parents, themselves acting under the Discourse of the Master - not telling students what they want from them, but making plain their unconscious desire, which is that the students should be a) creative geniuses, b) make lots of publicity and money for the school c) not cause trouble or appear to fail in attendance – in summary be a success and produce something new from nowhere. This is the bad side of film schools and the side we should try to avoid, by being clear, and also by understanding our own unconscious motivations to force the productivity of our students. The Master, also, too often degenerates into a primal figure, inhibiting the students through powerful super-egoic constraint. It is not enough merely to discipline students, I think we need to love and nurture them. Too often, the Master offered to film students and filmmakers is a masculine one. The teacher, the film director as father, and this, in my personal experience, has been more frequently foregrounded, with less than perfect results for those women who wish to enter filmmaking. We need a mother figure as well as a father, in order to establish a more properly Lacanian symbolic triad. Thus the lecturer holds the students and the institution creates a symbolic which is not arbitrary but consensual. With increasing student numbers and financial pressures, and with the complexity of film practice courses, this does not always happen, and I believe we cannot have a successful student community without a functioning academic body within the discipline as such and within individual institutions. Here, the historical dysfunction between film theory and practice and between theoreticians and practitioners can hardly be doing our students any good.

None of Lacan's Four Discourses are either good or bad, but have both good and bad consequences. The helpful part of The Discourse of the Hysteric is that it promulgates healthy rebellion. Handled carefully and with the other discourses it can create a fertile intextual relationship between rules of genre and its performance. In *La Nuit Américaine* the poor prop man, faced with the knowledge that he should have produced another cat, trapped by the situation ($), a moment where split subjectivity comes into the open, expressed as hysteria, uses this to gain a closer access to the make up girl who he desires. The lead actress, traumatised by the death of her male co-star, produces the dialogue that enables the film to be successfully completed. Surely, film education must have some element of this, to force students into really committing their subjectivities to their work. For me, this is through our operation of the Discourse of Mastery with as little hysteria as possible. Hysteria is an inevitable part of the production process, and we do not need to increase it with our agency as teachers. Rather we need to manage it and hold the students so that they can place their insecurities within a solid framework.

The Discourse of the Hysteric provokes the agent/film-maker into a confrontation with their own trauma and sometimes a resolution where they reinterpret the trauma in the light of their current understanding. Thus the Discourse has to be entered into in order for a psychoanalytic subject to achieve a 'working through'. In the psychoanalytic session, therefore, the analyst may need to provoke the patient's hysteria in order to make them reassess their behaviour and bring them to a more pertinent self-understanding and self-narrative. In filmmaking, this is exactly what we need to do with students and their scripts. We need to make them discover what it is that drives their scripts. We encourage them away from convention and towards the expression of experience and of imagination. Thus we may need to provoke their hysteria in order to resolve it. However, in provoking them into the Discourse of the Hysteric, there is a danger that we ourselves accept our role as Master and tell students the answers to the questions of their desire. This is terribly dangerous as we cannot know this and we will only provoke them to overthrow us as Masters. Instead we must show them how to find their identity. This is the Discourse of the Analyst:

$$
\begin{array}{ccc}
& \text{impossibility} & \\
\text{Desire (a)} & \rightarrow & \text{Split subjectivity (\$)} \\
\uparrow \; \text{------------------} & & \text{-----------------------} \; \downarrow \\
\text{Knowledge (S}_2\text{)} & // & \text{Master Signifier (S}_1\text{)} \\
& \text{inability} &
\end{array}
$$

Thus, the teacher in the position of Agent addresses the student in their split subjectivity, and offers them a set of interpretations which enables the student to discover their Master Signifier, i.e. what is driving them. In *La Nuit Américaine* this is actually what Julie (Bisset) does for Truffaut. In talking, she presents him with what he needs for his script. He is then able to continue. He also does this for her. When she is hysterical with grief at the supposed failure of her marriage, he gives her what she most wants – the illogical and nonsensical object of desire (a), the pat of butter. As teachers, we do this for students through our feedback processes, on their scripts and their films. By a simple, almost Socratic method, we can read their scripts and interpret back to them how the scripts are producing meaning, but we must do this, not just through the Discourse of the University, but also through the Discourse of the Analyst, listening to the students' desire expressed in their scripts and in what they say about them. The question 'I understand the script to mean this, is this what you want?' is how we might approach a student's work. It is for this reason that we need subtle and complex frameworks, like a psychoanalyst, to register what is lurking latently within the script as well as its attempt to fulfil a brief or conform to a template. I am not at all in favour of psychoanalysing students or subjecting them to obtrusive personal investigation. This would not be treating them as subjects spoken by discourse. Instead, what I'm suggesting is that we treat the work, the film, in this way. It is this performance which needs to be subjected to such an analysis, and then referred back to the student. This way we enable to the student to find their Master Signifier, what they need for the film to work. Of course, in encouraging the exercise of filmmaking authorship we would be encouraging the students' ability and independence to become adept at this practice both within their own work and in their work with others, as crew, as fellow critics, as friends. The sophisticated filmmaker engages with this practice as central to their filmmaking, whether they are conscious of it or not. Our encouragement of this 'Authorship' skill within the Academy is central, and I believe should be our core skill, carried out through an iterated practice of close textual analysis of all kinds of films and texts, not just student texts, so that students can see that all filmmaking is governed by the same activity.

The Discourse of the filmmaker is thus like the practice of the analyst. We must place our desires on the line, supported by our knowledge of film practice, theory and history, and use this to find a Master Signifier, in our textual palimpsest (our working copy of our film) and then we can use this understanding and connection to meaning in order to make a film which communicates.

The danger in the way I have been talking about authorship skills as discursive performativity is that this is too easily misunderstood to mean that the surface of communication means everything. When training filmmakers we need to arouse their imaginations bodily and experientially and we can only engage with their feelings and desires if we do so. Teaching students filmmaking only from a text based approach is like being an actor who only acts from the neck up. Nevertheless, Lacan's insight is to treat these emotions, these bodily experiences, as imbricated and bisected by language, made meaningful by language, and this again enables us to find a conceptual framework within which to work with emotion, experience and performance.

At the end of *La Nuit Américaine*, one actor is dead through an accident. The love affairs created on the film go wrong and Alphonse betrays Julie through The Discourse of the Hysteric when he phones her elderly husband to tell him about their one night stand. He tries to destroy the filming process and almost succeeds, yet goes on successfully to star in other films. His primal influence is negative, and perhaps it is not our job to teach students not to be primal. Yet, our example should enable them to surmount the hysterias that beset filmmaking, and enable the 'family' of the film to be a functional and a 'good enough' team. Yet, at the end of the film, one of the actors is dead, lost through the process of filmmaking – he is killed in a road accident provoked by hard work and the film impinging on his personal life. Surely, this shows us that filmmaking is all about loss, and about making good this loss. The action of the therapist and the therapeutic relationship is frequently to accomplish the act of symbolic castration, so that patients understand the nature of trauma and loss, and accept it. Anything we can do to treat our students work likewise will enable them to create a fictional world that repairs their psychic world, and this is surely to be desired.

BIBLIOGRAPHY

Barthes, R, (1977) 'The Death of the Author', in Barthes, *Image-Music-Text*. Glasgow: Fontana, 142–9.

Bronfen, Elizabeth (1998) *The Knotted Subject: Hysteria and its discontents*. Princeton, NJ: Princeton University Press, 8–12.

Bowie, M. (2000) 'Psychoanalysis and Art: The Winnicott Legacy', in L. Caldwell (ed.) *Art, Creativity, Living*. London and New York: Karnac Books, 11–29.

Burke, S. (1998) *The Death and Return of the Author: Criticism and Subjectivity*. Edinburgh: Edinburgh University Press.

Butler, J. (1997a) *Excitable Speech: A Politics of the Performative*. London: Routledge, 129–33.

_____ (1997b) *The Psychic Life of Power: Theories in Subjection*. California: Stanford University Press.

Lacan, J. (2007) *D'un Discours qui ne Serait pas du Semblant*. Séminaire XVIII, Paris: Seuil. 1970–1971.

_____ (2001) 'Radiophonie', in *Autres écrits*. Paris: Seuil, 1970, pp. 403–448.

_____ (1999). *Encore*. Séminaire XX, Paris: Seuil,1972–1973, pp. 1–135.

_____ (1991) *L'Envers de la Psychanalyse*. Séminaire XVII, Paris: Seuil. 1969–1970, pp. 1–246.

Laplanche, J. (1998) 'Notes on Afterwardsness', in J. Fletcher (ed.) *Essays on Otherness*. London: Routledge, 265.

McKee, R. (1999) *Story: Substance, Structure, Style, and the Principles of Screenwriting*. New York, London: Methuen.

Rose, J. (1998) 'Negativity in the Work of Melanie Klein', in J. Phillips and L. Stonebridge (eds) *Reading Melanie Klein*. London: Routledge, 126–59.

Segal, H. (1991) *Dream, Phantasy and Art*. London: Routledge.

Verhaeghe, P. (1995) 'From Impossibility to Inability: Lacan's Theory of the Four Discourses', *The Letter*, 3, Spring, 76–100.

FILMOGRAPHY

Augustine (1993) Directed by Coral Houtman [DVD]. Newport: Coral Houtman (coral.houtman@newport.ac.uk)

La Nuit Américaine (1973) Directed by François Truffaut [DVD].Amazon: Warner Home Video.

NOTES

1 For a comprehensive exploration of postmodern authorship theory, see S. Burke (1998) 'The Death and Return of the Author: Criticism and Subjectivity', in *Barthes, Foucault and Derrida*. Edinburgh: Edinburgh University Press.

2 The Discourse of the Master is primarily concerned with the implementation of orders; The Discourse of the University is overtly about the imparting and discovering of knowledge; The Discourse of the Hysteric challenges the Master Discourse; and the Discourse of the Analyst offers the analysand the secret of their desire. Verhaeghe has condensed the theory from several short mentions in Lacan's seminar *L'Envers de la psychoanalyse* (1991: 1–246), *Radiophonie* (2001: 403-408). They are also discussed in the next seminar: *D'Un discourse qui ne serait pas du semblant* (2007), and in Seminar XX, *Encore* (1975: 1–135).

3 I have interpreted these symbols fairly freely within the equations cited here in order to interpret Lacan for a general audience not familiar with his psychoanalytic concepts. Lacan himself uses these terms in a structural way, enabling each one to be interpreted in several ways according to position and context. By choosing more easily understandable terms and contexts, I am aware that I may occasionally be filling his 'structure' with inappropriate 'contents' or narrowing down the scope of interpretation of the equations.

4 See also Butler 1997b.

5 Wilfred R. Bion coined the term container as the result of the interaction of projective and introjective identifications between mother and infant, or more specifically between the infant and the breast. The maternal container must be robust enough to contain and accept the infant's projections. (See Segal, 'Mental Space and Elements of Symbolism' in *Dream, Phantasy and Art* (1991: 49–64.) However, the idea originates in Melanie Klein and is also further developed by

Donald Winnicott. In her article on 'Negativity in the work of Melanie Klein', Jacqueline Rose argues that a fundamental tenet of Klein's work is the void at the heart of subjectivity and the need for both mother and child to create a space which is not void and which enables creativity (1998: 126–60). Winnicott argues that the object of creativity is a transitional object – between self and other, and that the object can only be created in the space occupied both by the patient and the therapist (see Bowie 2000: 11–29).

CHAPTER 10
JUST BECAUSE YOU HAVE EYES
DOES NOT MEAN YOU CAN SEE

Peter Greenaway

This is an article written for the Italian newspaper *La Republica* on the occasion of the projection of an elucidating light programme onto the original surface of the da Vinci painting of *The Last Supper* in the refectory of Santa Maria del Grazia in Milan.

There was considerable opposition to this project in some art circles in Italy on account of fears of deteriorating the original fragile painting by the projection of light, by excessive peopling of the refectory space, and on account of academic prejudices arising out of a perceived assault on the orthodoxy of standard art historical practices.

In the event, the prejudices were overcome and the projection went ahead with great success and delight. It is the second event in a series of nine investigative dialogues to be held between the languages of painting and cinema that started in 2006 with Rembrandt's *The Nightwatch* in the Rijksmuseum in Amsterdam and will finish with Michelangelo's *The Last Judgment* in the Vatican, Rome, in 2012, via, amongst other paintings, Veronese's *Marriage at Cana* in the Louvre, Paris, Velasquez's *Las Meninas* in the Prado, Madrid, and Picasso's *Guernica* in the Reina Sophia, Madrid.

Peter Greenaway, Milan, June 2008

The business of seeing and looking is curious. Just because you have eyes does not mean that you can see. We all have to learn to see. We have all watched a baby lying on his back staring fascinated apparently at nothing or at very little, a space of light on a ceiling, a conjunction of simple shapes where ceiling meets a wall. We have tried to follow his eye line and wondered what it is he is actually staring at with such intense concentration, repeatedly returning to examine and make sense of what he is looking at, at things that to us seem extremely minimal and ephemeral. These early stages of looking are often physiological, intensely retinal, grappling with the muscles and the lenses of the eye, discovering how they can be used and to what end, and when the baby moves his head and slightly changes his point of view, we can often see him start and stare with a newer surprise and a greater sense of discovery. If we are going to be successful at manoeuvring on Earth, we need to understand with our two eyes, our bifocal vision, how to understand and appreciate space, how not to fall downstairs, how to negotiate a corner, how to distinguish light from dark, texture from a plain surface, one colour from another. In a sense this education never ceases, though it is surprising how very quickly we gather in an ability to visually comprehend our surroundings.

We can talk about these things, give these experiences names and explanations, we can in effect discuss them as a grammar of seeing, two dimensions against three, geometric and aerial and false perspective, colour-coding, true and false representation, visual exaggeration. We can get even cleverer and start talking in technically visual terms; we can discuss and explain anamorphosis, entasis, chiaroscuro, sfumato. To make an analogy, we can in effect manoeuvre in speech communication very effectively without knowing consciously about grammar. Understanding what a gerund or a past infinitive or the dative case is, is not essential when ordering the groceries and it is not essential, though it is very fascinating, to know that when we stare with admiration at a tree on a hill, that our bifocal vision is offering our brain extraordinary sensations of light against dark, flat against solid, gradations of highlights down to glooms, minute shifts of colour concentration.

This sort of examination of our environment is the stuff of the really professional lookers and watchers and see-ers and these people for at least eight thousand years have been painters. Until the invention of photography, and then the whole plethora of visual artists that have followed on the invention of photography, these people, the painters, were responsible for training our eyes to see and to look, and of course along with their newer cousins with all their mechanical and photographic toys, they still are. We underestimate their contribution to our understanding of the world. We are always seeing the world though their eyes. We have been trained by them to see the world. It has been said that your grandmother (without in any way underestimating her good intentions and bright insights) knows practically nothing about Picasso, but Picasso, you can be certain, knows everything about your grandmother.

These painters are the grammarians of seeing and looking, although there again, although Della Francesca and Poussin and Seurat and Paul Klee might know and understand the minutiae of what they were doing and be able to talk about it eruditely, many painters would not find it necessary to elucidate such things intellectually, but would have learnt them nonetheless by intense concentration and endless observation. It has often been said that they best way to visually understand an object is to draw it. And we owe these painters an enormous debt. They have taught us how to see and to look, and our cities and architecture, our objects and artifacts, and our man-manicured landscapes have been arranged and constructed according to what they have taught us. To understand what they have taught us is important and in the huge burgeoning of contemporary interest in painting is evidence that we are starting to understand the significance of what their contribution has been, and still is, all about.

The sophistications of the laptop generation which is now practically everyone in the world aged between 13 and 30 and who have access to electricity, are profound and intense. They have rapidly become excessively familiar with today's tools of communication. And they expect the world – and I believe quite rightly – to respond to their sophistications. What they see and experience in the commercial marketplace which teaches them what to appreciate, value and buy and imitate and consume, sets them up with interpretive languages which they are going to use everywhere on every occasion. If we are going to wish to educate these people to a greater comprehension of what we believe to be valuable, then we are going to have to use the sophisticated tools they know and use and expect and can understand.

There have been a series of profound visual works in the world in the last two thousand years, benchmark works that have expanded and developed and enlarged our vision of ourselves. Da Vinci's *The Last Supper* is undoubtedly one of these profound works. A benchmark painting invariably makes a leap forward and embraces and consolidates an idea or series of ideas in encapsulated economic substantial form. Life is amorphous, often unshaped, multidirectional, full of ephemeralities and inconsequences, discontinuities, dead-ends, cul-de-sacs and long stretches of tedium and repetition and reprising. It is the very nature of life. A successful artwork takes this stuff of life and gives it shape, drops out the irrelevancies, sieves away the inconsequences, invents systems and economies to make an overview and recapitulation of what is essential.

Leonardo has a number of strategies in *The Last Supper*, some old and familiar, some new, and he uses them all with great skill to make a presentation, an exhibition, an image of steadiness and harmony, an image designed for contemplation. What he puts in, we must take out. What he engineers we must fathom. What he builds and constructs we must comprehend. To do this we must use, as all artists and their communicators have always done, the technological tools and comprehension of our contemporary times. Painters as various as Uccello and Leonardo used the new geometrical aids and navigational and astronomical technology of their age, Durer and Canaletto used the optical tools of their age, Vermeer used the camera obscuras of the 1660s, the Pre-Raphaelites used the newly discovered colour-dyes, the French Impressionists used photographic tools, the Italian futurists used the cinematic tools.

That is our intention here. We aim to utilise the technological tools of our age, the tools that the laptop user is familiar with, to elucidate the visual world of our heritage of which Leonardo's *Last Supper* most certainly is part. We use these tools to emphasise, explain, demonstrate, underline, suggest and explore what Leonardo was doing, show his intention with the dance of hands, the turning and twisting of the profiles, show how he posited these thirteen figures in a given architectural space, show how the lines of perspective in two dimension are carried on in three dimensions, show how his symbolic Christian use of the grouping of threes gives metaphor to the unity of the painting, God the Father, God the son, God the Holy Ghost, a visual litany of Christian mythology based on something much much older which also suggests the triangular nature of stasis and harmony and equality; show how he used his vocabulary of different comprehensions first for the table and then for the figures, then for the architecture, bringing them all into alignment; demonstrate how the outline and the silhouette is used for dramatic effect, even hinting his apparent prophetic construction of cosmographies. This painting is no mere rendering of surface, no mere recording of visual ephemeralities; it is not a Polaroid photograph picking up visual anecdotes by accident, it is not a frozen frame, it is a fully rational and very careful construction, a thing made, a thing extremely well-wrought, well manufactured, well and intelligently engineered in all its parts, in all its substances.

In the end it would seem to be perverse not to do these things, not to use the new tools and their concomitant characteristics and the philosophies that are constructed around them because of their appearance on the human landscape of comprehension: it would be a dereliction of opportunity not to use our best abilities and greatest intelligences and most sophisticated tools to acknowledge his best abilities and great intelligences. The sceptical critics, reluctant to let contemporary sensibilities tackle Leonardo's insights, because they believe the preserve is theirs to enumerate with old tools and out-dated curiosities, are satisfied with too little. They want a dead monument, sub-scribed by academia, to be made untouchable, the book of understanding closed, because they think they have closed it. They mis-use, mis-understand, and mis-apprehend the heritage. Leonardo would be the first to make them a caricature of fusty misinformation.

Let us exchange intelligences, spiritual, intellectual, emotional. To acknowl-edge in a dialogue from us to him, we can offer intellectual exchange with our tools to his tools. To say in effect we understand and respect and admire without constraint this extraordinary thing you did. How you made this great thing that sings to us, resounds with us, believer, unbeliever, Christian, non-Christian agnostic, atheist, that makes us proud and confident that such things can be made, comprehended, understood. We are capable of this. This is no mere Son et Lumière cheap and vulgar exposition of externals, exploited for a five-minute wonder, it is to be a dialogue to be held with pride that we can be so civilised and exchange such significances. Despite all inequalities, medioc-rities, inadequacies, injustices – hey! this is us. Civilisation can do this. This is what we can do. Through you, we can do this! We can make this thing. Make, mark and view this thing together.

In the world at large there is a fascinating revolution taking place. Some talk of it as a seismic shift in understanding. For eight thousand years it can be said that the information gatekeepers of civilisation have been the text-mas-ters. These word practitioners, the advocates, the orators, the speakers, the word-smiths, the word engineers, have created our politics, our holy books, our laws, codified our thinking, fashioned our vocabularies. Now post the digital revolution, these guys are going to have to move over and make way for the image-masters, the gatekeepers of the visual. This presents us with a problem because our visual education in the world is undernourished, impov-erished, and not prioritised in our education systems. We have to seriously get going and really do something about this state of affairs. In the end it will always be true that the image always has the last word - indeed the written word is an image. The word is an ineffectual insubstantial temporary tool of historical and geographical limitation when placed alongside the image. We must transform our visual illiteracy.

CHAPTER 11
THEORY FOR PRACTICE: CECI N'EST PAS L'ÉPISTÉMOLOGIE

Brian Winston

If one is in the business of teaching documentary film production, it is a very good idea to ensure one's students avoid early editions of Bordwell and Thompson's cinema studies textbook, *Film Art*. Suddenly (for instance, on page 128 of the 3rd edition (1997)), in the midst of a theoretical discussion of non-narrative films, these eminent scholars are pitching, by way of example of a documentary type they have identified, a movie:

> Suppose we are setting out to make a film about our local grocery store ... We could go through the store and film each portion, to show what sort of things the store contains. We might show the meat section, the produce section, the checkout counters, and other categories within the store. (1997: 128)

And, if they were your production students presenting your class with such a film, you would have to give them a 'C' – or worse.

What is awry here is that this procedure does not suggest a documentary. It suggests rushes and to be fair to them the passage has been dropped in later editions. (They also, however, suggested a film about butterflies which 'might use scientific groupings, showing one type of butterfly and giving information about its habits, then showing another with more information, and so on'. This collection of rushes, willfully ignoring the compelling narrative of pupae to flying insect, they are still pitching (2004:123). 'C' again, I'm afraid.)

Pregnant though this example from *Film Art* is for those who would dismiss the usefulness of film theoreticians to the business of practice teaching, this does not mean that there is consistently nothing in theory of value to the production class. After all, the very possibility that theory must be inevitably irrelevant to practice is, pace *Film Art*'s documentary proposals, an Anglo-Saxon absurdity – a riff on the 'those who can do, those who can't teach' crassness than which little is as stupid. The Bordwell-Thompson grocery store and butterfly films are rare examples of high theoreticians essaying what amounts to practical guidance rather than the usual analysis of existing texts. This later work, however, is crucial to our understanding and, it must be said, it has few practitioners (as it were) as acute and astute as Thomson and Bordwell. Analysis necessarily informs the sensibilities and responses of students and practice teachers without due consideration of which they would be potentially doomed to live the unexamined creative life. Of course, this is self-evident. Without analysis we are compelled to repeat history as farce, reinvent the wheel, be *Groundhog Day* prisoners.

The clue to the hostility to theory often (and vehemently) asserted by practice teachers lies in the definition of the very word. In English, one meaning of 'theory' is that it is the extraction from practice of a body of 'rules, ideas and principles and techniques that applies to a particular subject' (to quote the OED); and these (the obvious result of analysis) are distinct from the practice itself. Alternatively, a second meaning has it that 'theory' can be divorced from practice and relates to abstract thought or contemplation. (There are other less pertinent meanings but in this context these will suffice to illustrate how the supposed theory/practice chasm in Anglophone film education arises.) What practitioners (and those who teach practice) commonly mean by 'theory', it would seem, is only the later second meaning – the abstract stuff which is allegedly such anathema to the practical Anglo-Saxon mind. Continental Europeans seem less inhibited with their *auteurisme* and *dogmes*; but in Anglophone realms theory that can be abstracted from practice, the first meaning, is somehow not considered 'theory' at all.

Take Alan Rosenthal, as crucial a pioneer of documentary film studies as anybody and, I must confess, a colleague with whom I have had the honour of making a documentary or two. Rosenthal, an Oxford and Stanford graduate with more than three decades of filmmaking and sixty titles to his credit, has consistently maintained his hostility to what he thinks of as 'theory' even as he has, with book after book, contributed to it – or at least to its unacknowledged first meaning.

His handbook, *Writing, Directing and Producing the Documentary Film*, for example, promises that: '*Rather than dealing with theory...* he tackles the day-to-day problems' (1990, emphasis added). The negative part of this claim is more than a little fraudulent (and a good thing too, I would have thought, given the book comes from an academic press). This is primarily because Rosenthal is at pains to stress the importance of structuring material; and, both as a filmmaker and a teacher, he knows that without story – narrative -- documentaries will always work (to use a phrase of Dai Vaughan's) 'better in the head than on the screen' (1983: 75). Bordwell and Thompson's search for non-narrative documentaries, when it is not ignoring narratives in documentaries they claim have no such thing, cite films – Les Blank's *Gap-Toothed Women* (1987), for example – which perfectly illustrate the truth of this. Such documentaries, even the best of them, Humphrey Jennings' *Words for Battle* (1941) for example, always play 'better in the head than on the screen'; and I know from my own experience of Rosenthal how well he understands this and how meticulous he is about avoiding non-narrative difficulties.

When working with him on a film about the Holocaust, in a footling (albeit unconscious) attempt to apply *Film Art* principles of the 'categorical' documentary, I decided that the way to deal with the history of Nazi persecution in the 1930s was by utilising the following format: medieval Anti-Semitism said 'you cannot live amongst us as Jews'; modern 'political' Anti-Semitism argued 'you cannot live amongst us'; the Nazis said, 'Jews, you cannot live'. This led me to produce a draft script in which an account of the development of Nazi Anti-Semitic legislation ('you cannot live amongst us') starts with the Nuremburg Decrees, 1935. These were therefore placed in a draft script before the start of the 'you cannot live' phase, dated to the establishment of the first concentration camp, Dachau, 1933. Alan was quick to point out that the script, however elegantly obedient to these categories, deeply offended the chronological imperative of the narrative. 1935 has to come after 1933 if the audience is not, as it were, to loose the plot. This quite proper insistence on chronology rather than clever, clever 'categories' was of course exactly the result of his extracting from his experience of creating effective communications ('practice') a specific theory of how to do this when making history documentaries.

Of course, he did not see it this way. In rejecting my draft, Rosenthal did not bother with any of the extensive theoretical work on narratology. Barthian hermeneutics, Genetttean iterations or Seymour Chatman's chrono-logic and so forth were not played into the argument. He was merely being 'practical'; but what he presented as (*de facto*) experiential is theoretically grounded all the same. Rosenthal has a theory, whether he calls it that or not. When the blurb on the latest edition of his handbook states that he stresses 'story telling' (2008) (while, by the way, abandoning that rather silly claim to be eschewing theory), it is merely acknowledging this fact. All practice-based teaching of, exactly, writing, directing and producing any film is necessarily theory-based in the sense I am suggesting the word must be used.

And so what is more useful – especially to those (students, say) who lack the decades of practice of a Rosenthal? Just being told that experience, which must be obeyed, says 'do this'; and that those (film studies theoreticians) whose experience is merely of watching the screen have nothing to say on the matter? Or, instead, being taken through theory-based analysis which offers reasons for obedience but at the same time lays a foundation of insight that allows for rules to be questioned and, indeed, broken? This choice is, to use a theoretical term, a 'no-brainer'.

I would argue the need for theory does not just apply to documentary nor just to narratology. All of theory (even 'post-theory' musings) can be of value to all of film production teaching. It does, however, need integration into the practice strand of a programme and, certainly at university level, this melding can be hard to come by.

First there is the hostility between the two camps most vividly expressed, if the faculty is large enough, in different departments. The film production teaching staff are often at odds with the film studies professors or visa versa. The theory lot can be merely a service department providing 'Film 101' and a bit here and a bit there to satisfy the overall institutional requirements of traditional pedagogy – book-based learning delivered in lectures and seminars and assessed via papers and exams. The only gesture to the specificity of the subject is the augmentation of the reading list with screenings.

The theory people can regard the practice teachers dismissively as (to use a term once current at one institution where I have laboured) 'woodworkers'. For a practice teacher, making one's way in the academy on the basis of one's professional qualifications alone is still hard. Continuing to work as a media professional can count for little. This is in contrast, it can be noted, to the acceptance, as legitimate academic enterprise, of other artistic performance of all kinds, say in music as well as the plastic arts.

In more traditional universities, student practice is only grudgingly admitted as assessable. One finds extraordinary cavortings – a course on film sound which is forced to require written descriptions of hypothetical soundscapes when what should be (and easily could be) created and assessed are the soundscapes themselves. In another, final projects, which were made but deemed unsuitable for assessment, had to be outlined on paper under exam conditions. The university in question had regulations which demanded no less. And this is also true of doctoral work. The solution to the endless debate around allowing 'practice-based' theses in the arts is easily solved. Just demand 100,000 written words of commentary (preferably with lots of footnotes as well) and the institution can pride itself on its academic adventurousness.

For practice teachers caught in such a position of enforced inferiority, a defensive hostility is a quite natural and, in my view, excusable reaction. After all, why are institutions hosting production courses at all? Why are they hiring people (scandalously unacademic!!) whose only value is the small matter of them knowing how to teach practice on the basis of their own experience? The answer, obviously, is student demand. The hypocrisy of the universities is self-evident; but this doesn't make things any easier to bear. The despised practitioner is made not more happy with her lot knowing that without her efforts the finances of the university's media education operation (and the 'areas studies' department in which it is often embedded) would collapse. The institution, also understanding this, can be nevertheless ever more adamant that insistence on its traditional ways and 'standards' is justified.

So is the answer then the free-standing film academy? Well, not entirely. These can often seem to be intent on twisting the concept of the conservatory into a trade school so firmly do they turn their face from offering anything other than practical training. They are aided in this by the fact that, when Anglo-Saxon practitioners within the film industry come up with something recognisably theoretical, it is likely to be nonsense. Take the shibboleth of 'three-act structure', as artificial a construct as any produced by scholarly theorising. It is clearly a theory, a paradigm supposedly explaining how mainstream narrative films are structured. It is offered up with a promise that utilising the formula will produce the grail of saleable commercial scripts (for example, Syd Field's *Screenplay: The foundations of screenwriting* (2005) – 'a bible of the trade'). Nevertheless, even praying in Aristotle does not alter the fact that this is to the analysis of narrative what flat-earthism is to astronomy. It does not begin to explain the structure of even Hollywood movies. The 'three-act' 'trade' gurus have extracted a theory from practice but having done so in so simple minded a fashion as to make their conclusion about as useful in helping a production student understand story-telling as Ptolemaic astronomy is. Collectively, Barthes, Genette and the other narratologists simply do an incomparably better job.

Film students, like their practice teachers, often simply do not want to know. They can be eager to support their instructor's prejudices against film studies and not just simply because they disdain traditional academy learning requirements. They are, after all, also bolstered by that nineteenth-century rhetoric about art which makes them, to use Coleridge's term, a 'clerisy' wherein artists are deemed to be 'the antenna of the race'; or rather, they are novices to that clerisy. Although the privileging of art as the 'the best that has been thought and said in the world' does not, obviously, preclude the legitimacy of training, it can suggest that creativity springs fully-formed from the students' mind and this can be stifled by externally imposed more formal knowledge. It is as if there is an assumption that the analysis of creativity somehow destroys it. Intuition trumps inference. Sustained by this vision, film students can be so intent on their own creativity that they have little time and less patience with any distractions from this – even, say, the straightforward screenings of the work of others, much less the more cerebral considerations of what others have done before. Far from avoiding reinventing the wheel, reinvention is what too many of them aspire to (and, indeed, is the only thing with which they are at ease). This is true of those within the university and is possibly even truer within the free-standing film conservatory

This, then, is the environment of film production teaching. The practitioners pour scorn on the scholars and hold their analyses to be incomprehensible irrelevances. The academy barely tolerates practitioners and thinks their more abstract musings are inadequate inanities. Students, 'great artists' in the making, are in the middle. What, as the man once said, is to be done?

Well, first, I suppose, the entire Anglo-Saxon structure of the theory/practice divide needs to be acknowledged for the debilitating distraction that is. This does not mean, of course, the wholesale acceptance of the entire corpus of film studies. One is more than entitled to pick-and-choose, accepting one opinion or approach while rejecting another. After all this is what the scholars themselves do, sometimes with venom. Scholarship is not static and, indeed, its dynamism is often seen as a species of faddism, with one paradigm or focus (replete with its own arcane neologisms) succeeding another in popularity. Confronted by, say, post-post-modernism it is easy to mock; but so to do is to ignore what in the academically fashionable (or, indeed, in the previously fashionable) might be useful for the teaching of practice.

The choice of any particular theory, after its fundamental efficacy is determined, obviously depends on the practice teachers' own predilections. Psychologically-based theoretical approaches might be more acceptable to some than are formalist ones; and visa-versa. Apart from history, which it is very hard to see as anything other than foundational, variety is to be welcomed.

Beyond the teachers' preferences, though, there is the need to offer theory which makes sense to a particular student and a particular project. While not accepting that intuition backed by only an unexamined experience of the screen will liberate a student's creativity, nevertheless it must be acknowledged that different students with different projects will find one set of theoretical insights of greater value than another. The instructor's theoretical preferences should take second place to the student's particular needs. With film production, as with all teaching of creativity, the student, not that unusually, can bring to the table material of a highly personal nature. Perhaps it is especially true of documentary, where the possibility of aping mainstream genres is attenuated, but projects so closely related to personal circumstance that dealing with it on film begins to look like therapy is not unknown (I recall a conversation with the Polish director Kristof Zanussi discussing a film-school at which we had both taught. 'Tell me, Brian', he said, 'in America, psychiatrists are paid more than film professors, no?' I concurred that I believed that this was so. 'Next time I go there', he went on, 'I ask to be paid as psychiatrist!!').

The instructor, of course, is the prism through which the student comes to theory but, and this is completely utopian, it would be ideal if the student encountered only those theories which worked for them. In other words, aside from a requirement to experience the history and range of the cinema, rather than a wadge of courses covering, more or less, all the rest of film studies, the student, guided by the instructor, should also be free to pick-and-choose what matters to her or him. And (this is the utopian bit) that alone should be what they are examined on.

This, though, is not entirely impossible but it does involve redesigning the curriculum or (as is far more viable) redesigning the curriculum but not really telling anybody one has done so. The clue is to make the sequence of practica the backbone of the course and to introduce theory as and when needed. The paper trail can show discrete modules on this or that theory but the content of those modules (and their assessment regimes) are folded into the practice sessions. In an informal sense this is far from uncommon. Practitioners sensitive to theory are always citing it in connection with the assign-and-critique process of production teaching. My experience suggests that in the course of working through a selection of projects with a class it is not very often that one finds oneself thinking of a theoretical concept one has not addressed. (This also applies, of course, to more practical but still abstract matters such as relevant media law). It is a question of doing this integration in a systematic way; and in the belief that there are few things of more practical use to a student filmmaker than a pertinent theory.

PS: All the above has, heaven forefend, nothing to do with epistemology.

BIBLIOGRAPHY

Bordwell, D. AND K. Thompson (2004 [1997]) *Film Art*. New York: McGraw Hill.

Field, S. (2005) *Screenplay:The Foundations of Screenwriting*. New York: Delta Trade Paperback.

Rosenthal, A. (2002 [1990]) *Writing, Directing and Producing Documentary Films and Videos*. Carbondale: Southern Illinois University Press.

Vaughan, D. (1983) 'Portrait of An Invisible Man: The Working Life of Stewart McAllister, Film Editor'. London: BFI.

FILMOGRAPHY

Gap-Toothed Women (1987) Directed by Les Blank [Video]. Amazon: Flower Films.

Words for Battle (1941) Directed by Humphrey Jennings [DVD]. Amazon: Image Entertainment.

PART TWO

CONVERSATIONS

CHAPTER 12
FILM AND PHILOSOPHY:
AN INTERVIEW WITH MIKE FIGGIS

Clive Myer

Clive Myer: Having explained the premise of the BEYOND: The Theory of Practice conference I'd be very interested to know your thoughts on the relationship between theory and practice for filmmaking students and, if you like, the impact of philosophy on film practice.

Mike Figgis: On one level I have a big problem with film theory and the kind of focus on film theory in that at the end of the day filmmaking is a very practical business and in fact I remember at one point being rather insulted when someone said to me 'Mike you're not an intellectual, you're a filmmaker' or 'you're an artist but you're not an intellectual'. I was annoyed at the time, although I understood it. My observation as I've grown up and worked in music and then in theatre – experimental theatre and experimental music and then in film, initially fairly experimentally and then as soon as you get into the mainstream you realise that you can't really function experimentally within the mainstream, so you have to bite the bullet and actually get down to the very time consuming and energy consuming business of practically making a film. As you progress obviously you're going through a period of education, every time you make a film you absorb things yourself, you also watch films and so you are constantly trying to answer questions for yourself, but questions that in my case always come from a practical necessity of I want to do something and say something in a different way, I don't want to repeat an idea, although the central image or the philosophical idea behind the image may remain within a very small group – as Louis Bunuel said, three or four ideas may occupy most of your life in terms of your obsession. In general though it's interesting to me when you mentioned in your introduction that at one stage Britain took over from France as the leading theoretical platform for thinking about film in a theoretical way; unfortunately Britain didn't take over as the leading filmmaking community, which I think is a somewhat telling point.

CM: But could it ever have done that, because of the strictures on production and economics and cinema ownership and distribution, exhibition and so on. France and New York had lots of independent cinemas, was Britain ever in a position to be able to do that?

MF: I think so, yes. Britain, like every country in the West or let's say outside of the third world, had as much of an opportunity to become the leading base for film production as anywhere else. It's not an economic problem and it's not particularly a structural problem, although tangentially it is because filmmaking is complex but simple – you need a structure which contains filmmaking, film distribution and film criticism as being an homogeneous body that works together, because once that happens the ability to find or create an independent cinema and screen things is relatively simple because there's a lot of energy going in one direction and if you need an independent cinema, you're making great films and want somewhere just to show them, if they're good films then the place you get to show them will soon be full of people, but that being the very sort of basic law of supply and demand and as with many other things within British culture during the 1960s and early 1970s and so on, and certainly the music scene, that did happen. Of course much simpler; you don't need such big sort of structures – you just need a record player or recording studio or whatever and some venues for bands to play and I've always felt that an inherent problem in British culture to do with its postcolonial intellectual basis was that intellectually we always seem smugly happy to talk endlessly in a very rarified and kind of elitist language about culture and art, very aloof, very Europeanist in a sense that whilst there were very interesting things happening in France certainly, look at the reaction amongst a large number of critics to the Nouvelle Vague and to the work of Jean Luc Godard – fairly contemptuous, fairly dismissive, as if just the French somehow weren't good enough, they didn't cut it for a lot of critics here. As someone who cut my teeth on experimental theatre and performance art, I know from experience that the process of going through British cultural criticism through the magazines, newspapers or whatever the venues would be, was pretty much negative all the time and had I not been in the fortunate position of being able to work in Holland, France, Italy and America most importantly, and in all of those countries to get a very positive, high energy feedback from critics. So working within a group where the feedback was so strong that like a lot of British artists you come to just accept the negativity that comes from British cultural quarters, because you are being sustained in New York, Amsterdam, Paris and Rome and so on.

CM: That's very interesting because you mentioned music and theatre and I suppose we're talking about the late 1960s, early 1970s as the genesis of it. We tried in film and we had the London Filmmakers Co-op, we had Co-ops around the country here, the British Film Institute Production Board was developing and was quite radical though had very little money but the Arts Council were giving out some, yet it happened in music and it happened in fringe theatre. I remember seeing many different productions of fringe theatres, way outstripping the number of possibilities and venues and work coming out of film. Actually I don't understand why it was possible in theatre and music and why wasn't it possible in film do you think?

MF: Because of what I touched on before. Film has a unique position in that it structurally is more lumbering, or it was then, it's no longer but there's interestingly the same problem in theatre, which is that the amount of equipment you need to make a film and project a film and post-produce a film at that time, even if you were shooting on Super16mm or on 16mm, was still a fairly daunting prospect. You needed a budget that would be more than the budget of a theatre and organisationally you needed more. Therefore it required the unification of a certain number of key elements; production, post-production, criticism and it seemed that we had a problem unifying those things outside of a kind of elitist kind of ghetto, like the London Filmmakers Co-op or elements of the old Arts Lab and as you pointed out, certain kinds of places such as Amber Films in Newcastle. Films were produced that were of interest and of note, but we never managed to get together something like the Nouvelle Vague or Dogme now. I still think that the problem is a problem of criticism and of the way things are talked about, but if those factions persevere in maintaining the sort intellectual elitism and snobbery and insist on using the kind of language which when you read about film theory, unless you are a really dedicated intellectual, that sort of idea of a sort of artistic, philosophical, intellectual debate, which to a person who I would call a filmmaking beast, is of no interest really. The energy is completely different; the practical ability of the one person versus the other is completely different. Unless you can find some kind of marriage between those factions, it's never going to be possible to create a vibrant film industry that is an alternative to just importing American films and making clones of them within our own culture.

CM: Apart from the London Filmmakers Co-op, a few film groups and the single filmmaker doing his or her work, which still exists to a certain extent, there are a couple of feature filmmakers who came out of that period – say for example Sally Potter and I suppose Peter Greenaway – I can't historically put Mike Figgis there because you weren't a filmmaker then, but you came out of that period not coming from films, which is very interesting.

MF: I came into film not through a theoretical love of film, in fact I really was much more interested in sound and the use of sound in film and using film as a platform for and I still believe that – the phenomenon of contemporary film is more of a sound environment than necessarily a purely pictorial environment. It's the combination obviously of those elements that make it interesting and unique. When I first came in to film I was working with Diane Tammes who was very closely involved with Laura Mulvey and Peter Wollen, so I was aware of the early Greenaway kind of work, I wasn't really interested in it – I certainly listened and I observed, I didn't find it exciting in any way, whereas I did find Godard exciting and I also found a film like *Bonny and Clyde* (1967) to be very radical and exciting, a film like *In Cold Blood* (1967) had far more influence on me than say *Riddles of the Sphinx* (1977).

CM: The films that came out of that period in the UK have hardly been seen or written about, giving the impression that there was almost no indigenous cinema at all during that period other than a reflection on the European or New York films that were around.

MF: And also there wasn't and there still isn't to me a magazine that wrote about film that satisfied me. There was nothing, and I still feel that way – there isn't a newspaper that I turn to with a sense of enjoyment or I wonder what he or she is going to write about this week that I can engage in – I mean nothing and I find that in general about the way films are written about and certainly, although I faithfully get *Sight and Sound*, I haven't read *Sight and Sound* for a couple of years now. I used to read it more – when I first started making films, to me it was more interesting than all the other magazines that to dealt with film, *Film Premiere* and all those sorts of things, they just seem dreadful. So I really feel there's a huge gap in the market for intelligent conversation about film that isn't so elite it stands to be disconnected.

CM: Where I want to take this is really not to talk about art at all, actually the reasons we were all involved in doing it at that time, which, and tell me immediately if you disagree, but it was actually to do with a political consciousness more than it was to do with actually producing a piece of artwork. The two compounded in some way with an attempt to actually examine art politically.

MF: I think probably the collective philosophy of that period was obviously far more politically radical and open. The result of that was a climate, an atmosphere of genuine interest in the way things functioned and a very healthy idea that questioning was a good thing to do and that process of using whatever it was – film, theatre or music as an extension of one's own desire to look at the world.

CM: And change it?

MF: Not necessarily change it as a kind of goal, in fact that would be the result if you were healthily interested and I would actually make a huge differentiation between those who thought what they were doing was going to change something, which I would never subscribe to, I always found that naïve because after all its art. Art to me can signify change and in some cases can actually be very instrumental and be part of a change, but the function of it really is to ask the question in the first place within the license of art, which is considerable and a privilege and luxury to be part of and I would say the second group were the people who were just genuinely inquisitive and full of a love of life, which automatically made them ask questions and through that energy automatically make changes or open the way to a wider consciousness of wanting change. That to me was very healthy, I was always very wary of the so-called artists who saw themselves as politically significant, because I think that nothing dates a piece of art more than either flared trousers or the awareness of one's own political significance.

CM: Yet you are an admirer of Godard.

MF: Yes, but Godard specifically I think – I just watched *Weekend* (1967) again, projected at the Godard season. I introduced it at the French Institute and thought I'd stay and watch the first twenty minutes, but ended up watching the whole film again. What really struck me about that film and it is my favourite Godard film, although it's not generally thought of as being his best, but it contains so much humour and his view of political change. I think it is exquisitely judged and he never to me has both his feet in the mud – he's always dancing on those things and to me all signifying that he has the right to change his mind a week later if he wants to. So he's never coming in there with this kind of slightly more Germanic kind of force of 'this is what I believe and I will be counted for this'. And he remains an artist.

CM: Except for the period in his life and certain musician's lives where Maoism played a very important part and he made films like *Sympathy for the Devil* (1968).

MF: Sure and even those films remain absurdist in a way, so that to me he's never saying you must take this absolutely seriously, these are ideas that are going through my mind right now and I'm expressing them and I think that's the genius of Godard and I think that is the thing that separates him from all other filmmakers – his ability to keep, even now when we look forty years later, to me he's still dancing on those issues, he's not drilling.

CM: In music some people dealing with those issues went on complete journeys of change and never came back, I'm thinking of Cornelius Cardew for example and the Scratch Orchestra, the Portsmouth Symphonium and the sort of radical, post-John Cage movement.

MF: Again, the problem I have with all of that post Cage radical work is that they started off married to a premise. I mean the group I played with, The People Band, which was a radical avant-garde free jazz group, completely open to any possibility every time they performed, although very quickly like all human groups, it creates a sort of house style and you become aware that certain personalities become alpha and beta and so on. But initially what drew me to them and got me into the People Show and then got me into filmmaking was the openness, conceptually the openness of the possibility rather than to me the leaden British cliché of with trepidation walking into a preconceived intellectual plot, which to me characterises intellectual British life in all walks and I find it deadening, boring, limiting and one of the reasons why the beast doesn't move forward at any speed – it always limits itself before it even gets anywhere by somehow desperately needing the endorsement of an intellectual concept.

CM: You see it's had a big impact on education in as much that's there's now a big subject field called Cultural Studies and that subject field has not only produced theory, it's producing practices within universities, art colleges, film schools and so on, which contributed to the UK Film Council decision to set up the Screen Academies to try to separate out where is the practice and where is the theory. But not to dismiss that, from my perspective because there are some very fundamental interesting issues, alliances and contexts that are outside of the cinematic, shall we say, and in the world of other problems, the world of the subject that you are filming. In the last thirty years because of globalisation in particular and because of how postmodernism recuperates all the radical looking work, then a certain essence from then might remain important rather than dismiss it and say it was useless to us, because how do you counter, an unfashionable word, but how do you set up against an ongoing development which almost isn't possible to mitigate against. For example, I think you personally, if I may say so, handle it in a very interesting schizophrenic way by having one foot in Hollywood and one foot in experimental filmmaking. Other people find it very difficult – I was talking with Noel Burch about George Monbiot who is a Guardian writer and part of the Green movement and wrote a book about globalisation, *The Age of Consent* (2004) on the basis that they've taken everything from us really except our consent, they didn't ask us if they could take everything from us and in some ways Hollywood cinema, 'dollars' cinema and television have not only taken the pound out of our pockets, they've also taken the spirit out of our lives. It's like the Native American idea of not wanting to be photographed because of losing your soul and a certain philosophical level I think that's what film does, inadvertently on one hand, but also with the acquiescent consent of the people on the other hand.

MF: Well it's a strange form of consent because it's a consent that comes from giving people a very limited choice, knowing that there is a desire for the product, it's what I used to call the Marks and Spencer principle where everyone seems very happy with those designs on sweaters with little insignias on. I used to say clothes are much nicer if they don't have insignias on them and somebody said everyone seems to like them and everyone is wearing them and I said they're wearing them because that's the only thing – if they go to British Home Stores or Marks and Spencer's that's all that's available and I feel that way about films. Therefore my point has always been that any kind of radical change in cinema has always got to be the result of the coming together politically if you like of what I said before, the factions of production, post production, distribution. Because unless you strive harder in the more unfashionable areas of cinema, which is distribution and projection and so on and unless someone says I will dedicate myself to that element of future cinema, unless that happens we'll just continue bitching about how Hollywood is stealing from us and so on. The fact is they are doing it quite openly, it's not a secret and it is, particularly now more than ever, within the power of people to really easily create their own cinema and their own ways of projecting films. One also has to take into account, and I had a very interesting discussion with Jeff Wall about this a couple of weeks ago, the world has changed considerably, we have become used to the way films are edited now – they're much quicker, the editing processes, much quicker, than they used to be and its no longer good enough in my opinion to make a slow film and call it an 'arthouse film' and say its deep and meaningful, but of course its not for the mainstream, another form of elitism, if its not for the mainstream then quite frankly its not really for anyone anymore because you're making a film that is kind of an homage to a style of filmmaking that no longer exists. It's fine if that's what you call it, but if you're actually hoping to engage with a tricky subject and with some slightly more profound concepts within a film than as a mainstream Hollywood film, and you'd like it to be seen by as many people as possible, certainly a wider audience than just an elitist gallery audience, then you have to also take into account technically the way you're making the film and it brings up the whole issue of 'is style within itself aesthetically, intellectually a good enough thing or is it merely the thing that services an idea?' and if it's the thing that services the idea then we can't really afford to be so precious about the style elements and then it asks a wider question of the art community in general, the way in which art is developed and presented and iconised very quickly to an elitist audience is surely a kind of rather negative hangover from a time when art patronage, economics, capitalism were functioning in a way that we had very little control over, so we weren't able to influence it in that way. However, that has completely changed to the idea of the single object versus the multiple image and mass reproduction of images, which is a far healthier concept and a logical extension of the printing press and all the other ideas gives us a certain freedom and yet artistically we seem to want to cling on to the idea of elitism, the single image, the iconisation of things, with the idea that the fewer people see it, quantifiably its probably a better thing, it's somehow a more pure object or a more pure art object. So as a filmmaker I come up against these ideas all of the time, one of the most frustrating thing as a filmmaker and as an artist - I really see myself as an artist who makes films or makes music or whatever and I don't feel that's something I really want to spend hours and hours having to justify and yet within the art community the subject of filmmaking is very loaded. They somehow find it very difficult to come to terms with – to me *Bonny and Clyde* is an art movie, it had a huge influence culturally at the time, and it influenced all the films that followed it. It had artistic moments that were more profound than most art films and so on, so to me, although it's a mainstream film, it functions really as a sort of seminal piece of filmmaking and there are other mainstream films one could argue, like *The Godfather* (1972) or whatever, that occupy that same sort of area and yet it's a tricky area and at the end of the day I don't know how important it is that one should care one way or the other, whether it is seen as a piece of art or seen as a functional piece of entertainment and why do we get so concerned about this and why is it so important to us. But it is important because at the end of the day art is important and it matters how work is classified. But all these issues seem to relate to each other.

CM: But as some radical filmmakers and theorists have moved towards content and away from form, you seem to be moving more toward form, not away from content necessarily but more towards form.

MF: Because I think that unless you are aware of form - that the function of form is to reframe ideas on a regular basis, so that you are in the best position to stimulate your audience. An audience that is seeing something that is using form in a newer way will look at that idea in a fresh way. If you constantly repeat the same form, which is the problem of cinema, I mean it's repeated itself to death; you have very little chance of communicating a genuine idea because it's too familiar.

CM: You see Noel Burch, who did used to encourage students in a way to make unreadable films, to deconstruct the codes of Hollywood cinema within our films, has done a *volte face* and gone completely the other way now and is very against any films that are difficult to read, any film that can't get through to the masses and so on, and he loves Michael Moore and that's fine – everyone loves Michael Moore to an extent...

MF: Not this person!

CM: ...but when I went to see *Fahrenheit 911* (2004) the most exciting part to me - and I've seen his live performance on stage and his other films and agree with you in the sense that, well, weren't we doing that in Agit-prop films in the 1960s and 1970s and what's the difference except that he's a personality and he can use his presence in his own films – my point is that there's one scene in *Fahrenheit 911*, the Twin Towers attack, where he's not showing the planes going into the buildings and actually there's no image, he's just got a black screen and you're hearing the sounds instead. So in terms of it being a straight-forward documentary really, there was a moment where suddenly form is intervening and actually saying that if you use form then its dynamics, the dialectic that come out of that for a viewer, actually gives you an attentiveness which allows and encourages you to participate in the work of the film.

MF: I would agree with what you said earlier, that not being a huge fan of a film where form is something that is stopping you allowing the audience to connect with the film and I would say that is quite true of many art house films. However I think there's a way of using form where you can create a freshness. In *Time Code* (2000) for example, people's first reaction before they see the film is that it sounds like it's too much work. Inevitably they say after twenty minutes it was very easy to watch and I knew it would be, but I did know that it would also make them very attentive because I just know scientifically that the way the eye-brain relationship works if you present people with more than one image, they are bound to scan all the time, if you present them with four images then they're scanning relatively simple tasks for the brain and the eye, and it's all in one square anyway. But they are scanning four images all the time, that's four times more work than they normally do with the single screen. They might scan a single screen but basically they're looking at a composite image, so they're never thinking I might be missing something and so I knew theoretically initially and then as soon as I started screening it, I proved it to myself, that the result being an attentive audience that are sitting on the front of their chairs not slouching backwards already meant you were getting more focus than normally you would get in a conventional single screen and that was the purpose of the exercise for me initially and then having set off with that technical exercise in mind I then, as a filmmaker realised it was my duty to tray and make what was going on as interesting as possible as well. So it was for me a healthy combination of an experiment in form and a convention of still telling a linear narrative – running on four screens, but it was still the same issue, it was a film with a start, a middle and an end.

CM: I was asked to do a presentation about *Time Code* at Chapter Cinema in Wales two or three years ago and it was great, but I did need to point out to them that there was a filmmaker called Abel Gance who in 1927 made *Napoleon* with four or eight screens.

MF: They varied didn't they?

CM: I think the difficulty with film and the reception of film is that people have more of a sense of history of art, painting say, and feel they understand some things about it because they've seen a Renaissance painting, so they can relate even to conceptual art, but in terms of film - maybe it's a school education problem that film isn't taught well enough if at all in school - people don't grow up with a historical understanding of the medium and therefore *Time Code* looks completely innovative to them, when it's a very interesting film but its not a new technique.

MF: Well it is and it isn't. There was never a claim that splitting a screen was an original idea, Erwin Piscator did it in a live theatre environment in 1925 and in the 1960s a number of filmmakers such as Andy Warhol did it. So anybody who has a vague understanding of the history of film would know that there have been these periods where more than one image has been projected.

CM: But that's an elite understanding because most people don't.

MF: Yes OK, but all things will function. A book will function on the basis of does it work now for someone reading it who knows little about the subject and does it also function for someone who will have a wider intellectual, historical understanding of the context of the book? The fact remains that what was unique about the film was that it was in real time on four screens, which had never been done before. So, in fact as an exercise it was a real time film. As a filmmaker, when I set out to make a real time film I thought, going back to what I said before, audiences are now much more aware of editing and the need to move forward with narrative in terms of visual change, so if I make a real time film, which I now can because video will allow me to do that. In order to maintain visual interest, single screen isn't going to do it, they're going to get bored by single screen and the camera is going to have to gyrate to such an extent to find new and interesting images, that actually splitting the screen is going to be an interesting alternative. So they are getting information, only they're not getting it in cuts, they're getting it in sound edits in a way and so on and then I went to four screens. So it was never a film that was going to claim that splitting the screen was an original idea, however it was a film that was going to claim that splitting a screen in real time was an original idea.

CM: Within the context of that, is what the film is about important, or not?

MF: It's as important as in any film that's ever been made. For example take a musical analogy – if you say I've come up with a new chord sequence using the whole tone series and I want to change the time signature. So the audience who hear this in a concert hall are going to be alerted because the time signature is going to be odd and changing and their ears aren't quite used to this kind of harmonic progression – that's the context of what I'm going to attempt to do, it's a forty minute piece of music. Now I'm going to start writing the music, within that I still want moments when I touch them emotionally and other times when I stimulate and excite them in a different way as I would with any film, to me its just by changing the form it gives you a kind of a fresh pallet. But once you start making the film, as a filmmaking animal you're going to be very quickly saying to yourself okay I know the theory of what I'm doing, I'm actually now bored by that theory in the sense of that is no longer enough to sustain me as a filmmaker, now my challenge, as with any film I've ever made, is to try to make an interesting film with interesting characters, with humour, with some tragedy.

CM: So what exactly did you feel you were losing interest with and for what reason?

MF: Technically you mean?

CM: Yes, that's what you were saying.

MF: Because form is only form, that's what it is and it's not enough. It's your duty to try for yourself to reinvent form all the time. It's a limited choice; there aren't so many things you can do. Because the minute you write a piece of music or you make a film you know you're dealing with certain limitations that aren't really that negotiable – how a camera functions, how a microphone functions, how light functions, how those things function together and so you just try think of ways of combining them in an interesting alternative and then once in a while when a new piece of equipment turns up, for example a camera that will record more than 90 minutes without stopping, which was entirely the basis for *Time Code*. Just the realisation that now there is a piece of equipment that is technically able to do something that filmmakers have wanted to do for a long time, which is to keep running for the convention of the length of a feature film, let's say 96 minutes. So sometimes a piece of equipment will inspire you – the size of the cameras is inspiring in the sense that you can get into areas that you couldn't before and their auto abilities that will let you auto-focus and auto-record sound and in a reasonably sophisticated way allows you to work without a crew. So again in terms of the form and the way you make the film is quite radical and offers you a very exciting scenario as a filmmaker. But once you've had those ideas, which are the 'what if' and 'if I did it like this' and 'if I didn't use any lights and shot the whole thing in three days', you've still got exactly the same problem you've always had if you're doing a 3 month shoot for Disney, which is - what is the content and how can the content be strong enough to transcend the form so that you're not looking at an exercise in form, even though if you do something radical enough people will still come out and say yes but the amazing thing was it was all shot upside down in a barrel of oil.

CM: You mostly write your own film work?

MF: Yes, you have to.

CM: Otherwise it's not your own work?

MF: No, not just that, really it's a necessity that if you're interested in working with form in as radical a way as you can, then really the only person who is going to know what to write for that format is yourself. Otherwise you end up spending a huge amount of time trying to explain your ideas to somebody else, when really if you're able to write, the easiest thing to do would be either to write it yourself or create, as with *Hotel* (2001), enough of a template so that once you've explained it to the actors, what their technical world is going to be and then say we're going to improvise around these structures and you choose actors who can do that, then those improvisations would be improvisations on a theme. So in a sense you've written a structure and now you're using their talent to improvise. It's pretty much like taking a piece of improvised jazz in whatever form that would be.

CM: Would you see content as something that is a theme about the world as opposed to the traditional idea of telling a story?

MF: Again telling a story is a very convenient way of discussing themes about the world and it's really a priority issue. I would say in Hollywood the problem is that the elements that are ruling the production of Hollywood films are technical innovation and the stranglehold that technicians have over the filmmaking process. It's very hard to block that. And secondly the cliché of a small number of stories that seem financially to function well within the Hollywood system, but that's a self fulfilling prophecy and I don't believe it, but its enough of a self-fulfilling prophecy to convince the executives who hold the purse strings. So therefore you have a pretty unhappy marriage between story repetition and technical stranglehold – it's very hard to get beyond that within that industry.

CM: Otherwise what you have personally is a strategy to approach that, like in *Leaving Las Vegas* (1995)?

MF: Well it was made entirely outside of the system, it was French money, it was Super 16mm, it was shot in three weeks on location as a kind of completely independent film and nothing to do other than the fact that it was American in subject and was shot in America with American actors. Aside from that it had nothing to do with the studio system. It was then bought by a studio and distributed by a studio and got nominated and ended up smelling like a Hollywood film, but it entirely wasn't.

CM: It was an accidental strategy then and that's very interesting to me because at that time I didn't know it was your film and had hired it from a video shop, probably because of Nicholas Cage after seeing him in David Lynch's *Wild at Heart* (1990) and I watched it and thought, this is not an ordinary film, this is the most interesting drunken scene I have ever seen in a film and whoever has made this film really knows how to work cinema. So it was like a Hollywood film, I was looking at the box thinking what is this! But I think that's great, you really entered the system and twisted something in there.

MF: Having worked in the system for three or four films before that, *Leaving Las Vegas* was quite clearly to me the film I needed to make in that environment, but entirely outside of the environment as well in terms of the industry, to prove something or to satisfy something within myself that I'd been completely denied and also to either prove or disprove something to myself. I kept looking at the way I was being expected to work within that system and being deeply unhappy with it and having just one confrontation after another with executives and producers in the process of getting a reputation as a troublemaker and as someone who would not bite the bullet and I wasn't doing it for that reason, I didn't want to be a rebel, I was just trying to make films and I was trying to make interesting films and working on the basis of that really the biggest plus you have if you're a filmmaker is your own instinct and if that instinct is constantly being asked to go to sleep while you have a consultation with a technician or executive, its not going to lead to anything creative, so it was important to me to make the film in that way.

CM: Would you agree with me when I say that I get really fed up with people who oppose any new ideas by saying 'look its all about telling the story, film-making is only ever about telling a story', to which I always reply 'no, it's not about telling a story, it's about how you tell a story'?

MF: Yes but it's about story telling. For me *Hotel* for example, having made *Time Code* and in the process of making *Time Code* I asked a lot of unan-swered questions of myself, like how interesting - if you use these cameras you can do this, if you don't use a crew you can do this, if you don't need to light it that means you can go anywhere and use the actors if they want to suddenly go into a room that's dark you can do that too, I see. Instead of thinking well I need to now make a film that has all those possibilities as possibles, not as givens, and in that case the story that's important in *Hotel* is the story of *Hotel*, it's the story of the film and what's very interesting to me about the film is it's a film about filmmaking. That happens to be the most interesting story that's going on, that's the most consistent story that's going on within that film. So sometimes, as with Godard when he's really on form, the film itself is the story, Godard is the story and within that there may be little bits of stories. I personally, in terms of my appetite, don't need a three-course meal, some-times I quite like a bit of this and a bit of that and some water and I don't mind falling asleep in it either, I really don't.

CM: Do you think you've come to that view, if that's a general statement in a sense about all of your most interesting films, that they are films about filmmaking. Do you feel you've come in a sort of circle – a bit like Sartre did when he started off as a Marxist, got into Existentialism and just by the end of his life came back to being a Marxist and that's what I meant earlier about whether you're finding something now that people found thirty years ago but nothing happened and you're coming to that conclusion.

MF: Yes I would say that to paraphrase a friend of mine Billy Forsythe who runs the Frankfurt Ballet that I think has just folded now. He's about to run another company and he's a very interesting man, we're the same age, I think we probably culturally come from, although he's American and I'm British, the influences from spending a lot time there are consistent and he said a very nice thing when I was interviewing him. He said 'As a Choreographer I quite like to watch the way rain falls and hits leaves and then drips off leaves onto other leaves and you get these kinds of rhythms that are not in time to a metre but within themselves as a phenomenon are really interesting'. So I'm fascinated by natural phenomena and the way it falls. Other people are much more interested in control phenomena, they like it to be in time signatures and they like it to loop very quickly almost. I would agree with Billy in a sense that I would say that in all aspects of life and culture, I am very interested in natural phenomena; therefore I try to resist the clichés of falling into the storytelling trap. There are moments when elements of stories in themselves are just amazing. For example Paul Auster's book *Oracle Night* (2004) he is very interesting as a novelist. He's writing 3 stories at the same time and one of the stories he just abandons, it's just never resolved, it's a story within a story within a story. The character is a novelist who is writing a story and then he abandons the story, but the story in itself is interesting and you want to know, then you think that's fine because I can sort of see where he was going with it, he didn't know how to resolve it, but that in itself is fine as an image, I like that.

CM: John Fowles was my favourite novelist and in his work it's the space between fact and fiction that is challenged.

MF: Of course. Right now what obsesses me is this: let us take the phrase 'the suspension of disbelief', which is the basis of our relationship with theatre and therefore it's also the basis of our relationship with cinema. We make a pact with ourselves to go into a dark space – a theatre or a cinema, and watch a drama where we know for the most part that there are people pretending to be people that they're not, in situations that aren't real, but are parallels to situations that have some reality to them. So we're watching some kind of parallel life drama that maybe is going to inform us in a good way about ourselves. You know that works quite well I think as an intellectual human contract. However, if you make a contract and after all these things have births as ideas, they're not natural phenomenon. At some point the Greeks said how about if we have this contract and then you have a proscenium arch and so on and then at certain points you are going to go say fuck the proscenium arch, let's go with theatre in the round, let's do street theatre. Now when you do that you kind of call into question the suspension of disbelief contract and you say OK I'm not going to directly ask you, but what I'm saying is can we renegotiate this contract and can it now work for you 360 degrees rather than *en face* and a hip audience will kind of go 'yeah that's cool and we'll go along with that, in fact this works better for us because it's fresh' – going back to my idea about the need to change form. If you just assume that it's a given, that you have the privilege of this contract and you never bother to ask the audience ever again if its okay with them and you have an industry that's developing the hi-tech potential of a camera, the hi-tech potential of recording Dolby sound, a huge screen and so almost like a pure Christian would say 'is it time to kick the money changers out of the temple, and are our churches now too full of images of God, do we now need to go to a plain room again and just sit and close our eyes and think about the meaning of our relationship with God?' and there is a parallel there. I hate to make it sound pompous, but if you just keep putting more and more images into the temple and never bother to ask the population whether that's okay with them, then I think you have a problem and therefore it's time to renegotiate that contract of the suspension of disbelief. Going back to what you said about the relationship between the story and so on and whatever form cinema is now going to come up with, it has to have that dialogue with the audience as part of its honeymoon period. It doesn't have to be a direct question, but if the question is at least posed in one's head it will, all be it abstractedly, answered by the audience. But if you're not thinking about it and you just assume that it is your right to have that relationship with an audience I think you're in trouble, really in trouble now and what's interesting now about the new digital technology and shooting films on cameras like this is that it is a good time to do that because all the rules of cinema are crying out to be broken because of the equipment, because they were created because of the equipment in the first place. So to me the next period has to be about that question and the relationship between documentary feature filmmaking, independent filmmaking and distribution, the multiplicity and availability of imagery, the fact that on one level – on a banal level, the audience is very educated, on another level they're very ignorant. In order to move forward into the new era of multiple imagery, and that's what I meant by multiple imagery – I didn't mean on the screen, I literally meant if you wanted to you could make a thousand copies of this fairly easily and relatively inexpensively and distribute them. That's what I meant by multiple images, as opposed to a limited number of prints if you like, one negative and so on. Cloning is not a possibility; it's a fact of life now.

CM: That brings us round in a circle. I think we've come to the crux of the matter, where we are and how film works on consciousness. It's certainly an area that I'm looking into with my own research and it's to do with collective consciousness and we've touched upon it. You also touched upon it at your Royal College of Art talk a few months ago, when you talked about your interest in dream. But I see a slight contradiction, very interesting and exciting what you've just said, but there's a slight contradiction and difficulty with your interest in natural phenomena – what is natural, but presumably in society, not just rain falling on a leaf, but actually from a filmmaker's perspective and interaction with people.

MF: Let me put that into a frame in itself – rain falls gently and hits a leaf and starts to cascade in a sort of natural way from one leaf to another making a sound and making a visual image. I can stand forty feet away and frame a wide shot of this whole event or I can choose to come in fairly close and look at a section of the tree and the leaves of the bush and go 'oh that's particularly interesting there', that one section of it because aesthetically this informs me in a certain way – I frame up, I've now made a choice, I've now changed it by specifically choosing that part of the image and the minute I do that I've turned it into something else and I think in the same way as if I'm making a drama, I try to find natural phenomenon and then I focus on it. The minute I do that I've changed everything, of course at least I've started from something that doesn't look fake and I have some chance of engaging with it in a way that to me is fresh and that my actors maybe are in an environment which is non-artificial to them. So therefore me, them, the situation and the relationship of suspension of disbelief, at least to me has a freshness and is asking a question of that contract.

CM: How do you do that with actors in a bare room, no windows?

MF: I do it by trying to take away as much of the kind of ritual of filmmaking, rather than worrying about the room itself. So if you think about the conventional ways of shooting a dramatic scene, the preparation, the build up, the tension, the 'are you ready, the lights are on', the this and that, that everyone is focused in a certain way, stand by, ready steady, clack, go, action – you know all the things that build up to that - to create an artificiality in terms of an over-hyped, overcooked environment where its very theatrical, its very old-fashioned in a way. The camera is like this. If you can sort of get rid of as much of that as possible and take away as many people from the room as possible, then the room at least resembles a bare room.

CM: Almost Grotowskian theatrically?

MF: Yes.

CM: My favorite Derek Jarman film is *Edward II* (1991), where there's almost no set really. I think he handled that incredibly well in the way you're describing.

MF: Interestingly in a Godard book that came out, *The Future(s) of Film: Three*

Interviews 2000/01 created in Switzerland by journalists from *Cahiers du Cinéma*. It's a very short, small book and in that Godard is asked about digital technology and he's very negative about it. I think because here's the man who developed, if you like, the use of video almost single-handedly within that context and I think that's his domain and now there's this interesting idea that actually millions of these cameras are now available, the very thing he always wanted and he doesn't really want it now because its too out there, its not specific enough somehow.

CM: So he's gone back to 35mm film?

MF: He's almost being a Luddite in the sense that he says there's no depth-of-field and that's absolute bullshit; if you want depth-of-field you create depth-of-field as you would in a film camera. However I do understand where he's coming from and he talks about the fact that it's impossible to make a film with one person, you do need the crew and he's now going against so many of the ideas of the *Nouvelle Vague* and his own ideas. I understand why, but at the same time I say he's wrong. In fact it is possible, it's entirely possible.

CM: Just to continue that question of the example of the natural. You've also talked about a parallel world in a way which connects to your dream theories about consciousness. The parallel world involves the world that is being filmed and then the world that's on the camera as two different things, seeming to be corresponding, but in fact they're miles apart.

MF: Well they're miles apart because the minute you start controlling the camera, and that after all is your pallet and is your voice, particularly a camera like the one you are using now that is recording the sound as well, the minute you start making decisions about where the microphone is, how far your zoom is, the speed of your zoom, the type of movement of the camera, whether it's the deliberate kind of jerkiness of Dogme or the controllable fluidity of something that's a bit less obvious in that sense in terms of the filmmakers hand and how you choose to expose - black and white, slow shutter speed, even the corny things like old movie effects or negative or solarisation, they're all rather wonderful, quite stunning as visual tools if used in a certain way, like anything else the minute you make those decisions, you know what you have on the camera even though you're in the same room as the subject, it's a completely different world.

CM: What concerns me mostly is that the viewer, the subject in the world, I fear no longer quite knows which of those dimensions they're in – the live world or the lived world of cinema and they relive their lives through television and film.

MF: That's entirely my point when I say the need to re-examine the contract of the suspension of disbelief, it in a way is your duty to inform the audience as much as possible of what you're doing stylistically in order for them to be able to interpret and understand what it is they are watching and the problem with reality and the fact that these cameras approximate reality rather well and relate to the so-called cheap TV shows about reality and so on, is that that line is now so blurred and that becomes the model for most people when they're growing up, the model of their experience and they will impersonate elements in these visual documents as part of their life experience as we always did with film. But film before was so clearly a theatrically different world with a certain look and sound to it, that one always knew the cliché of coming out of a cowboy film and feeling like you're a cowboy and all of that, your relationship with unreality is very clear and that's why in a way I favour a kind of return to it, almost like a Brechtian drama where props are minimal, stylistic elements of clothing and visual elements are clearly theatrical and the only thing that is of concern for the moment is the power of the drama. But the context of it, the frame in which it lives should be seen clearly as theatrical, not realistic, particularly never be realistic. However, as a poem it can function really well.

CM: As a poem?

MF: A poem, which is what film is it's a poetic visualisation isn't it?

CM: Yes absolutely.

MF: I mean, you know, you film your loved one. It can never be a substitute for your loved one. It can merely be a poem about your loved one or something that you love. It cannot replace that thing.

CM: That's a deep one, taking a photograph of your loved one into war, powerful.

MF: The poignancy of that is so strong so powerful, however it is not a replacement, it is merely a reminder.

CM: It's interesting though because you take the still image with you and you only remember that person through that still image in the end, and that again is the same thing about film and OK you could say it's a pleasure but it's a very dangerous pleasure, it could be a very dangerous plank to be walking on, to not really know who we are, let alone who we're talking to anymore, through our own kind of make-up and that's my problem with the natural elements. I understand what you're saying about framing and re-composing the world and being very open about it and that we must be very open about it, and we've always said that from our perspective of whatever you call radical filmmaking.

MF: I suppose to bring those two ideas together, you need to make a balance. Natural film is so seductive that the minute you use a very evolved eye and a brain, which after making films for a while you should have, the ability to get in and seduce with imagery is very tempting, it's very powerful and needs constantly to be tempered and again I would go back to Godard and people say well he's boring and I say yes he's boring in sections and then he will give you an absolute gem of an image or an idea and you walk away with a very clear idea of the context of those gems, rather than the kind of obsessive goal of most filmmakers now, which is to give you a hundred minute seduction experience where you're never let off the seductive hook and that ultimately is an entirely frustrating experience because you come out with your brain having been, up to a point, fooled into the idea that it's had an experience when it hasn't had an experience, it's merely watched a film. Therefore it's very important dynamically, I would say, to filmmakers and students 'wow I read your script that's an amazing first ten minutes, it's simply in the wrong position'. You could afford to have a dull first ten minutes, an audience will forgive you for that, but you really have nowhere to go after that and you're trying to be Spielbergian and of course what he's very good at is maintaining this sort of opening for the entire film by this sort of excessive and very expensive use of filmmaking elements. It's perfectly all right to be quiet and a little bit sleepy for ten minutes and really the challenge for any artist and certainly a filmmaker is where you put those moments. So a successful film could be regarded in one way as one that has a satisfying ending but somehow in the last ten minutes there was a degree of engagement that really allowed the audience to leave the cinema in a kind of fulfilled way and there were three or four moments in the film that really were very poignant and moving or frightening or whatever and they were connected by other quiet scenes which clearly allowed the audience to back off from the experience in a certain way and remind them that they were in a film and then take them out of that and then you are playing with those elements in a way that results, I think, in a healthy perspective of what the experience has been. Because as I said, one of the worst things about film is the temptation to seduce, it is the most seductive genre that we as a race have ever been able to come up with to satisfy the greatest number of people in the largest dark space possible – more than opera I would say and more than theatre, other than certain tribal events where everybody joins in and chants in the same rhythm. Cinema isn't like that.

CM: It's a sort of fulfilment of narcissism, you see yourself up there and you're very pleased to see that.

MF: Absolutely and I would go back to the kind of biblical analogy, which is - it is also dangerously the worship of the false God. It has always been the sinner's cinema as well and maybe a kind of combination of a sort of protestant ethic and a catholic indulgence is somewhere where cinema interestingly can sit. If you look at Bergman and Bunuel, the icons of cinema, they seem to have been able to produce interesting mixtures of these elements, so that you know what it is, you know you're watching a film but you are able to carry it with you for quite a long time.

London, July 2004

BIBLIOGRAPHY

Auster, P. (2004) *Oracle Night*. London: Faber and Faber.

Cahiers du Cinéma, available online in English at http://www.cahiersducinema.com/ rubrique84.html (accessed 9 November 2008)

Godard, J-L, (2004) *The Future(s) of Film: Three Interviews 2000/01*. Bern: Gachnang and Springer.

Monbiot, G. (2003) *The Age of Consent: A Manifesto for a New World Order*. London: Flamingo.

Sight and Sound: BFI Publishing.

FILMOGRAPHY

Bonny and Clyde (1967) Directed by Arthur Penn [DVD]. Amazon: Warner Brothers/ Seven Arts.

Edward 11 (1991) Directed by Derek Jarman [DVD]. Amazon: S.A.V.

Fahrenheit 911 (2004) Directed by Michael Moore [DVD]. Amazon: Ufa.

Godfather, The (1972) Directed by Francis Ford Coppola [DVD]. Amazon: Paramount.

In Cold Blood (1967) Directed by Richard Brooks [DVD].Amazon: Columbia Pictures.

Leaving Las Vegas (1995) Directed by Mike Figgis [DVD]. Amazon: MGM.

Napoleon (1927) Directed by Abel Gance [DVD]. Amazon: Universal.

Riddles of the Sphinx (1977) Directed by Laura Mulvey and Peter Wollen [DVD]. London: Mulvey.

Sympathy for the Devil (1968) Directed by Jean-Luc Godard [DVD]. Amazon: Abkco.

Time Code (2000) Directed by Mike Figgis [DVD]. Amazon: Columbia/TriStar.

Weekend (1967) Directed by Jean-Luc Godard [DVD]. Amazon: New Yorker Video.

Wild at Heart (1990) Directed by David Lynch [DVD]. Amazon: MGM.

CHAPTER 13
PLAYING WITH NEW TOYS:
AN INTERVIEW WITH PETER GREENAWAY

Clive Myer

Clive Myer: I know you have lectured at film schools and you have an active relationship with the Netherlands Film and Television Academy and the International Film School Wales so Peter, can you imagine why so many film schools are actually propagating entertainment rather than 'ideas' as a way of making films?

PG: Well we have a subject here which we could take ten hours couldn't we and I think it is related to general education around the world and through our perceptions of what we think is necessary. We educate very much within a capitalist, money-based system which in the some senses, in practical terms, make a huge amount of sense. The necessities of first of all finding a way to live. Whether you look at that as a series of jobs or career, or a vocation is highly problematical and I don't really think our education system can deal with it very well. So what do they do, they teach us how to be economically successful, isn't that the point of most western education and the far reaches of philosophical import and the meaning of life etc, largely is either an auto-didactic pursuit which we do because we are fascinated about living per say, but I don't think our educational system has really taken enormous amount of account for that. But then again, on the other hand, that is how 99.999 per cent of the world population lives anyway. You and I are part of an extraordinary

privileged minute minority who can engage in intellectual pursuits, can associate ourselves with the rarefied areas of philosophical examination and to
life; you can't possibly expect the whole world to think in the way that we do.
I am always very much aware that all the high points of civilisation of which
I cherish, have basically created the situation of 3 per cent of the population
supported by 97 per cent of everybody else. I spent a lot of time looking at
the Heian dynasty in Japan, I made a film several years ago called *The Pillow
Book* (1996) and was fascinated by the recherché nature of that civilisation. It
was one of the most sophisticated civilisations that's ever existed. The population of Japan then was about five million and it really supported an elite of
about three hundred thousand. Look at Versailles, at the Weimar Republic or
the Han Dynasty in China, it's always the same so I am always aware of this
incredible dichotomy about privilege and not privilege. You might say that
we've found our own particular ways to be where we want to be by hard work,
but there is always an awful lot of good luck in it. I used to believe that once
upon a time that talent will out, but that's absolutely not true, totally not true.
If you think about it, 51 per cent of the world's population are females, and
there is an enormous pool of talent, and has it come out, hardly ever. So the
notion that talent will out is not true at all. But also I believe in the maxim
that fortune favours the prepared mind, and again you know and I know that
there are huge numbers of paper films that exist in the world which are vastly
disproportionate to the production of film making material. I have I suppose
three careers now, I still am a filmmaker and we are busily making films, but
I am also deeply interested in my first love which has always been painting
and I have a second career, which could be described as curatorship, so I am
associated now with many collections and galleries all over the world and I
am putting on lots of exhibitions, and I am always aware that every museum
we have contains about 3 per cent of what man has ever made, so 97 per cent
has entirely disappeared. Maybe it's a good thing, because where would we
keep all this work? But it always seems to be the same. Gore Vidal said that
the population of America is some 360 million people but there are only about
twenty thousand people who read books. So ever since I was 17 and saw the
Seventh Seal by Ingmar Bergman and decided to be a film director, I knew
right from the beginning that I was going to have to be associated with a huge
amounts of contradictions and paradoxes but I had to accept the notion of
being a highly privileged, elitist, overeducated Englishman, white, a member
of no minorities whatsoever, in a very privileged position and see if I could
plough a furrow through all that, so when you ask me general questions about
the notion of filmmaking education, in some curious way I'm nonplussed
because I can't possibly give you any answers. I can only talk to you about my

personal experiences.

My central bug is visual literacy. We have a text-based culture; we have a text-based cinema. I think that's very, very unfortunate. We ought to have an image-based cinema. Every time you see a film you can see the director following the text. Cinema knows this; cinema knows it is deeply impoverished because it always goes back to the bookshop. What are the big things of the last ten years – *Harry Potter* and *Lord of the Rings* – these aren't films, these are illustrated books, but this is a very obvious thing to say because the books and the films are out in the world at the same time, but you look at the 99.9 per cent of all filmmaking, that it's basically illustrated text, so I would say to you, you probably have never seen cinema all you have seen is 113 years of illustrated text, which is something completely different. But faced with those dilemmas there are a lot of problems and I think you have to negotiate where you think your intellectual position is in all this. I am now 66; I hope to live till I'm 80. I have, what, 15, 14 years left; I make a film once every 9 months, human gestation period, so if I'm lucky I can make 12 more films. I'm going to stick to that. I know my audiences virtually don't exist anymore, I know the cinema that I'm interested in virtually doesn't exist anymore; I know that the European art cinema is dead. I give you a date, it is 31 September 1983 when the zapper or the remote control was introduced into the living rooms of the world. Cinema's a passive entertainment, you sit in the dark, what the fuck are you sitting in the dark for, man is not an nocturnal animal, you have to sit still if you're watching a feature film for 120 minutes, and you're looking in one direction. Godard famously said, 'The world is all around you why on earth are you looking in one direction?' So we're living paradoxes, it is a totally artificial phenomenon that really makes no sense at all. One ray of light, I do believe that the modern technologies are opening doors and windows, and political doors and windows and social doors and windows which will radically transform the notions of what we think are cinema. But I think probably it won't necessarily help me, because I think the notions of where people want to take cinema are not particularly, and have never really been, apart from one or two Belgians and one or two Parisian French, the direction that I would like to take it, so I plough a very narrow furrow I think with a vastly diminishing audience and really I don't think would like to imagine that I was just a product for a film museum, though it is interesting, the film museum have taken me over here now and everything is being archived here. There is still a trickling of extraordinary intense appreciation, but to be counted in thousands and not tens of thousands. So all the questions you asked me, again I feel in themselves are deeply paradoxical.

CM: I'm going to keep bringing you back to film education yet at the same time move off into film philosophy and try and interweave them so that the questions of what kind of film theory and practice film students might get involved in begins to makes more sense. Going back to what you said earlier, that film schools probably teach the way they do because people have to live, points to a paradox for you, assuming that you are living off the filmmaking work that you are doing, not just the curating.

PG: John Cage said it normally takes 15 years for a passionate desire to promote a certain body of work to actually take off and become independent, and it worked perfectly. I made a film called *The Draughtsman's Contract* (1982), after 15 years from when I'd seen Bergman's *The Seventh Seal* almost to the month and since then I have been totally, totally independent, I have never made a commercial, and never ever compromised as far as I can see. Again it has to be a position of extraordinary privilege. There is a secret to this again. When I showed my films for the first time not in this city but in Rotterdam who used to have the best film festival, I'm quite convinced, in the 1980s I was discovered by a man called Kees Kasander, he was the pupil of an extraordinary famous film cineaste called Hubert Bals,[1] who was the most extraordinary film cineaste I have ever come across. There is a famous anecdote about him, he spent his entire life in cinemas, lived in the dark, ate junk food, and he knew absolutely everybody in the filming world at that time, and he had some minor operation, I think it was an in-growing toenail, and had to spend three days away from the cinema in a hospital, had a heart attack and died. It was like massive dose of cold turkey. His funeral was extraordinary, practically everybody was there – from Scorsese to Godard, to Rivette, to Hollis Frampton; the entire breach from top to bottom – as they just realised that this was the number one cineaste probably, the most extraordinary, amazing man. And I think he made the Rotterdam film festival extraordinary, but his pupil was a man called Kees Kasander, and Kees Kasander came to me and gave me this extraordinary offer, he said provided I didn't want to use Elizabeth Taylor in a Hollywood movie he would basically support me for the rest of my film career. Can you imagine, a desperately, struggling filmmaker given such an offer, I couldn't possibly believe it, rubbish, go away. How could you offer me this extraordinary resource? I met him again three years later and he made the same offer, so we tried and then we went away and we made a film in Rotterdam zoo called *A Zed and two Noughts* (1985) and he and I have been together ever since. He finds all the money, creates all the logistics, all I have to do is come with the ideas and make the movies. I can think of only one better relationship in the world, Raúl Ruiz, you know the ex-Chilean filmmaker, he had a producer probably Columbian which explains a lot, who said you only make films for me; I don't want the films you make for me to be seen by anybody else. So that really is Pope Julius II and Michelangelo, there's the ceiling, go for it, you have as long as you like, as much money as you like, do it. So this relationship again puts me in an extraordinary privileged position.

CM: Very simply, finding partnerships that work?

PG: But they're so rare aren't they? If you think of all the producer/director partnerships you can image, you know, Woody Allen had a long standing relationship with his producer, then Wim Wenders, Godard occasionally, but after 3 or 4 films they break up, the nature of human relations, etc. But we are now about to embark upon our sixteenth feature film and we must have made about 300 other films of other descriptions, so it's extraordinary, so you come to me worrying about film education about this most privileged business and I just throw this back in your face it's so curiously, I don't know, so distant from my preoccupation.

CM: You see, on these questions, the way film education has changed and universities have changed in the UK, I should imagine everywhere else as well, so many more film courses, so many media courses.

PG: So many more graduates, so many more film festivals than there are days in the year. All this is very bad for the health of the cinema. The balance has gone completely wrong, which is another indication to me why basically cinema is dead and we shouldn't really worry about it any more.

CM: On the other hand, you know, it opens up many more possibilities because if people are thinking in different ways.

PG: It's a bit like art school, I went to art school and the number of people going through art school who actually justify their promise is miniscule, absolutely miniscule. First of all, the arts schools even then would say forget all the women, they're not going to make it, the difficulties simply of being a woman in a patriarchal society, the problems of distribution and organisation, of the canon of good taste is probably going to predicate against it. I'm thinking back to the 300 art students I knew, there was only one who broke through and he didn't even break through as a painter, he came through as a musician, Ian Dury. But where have all these amazing talented people gone? How did art school help them? What did they do? Did it just make them better people? Did it just open their eyes to a more exciting, visual vocabulary? Where do these people go? In a curious way, though people were very derogatory about the females, there was a way that the females by being educated, would at least be in good position to pass on their education to their children if they should have some, which wouldn't exist in the male's orientated phenomenon. So I'm deeply, deeply critical of the point of making film schools or art schools anyway.

CM: I remember when I was at film school in the early 1970s and a Spanish student friend said that the universities in Spain were opening up and huge numbers of people were now being educated, The negative side being there wouldn't be the jobs for them but the positive side was that there would be very well educated lorry drivers and in one sense that's a wonderful thing, because there will be a more educated audience.

PG: OK where is it? The promise, apart from maybe Almodovar just did not manifest itself did it. It's a bit like Russia's now open free market enterprise. Have you seen any Russian films? I go the Moscow film festival regularly and its crap, absolutely crap, they might cover the Red Square now in artificial snow for three days, you might be able to borrow the Russian army, but that doesn't improve anything.

CM: But things only last a short period of time before they move somewhere else or on to something else, like the New Wave, like Dogme.

PG: But we are talking about a little tiny minority talking to another little tiny minority aren't we. I mean, one doubts about major cinema now, because happily that's collapsing all over the place isn't it. It's petering out everywhere seemingly, even Hollywood suggests now with the price of tickets that people just simply are not going to the cinema anymore. From 100 per cent of people I suppose something like 90 per cent probably watch their movies on television. Maybe, I don't know, another 5 per cent probably buy the DVD's, but that's collapsing as well now. There's only about 5 per cent of people in the world who actually go to those funny places called cinemas. I've just come back from Brazil. I thought all Brazilians went to the cinema; not true, I've been prostheletysing *Nightwatching* (2007) in Japan, I thought at least Japanese young people go to the cinema, not true. People just are not going to the cinema anymore. Mind you I would say that with a big shout that cinema really is dead. It's really brain dead. There is a whole phenomenon which I think is much more interesting which is a simply the notion of the screen and the screens are around us, there's probably five cameras in here looking at us anyway; were all on screen all the time, so I think that the mobile phone in my pocket is the phenomenon that's going to be really interesting. I'm now a devotee of Second Life[2] and I'm making movies now on Second Life so I think apart from the sheer excitement of handling a new material, the whole digital revolution, the phenomenon of the cinema high street really is either a totally fossil phenomenon or such a minority that it's irrelevant. People just are not going to the cinema any more.

CM: But cinema is a different experience to watching a film at home or in an art gallery.

PG: But you're going to have to change, you're going to have to manoeuvre. They said this about cinema in the beginning didn't they in 1905.

CM: Didn't they say this about theatre as well. Theatre still has an audience. OK, what's on in theatre may be problematic, we're not talking about that at the moment. But you know the 1970s when there was an independent cinema there was a kind of independent theatre as well.

PG: Yes but you know, what's your bug? What are you trying to say? What do you want? What are you visioning about? What are you prosthelytising?

CM: I'm trying to give something of a hope to people who are going to film schools or are having a film education or are independent filmmakers who can actually begin to bring, I will talk to you about theories of representation and your own work in a second, but who can bring theory and practice together and actually work on projects which remain dialectical, remain something which the audience can actually participate in thinking through.

PG: If you don't have a canon of appreciation if you don't have educated people who are going to be fascinated by this you are farting in the wind aren't you?

CM: But as there is such a large educational flow and OK one can be as critical as you like of Media Studies, Film Studies, Cultural Studies, but there is an educational awareness going on and yes of course it's still a minority.

PG: It was Giacometti who said that your grandmother probably knows nothing about Picasso but be certain Picasso knew everything about your grandmother. But again we are talking about the top three per cent the Gore Vidal twenty thousand people who read.

I don't know how in a curious way a cinema can sustain itself on that phenomenon. You might deride Hollywood and I might, but my god they are sustaining the world's industry. They're providing the cinemas that stay open for fifty two weeks of the year of which maybe if I'm very lucky I can squeeze in ten days somewhere. My cinema could never keep us and my filmmaking practice can never keep a cinema open. I am a total, total, highly privileged parasite.

CM: OK, I'll bring you back to that in a minute let me take you somewhere else. You talked about the first twenty films you made being about representation, I'm not sure what happened after those twenty, but can you talk a little bit more about that and what your thoughts are.

PG: Well I suppose again without going into massive detail I've always thought that my film career would have been organised in three parts, that sounds very manipulative and its only by hindsight I can say that. I wanted from a very early adolescent age to be a painter, I am absolutely convinced that painting is the supreme visual communication. I think the first mark the first notion of anything man made was probably a painting and when civilisation goes down the tubes as it surely will, the last mark will be a painting. Deridda famously said "the image always has the last word", but maybe that does not go far enough because after all the written word is an image anyway, so I am all for the notion of communication through the notions of visual representation. So I think all my early films certainly up to *The Draughtsman's Contract* are really the films of a painter. They are about all the things that makes painting so exciting, about notions of form, about notions of shape and colour, notions of abstraction all the things that basically you can't manoeuvre into a cinematic world which makes their differences. But I began to find that it was an extremely lonely world, full of practitioners who were often enormously hidebound. I was generously supported in the early days by the British Film Institute, but I could see how fashions changed every eighteen months. So I can see how these sorts of notions effect the educational institutions and practices as well, I suppose here too it's often the singer not the song, it's the person who manipulates the education and its systems. I was very lucky, Peter Sainsbury, a name you know, really went out on a limb to support me. He decided to leave and go to Australia, a guy who really set me on my feet, incredible.

CM: He also funded our first film *JUSTINE, by the Marquis de Sade* (1976). It was really the first narrative deconstructive feature film in the UK, which I suppose was being developed at the same time that Wollen and Mulvey were working on their films. But that period came crashing down for various cultural and philosophical reasons, I think, as well as commercial reasons. The BFI Production Board went through a series of changes and then was disbanded which was unfortunate for independent filmmakers.

PG: At that time I was dead lucky, because Channel 4 had just started. My first feature film *The Draughtman's Contract* ran out of money and Channel 4 came along and bailed us out. Still extraordinarily profitable for me I had an amazing contract; an association which still earns me money from way back when. The second part of my career, then, I was fed up sitting in an ivory tower, being so incredibly privileged and my movies going to all the film festivals in the world, patted on the back, no money, still living on carrots and chips, not finding an audience I wanted to talk to. Then of course we're talking about middle period Nouvelle Vague and the great middle period of Italian cinema. I thought my next ambition I must get a film at the Cannes Film Festival, I must find some credence here, I can't go on making the same movies over and over and over again, which only a very, very small number of people are look- ing at, but you know about that, most cinema, underground cinema never becomes above-ground cinema, and the number of juries I have sat on year after year and seen the same goddamn films over and over and over again. Because there's no knowledge, there's no understanding of the underground before. This is terribly unlike painting, underground painting always becomes over-ground painting. Think of Picasso, think of any well known painter, this is a phenomenon that just doesn't exist in the cinema. Then again I became very, very cynical. I can write scripts very easily, I'm highly literate but all the time I want to be highly visual but as you know I cannot go to a film studio or a producer with four paintings, three lithographs and a book of drawings they want know what the fuck I'm talking about as most people are visually illiter- ate and we have text based cinema. And if that text you present them with already has succeeded in the marketplace well even better, I mean how many Jane Austin movies are we ever going to have to stop seeing? So I became very disillusioned by that and in the early 1990s I virtually gave up. I didn't want to do it anymore, there was no purpose in it. But then at the same time I started doing a huge amount of museum curatorship and we had a whole series of big exhibitions all over Europe about different aspects of notions of what I thought the connections were between general ideas about art with a capital A and cinema and I began to discover the excitements I suppose of the new digital technology and slowly I crept back in again. So now I think the main push of my excitements really is an old filmmaker playing with new toys and I have an enormous following all over the world who are interested and want me to be some sort of a flagship video performance artist – this grey-haired old man who now has huge career as a VJ. We were in Moscow last week giving a big VJ show, I am in Bari next week, we go to Montevideo in three weeks time, so I am now a VJ for my sins so why is that, because I argued you know we need to change cinema and this is one of the ways to change cinema. There's a way in which the recapitulation of the audiences now are attaching themselves to the notion not of cinematic cinema but of notions of the screen and the screen outside the cinema. It is like cinema outside of cinema where I think things should really be now.

CM: Does it matter where the screen is? Can it be anywhere?

PG: Not at all, preferably not in a cinema.

CM: Why are you so against traditional cinema?

PG: Because they are small included, occluded places which have a reputation and a taste which I'm not very interested in anymore, because I think they still fulfil the same function. Martin Scorsese makes exactly the same films as D. W. Griffiths, the only big difference is the publicity value. We still play with the same tropes the same paradigms, the sort of narrative insistence of continuity with beginnings, middles and ends, psychologically based characters which are already predicated in reel one, Christian mythologies again moving from a position of negativity to positively – a very simple way of saying happy endings, or let's say endings with some sense of resolution. So I still think you know cinema has not moved at all its been pathetic its always been slow its always been lazy and I don't think it's advanced. If you really believe cinema began in 1895 look how far literature has travelled, look how far music has travelled, look how far painting has travelled, Van Gogh to Andy Warhol, where is that comparison to be made in the cinema? I mean H.G. Wells was writing in 1895 and now we're post-Perec, post-Borges, post-Márquez. Huge changes, when you think of music Strauss was still alive in 1895 and now we are post-Stockhausen so where has cinema travelled in that same period?

CM: Let me get you away from cinema as an entity and get you back to cinema as a kind of philosophical relationship with an audience, with a viewer, with a thought system, with ideas, because really I'm interested in a more sophisticated understanding of what representation is. It's not to do with whether it's visual or whether it's literal but actually the way knowledge is transmitted and perceived and in a sense the way we interpret the world, so I want to talk to you a bit more about your notion of the relationship between film and philosophy and that if cinema is based on the notion of the idea and is a form of philosophy, which I think you would probably suggest it is, that the viewer would implicitly use the equation, philosophy over imagination is equal to representation over understanding.

PG: Yes well, how shall I answer this big question? There is generally in the world now a feeling isn't there post-digital revolution the last eight thousand years our civilisation has been organised by the text masters. He, or she, can handle texts which created our culture, created our laws, created our holy books, created the whole way we perceive ourselves. But maybe there is a feeling now that these textual gatekeepers have to move aside, they really have to move aside and we are now seeing the very beginnings of notions of a visual communicative world. If that were to be the case, I am not saying anything new here, Umberto Eco aimed primarily for the same phenomenon, then we are faced with a dilemma because if I believe that most people are visually illiterate who are now going to be the highly sophisticated organisers of the phenomenon of the primacy of the image? You see there is an important notion about English culture which is very, very un-visual. We have a very strong literary culture we can probably offer the best literature in Europe. But who could we export as a painter? There are many, many English painters but maybe Constable, Turner and if you're lucky Francis Bacon but that's about it and then if you do a return phenomenon and think of what France, Italy and Holland can offer in terms of painting it's huge and they do manage in this city especially, I think they say in the golden age of Dutch painting, which is about 1600 to about 1670, there were probably a million paintings painted in this city by at least twenty thousand painters. Extraordinary heritage you can't find that. You know, was it Truffaut who said that English cinema was a contradictory term what he was really saying was English visual imagination is a contradictory term, where is it? It is very, very little on the ground. You know when Reynolds actually wrote his discourses everybody thought this man's a painter he can't possibly write, he must have had a ghost writer and you know the terrible way the English establishment attacked R. B. Kitai which eventually drove him out of the country this extraordinary painter and they dumped down on him because he was too clever because he was too much associated and too articulate with actually what he was doing as a visual phenomenon. So there is an enormous amount of, I can't really say its anti-visual because it is an enormous amount of ignorance and I think that permeates English cinema which is very, very un-visual and notions I think probably of English art education which is also highly problematical so we have some really, really serious problems here. What am I saying? Let me try and wrap it up. I believe that all of us are experiencing some sort of cusp of an educational phenomenon which is basically moving now from the primacy of the text to the primacy of the image. I hope even consciously or subconsciously that I am somehow wishing to be associated with that so my products would be relevant to that phenomenon. There is a way that those people who command text are highly respected because of the traditions and the 8,000 year backup but now we really seriously have to consider the notions of philosophical discourse being a phenomenology that is associated with visual communication and it has not been in this country and I rather suspect, which I can associate myself with in educational terms, I can do a lot of teaching in Belgium, I am off in three weeks time doing Harvard university lectures, everywhere I go I give lectures in film and I constantly meet educationalists like yourself who feel all this sort of change, this cusp, this confusion, this deep dissatisfaction with the notions of the status quo. I will argue and constantly argue that the notion of cinema has not realised its potential. You listen to Bazin in 1921, it hasn't become the great twentieth-century medium, cinema has not become the medium of intense philosophical discourse, it's somehow lost it's way, it's missed the point. If you think about the last great splurge of philosophical consideration it's French, and it's basically textual again. It is so semantically textual it's really only about text talking about text, so we haven't made any serious notions of ontological research into this new phenomenon but, and I think everybody says the digital revolution has touched us and is touching us in ways we don't even remotely understand yet. If you think it began in September 1983 that's not so long ago, so maybe we are in a massive, massive learning curve.

CM: What about if you draw a line from say John Berger who was looking at images not words in *Ways of Seeing* and cross over to France where you've got Godard and writers/academics like Jacques Aumont, back to the UK with filmmakers like Sally Potter and yourself, then there is what one might call a body of work. You are putting over this very pessimistic view and I am constantly pushing back to you this optimistic view that says actually it is possible to work and it is possible to do it in not quite such an elitist grand English gentleman manner that you are suggesting in your discourse. And where you talk about technology this could be seen as democratised access to knowledge in the form of the internet. You asked me what my bugbear was and I think it would probably be better if I tell you more directly, which is that I'm not sure if it's about image or text or whether actually it matters that much because what it is about is the position of ourselves as subjects in the world, subject to a knowledge which has, what Althusser used to call dominant ideology, the dominant knowledge and therefore how can we think outside of that perspective. My own work is about collective consciousness and the idea that it's very difficult, because of notions of representation and philosophy, to actually think and behave and make films and watch films outside of that collectivity. My interests in Noel Burch was about something I am trying to redefine at the moment both academically at conferences and in writing but also in my films which is the notion of diegesis, the notion which is not to do with Plato and Aristotle which it was originally, the narrating, the telling of a story which you know a lot about and you've addressed that in lots of different ways. But actually it's about the way we understand ourselves inside that narrative or that space or that reflection of the world and that if one tries to open up that diegetic space and make it more amenable, whether it's through formal intervention or whether it's through even the content of what is within a piece of moving image. Let us call it moving image and let us assume for a moment that moving images are more relevant to our discussion than still images or even paintings because moving images actually address that notion of our consciousness in every dimension.

PG: There is another argument but I doubt that because there is very little contemplative value.

CM: Godard's *Histoire(s) du Cinéma* for me is probably the best example. Godard has managed to open up questions of consciousness by taking images and sounds apart and sowing them back together in order for new meanings to come out of them. Jacques Rancière writes about the concept of re-figuration, of taking images and sounds and adding further meanings to suggest there further readings, not in a postmodern, 'anything goes' way but in a way which is quite fixed politically and culturally yet provocatively opening up areas where we can begin to think again. I believe that's been a problem in recent European cinema.

PG: So you are really arguing for cinema as thinking medium.

CM: Very simply put, absolutely yes.

PG: Well of course I am not going to disagree with you remotely, but you must also be aware of all the contradictions and all the paradoxes? Are you sufficiently happy with cinema as a thinking medium if you are only talking to one person?

CM: Well I am not sure anymore whether it's necessary to think like that because yes I used to make films where only one person might remain in the audience, but not anymore. Peter Gidal was once the only member of my audience to stay and watch my film and he didn't like the bits that were actually in focus because it distracted from the purely cinematic qualities and interfaced with meaning. It is exactly meaning that needs to be brought into the world and extrapolated but, thankfully, that idea of one person is no longer inevitable because of the technology that you are working with. The internet has a worldwide audience and there may well be a small audience compared to that of a Hollywood film – but it is by no means only reaching one person.

PG: Yes but when I examine my fascination, I made a painting once which said if only cinema could do what painting can. Cinema can't even approach this. How do I explain these extremely rarefied areas of excitement? Do you understand the excitement of putting one pink tone against another pink tone? What has that got to do with my grandmother? What's it got to do with the people in the street? You know it's almost imperceptible for me to celebrate and become excited and communicate that notion. Who am I talking to? So in the end it becomes a form of excessive intellectual masturbation.

CM: Of course this question of jouissance is very important. If you visit the Picasso museum in Barcelona, you will see 58 of his reproductions of Velásquez's *Las Meninas*. You'd think every one would be the same but it's a completely different painting every time. The intellectual pleasure he must have experienced and the pleasure he gives to others is enormous.

PG: When you say that I recall what we were saying earlier. You were actually implying that the moving image is more important than a still image. I would disagree with you. A moving image allows very, very little space for contemplation. The particular excitement about a painting is this iconic notion of contemplation. Wordsworth's definition of poetic creation was "recollection in tranquillity", that I translate as a profound ability to communicate with a still image which is very rare in cinema, very rare in emotions. I have tried very hard to encompass that and to demonstrate it, you know sometimes my shots are ten minutes long because I want you to look, to look for Christ sake look, don't be disengaged by movement, don't be disengaged by the ephemeralities of notions of narrative and anecdote, just look. But it's very, very difficult to get people to do that, you never make a film ever again because nobody ever gives you money because nobody knows what you're on about.

CM: If you are passionate about that, which you are, you can make films anyway. Actually you don't need a lot of money to carry on making films. If no one funded Peter Greenaway ever again I know you would carry on making films. This is happening to Ken Russell at the moment, you know that he is now a professor at the International Film School Wales. He makes films in his garage now with a small digital camera and he's making them because the notion of work and the 'pink next to the pink' is vitally important. It is what gets you up in the morning and it's what I was trying to say about the Picassos and *Las Meninas* or the Godard film in the Rancière way, taking something that already exists and refocusing its meaning.

PG: Let's talk about *Las Meninas* because we are going to go and tackle that. It contains the most exciting piece of painting in the whole history of Western art. There is an area in the top right hand corner which is a painting of air and nobody has ever managed to paint air so convincingly. That's extraordinary, then when you talk to people about the painting of the air they ask what on earth are you on about? You know, how recherché, how elitist can you get?

CM: Turner painted air. There was an English moment when he was moving potentially I guess towards a cross between Expressionism and Impressionism in some ways but I think these things have been attempted.

PG: It all came from this man over here, Rembrandt.

CM: Rembrandt's brushworks are incredibly painterly. The first time I came to Amsterdam and had a look at Rembrandt I was shocked at how in a sense 'deconstructive' his works are, they are not at all the illusionistic images that art school had taught.

PG: There's this phenomenon called the Stendhal syndrome you know when you finally see a work of art like Stendhal did in Florence at the Uffizi gallery. He fainted. There was something about seeing the natural phenomenology of the real thing. Once upon a time we had Vivienne Westwood who was going to do the costumes for *Nightwatching*, it didn't happen in the end but she came and did her homework here and I took her around and she came and saw Rembrandt's *The Nightwatch* for the first time. She didn't faint like Stendhal but she burst into a series of uncontrollable giggles which she couldn't stop, it was something to do with the sheer presence of that extraordinary painting.

CM: Yes, absolutely. Lynda[3] burst into tears watching Godards` *Histoire(s) du*

Cinéma. All that was happening on screen were a few dissolves going from one painting to another. But the emotional impact was immense. I know you have spoken elsewhere about the idea that commercial cinema is this kind of pretentious attempt to extract false emotions, or put another way, the emotions which are present in the viewer are being induced to be exploited. So I would still argue that the moving image today is more important than the still image. I know it is a very, very difficult argument because Barthes wrote his essay about stills from an Eisenstein film not about moving image scenes themselves. But the wonderful thing about the VCR recorder when it was invented was that you could stop a film and you could go back and look at it, scenes, shots, frames again and again. So you can contemplate on moving and still images. You know we have come much further than that, but the point philosophically seems to me, and I think your work is doing this overtly, the affront that the moving image has on our sense of understanding the world is similar to photography when it first arrived. This whole idea that from that moment painting was dead was a realisation of the quest for similitude, the production of false consciousness. Your suggestion that cinema is dead is contradicted by the inevitability that painting is indeed still alive.

PG: The basic six media of the ancient Greek forms of communication will never perish, but my criticism about cinema is that it's a little local technology which is very much dependent upon sophisticated machines and if you pull the plug out on the wall it all goes, but you wouldn't say that about theatre. But I don't think we should think about theatre in an English way, I think we should think about theatre in a much more open way. We have a very text based theatre here but the rest of the world doesn't. Go to South Korea or China, their theatre doesn't operate like that, but that will be there for ever. I think also that our notions of literature will always stay but it is the local technologies like cinema which arise virtually from nothing, become highly evolved in a very sophisticated way but their sophistication is their own downfall in a curious way. And I think for all the reasons and we have talked about twenty of them here, the notion of the cinematic as an art form this pretence of it being the seventh art, sorry it's not going to work. You've made deconstructive films, all cinema could be deconstructed down to something else and the condition, species driven, of a new art form surely must be it cannot be deconstructed down to any other art form, it must surely be autonomous. It's a bit like the evolutionary comparison that zebras and horses can't fuck to produce any decent offspring but cinema can fuck with anything so therefore it has no autonomy.

CM: When I first started teaching filmmaking I would praise cinema for the fact that it contained the codes of all the other art forms. What you're saying is that it is the death of cinema that it contains all the other elements and it contains nothing of itself.

PG: It has no backbone it can't stand up.

CM: On the other hand, this is getting back to the point, I'm working with nonfiction work at the moment, I don't like calling it documentary because I don't think it documents, it does something else.

PG: It's about text again isn't it?

CM: Yes exactly but nonfiction, this is again getting close to my bugbear, the elements within let's call it art, or philosophy, or imagination, but the elements which bring us as living people closer to that expectation of what life is about, and why cinema or whatever you want to call it, moving image, the capturing of live action - again there is no word which is not tainted, this is the problem, live action is impossible, there is no live action in cinema other than the prefilmic and the act of viewing.

PG: What we're talking about is a visual world in words, how can we do it otherwise? How can we do it now, I mean that's the whole point isn't it? We need to be able to do that, we need to find the language to really open all the doors and windows and successfully communicate in a brand new way.

CM: Would this brand new way then, not be one that is still problematic because any form of communication is a form of representation. Any form of representation, in the equation that I put to you earlier, is a form of philosophy. Any form of philosophy has a form of bias to it and any form of bias therefore already has built within it something which is telling a viewer, to whom you are passing this knowledge, to think in a certain kind of way even if you are saying 'I want you to think in your own way'. You cannot because they cannot, because they are trapped in that circular ideological conundrum. And any form of representation, whether it is theatre or a form of communication that hasn't yet been invented, is lost and trapped in the sense that we are containing people in a certain ideological precept. The liberation of the pink next to the pink, the emotive subtlety, is the key which actually switches on a passion and that passion, if we go into one of your exhibitions, or if we go to a Warhol exhibition, turns on a certain switch in the viewer which says there is more to the world than the world I am given and the world I perceive. In a sense it gives people hope.

PG: Despite my little sort of tremor of I suppose you might say negativity I am a total, total optimist simply because there is no point in being pessimistic, we are beholden and we are obliged to be optimistic.

CM: Are you referring to human nature? In order to reproduce we must be optimistic?

PG: Well it's why we don't jump in the canal, there is no purpose, there is no reason to get up in the morning if you are pessimistic. But you can see my dilemma can't you? How can I, advocate of notions of social communication of cinema, argue cogently because I keep falling back into positions of extreme privilege every time, there is no way that I can put my theory honestly, honourably, creditably, into practice is there?

CM: But that's a kind of excuse isn't it? All great artists have said that they just do their thing in a garret and hope someone will see it.

PG: Yes but wait a minute, don't accuse me of that because I hate people who refuse to try and explain themselves. I am what I am because I am doesn't wash with me, I'm sorry it has to be something more prescient. I was in Lucerne a couple of weeks ago with urgent, urgent filmmakers, they were all architectural students as well, my cinema seems to have a particular excitement for architects, and I was saying, you know, forget cinema and concentrate on architecture, you can live your life without ever going to a picture house you'd be impoverished but you can do it but you cant live your life without architecture. You simply can't, so if you want to work out where your social responsibilities are, where your aesthetic control is over people, worry about the architecture don't worry about the cinema. You know we have apparently enormous amounts of aesthetic freedom now don't we and that is the most difficult thing to handle. There is so much aesthetic freedom that often these poor students, you look at them with sort of angst on their behalf, they don't know what to do. They can't focus there are huge amounts of extraordinary floundering. YouTube is probably the greatest thing that has happened in the last four generations I really am convinced that it is an extraordinary phenomenon but in a way it's opened so many doors and windows people don't know how to handle it. Within six months there was more footage on YouTube than 200,000 people could see in 200,000 lifetimes. Isn't that extraordinary? I really pity the archivists in a hundred years time. How on earth are they going to handle that? And it's so instantaneous. I was showing in Milan on a Friday night and on Saturday morning it's all over the world on YouTube. We had a VJ show in Moscow and I was looking at the audience and they were all holding up there mobile phones and there must have been 300 films on YouTube the following morning of our event. That's amazing isn't it. But here I am this English privileged bourgeois gentleman worrying about pink against pink and you have this phenomenon of YouTube. How do you match those two things? My question to you.

CM: Here's the match: you've now crossed over from being a pessimist in this conversation to an optimist and the hundreds of people holding their mobile phones up, no longer just at pop concerts but at art events, means that there is in fact an audience that even though you decry the idea that there is no audience for films anymore this obviously means there is and it is a growing one. It is a different sort of audience and they are ones who are appreciative of new inventive forms of art that excite them. So you can still be excited by two pieces of pink placed next to each other and you can be equally excited by a million hits on YouTube.

PG: So what's our responsibility then, keep up the pink against the pink?

CM: I think the responsibility isn't about the form and I don't think it is just about the content. It's a responsibility that I'm trying to dig into with this book which says how do you bring those two things together? Most film schools are about the teaching of film crafts and they are shy about the teaching of film theory or film philosophy, which is different to film history or film studies. So how do you actually have a discussion like this in a film school which then excites students who are in this elite and powerful position of being able to take their cameras into the world and engage with other people? How do you get them to take responsibility for that?

PG: This has to be a rhetorical question because you know how it might be possible.

CM: But I want to know how you think it might be possible with the work that you are doing. We are not in the 1970s or 1980s, there is no political context for doing work that allies itself with new radical political movements. We are in this blancmange of a postmodern world where anything goes and the more that goes the better and as it goes the industry absorbs those things into its own pocket, its own purse actually. Now you could say forget it, give up, don't bother making films everything you do is going to be absorbed into the industry anyway, we talked about the zapper in 1983 which is exactly what Noel Burch also thinks. As far as he is concerned there is no point in making avant-garde cinema any more because since the zapper was invented everybody is making deconstructive films, everybody is deconstructing narrative so the best thing you can do is to make films about politics rather than taking on Godard's point about making films politically. I think he was also being too pessimistic, that it is still possible to work with aesthetic consciousness because as the world changes as you've mentioned, you've given very good examples about the way people in the audience film your films and taking their own decontextualisations and recontextualising them their own way by sending them to their families and friends saying look at this, look where I was last night, and then it's sent on again by a third party and it becomes another piece of representation which is on a journey somewhere and that journey is an exciting one. Why is it then that film schools are moribund and still teaching people to make uninteresting films? Yet in this elite group of a hundred people in a film school, somewhere in there is another Peter Greenaway, another Godard, another Sally Potter who actually might be struggling against the status quo and beginning to understand how they are misinforming the world. How do we deal with the problems of the misrecognition of representation? The problem and the excitement about the moving image is that it looks like the real world but is saturated with ideological meaning. So where do we go from here? We can't effectively deconstruct because Postmodernism has taken that over from us. We can't just make films that overtly tell us to think politically like Noel Burch suggests because no-one welcomes didacticism and yet there remains hope. You were talking about why there are so few women filmmakers, well you know there are there are going to be more and more women film graduates and the more interesting it is possible to make the film schools the more interesting filmmakers will emerge. At the moment the West is still male white dominated but in the South there are still political excavations to engage with, there are still things to bang against because there is repression, there is hunger, there is prejudice, there is injustice.

PG: Yes and you and I are talking in probably the most sophisticated pinpoint in the whole of the world, in this city of Amsterdam, this country with its great liberal democratic choice for freedom and power, where all the hospitals have ethical departments, where homosexuality, abortion and euthanasia are breakfast-time situations. You know I can't overestimate this, I know I live here of course for all sorts of reasons, some good some maybe not so good, but this really is the most extraordinary place for actually having this argument. I wish people would understand that too.

CM: I can absolutely understand and sympathise with why you have moved here and I think there are probably other places in the world I believe

Montreal is pretty good too. There are cities which are very culturally and critically aware and that's what people talk about, not what you do for a living and how much money you earn, which is the English and American way of introducing yourself.

PG: And your film schools too are really like that aren't they? Because I doubt whether they really are teaching even craft are they? They are really saying how can I get a job at the BBC?

CM: When I started teaching as a practitioner at film schools in Wales I taught modules called 'Discourse' to first, second and third year students. I believe that you should teach theory and practice together. The first film I would show to a new first year student was Derek Jarman's *Blue* (1993) and of course the first thing they would say is this is not a film, I hate it. You have a show of hands, or in my case I actually ask people to move to the left or right of the room to see if they thought it was interesting and of course 90 per cent were just totally appalled by it. Then followed a one hour discussion and after that I asked the question again. By now students had become totally fascinated by it – they had neither seen nor considered such a film before. The outcome of the second move around the room at the end of the discussion was a total reversal. Most of those students went on to make really interesting films.

PG: That didn't have a lot to do with the film though in a curious way did it? It had to do with the powers of your oratory and discourse.

CM: OK so students are as susceptible to new ideas as they are to established ones. *Blue* was the equivalent of our 'pink on pink' discussion. And maybe teaching can be as effective as an interesting film but reaches the real minority that you have talked about. You've used colour in your films you've used all sorts of devices to do with dialogue.

PG: Maybe you are right but your questioning is rhetorical isn't it? Because you know how to do it don't you.

CM: Yes but who am I? I can't do it on my own.

PG: You have power, you have access to student minds don't you through your teaching? The way I think about it is that I know my cinema is problematical and difficult so wherever possible I would always take up the opportunity to go along with my film so that they could see the author behind the film, and that I could talk about the film just in the way that you've done. Exactly the same way but then the most interesting part always is always badly organised by the organisers is the dialogue at the end the Q and A that is what gets really exciting and of course it is the females who ask all the interesting questions do the most probing and the most critical, always, always and maybe that's a positive notion for female filmmaking of the future. So I suppose if you do really want to ask me what is my methodology? There are many, many things in my life I have a young family, I have a seven year old daughter I am a very domestic man I do huge amounts of intake as well as outtake in terms of reading and looking and listening, but where I can and where it's possible I am more than happy to take up invitations but what does it mean? I can't be in fifty thousand places at once, I can't on the whole talk to more than one thousand people at one go. But I do feel doubtful about it because does that mean that my films only exist if I come along with them?

CM: I came to the conclusion about my own films which have no market value like yours do, that the only place for them is at conferences because I can be with my films and talk about them and I have resigned myself to this idea as half academic and half filmmaker. But tell me what you think of Godard's films? Particularly *Histoire(s) du Cinéma*? Where would you place that kind of dialectical work?

PG: I have a problem with Godard now. I have a lot of problems with Godard's lack of pleasure principle. Though I am regarded as a film intellectual there is a great sensuosity a great physical sense in the world I create in my cinema and I find him dry. I can admire his intellect but the emotional associations are poor.

CM: If you consider the example of Lynda crying during *Histoire(s) du Cinéma* it would indicate that emotion is there. There is such a joy in that rediscovery as in John Berger's *Ways of Seeing* which I ask Foundation students to read when really it should be given as a text to 11-year-olds at school. And then to open up some knowledge to the history of the movements of World Cinema which have changed the way in which we perceive the world through cinema. That's why I teach film.

PG: Yes I suppose that's one of the excitements of my approach and dialogue with painting again. You know there are an awful lot of people going back to art galleries but they don't really look at painting before about 1900. They are all associated with the excitements of Pollock and the twentieth century which is very valid but, to pick up your last comment, there have been benchmark images made, which are so powerful, even though we don't necessarily realise it that have taught us how to see. The whole concern about English landscape has come out of painting, Italian painting very largely, nobody understands quite how that all happened, though the English landscape is highly artificial and deeply manicured and really is the result of a painting illusion, and you can say that about so many things and its painters who teach us, but we don't give them credence certainly not within the English educational establishment and hardly in the European establishment and basically, I don't know because we feel we have got eyes we can see and its not true. Just because we have got eyes in a curious way it makes us blind.

CM: That's very interesting

PG: You know it's like the problems about human childbirth there is a mismatch in evolution the embryo has grown too big too fast and the female pelvis hasn't caught up with it. So they now say the eye is lacking demonstrably behind the brain so that the brain is rushing ahead in evolutionary terms and the eye hasn't caught up.

CM: That's extremely interesting and I think it would have to be another conversation. Given all the things you have just said how would you transform film schools to teach them elements that are not just about craft?

PG: Well I suppose you are going to have to make a big sea change to actually put it on the agenda saying, look this is important, this is really important. Forget your job at the BBC, don't worry if you never even make a film. You know one of my heroes Etienne-Louis Boullée (1729-99), a brilliant architect, never made a building but still perfectly valuable because he influenced and virtually created I suppose nineteenth century architecture. So I think you just have to lay down on the law in a sense to educate the educators don't you?

CM: One is trying to do that but I mean would you do away with films altogether or would you slowly transform them?

PG: If you look at what their products are, I mean it's a bit like advertising, how do you evaluate how successful advertising is? It's very, very difficult to do that. How do you evaluate what education is? I don't know. How do you make sure? Do our films get better because there are more film schools? Do our films get better because our film schools are getting better? Very difficult to evaluate isn't it? I mean Godard never came out of a film school did he? Eisenstein was an absolute brilliant filmmaker an extraordinary teacher as well but where is his legacy?

CM: In montage – I'd say it is being taught in the best film schools.

PG: I think it's the only thing that perhaps the cinema ever invented. And it is so cinematic it's one of the things that didn't come out of a bookshop thank God, most everything else did. I don't know but I mean you probably know the answer to your question but it's back again to the top end of our conversation, you know there is three per cent of civilisation that somehow endures and is valuable and the rest goes to the wall but maybe you have to have that 97 per cent in order to have the 3 per cent. You have to have Hollywood to provide us for the legitimacy of this conversation.

CM: If society inevitably works like that do you advise independent filmmakers to stop making films, that there is no point because Hollywood absorbs all the ideas anyway? Jeremy Isaacs, the first Chief Executive of Channel Four famously told independents to become chicken farmers.

PG: No, No. I think you have to do a David Lynch, get in there and try and change it and do your thing within it but continually be aware incredibly self aware of what it does and how it does it.

CM: Well that is my view in a nutshell absolutely. Which is why I still have faith in film schools, in fact a film school gives a student three years to think about these things.

PG: Or does it? Or does it make students worry about how to make the documentary that looks as though it's shot by Vittorio Storaro, and organised and lit by so and so, you know.

CM: Well of course you are absolutely right it depends who teaches in film schools. A university or film school is only as good as the people who teach in it.

PG: It's the singer not the song again every time isn't it.

CM: You know a colleague and I recently set up a Skillset Screen Academy in Wales and of course, quite rightly, their mission is to bring in skills and talent from professionals in order to get graduates into the industry and several skilled professionals have given their time to pass on their knowledge. But do you think one ought to push for independent filmmakers, if they are grant aided and government funded, to actually spend a whole semester in a film school as part of their government aided funding? In other words to make it a requirement of the filmmaker's funding and build it in to the financial aid in some way, perhaps by collaboration with the schools.

PG: Well there is a very big film script situation going on in this country which I have to say has a very poor filmmaking reputation and I am constantly asked to go there and they are all so proud of being scriptmakers, film scriptmakers, who never made films. Some curious thing. I always remember in Brussels some years ago people arguing that the script Bergman wrote for *Wild Strawberries* (1957) was ten thousand times better than the film. It's that sort of funny notion which also upper edges of art schools and educational establishments tend to push as well, which is offensive in a funny way and non-productive. And people still argue don't they in England for scriptwriters' conferences you know. We don't need scriptwriters you know we need filmmakers and script writers aren't filmmakers but it's very, very difficult to explain that to anybody, but you just have to keep proselytising. Maybe the best way to teach film is to make it even more so than to talk about it.

CM: You have arrived at a question which is really about narrativity and scriptwriting. You have talked many times about the problem of the narrative. Actually it's probably more about narrativity and the problem of how narrative itself is constituted, but then with those problems and with the issues that you are interested in, how would you recommend one teaches scriptwriting?

PG: Well I don't, but you know it is a big irony because I am a very good scriptwriter, I can turn scripts out dead easy I am very facile and I'm able to do that. Most of my films are catalogue films, if I make *The Tulse Luper Suitcases* (2003-04) it has 92 films within it, and they come rolling off dead easy so I am naturally very suspect of that. It's an English characteristic but cleverness should not be part of our vocabulary or the downside of that, but that also means I have to fight the literary in myself all the time that is why I argue so strong for the painterly, so it is a problem. Most people think that narrative is essential, I don't. Cinema is really more about sequence not about narrative and you can't have narrative without sequence but you can easily have sequence without narrative, and that I think was part of the filmmaking process which you and I were worried about in the 1970s and maybe we've lost that now, that interest, but it is still very profound for me. One of the reasons why I'm VJ-ing now is because I can make a presentation of multiple image excitements without notions of narrative, or at least let's say extreme minimal narrative. I don't know, do you believe that one, two, three, four, five, six, seven, eight, nine, ten is a narrative? I always think a better narrative is ten, nine, eight, seven, six, five, four, three, two, one.

CM: But there is always linearality.

PG: Well there is temporality too and you have to take account of that which again painters don't have to. That is why I say the DVD is absolutely ideal for me because as a painter and as a filmmaker I am both sides of the coin. You know I can go and look a the *Mona Lisa* for two seconds, two minutes, two hours, two years if I wish because the power is mine. I have the power of the viewer, but if I make a film of the glass on my table I will only give it to you from the angle that I want and for as long as I want so the power is mine as creative maker, but the DVD shares that power or theoretically it shares that power. It can allow you to be king viewer or it can allow you to be king maker. And I am searching, searching all the time to try and make that happen. And I suppose again succinctly, but again I am only quoting *Time Out* which some years ago now, suggested that Greenaway is struggling against the odds to turn cinema into painting. Because painting does things so much better it strikes me. The act of contemplation again – use your eyes.

CM: But you're taking painting into cinema.

PG: Well, the jury is out but it's an ongoing process often very, very entertaining and often extremely problematical.

CM: When you used to talk about three sorts of cinema: historical; Walt Disney/Holywood; and the third way, you said the 'historical' attempts to conserve the past and that's going to become an archive. Do you still hold with that view about three forms of cinema?

PG: Well maybe, but I suppose the whole of *Tulse Lupa* really was about there's no such thing as history there are only historians, so it's all highly subjective and manipulable and manoeuvrable according to subjectivity. I read enormous amounts of history, I am now engaged in a huge hundred book cycle for a Parisian publisher, 100 books about different aspects of a given phenomenon, an impossible megalomaniac task which I know I shall never finish but then that's no reason not to start.

CM: I think what I am trying to draw out, in a sense it's not about you, it's not about your films, it's about your philosophical impact on how one's film work can potentially change how we understand the world, and you know we have to give ourselves credibility and credence for that because in the end it does make a difference. So what is that difference and can other people, this is the bottom line, can other people make a difference? And that is why I value film schools; I still think they are a potential kindergarten.

PG: Maybe it's like the inadequacies of democracy, it is a deeply, deeply flawed system but it's the best we've got. I don't know let's try and wrap ourselves up together in some kind of final reprise if only to leave this meeting with some sense of satisfaction, having achieved something. Your position is you still want to feel that film schools are valuable and you are trying to find a justification for it, yes?

CM: I don't think they need a justification but I do think they need philosophical methodologies.

PG: Ok, well then maybe just to repeat again what we have already said, it's a bit like in our society. I had a big exhibition here in Rotterdam once it was called *The Physical Self* , because I was worried that there's nowhere in society where you are legitimately allowed to look at a nude figure. Ok you know you go to art school but a very, very small number of people go to art school, strip clubs are not the same thing, something else is going on there. Where is there in society an opportunity to legitimately just look at the naked human. So we put on an exhibition which did really make a presentation of naked humans, and we had a roster, it went on for three months. We compared it to beautiful Rubens drawings of the nude and paintings by Odilon Redon and Picasso so there was a way of using their collection to focus on the nude. And it was very successful in a very public way it may have been in a sensational way but at the very end almost before we closed after three months a little old lady, she was 70, came up to one of the janitors and she said 'I never married, it's a long time ago since I ever had a boyfriend, I am going to die within the next five years but you have given me a legitimate opportunity to look at a naked man before I die', she had a thousand reasons but it is a bit like the Christian phenomenon isn't it, one convert satisfies the globe. And I suppose it's back to pink on pink again.

CM: And one film student who has time to think about, contemplate, produce work.

PG: It justifies your use of an art school.

CM: I know you are interested in concepts of life, sexuality and death which are more-or-less the three elements of which philosophers have always talked about and can therefore also lead more clearly to questions about what students make films about and why they make them, other than as ways of getting in 'the industry'. It seems to me that there is no such focus.

PG: What else is there to talk about. We just had an exhibition at a place called Zwolle here in the east of Holland and we simply called it *Sex and Death in Zwolle*, a little tiny community but a big subject. We interviewed 100 people and asked them three questions. What do you know about the circumstances of your conception? Which flummoxes most people. What do you know about the circumstances of your birth? Although that is really a minor question I suppose because birth is virtually involuntary, and the dangerous question how do you think you are going to die? Zwolle is in the Bible belt so we had a lot of religious sort of justifications but it certainly made people think. Do you know the circumstances of your conception?

Amsterdam, July 2008

FILMOGRAPHY

Blue (1993) Directed by Derek Jarman. London: Artificial Eye.

Draughtsman's Contract, The (1982) Directed by Peter Greenaway [DVD]. Amazon: Fox Lorber.

JUSTINE, by the Marquis de Sade (1976). Directed by Stewart Mackinnon. London: Film Work Group.

Nightwatching (2007) Directed by Peter Greenaway [Video/HDTV]. Amsterdam: Benelux Film Distribution.

Pillow Book, The (1996) Directed by Peter Greenaway [DVD]. Amazon: Film Four.

Seventh Seal, The (1957) Directed by Ingmar Bergman [DVD]. Amazon: Kinowelt Home Entertainment/DVD.

Tulse Luper Suitcases, The (2003–04) Directed by Peter Greenaway [Video/HDTV]. Amazon: A-Films.

Wild Strawberries (1957) Directed by Ingmar Bergman. Amazon: Criterion.

Zed and Two Noughts, A (1985) Directed by Peter Greenaway [DVD]. Amazon: Zeitgeist Films.

NOTES

1   The founder of the Rotterdam Film Festival in 1972.
2   The internet-based virtual world where people socially interact through avatars.
3   Lynda Myer-Bennett was on camera recording this interview.

CHAPTER 14
AN INTERVIEW WITH NOEL BURCH: PLAYING WITH TOYS BY THE WAYSIDE

Clive Myer

CM: There was a certain conjuncture in the 1970s where film and philosophy joined up, at least for a while. In the last thirty years there has been a huge dissipation between the two spaces which is why I called this conference *BEYOND, the Theory of Practice* in order to bring back together some of the original thinkers about the nature of a theoretical practice with some new people who are interested in both theory and practice and to see where we might go from here. The main questions are very simple – what sort of theory do we teach our film practice students now and why has film practice gone in one direction, towards a mini-industrial process while theory has gone in a different direction, which is more-or-less to avoid practical work altogether. That's the kind of general premise for the whole conference.

NB: So I'm supposed to respond to that. Well look, as for the why all this has happened, just look at the world. This mostly concerns me in a very anxious and I would almost say sickening way. What's happening to the world is why I'm getting politically active in the Green Party in this country, part of my life as it is now, but as far as apparently the nostalgia that some people, maybe not yourself, but some people seem to still have for the 1970s I want to tell one of many anecdotes that took place around 1980 and for me in any case sums up my own revisionism.

I went back to the States for a couple of years after the defeat of the left in this country after 1979. I absolutely hated it, it made me quite ill and now I'll probably never return. When I was there I was teaching undergraduates Film Production and Film History. It was actually the last time I ever taught elementary film making. One day I was showing Dreyer's *The Passion of Joan of Arc* (1928) to a class of around a hundred students and I gave this speech about the abstract space and the relationship of the frame, etc. and then I went out to do something in my office and a student came by and said 'Professor, this film is absolutely wonderful, but tell me something – what does that girl want?' Then I have to say the penny dropped and I went back and asked these 75 kids who Joan of Arc was and there were two who knew and I said to myself there's something wrong, I should be perhaps talking about what the films are about. This and some other experiences in retrospect were moments of absolute truth. If I had to teach students film production today, I would be teaching them how to be inside the codes of what we used to call dominant cinema, because I think it's the only one that's readable. Today I've become very critical of avant-gardes in general, be they political or not – the historical interest of Vertov, etc. Okay but nobody was interested in those films, they had absolutely no political effect. The point is that it was all wrong-headed to my mind, the only films that I have personally made that I still feel have any value are two documentaries, which I'm sure you have not seen because they are never shown. They were co-produced by Channel Four, it was the Head of Independent Film Alan Fountain's last project and he left before they were due to be shown and they were never programmed, but not because they were anything like avant-garde, one was a film I made on the American left, *Sentimental Journey: Refuzniks USA* (1994), it was viscerally anti-American, it was shown here on TV with a certain amount of success actually. I made another film a couple of years later with Michèle Larue, *Cuba: Entre Chien et Louve* (*Cuba: Mothers and Machos*, 1997) which was about male/female relations in Cuba. It showed here on Planète, a documentary cable channel, as they co-financed it and I think it's really interesting but some of my formalist friends thought it was like a radio programme.

It's nice to have films look OK and know how to put the camera where you should put it. These are the things that one has to teach students – anybody can teach them who has any kind of pedagogical capacities. I was actually blackballed from teaching in film school in France and England because of my interest in revolutionary formalism at the time – IDHEC[1] [now La Fémis][2] didn't want me because I was a Communist and The National Film and Television School [NFTS] in the UK didn't want me because they felt I was trying destroy the British Film Industry, which was rather flattering at the time but they were totally correct, it was totally useless. As far as my writing is concerned, I have published one book, which I really am proud of which I wrote in collaboration with a woman, Geneviève Sellier – I prefer working with women and have for a long time as a matter of fact. The book, *La Drôle de Guerre des Sexes du Cinéma Français : 1930-1956* (1996), is an analysis of the representation of gender in French classical cinema during that period, which I really think is a good piece of path-breaking work in this country, because nobody has ever done that here or anywhere for that matter – it's not exportable because nobody cares about that cinema anywhere else but here it's a big success, which is interesting because here people are very anti content analysis, but it is cinema that is so despised in this country, all those 1930s and 1940s films, anything before the New Wave is in for a dig.

CM: What about the book you've just finished?

NB: The book I've just finished [*De la Beauté des Latrines* (2007)] is a critique of Modernism. It's about cinema criticism; it's a critique of the historically modernist bias of French film criticism since Louis Delluc and even way before that. On the one hand it is a sort of plea in favour of a gender-based grid of evaluation of films, which is no longer aesthetic but which is political, content orientated and concerned with ambiguity. It's about different things, it's a big book but it is primarily a critique or at least the offensive part of it, in both senses of the word, as far as French criticism is concerned. I found a few people who actually quite like the book here; it's a sort of a deconstruction, as they say, of the dominant thinking about film in this country, because we're dominated by aesthetics basically from the word go, something which I contributed to in my sort of naïve way, without knowing it. I thought everybody here was into content when I was writing *Theory of Film Practice* (1968/1973), but of course it wasn't true.

CM: Your anecdotes are interesting, but of course came at particular moments that have now moved on. From the idea of looking back at *Theory of Film Practice* I would put it to you that some of the main concerns in that book and possibly some of your recent concerns, not for you personally, but as a problematic in the world in fact have not moved on that much and have not been resolved, such as the question of dialectics, the place of Marxism within the general space of the shift from Modernism to Postmodernism.

So I wonder whether making this absolute shift from form to content, which seems to be what you're saying, is in a way avoiding the kind of responsibility for the contribution you actually made to that work historically and which has been fantastically important. As for your anecdotes on moments of truth, these could be balanced by other more positive instances such as shifts in the school curriculum adding materialism to the history lesson as well as the development of Film Studies and Media Studies. People that have come out of that period of the 1970s, who themselves are now either filmmakers, teachers, professors or researchers have passed on methods of working, methods of analysis – a critique which was not just to do with cinema but was a political critique. We've come to a position – as suggested by Terry Eagleton in *After Theory* (2003) – that has simultaneously attempted to instigate debates on questions of the production of meaning but actually makes them even more problematic and recuperative in today's context. Media Studies has become a dominant subject choice for entrance to universities. Whereas in the 1970s people were looking at classical texts for their Doctorates, they may have been looking at Bram Stoker, now they're doing their theses on *Buffy the Vampire Slayer* (1997–2003) and popular television. Eagleton suggests that whereas in the 1970s and 1980s Cultural Studies students were interested in sexuality, now they are interested in sex. There is a kind of overdetermining of the problem alongside the development in the world of globalisation, there no longer being a dichotomy of the struggle of two superpowers (though there may be newly developing superpowers). The grand narratives which themselves were based in form rather than content have gone, so rather than go backwards into finding the other space (of content), to enter that other non-formalistic space – where form and structure are no longer dominant over what they're actually portraying, Eagleton concludes by suggesting that we should look for new spaces, ones that are now being created by globalisation itself. My fear regarding your position is that if one leaves these issues of form alone, you are going to find in another 10 or 20 years that students of today will not have been enabled to deal with future reconstructions and myth.

NB: I'm fairly familiar with the argument and I read Eagleton – I haven't read *After Theory* but I know most of his previous work and I think his analyses are on the whole quite accurate, certainly his critique of what Cultural Studies has become. Last year I was at the SCS [Society for Cinema and Media Studies] conference for a prize for my life's work – it was absolutely ghastly. I mean it was all *Buffy the Vampire Slayer* or the equivalent. It was the run up to the Iraq war and there was even a seminar devoted to that, but they had nothing to say, they couldn't say anything – it was terrifying. I am so completely and absolutely pessimistic about the possibility about these new spaces – the new spaces are conducive to this fragmentation, individualisation, narcissistic jouissance, things that precisely inform Cultural Studies. The marginalisation of Marxism, the marginalisation of feminism in so far as it was a critical space. My own feeling is that, as far as audiovisual production and more largely artistic production is concerned, well I do believe that probably in the South – what we used to call the Third World there is a sense that new things could possibly emerge that precisely are in many respects renewing the kind of thinking one was doing in the sixties and seventies. But as far as the countries of the centre are concerned, forget it – I have become completely cynical about that. I think that, for example US hegemony is almost irreversible until the decline of the US is such that the whole thing implodes and there will be a crisis, out of which will emerge undeniably perhaps other things, other possibilities, but as far the actual current tendencies are concerned, no. I ought to say for one thing I do feel, strangely enough, that it is not through documentary that anything politi-cal or culturally dynamic and provocative and expressive of dissident currents can express themselves, but rather through fictions and I have to say that there was a rather remarkable period in the nineties of about seven or eight years, it seems to be over now for reasons which everybody understands, where as far as the North was concerned, it was in the US, a sort of semi-independent film production, totally within Hollywood codes. I'm not interested in the under-ground, but films like *Freeway* (1996), which were startlingly expressive of political correctness, which I take to be a good object – I'm 'politically correct', at least in the face of people like Bush you understand, i.e. I share the ideals of the Western left – I've even written a bit about that. Anyway I've seen twenty to thirty films from that period of independent production in the US, but today that seems to have died on the whole and obviously the climate in the States has become what it is and it's become much more difficult apparently. Besides which, those films were, I learned more recently, practically unseen in the US, they were shown on videocassettes basically and who knows how, where and when. My friend Jonathan Rosenberg who is a critic in Chicago had never seen most of these films – they only came out in LA, maybe New York and nobody's interested and so they go to video.

CM: Can you mention any other names of films you're talking about?

NB: *Signs and Wonders* (2000) by Jonathan Nossiter, *Very Bad Things* (1998) by Peter Berg, *There's Something About Mary* (1998) – I thought that was an absolutely remarkable film about male sexuality and the way men create women as images, etc. *Nurse Betty* (2000) is another remarkable film and oth-ers you probably haven't seen.

CM: Would you pose those against films coming out of New York in that period – like Harmony Korine's *Gummo* (1997) or Darren Aronofsky's *Pi* (1998) – independent low budget feature films?

NB: They haven't come here, as far as I know.

CM: What about work coming out of Denmark – Dogme films, have you seen those?

NB: All I know are films, where this guy makes these terribly misogynistic films, which make me vomit every time I happen to see one.

CM: Not necessarily films directed by Lars Von Trier, but films like *The Idiots* (1998) and *Festen* (1998) – films on the edge one might say.

NB: I saw them and I think they are just nonsense. On the whole I think European cinema is partly nonexistent as far as I am concerned. I saw a Stephen Frears film a few weeks ago, I think we sat through it but I thought it was an absolutely revolting and exploitative film. I hardly go to the movies anymore, it just depresses me – I go to the opera if I can and that's about it.

CM: Let me go back to something that might interest you. George Monbiot, a journalist, and environmental activist in the UK, wrote a book called *The Age of Consent* (2003) in which he says everything has been globalised except our consent. I think he'd agree with you in as much as you would suggest that America has won, there's no kind of argument that averts the way that world history has developed economically. But rather than attempt to counter that, which would be futile, flow with it, which in a sense is a parallel to your entrism of going into the film industry and flowing with it in order to ride on the crest of globalisation, use its opportunities to actually develop this realisation of one world, where there is the possibility through communication of being in touch with African countries, Asian countries, and lets face it, a lot of interesting cinema more than anywhere is coming out of those countries now.

NB: OK, look if we're talking about art, I should counter that by saying my judgment of films has essentially become a political judgment. Not so much because I appreciate films that put forward positive messages, but I appreciate mostly films that put forward real contradictions. In other words because I think that is basically what art is about and in a way if I'm going to judge a film or a novel as a work of art it's on those grounds, it's in the way in which it works through real contradictions in the world. OK, that sums up half of the book I just finished, but to be frank with you, I do not believe that art has any political effect – I don't believe that anymore, I think it's absolute crap. I now think it's about political action, 'altermondialisme' we call it in France, we don't call it anti-globalisation any more – because obviously globalisation, there's something wrong with that. What's wrong with it is the fact that it's Adam Smith's dream come true, so to speak. The question is how to combat that – right now for example I am trying to put together some work with Allan Sekula who is a photographer who has been working on the political and is a theoretician, a Marxist/feminist like myself, he's been working on the political economy of the sea for many years. He made a travelling exhibition of photographs called *Fish Story* (1999) – he is quite famous in photographic circles, he has sort of infiltrated photographic circles, he's not really an artist, he's an agitator and we've been trying to put together a feature length film on the political economy of the sea through his vision. The point being that it's been impossible to find any money for this, because this is indeed an attempt to talk about what's really going on, i.e. the way the sea is the place of exploitation; the worst exploitation and the basic exploitation, the whole infrastructure. All this globalisation is because of these ships that go back and forth with shoes made in China, etc., this is really what its all about. The sea also has a mythological aspect that we're embracing, this reality of containerisation, the reality of work and transportation – all that is hidden from view; the working ports are further away from the cities and other ports are being turned into places of leisure and into places of a kind of sublime of the sea. One of the most interesting examples is the Gary Museum in Bilbao [Guggenheim] – this ancient shipyard/seaport was completely destroyed by the IMF [International Monetary Fund] and European dictates to Spanish economy and they're now trying to turn it into a leisure spot with this ghastly pretentious museum that Guggenheim put up there and somehow tried to turn Bilbao into a tourist spot – it's not really working and they're trying to build these museums all over the world, like hamburger joints. We got some money from an art foundation in Holland, we got half the money. No television channel here will even contemplate putting a cent into this thing [The film went into production in 2008]. I still am motivated by the idea of saying it through television preferably, because cinema is not I think on. It's true that *Bowling for Columbine* (2002) I guess has had some impact, which is something I admire.

CM: Where would you put Chris Marker now?

NB: Which Chris Marker?

CM: If you're talking about content, the potential of using the contradictions of art to actually politicise a particular space, then the Chris Marker of the essay film, which in a sense is what you're talking about, it means that you could actually produce this film within a context.

NB: It's becoming so difficult to do them. In this country it's become, I would say, absolutely impossible. Chris Marker is a great man, go talk to him and he'll tell you how it's absolutely totally impossible to do anything like even what he was doing. He did make something not too long ago, but he has a name, Godard still makes these crazy things that nobody understands. But today I have many friends who are coming up against stone walls trying to do anything which has any kind of ambition like that. The producer who was going to try and produce Sekula's and my project here just failed to find any money at all and has given up making TV documentaries because he feels that it's totally impossible to do anything that he wants to do. He told a terribly revealing story, which I think feeds in a bit to this issue here. Last year he produced simultaneously two products, one of them a documentary where a guy drove round in a taxi and talked to his customers and it was cute and was raved about in all the press [*Taxi Parisien*, 2002]. At the same time he produced a very remarkable film by a Belgian woman, Bénédicte Liénard called *Une Part du Ciel* (2002) somewhat in the tradition of ultra-realist Belgian films, which I find kind of interesting in a way but often very boring. Her film had no positive criticism worth mentioning and it was a beautiful film – I'm sure nobody heard of it anywhere and that is a film he spent three years on – down the drain, nothing. I'm talking about Jacques Bidou the most prominent left-wing producer in France. The penny dropped and he realised where we're at today. So this whole question is in an impasse and one can dream about riding these waves and all the wonderful things that are going to happen in the future and so on, one can fantasise about Braudelian cycles of decline and suggest that Iraq and all that is a sign of America's weakness. I'm sure it's true and in the long run obviously civilization is not going to die but it's going to shift to another place.

CM: There are fiction films still being produced in Europe and elsewhere that could be considered as radical, dealing with social issues rather than overt politics. I think of Abbas Kiarostami's film *Ten* (*10*, 2002) and the French film by Claire Denis *Vendredi Soir* (*Friday Night*, 2002), which are also rides in taxis. Also interesting is the work of the Dardenne Brothers in Belgium such as *Le Fils* (*The Son*, 2002).

NB: I haven't seen them, but then who does see them? I'm sorry, that's the other side of the coin. Their audience is solely made up of bobos – the bourgeois bohemes, the people who are in this party that I'm in [the Green party]. There isn't a worker in it, that's one of the problems with this party; it has only this middle-class constituency. And this is the problem, if you like, with 'committed art', even the Columbine film, I'm a very great fan of Michael Moore obviously, but at the same time this is not mass audience stuff because it just cannot be. It is by definition, for all sorts of reasons, even if it runs on television it runs on ARTE[3] so it's really looked at by the same people. The complexity of the forms of domination are such that it is difficult for people to be able to understand that it's not nature taking its course, which is what most people today have been taught to think. That's one of my main concerns in writing little tracts that we distribute in the neighbourhood to try and link all these things together but it's extremely complicated and these linkages are only, I think, perceptible by the enlightened middle classes. You tell a worker who has been out of work for a year that a fulfilling life is not one devoted 100 per cent to work and that work itself should be less alienating and they look at you – yeah but how am I going to pay the rent? All the things that are happening today are making it more and more impossible to put across these complex reasons for struggle and areas in which the struggle can take place and so on. So I do think the dynamic today is totally opposed to that and explains what cinema has become, because just have a look around us and look at what plays – this mass of American spectaculars, very sensually fulfilling things, which the young people are totally involved with in a totally uninvolved way, if I may say so, this extraordinary idea that everything is kind of a joke – the biggest success on television here over the past few years was the French equivalent to *Big Brother*. I have a student who has been doing work on these reality shows and kids watch them in order to laugh at the people in them. In other words it's this mixture of distance, a sort of Brechtian distancing, everything is now distancing. I have to say I wrote a piece about that in the early 1980s, which Miriam Hanson trashed at one point, accused me of cultural pessimism, but I think I was bloody right, distancing has become one of the weapons of the ruling class, distancing with regard to almost everything has become really dominant. There's one point in which we were totally wrong – the whole idea that distancing is a radical tool, the most subversive things you can make today are the most involving things.

CM: Is it distancing or is it voyeurism?

NB: Voyeurism is a kind of distancing, I'm not sure there's a great difference in a funny way. Voyeurism implies an erotic dimension to it, OK let us call it indeed a kind of erotic distancing. Obviously it no longer has Brechtian content, Brechtian distancing this certainly is not, but at the same time it is – there's no question. Look at all this American Tarantino and David Lynch kind of stuff, which is distancing for the chic middle classes who are laughing at mass culture. Also even films like *Mars Attacks* (1996), I don't know if that had success, I think it did whereas *Starship Troopers* (1997) did not, but they function the same way – this kind of distancing where in a sense people are laughing at their own pleasures in a way. *Scary Movie* (2000) is a movie in which people go in order to laugh at their own relation to *Scream* (1996). It's all very fascinating and Baudrillard and people like that can write fascinating books about it. It is totally fascinating but it is totally revolting.

CM: Can you bring that back to the philosophical, political critique that we talked about, whereby in a sense what's happened is a popularisation of Postmodernism? In the 1970s one was really still a Modernist and this notion of the pluralism of meaning had not yet evolved. One was battling between two fixed spaces; the left and the right and then the relationship with Cultural Studies. The people who are making these programs are in fact our own students who have come out of film schools, which have now multiplied in number and output a hundred fold. They've taken on board some of the things that we have taught at film schools, they are semi-politically conscious, I won't deny them that, but they have lost a kind of space in which there is a focus; there is no longer a focal point towards which the reasons they're doing the things they're doing are moving.

NB: Then we're going to have to talk about Postmodernism. In a sense, Postmodernism, if it exists, is a reading of what is happening *to* the world. It is not the definition of what is happening *in* the world. Postmodernism, in so far as it is an intellectual framework or in so far as it is an artistic practice, is simply opportunistic - if you can't lick 'em, join 'em. All the things that we've been talking about today, for example in cinema, these Hollywood films that can be qualified as Postmodernist, Tarantino, etc., how should I say? They are basically I think the products of a certain cynicism, which has become in the US a dominant political ideology. It is no longer a question of believing the great myths of America, man and his destiny and all that, it's a matter of believing *nothing* and that's enough to keep the system going. I'm quoting my friend Thom Anderson in the film I made about the American left. That's how it functions and that has produced, for various levels of consumption *Scary Movie* at one level and lets say *Starship Troopers* at another. This was a film that failed at the box-office but which here was regarded as a great progressive movie by the critics, believe it or not.

The point is that indeed the collapse, the betrayal of the left, the social democratic left, is absolutely fundamental, as much as the collapse of the Soviet Union has been to the current hegemony of market society. I'm very much in debt to Christopher Lasch's analysis, not his stupid remarks about feminism, of course – he was an older man when he wrote that stuff - but nonetheless basically *The Culture of Narcissism* (1979) is really a description of what has happened in our societies. So we have this sort of ideal, this atomisation and so on, which is happening, whereby everything is everywhere. There are a few who celebrate this sort of generalized relativism, I feel they are really vile – Richard Rorty and his work simply appals me. But the real problem of course is that there's this imbrication, Eagleton alludes to it a little bit in *The Illusions of Postmodernism* (1996), of indeed new forms of struggle which have arisen in feminism, ecology, ethnic groups and so on, which are perfectly legitimate struggles and indeed are part of the general picture of oppression and so on. But at the same time, particularly because of the way America is, always has been, having no tradition of class struggle really, at least one which has completely been perverted for so long, that these progressive ideals have become fundamentally confused with the values of liberal capitalism, everything becoming marketable and culture itself becoming simply another market value. The confusion is such that it is almost impossible to extricate the one from the other and this is what has broken down, I think, any kind of serious cultural or political resistance. If you want to call that Postmodernism, OK, let's call it Postmodernism, but it's a scam essentially and it is something which I think has become practically impossible to combat as well because it's so omnipresent and the confusion is so extraordinarily great. Of course what has also happened, one of the things that strikes me the most, as Jameson points out at one point early on in his writing about Postmodernism, is that Postmodernism is indeed a recycling of certain aspects of Modernism and in particular, despite all the attentiveness to mass culture and so on, it is essentially elitist because it is this kind of camp reading of *Buffy the Vampire Slayer* for example. I counted that in America at that SCS thing there were 10 seminars on *Buffy the Vampire Slayer*, with young feminists apparently giggling over the kinkiness of this thing. It was absolutely fascinating how that elitist attitude has been 'massified' in a funny way. So it's all very democratic in a terrifying way, but it is totally and fundamentally depoliticised in so far as politics is about power relations and I do still remain a Marxist fundamentally about the economic power relations. You see I've refused to accept the idea that everything is equivalent.

CM: Well here is a view of where I think the problems are with the more recent generations of film students in the UK and America. Since I left the RCA, I've been teaching in film schools and universities for the last 30 years. I've seen students, say from 1979, young people who had come to understand the world only during the premierships of Ronald Regan and Margaret Thatcher. These students grew up in a completely different social and economic environment, and therefore ideological environment, than I grew up in and I've seen, as I'm sure you have, the nature, the essence of the student itself change and develop from a very different sort of person; one almost without a sense of desire. They have become absorbing, instead of developing and that to me is a tragedy caused fairly directly by the economic and political system through which they traversed. Instead of developing their individuality they have absorbed the ideology and developed as the self-centric individual. However, I think that is changing and that's why I'm more optimistic, not pessimistic about it. I'm very interested to know that you would still consider yourself a Marxist, because slowly but surely, in a strange sort of way, people seem to be now coming back to it, particularly in America. I gave a paper at a conference 5 years ago and some American sociologists were there. I was talking about Emile Durkheim and collective consciousness - which I'd like to discuss with you shortly - and they were saying do you know for the first time we can talk about Marxism in America, because we haven't been allowed to until now and now people are beginning to be interested in that academically. I just want to hold onto that on one hand and on the other hand talk about what you said about the elitism of Postmodernism, because you touched on it; it's both elitist and populist at the same time and that kind of contradiction produces its nothingness that you're talking about. I think what we're witnessing and why I'm quite excited still, is that I think we're seeing the end of Postmodernism and I think that's going out with the development of globalisation, because there is nothing to any longer disentangle and pluralise; you don't need to pluralise it anymore, we're going somewhere else. Where is that else?

NB: I suppose I can talk a little bit about France, though in a way somehow I tend to focus on America, even though I don't go there and intend never to go there again actually because it just makes me ill. Here it's considerably different in the sense that Postmodernism exists only in certain avant-garde circles – the universities don't give a damn about that, they're much more conservative in a sense, which is in a way perhaps almost positive. For about seven years I was a Film professor in Lille – and taught young students, most of whom came out of a lower, middle and working class background, which was new to me, before that I had only taught in Paris where they were all trendy middle class students. After a while I began to realise these kids were very open to a lot of things; they were perfectly aware that Godard was just shit, whereas in Paris the students were saying 'oh you can't talk about that' – I'm referring to what he's done for the past 20 years, not his earlier work, which is problematic, but certainly not shit. Because of their class background, often they were of North African extraction, they were incredibly open to a sophisticated feminist discourse. I and my friend Geneviève Sellier with whom I wrote that book [*La Drôle de Guerre des Sexes du Cinema Francais: 1930–1956*], were the only people who have ever taught Film Studies in this country from a gender perspective – two people – and she had a great deal of difficulty getting into the university at all and then finally was appointed a professor at the age of 55. So it's been ridiculous, but when you do bring these ideas to kids like that, those kids; their response after a few years - it took a while - was amazing but it died because they replaced me with some formalist of the worst kind. It's another matter all together in the States. The same sort of students there, even Doctoral students, were aware of their own historical oppression and its continuing impact today but they were totally unaware of the affect of these American policies on the rest of the world. Surveys show that only 20 per cent of Americans have passports and in Congress 85 per cent are proud never to have set foot outside America. There are 60 million born again Christians who are the base of the right in America. The right may lose the next election but they aren't going away. They may, as you say, be teaching Marxism again in universities but the university world in America is so isolated that it doesn't mean a thing to the rest of the country.

CM: Here's another major contradiction you've just put your finger on, that 80 per cent of America has not travelled outside of America, while 100 per cent of American culture has travelled outside of America, which is still, if one can use the term, dominant culture. It brings me back in a circle to this question of cinema or film or if you prefer, representation, because we haven't talked about DVDs or the internet or other methods of the circulation of representation. I can understand your anti-art discourse, what I can't understand is, given what you said about the metadiscourses going around, which is going back to *Buffy the Vampire Slayer* and the fact that American culture dominates the world. I can understand your decision to stand inside politics and political struggle, but I have to say I would challenge your position, which comes from the very first thing you were saying about your revised perspective, which now rejects the struggle that is inside representation itself. It seems to me that it has become even more important during the last thirty years. Given that the hegemony is totally a cultural one now, don't the inadequacies of political expression become subservient to an ideological one? How can we not remain and develop as film representational makers in struggle?

NB: For me, art is dead, art as it was understood for many centuries in the West, I think it is really dead. It is dead because in a way it has, how should I say, I suppose it's because anything goes in a way and that includes any kind of aesthetic innovation in so far as you consider art to be in the socially linked tradition of aesthetics, it is dead, which I'm happy to accept. I watch old movies on TV and, gee, they don't make movies like that anymore, but that's not important, I'm not worried about that, but the problem is as I say, since anything goes, you surf on the net and you can find anything, it's all there in this fragmentary ultimately meaningless way, you see.

I remember we had a teacher at IDHEC, who was sort of a conservative composer, who used to go on about 12-tone music – how it was like grains of sand in a glass, some black, some white, you shake it and it all gets together and becomes grey, but you can keep on shaking it forever and it will never get black and white again. I didn't understand at the time what he was on about because I didn't even know about 12-tone music yet. In a sense that is what has happened today, it's all there indeed – just look at the television programmes. There are something like 500 films a day, there are seven channels showing old movies, it's much better than America if you're a film buff, it's just incredible. It's mad, it's totally insane, you go into a shop and you have hundreds of different kinds of mobile phones and this has broken down the possibilities of constructing meaning about the world. I think this is really the difficulty and I think in a way art, in so far as that was what it was about ultimately after all, that's what Rembrandt is about in some way or other. I think that the problem is value, the whole question of artistic value, aesthetic value, all that is gone. So what have you got left, you've got this communication, this information, these flows of information and who controls them and so on and everybody gets excited. People get all excited about the internet, these cyber anarchists – the whole idea that they're going to break down the system, they are the people who are going to send viruses because that's what they're about, it's a kind of anarchism. Okay and I'm sure they bug the big companies, but department stores have always integrated 30 per cent loss for shoplifting, its no big deal, there's always some way of incorporating that, all that's absolutely hopeless it has no use. The circulation of information indeed, one can find out all these things Americans don't know, but it doesn't matter in a way because of the way it's out there you see, a headline in the *New York Times* or *USA Today* has a million times more impact than what you could read on *Truthout* for example, to take one site I happen to look at from time to time. That's going to keep going, because the whole point is in the great achievement of capitalist globalisation – 'late capitalism' I don't think it can be called – is precisely this enormous fragmentation, this diversification, this thing in which the individual picks out his/her little thing, and that is 'their' great victory in a sense, because 'they' have completely disorganised everything, including I would argue the possibility of creating meaningful art. Because of the context in which everything is being produced today, such that it is going to be diluted into this general circulation of 'merchandise' that this is why, I'm sorry to say it, but when I read the programme of your colloquium I find this playing with toys by the wayside. It is sure that if I were young today and had the same level of awareness, I would certainly not choose to be a filmmaker, I would certainly not choose to teach filmmaking, I would be a sociologist or perhaps an historian.

CM: So, if you were starting again as a student you would want to study Sociology or Anthropology, Psychology, Psychoanalysis, but not Film? Just talk a little bit more about that because I think there's an interesting clue to how film might ally itself to certain other sciences, if you want to call film that for now. If you could talk about why you would want to do this.

NB: Because I would not be concerned about film, I would treat film in this other alternative, impossible existence of mine as the way anybody does. You look at a movie from time to time and maybe a documentary of some sort, though I look at very few of them because I find that it is in documentaries that there's the least politics oddly enough, except for the occasional exception. I'm saying that I myself, the reasons why I got into film had to do with being a great artist, there's no question about that, and sort of going down in history as someone who created something unique and irreplaceable and all that crap. For the exact same reasons I began writing about film; I couldn't make films so I began writing about them and about how I ought to make films that would have that quality of uniqueness and be irreplaceable. This motivation I find absolutely absurd today and I find it very, very depressing when I encounter it in young people, as of course one does, because young people still have these ideas of becoming great artists essentially and in fact the attraction in a funny way, there are two kinds of attraction which the profession exerts on people – one of them is to become a great artist, I think actually perhaps less than before, and the other is the prestige attached to being in the media. So all of that I would be able to eliminate and I would be interested in trying to contribute to understanding, particularly understanding history, I'm very much into history today – I used to hate history, when I was a kid , American history was taught in an absolutely shameful way so that you would hate it, Edward Said talked about that very brilliantly in a piece he wrote about the Iraqi situation. It is absolutely true; history-teaching is one of the essential keys to the understanding of American alienation.

CM: Absolutely, but if we park art and let's make the statement 'film is a branch of philosophy'.

NB: That's what Deleuze would say, but the point is look at Deleuze; those books, I feel sort of embarrassed about Deleuze because Deleuze was a great fan of mine, he was the first famous person who ever wrote me fan mail and I then realised after a year or so that he was, not ripping me off, but in a way he was precisely translating *Theory of Film Practice* into philosophy. I'm being pretentious there, but I was struck by that and then I realised when I tried to read it – I can't read that stuff, it falls out of my hands, but nonetheless I realise enough about what's going on in there to see that he is indeed, it's true what he told me, that *Theory of Film Practice* was like a big revelation to him. That's the problem you see, in a sense its philosophy getting turned into art, because in a sense, where as for me Marx said it and I repeat it, philosophers want to change the world and OK maybe people making films want to do that, but it seems to me the whole problem is that the social status of the audiovisual object today is such that it can only be aestheticised philosophy. I do not think that its inscription through television – the only way to reach a lot of people is through television - the very nature of television is such that I think nothing vital can be conveyed. In the 1970s I think I told this to you guys as students, that I do not believe in any case that film can have any kind of positive ideological impact, except in let's say a revolutionary situation – Cuba 1960s, to some extent perhaps the Soviet Union in the 1920s – there are a lot of questions to be asked about that and perhaps some other examples I can't seem to think of right now. But otherwise it's just art and entertainment.

I honestly think that its OK to teach students to think about film, think about form – why not, obviously in these film schools they've got to do something right? They might as well give some satisfaction to their teachers and so on and students may get into this even if later on they're bound to be frustrated. But I have to say that I cannot, I have to be sincere about my own feelings about that, it has become this totally illusory activity. There's no reason why people shouldn't learn to make innovative entertaining, involving beautiful audio visual objects – why not, fine, it's an activity among others but I think that to want to privilege it, that's the big problem. That's one of the big problems about the film world, because we've always thought of ourselves as the centre of the world, particularly true here – being a cinephile is like a magic word, you're this person who understands that films are the most important things there are, this is really what the definition of cinephelia is. This is our big illusion and in France, in a way, this could be extended to all of culture.

There's a cult of culture in this country that the world envies because we spend much more money on culture than anybody else, we're fighting to keep culture out of the market and all that stuff, the 'exception culturelle'[4] and all that's fine. But the fact of the matter remains that the relation to politics and the relation to the horrors that the world is undergoing today, the poor people of the world as a whole – the rich are getting richer and the poor are getting poorer, all that is absolutely, in my opinion, impermeable to whatever innovations, agitations, that culture may provide. But after all, what I'm saying is totally in keeping with what the Pope calls the hedonism of the northern middle classes, which I have to say is something I feel totally ambivalent about, since I benefit from it, there are all sorts of pleasurable things available to me personally, which I certainly benefit from with a strong sense of guilt, but nonetheless what else is there to do, and at the same time I have a terrifying sense of what this really means in the larger view - with regard to the way we treat the peoples of Africa for example.

CM: It seems to me that you may have three balls in the air at the same time – one being the subjective self, the second is a desire for popularism, which may be the wrong word, but there is a large scale problem in the world, of which the aesthetics of film culture does not touch and there is the third which is philosophy and the theory of theory if you like, and probably all three have to exist simultaneously. But it brings to mind something Terry Eagleton wrote – 'ideology is around to make us feel necessary, philosophy is on hand to remind us that we are not' (2003: 210). I say that because if one remains within the notion of film as theory, for film as philosophy, for theory as theory, for the moment parking ego and self, parking mass world problematics, but working within the notion of philosophising philosophy itself then a branch of which would be the philosophy of culture. Then there are some serious real issues still in there.

NB: No I'm sorry, I don't know if I was ever really into what I would call theory for theory's sake okay – with the underlying belief that it's all useful, like mathematics. To the extent that I got into that, it is probably what I reject most violently today and I do feel that philosophy, in a sense by its very definition, that philosophers have always felt this way, I sound like a postmodernist, I guess in a way I am a postmodernist in the sense that I feel a very strong hostility to high Modernism and everything it implies. I realise that I'm not really into this Habermassian association between Modernism in the arts and the idea you can change the world. Okay, if that's a definition of it then I guess I'm still a modernist, but I'm a postmodernist in the sense that I certainly reject Adorno for example, with his hatred of mass culture and his belief that only the avant-garde is really dissident. Yes it's dissident alright, but it's dissident like philosophy in this sense, that is to say indeed it's sort of above the fray fundamentally and I feel that in a way for me what you've just described is a way of being above the fray and its been a long time now since I've been convinced that art is by definition, or pseudo-art that is to say, more above the fray than it was in the past. But then in a way the pseudo-art of today is probably less above the fray because it's so much in favour of the status quo ultimately in its way, whereas it's true that art at one point could seem to be oppositional in some way or other, that probably was true, but I think it was fundamentally an illusion because no one could find any instances in the whole history of humanity, at least I think, where art has actually been an essential part of any kind of progressive or revolutionary change. I think it has always been an accretion of it in some way or other – some often interesting, but only as such and not in terms of any actual practical thing. So I think theory should be much more concerned about how we're going to get out of this mess if you like.

CM: You see you took us back into art then and we've parked art because I wanted to take you from theory and philosophy into the areas you're interested in, which are sociology and anthropology. If there is a triumvirate relationship between various disciplines, still at a theoretical level, at some stage they have to de-theorise to the point of practice, because practice in that sense cannot be purely theoretical, it has to engage problematically with the world and no longer becomes pure theory and that practice is in this sense an audiovisual one.

NB: Okay, I would accept that there is probably some way in which in an ideal world, okay, I agree with that. Indeed, the articulation between these different forms of knowledge and audiovisual practice – yes, absolutely one could assume or suppose that there, in some ideal world, which is not this one, there are ways of rearticulating them perhaps. I continue to say that the environment in which the way that money circulates, I mean there are millions of determining factors in what can be and what is produced today and tomorrow and are such that this articulation can only feed the machine. I don't think it can in any sense be grains of sand – I don't believe that, I think that the hope that the tail can wag the dog is a vain hope and in the audiovisual production, as all other artistic or pseudo-artistic productions are the tail, they are superstructural, in the old Marxist sense and I do think that precisely because of what is called globalisation, but which is obviously something much more complicated than that. I think it's an illusion to think that one can change things, that this articulation at the School level lets say, of anthropology and history or whatever – I'm sure students can find ways of making student films which appear to be doing something, but its not going to be of any use to them afterward and I think whereas I used to believe fundamentally of course that they were all going to get together and change, indeed as the NFTS feared, for example the British Film Industry, well I mean look at Channel Four in the first years of Channel Four there were these illusions. I would say that one of the pennies that dropped about that same period was the following: my companion Hannah and I were watching the Channel Four thing where you could go into a box on the street and criticise programmes and a woman came in, sat down in front of the camera and she said 'there was a film the other night– on *The Eleventh Hour* I think it must have been, it was a feminist film and I was really quite interested. But then the camera began doing this... ' and she was on a rolling chair in this box and sort of slid in and out of the frame, it was Pam Cook who made the program I think and it was one of these deconstructive things. 'I completely lost the thread of the discussion and was really very annoyed with this'. Hannah and I slapped each other on the back and began to understand. This was mid 1980s, 1984 maybe, I mean the early Channel Four, you know I made the *Year of the Bodyguard* (1981) which was the first programme commissioned by *The Eleventh Hour* which was pioneering work. I saw it the other week, in Germany they did a retrospective of my oeuvre – it's ridiculous, so self-conscious and confused. It was a period when we did believe all those things, a lot of us did, you guys made *Justine [JUSTINE, by the Marquis de Sade*, 1976] but I do think it was utterly wrong-headed. The point is at that time there was a space and one dreamed about it, but of course in a way it was the tail end of that whole idea that television had from Keynes on, which was the idea that one could educate the masses through the mass media and of course it was all a tremendous mistake – one has to find ways of introducing politics into variety shows, but 'that'll be the day', as John Wayne puts it in some movie or other.

CM: You just mentioned that you don't know what use it is to students, which is the same question that the pragmatists in film theory and practice institutions also use when they insist that theory is of no use to practitioners who make films, which I would consider to be a theoretically misguided and potentially right wing discourse and they don't mean it the way you just articulated it, they mean it won't get them jobs in the industry.

NB: From their point of view that's genuinely how they feel about it, it's one of the reasons why on the whole you see I was teaching in Lille in this very curious situation, which is that in film departments in this country there is only one film school that is currently worth mentioning, the rest are private and are extremely expensive and on the whole the universities do not teach production because they don't have enough money, so kids who can't get in to La Femis will enrol in these film departments, where they spend some time fooling around with a little camera, but there are no classes in production, etc., therefore they are studying history and theory, but they have it in the back of their heads that they want to be filmmakers, well most of them, at least half of them anyway and consequently they're obviously bored by all this theory and history stuff. Now I was able to get them interested to a certain degree, precisely because it was so politicised and because of their class origins in part, so I would relate to that and some of them actually went out there and made some documentary films and so on. I haven't had an opportunity to teach film production students in about twenty years and I think once or twice I turned down the opportunity because I know I don't have anything to say they want to hear. I gave a series of lectures in Argentina to a university where they teach 500 students at a time film production – they had to attend, it was obligatory. So they were all there and they started walking out after about an hour and it was absolutely terrifying because they were all bored shitless you know and it was just obvious I had nothing for them, it was all about Hollywood and representation and women in Hollywood films, something like that, things I'm interested in writing about. They weren't the least bit interested and why should they be?

So the discourse you've just been putting forward is not simply a rightwing discourse, it is a spontaneous discourse of film production students, for all sorts of reasons they come in there thinking they've got all they need to know about the world and what they need to know is how to express this, how to express themselves. That's perfectly natural and spontaneous and so on. One wants to break that down, wants to give them some kind of political consciousness – that's certainly what I would be doing if I were teaching film today, as I did in Ohio State, I made those little macho bastards make films about rape and things like that and set them projects like that or else I'd show them radical films to illustrate technical sound procedures. That was just smuggling in my ideas, but this whole question about the battle of theory and all that kind of thing, I'm sorry I feel it is just part of the illusions that were ours in the days when we thought the revolution was imminent.

CM: But in the interim what do you make of the sort of film theory that's being taught in film schools now, which one could call cognitive theory – David Bordwell and people like that coming from America? I don't know how dominant that kind of work is, but it certainly goes against the post-Althusserian, Lacanian, post-Freudian kind of work and way into another direction.

NB: I hardly know Bordwell's work to be honest with you, but what I've read of it I found to be just another version of formalism – do you feel that's really different from that in some way?

CM: I'd say it was more based on psychology rather than psychoanalysis. Therefore in essence the tabula rasa isn't blank, that there is a subject in the world that isn't simply implanted upon, there are essences, and there are genetic implications. All these kind of things that have developed in the last twenty years, which suggest that we're more complex as human beings than we think we are. That has been said by some of the left and therefore in a sense that the left was wrong in the past and this is why that kind of Marxist and post-Marxist theory is of no use to film students. I think this is the battle that's going on.

NB: I don't know his work well enough to really discuss it, but what I've read of it seems to me nonetheless to be very much – I don't know how to say that – I feel more sympathetic to Janet Staiger if you like, although I feel there are problems with that too, she fetishises material traces and so on, which I think is a mistake because there are things that are happening in films that relate to people precisely through the unconscious but I do think contextual reading is what is most important. For example one of the key chapters in my book is about what I call the tendential ambiguity of the Hollywood movie and I feel that Hollywood has produced films with double and maybe triple meanings ever since the beginning you see and I think specifically Hollywood – I think other national cultures have done this much less, interestingly enough, and I think that's one of the strengths of Hollywood in a way; its one of the ways in which Hollywood manages to appeal to a large audience, to men and women for example, and that in certain points in time this has become materialist because these ambiguities become the portrayals of social contradictions; I think that's true in the melodramas of King Vidor, in Hitchcock and a few others. In a way I think that perhaps joins up somewhat with Bordwell except that fundamentally – you see for me what matters most is social realities and that films for me can only be evaluated in terms of their relation to the rest of life, the rest of social life and so on, but only that. The psychologisation,

Bordwell's psychologisation is for me a way essentially of disdaining the primacy of the real social world, which has been a tendency and has worked from the word go, even though it had other forms in the early days, it was much closer to the stuff I used to write actually. Robin Wood is someone I admire, up to a point, there are times when he's mistaken, but on the whole Robin Wood is the author who I most often refer to – he's been very seminal, I only discovered him very late in life and it's funny, we had a brief exchange on email and he explained to me how one day he'd come to the Slade just after I'd been there talking about Kenji Mizoguchi and had James Leahy slag him off because 'Noel Burch has just explained that Mizoguchi is all about form' or some shit like that 'and you're going on about culture and that type of thing is just out of date' and Wood had been very upset by this apparently. I only read his work five years ago perhaps for the first time, I think there are certain pieces of Robin Wood that I think are absolutely crucial, for example his analysis of *Taxi Driver* (1976), which was confirmation I found of this whole question of ambiguity in Hollywood film. His work on Sternberg, etc. So, Robin Wood and of course the women writers, on the whole there are a number of women who are for me absolutely crucial, such as Tania Modleski's work on Hitchcock and of course my friend Geneviève Sellier who is now writing a book on the New Wave, which is going to make a lot of people very angry, but which is absolutely spot on. It was Geneviève who taught me I suppose the basics of how do you teach film – 'what does it say and what does it mean' was the way she put it once and for me this is absolutely crucial and this remark has become in a sense my motto as far as teaching people how to look at movies. Obviously, meaning is produced by all means possible, form included, but nonetheless it is a question of how it inscribes itself in society in a given time. I'm slagged off very regularly in this country for preaching this notion, but I think my work is still very solid – nobody knows it in English because it's untranslated. It's sort of frustrating for me, what I've written for the past 15 years not a word of it is translated into English and it is work I'm proud of and work which if you like certainly articulates all this crap I've been saying here I think much more convincingly – I like to think so in any case, because its historically based and it is fed by a great deal of reading that I've done of basically feminist writing. I am at a point in my life where I can hardly deal with men anymore, I really agree with Louis Aragon about women and the future of humanity ['la femme est l'avenir de l'homme'[5]] and I really feel that, not just in film, in literature women's transformation of the landscape in general and this includes the history of opera, this includes a million things you could mention, it is absolutely decisive and I have basically been learning from women and I guess a few gays like Robin Wood, because I think its not irrelevant that he is gay and has an attitude that is so fundamentally anti-formalist; I mean as anti-formalist as I am. That I feel is not uninteresting in that the composers of the twentieth century who have written music that I find most amenable today are people like Benjamin Britten.

CM: I'm fascinated about what you're saying. In a sense what you seem to be saying is that there is an ontology of the make-up of human consciousness dependent upon its classification by gender – male, female, gay.

NB: No, it's a social phenomenon, I don't feel there's something ontological about it at all – it has to do with the place of women in human society over the centuries okay and this place has bequeathed to them, I should say, a broad spectrum of insights which they could not formulate for many years, but which now, actually for some time if you look back and discover what feminists were writing a century or two ago, but obviously it's been isolated and some don't even consider themselves feminists, but certainly Rachilde's[6] take on male/female relations is unique in her time and absolutely astonishing to us today still in a way. She considered herself anti-feminist but nonetheless she was a woman and occupied a certain space. Social space has nothing to do with biology, except very indirectly the fact they'd been consigned to taking care of kids and the family and this whole role of nurturing and all that kind of thing. But that was a social decision in itself wasn't it and it doesn't apply to all periods of history. But I absolutely fundamentally believe that, for example take one essential example of this – it was in the 1970s I first began to understand about the centrality of work and the male fetishisation of work and so on. And how to understand this I was in a textile factory in Eastern France doing a video for the Party and there were all these women and they began talking about work and their relation to work and how different it was to the men's relation – there were no men there, it was just a women's meeting – and it was extraordinary, they were saying men obsess about work and all the rest is nothing, we aren't like that. On the contrary work is work and the rest is the rest and we have many different activities and so on. These were not especially intellectual workers, but she had just understood that and understood that women have a different attitude toward work. Feminists do understand it and have written about it. But this is only one example. Feminists within Modernism, for example, Virginia Woolf's approach to Modernism is fundamentally different to that of Joyce as I think several authors have been at pains to develop, in particular Susan Gubar and Sandra Gilbert who wrote *The Madwoman in the Attic* (1979) and especially the three volumes of *No Man's Land* (1988 - 1994). This is about women in modernism and is absolutely fundamental. These books have been very important for me to understand that there's been a critique within modernism of the male tendency for abstractionism and all that kind of thing.

CM: Do you think people like Julia Kristeva were taking up a male discourse?

NB: There are things that people like Kristeva have contributed but it's always limited by the fact that they're part of the French University system – Kristeva has lived all her mature life with the most misogynistic of contemporary French writers, Phillipe Sollers, who has written a huge anti-feminist tract called *Femmes* (1984), so somehow she has to deal with this, so she deals with it in a way which my feminist friends find on the whole unsatisfactory. Real French feminists have no truck at all with what is called in England French Feminism, its something that people don't understand outside the country.

CM: De Beauvoir of course in the same context with Sartre.

NB: No, no, actually yes, de Beauvoir also had tremendous blind spots, she lived with Sartre and Sartre was basically someone who didn't really deal with women very well, okay he has a few insights, he learned a few things from her but not much. His Flaubert [*The Family Idiot: Gustave Flaubert, 1821–1857* (1971)] is in part informed I feel by de Beauvoir's sensibility. The situation here is very difficult to understand for anybody who doesn't live here. There's a militant feminism which is quite interesting, which even has working class dimensions today, but intellectual feminism is like what we call 'preaching in the catacombs', it's completely marginalised. Most of the feminist scholars are still teaching in secondary schools you know, can't get jobs in a university and can't get roles of authority, it's very difficult. It's getting a little better, particularly in areas like Sociology, but Humanities and Film Studies - forget it!, Even in Literature and that kind of thing it's very difficult for serious feminists to make any kind of headway.

CM: Luce Irigaray is an interesting French feminist.

NB: Well it's the same category, no. But you should have a look – I managed to translate the preface to one of the really important feminist books published in this country. It was a book published in 1982 called *La Poétique du Mâle*, by a woman called Michelle Coquillat who died a couple of years ago and had spent a great deal of time in America and this is an example of what I would call real French feminism. She does for French literature from Madame

Lafayette [1634-1693] onwards what Leslie Fielder did for the American novel with *Love and Death in the American Novel* (1960) a basic book for American culture and society in general, as this is basic for understanding French culture. I translated the introduction and the first chapter for a British feminist magazine. I added a little preface about this whole misunderstanding in the Anglo-American world about French feminism – what it is, where it is and who is doing it – historians of literature, sociologists or whatever and there's a lot of work - often extremely useful, stimulating work, etc., but it's totally unknown outside this country, absolutely 100 per cent unknown because it deals with French culture and I suppose that's one of the reasons because it doesn't deal with T. S. Elliot and Proust you see.

CM: You've talked about feminist theory and some gay theory – you haven't talked about black theory.

NB: The last two can be quite problematic, not just for me but for others too. Black history study is obviously extremely interesting, but let's put it this way – yes, I have been known to go so far as to say that as far as understanding questions of representation are concerned and I am obviously talking about questions of representation within the West, I looked at Japan but that was very trivial, the way I dealt with it anyhow - I would say that gender is primary. It has the same role in the private sphere as class struggle has in the economic history of the world, it's the motor. I believe this absolutely and there's a chapter in Theresa de Lauretis[7] where she suggests that indeed it's the male/female conflict which is the core conflict of literature and in general of narrative and I would say in representation in general, because its true of painting as well. I think this is absolutely true, it's one of the reasons why I have become primarily involved in questions of gender – not out of sympathy for feminism, which of course I have total sympathy at least for feminism as I understand it and as my friends understand it, which is not necessarily about difference but about equality, if you get the distinction that I make. It was when we studied French cinema and we confronted our work with that of the male historians of French cinema, who are sort of Marxist or crypto-Marxist, who are desperately seeking ways of seeing inscriptions of class struggle and history with a big H in these movies, and never really succeeding and we discovered that it was very clear why they weren't succeeding, because the films weren't about that at all, in any way. They were about male/female relations, that's all they were really ever about, everything else was secondary.

One of the main revelations in this book I have written with Geneviève

Sellier is that during the war, during the German occupation, films in France were far more centred around women and were indeed often sort of feminist, sometimes in a right wing way, but nonetheless, than ever before or since. Well this is a paradox and people hated us for that and particularly certain progressives and also for revealing that after the war French cinema becomes the most misogynist cinema in the history of the world for about five to seven years until things settled down. Of course it was also the Liberation, a moment of extraordinary social progress, (which the present government is trying to roll back), so here is a contradiction and this was not because society had become misogynist, but because cinema was reacting to a social evolution. The men making these films were terrified by what women were becoming and doing, so that's what they're making them about. Hollywood is exactly the same and I think this is also true of literature, which Marxists never understood. If you read Lukács' analysis of Thomas Mann's first novel *Buddenbrooks* (1901), it's absolutely fascinating to see that he doesn't know what to do with this female character who occupies half the book. He thinks she's a mistake in the book because he doesn't understand that Mann is actually talking about the oppression of women under patriarchy, but since this concept is totally outside his ken, he just thinks she's a mistake in the book. I want to write something about that because it seems to be an extraordinarily revealing moment of the blindness of Marxism in every way.

CM: I'm much clearer now about where you are and why and how you've got to where you are. What I can't clarify in your thinking is that there's a distinction I feel between film studies and filmmaking and a slight contradiction here between your admiration for films like *There's Something About Mary* and what you've just said. I can see the connection now, I can see why you would admire what I consider to be a dreadful film. However, coming back to the basics of what kind of theory does one teach filmmakers or film students who are becoming filmmakers, why would you not be able to make that transition from a development of feminist theory through to a development of filmmaking and forms of filmmaking, because film language has to be a male dominant language to start with.

NB: No, I don't believe that at all. Mulvey was all wrong, particularly with her idea that there was another language. It's like music, Serialism is all wrong because there is a socially dominant – I don't think it's necessarily biological, though it may have something to do with it, resonant bodies and so on - but there is a socially dominant musical system(s), let's say modality, tonality if you like, which is how people communicate and relate to music and the idea that one can abolish that or that there is any point to abolishing it, is just stupid. Mulvey's idea in *Riddles of the Sphinx* (1997) that one can abolish, as it were, the common language of the spatial relations of bodies, the things I theorised, originally to criticise them, but in point of fact I think the ultimate result of the work is not there and I'm glad about that. My book *Life to those Shadows* (1990) was about that, how one can go back to this 'primitive chaos' and find models for an alternative cinema. It's the same error as Mulvey's basically, which is somehow about how we're going to have to abolish the reverse field because it's patriarchal, the male gaze and that kind of thing. No, that's nonsense. My friend Jennifer Hammett, who I have a tremendous admiration for, has written a fundamental, philosophical critique of this whole critique of representation, the feminist critique of representation. It appeared in 1997 in *Cinema Journal*, it's called *The Ideological Impediment: Feminism and Film Theory*. She's a philosopher and it's an absolutely rigorous demolition of that whole thing and what she finally says is what feminist cinema needs is new contents, not new forms, not a new language in any case. I agree absolutely and that's what I did in so far as I was teaching students who had it in the back of their minds they're going to make movies. I was teaching feminist theory if you like – in other words what was really going on in all these movies, most of it detrimental to women, some of it not, and how to distinguish between the two and things like that. Hopefully, if they went on to make films, and a few of them did and most of them who did took this into account, because they were mostly women, because women were the most sensitive to what I was on about, who could understand it really. Some of the men tried to and pretended to, but it was very hard and I understand that - they have a different experience in relation to films, whereas women were not on the whole cinephiles you see. So they were able to go on and some of them have been making really very interesting films about the women who are around them and things like that. I'm talking about working class women actually. I would have liked to have had an opportunity to do that kind of work with production students. I've completely lost this tendency to setting forth prescriptive garbage, as I was once accused in print of doing by somebody in England, because I do think that basically the language is a common language, It's like an actual language and I don't believe at all, not for one second, in any kind of theoretical rethinking, global theoretical rethinking of 'the language' if you like. Because that's already been done by other video clips we see, this is going on all the time. Every music video you see now is a kind of implementation of all the critiques of continuity and illusory space – so who cares – it's obviously of no relevance whatsoever.

CM: I think it was Deleuze who said that our mistake is that in fact film is not a language and therefore in his notion of becoming, there is still a perspective of a consciousness which can go in a direction yet unknown.

NB: Film is not a language, that's absolutely correct. Film is a much more complicated affair than a language, but it involves languages, but nonetheless which have to be shared in common by the masses if you like because they're the only people worth reaching. Anyone who just wants to reach a few people I don't want to talk to, I want to talk to people who hope their stuff can be shown on television, because that's a fundamental criteria and therefore readable as it were in the Barthian sense – readability is not predicated on indeed a simple linguistic model, I've always said it was a question of modes of representation, but there is a shared mode of representation today, which is no longer that of 1905, or even that of 1935 as a matter of fact, because you show students black and white films and they don't understand them any more, literally – and not to speak of silent films. There is this problem of what I would call communicability or readability, I think the Barthian term is very well chosen and obviously it was a bad object for him ultimately, but who cares. It was an interesting concept and a very good distinction and therefore I am a great defender of readability, absolutely for me it is a basic thing. Well from that point on, how to be readable? It's something that an intelligent student will learn in any good film school, I'm sure we both agree with that. Beyond that, the ideal film school seems to me a place where indeed they are learning things which are in appearance divorced from film in a funny way.

I went to IDHEC the very first year after it opened, after they chased the communists out, in 1952. I remember at the time being very taken aback by this because we had courses on literature, history, art and music which had nothing to do with film. People were essentially not talking about cinema and I thought it was ridiculous, what are they on about? Whatever these courses were worth, I expect they weren't worth much because they were academic university teaching, but I certainly would say today, I could make an educational programme out of what seems to me to be necessary - political economy, indeed feminist literary history– I mean a whole continent of feminist work that is not of the theoretical kind, it wouldn't be Judith Butler, it would be as I say Susan Gubar and Sandra Gilbert and people like that. Susan McClary's book on *Carmen* (1992), this is really something in which one begins to understand how all this works, has worked and is working. Terry Eagleton obviously– *The Aesthetics of Ideology*, no, *The Ideology of the Aesthetic* (1990), interesting slip! There's a lot of different directions where it seems to me that knowledge has been produced that should be useful to a filmmaker, but on the other hand they should learn how to make readable films then they do with that what they want. Somebody who gets up and says the readable film is a bad object, which is what I was doing to you guys in the 1970s as you will recall; there was a strong lean toward the avant-garde and reading readable films as though they were unreadable, so that's obviously just completely wrong-headed and hopefully nobody does that today. Though I am sad to see that there is a tendency to use my work in that direction, I find it absolutely appalling; I don't know what to think about it. For example, people will tend to show *Correction Please: or How We Got into Pictures* (1979) but nobody seems to be reading *Life to Those Shadows* (1990). I see the curricula in the universities on the net, it's like the tail is wagging the dog there again, and it's completely crazy, meaningless.

CM: Actually I think there's an interesting bit of space opening up in the UK at the moment and in some other countries, for instance Finland, where universities are allowing and in some instances encouraging research by practice, though mostly they are tagged 'practice-based research' which is more containable within the general milieu of Media Studies and safer. There are a lot of Universities beginning to do doctorates in practice and it's a space where interrogative practice can be funded.

NB: Can you give me an example because I'm not sure I understand?

CM: For instance I'm doing a PhD part-time [completed May 2009], back at the Royal College of Art where the process can be called PhD by Practice because of the nature of the institution. These PhDs are 50 per cent theory and 50 per cent practice. But also conferences are developing, like *BEYOND, the Theory of Practice*, which I know is a small drop in the ocean but people are being able to get research grants to actually make films or to make art practices, not just to write. You might not like that idea.

NB: We do it here. I had a student who did a Masters on witchcraft and an amazing film actually, which was an hour in a prison with witches in the Middle Ages – they found a prison where they actually kept them and it's an extraordinary thing. He wrote at the same time a feminist essay.

CM: All I'm saying to you is there is a new space opening up where it is possible to do work at an advanced level now. People are using, or could use, the expansion in education of Media Studies, which is not without problems of course, but it is opening up again, in a sense a bit like it was thirty years ago, where only a few film schools were actually investigating ideas through practice – critical practice, dialectical practice, and engaging representation-ally with the social world. I will tell you more later about the Film Academy that I'm opening up which only has Doctoral students; it doesn't have under-graduate students, it doesn't take MA students – it will only take students who are committed to a certain development.[8]

NB: That's good.

CM: That aside for a moment, I want to re-engage you with this question of the development of what might appear to be false consciousness and what I am referring to as collective consciousness. I've gone back to Durkheim to look at his notion of the 'conscience collectif', in a sense running parallel with Marx and instead of religion one could substitute ideology. One of the fundamental things that you talked about many years ago was this notion of a diegetic space and that's something that if I were you I would now be very unhappy about the way it has been taken up in film schools and as you mentioned, on the internet as part of the curriculum, I think in a similar way that they look at your practice without your theory. The notion of diegesis is now being taught as simply either on-screen and off-screen space, or, what is internal to the narrative and what is external to it.

NB: What's important about that?

CM: What's important is that the correct definition of diegesis is not being taught, which I think is something you'll still be interested in. It relates to your question of understanding what really goes on in the world, this acces-sibility that you're talking about for a television audience, the space between the social world and the object itself. If one considers the diegetic space as the mental referent, the false world created within the frame, it has every-thing to do with how the reader understands the world through the film given to them. This is your explanation to me thirty years ago, which I have not forgotten.

NB: It's through Metz, its nothing to do with me.

CM: It may be Metz but you introduced it to us. It seems to me that if one is opening up the space of collective consciousness then there is a problem. There is a difficulty in this notion of a mass ideology, if you like, of freeing the subject/object into some notion of a 'real world' of consciousness. Given the hegemonic position of representation now, that people are born into the world where everything is given to them as a fact which is represented to them before their experiences in the world.

NB: That's right.

CM: It's a kind of basic Walter Benjamin and John Berger perspective that has become so sophisticated in the last 20 years, so pluralistic and used by both the left and the establishment right that makes me, in a theoretical or philosophical sense, go back to the question of where is the consciousness of the viewer in understanding their own position within the world when it has been primarily given to them by representation? And that's why I go back to collective consciousness. Look, for example, at the Mass Observation movement around the 1940s. They set out to document and photograph the working class; they photographed them with, in my view, a mistaken goodwill intention but then the statistics were used, amongst other things, for advertising purposes. This is where the diegetic space is important. It is a representational space on the one hand and a collective consciousness, which may not be just a representational space, on the other. The two of them work together, this is the problem. One could talk about false consciousness, but that's very unfashionable, so it's going back to this subject/object question of where is the subject in the world and how can one confidently actually ascribe meanings and readings to a mass television audience as you have suggested we ought to be doing?

NB: It's totally impossible. I'm not sure, but I feel that, how can I say, one has to realise when one is tilting at windmills. Look, *PlayStation* constructs a certain relationship to the self and to visual representations, very clearly as far as I can tell and what you have is a subjected generation of young men, even young women, though fortunately a little less and that's an interesting and important distinction. I think that one is really up against something that you can't do anything about and I understand now what you're saying about the significance of the confusion over diegesis. That's obviously because in a certain sense, it's 'all there is I see', it's this whole idea that basically 'dying is leaving the frame'. So, in a way oddly enough, it's a sort of cinephile vision which has become practically a universal reality. Like this idea that the world exists inside that little box, a world which is obviously not the real world – as Octave Mannoni theorised at one point – 'Je sais bien, mais quand même' [I know, but anyway] (1969: 9–33) – but at the same time it's the only one that matters and indeed that the isolation of it from any kind of larger imagination, which you were defining quite well there, I can't do it as well. The problem is that these are symptoms, symptons of something else, they are not like phenomena in themselves okay, that's where Marshall McLuhan was wrong. McLuhan has become fashionable again I guess, at least here – I don't know if he is elsewhere, but because everything he said seems to be happening. Of course it's true, but not for the reasons I think he believed you see, all that is happening is because of the universal merchandising and so on, the technological developments are in a sense a consequence also of the general production of the 'individual as commodity' I suppose, and individual consciousness itself has become commodity hasn't it? They seem to be trying to recreate a sort of eighteenth-century free electrons idea of the individual being this sort of Brownian movement in society. But obviously this is a fundamental economic requirement of this crazy flight forward, this blind accumulation, this whole idea that basically only hurtling forward with more and more things, more and more money, more and more and more and more, we're going to, I don't know, not die – I'm not sure what the fundamental psychoanalytical motivation is but it's obviously absolutely terrifying and it's something which hopefully the African countries will begin to realise as they are realising now. Many people in Africa realise there is something wrong, that they're being drawn into something which doesn't concern them.

CM: They didn't realise it during the development of Christianity did they? That's why I'm going back to Durkheim where the parallel would have been the missionaries.

NB: Absolutely. That's absolutely correct. But as I say again – you see if the feeling that my hostility, or at least my reticence before this whole problematic that you're representing here in a way is that for me the struggle to modify or to get people to think about modifying representations within this context is just a lost thing ahead of time. Only by modifying the context in some fundamental way, I mean whether people are going to do this or whether the actual logic of the system itself is not going to finally cause such a crisis that it will have to be modified. I don't know, but what is sure it seems to me is that in a way people will say the only thing to do is swing with it, they're certainly not entirely wrong, though even that, I feel, can only have some kind of marginal effect. The whole area is so much in the hands of the machine you see that I feel that to get involved with it, there are all sorts of reasons to do so, it's fun, you can make a lot of money okay, but to get involved in it because one wants to contribute to trying to stop this whole thing, this I honestly think is pure illusion today. I can't help it. I'm therefore trying to teach this to people. It is certainly important though in a film school to bring in other areas to enrich students politically and culturally with things they probably didn't get elsewhere.

CM: I will say that I partly agree and partly disagree with you. This is where I disagree. In a paper I gave a few years ago which was a critique of

Postmodernism within post-biological representation, I used the preferential term 'contextualism' and it is something that I teach within scriptwriting theory and practice today. I examine the notion of what I call the trialectic, which is form, content, context. There's nothing mystifying about that, but it's a triangular model rather than a binary model and in that respect enables rather than restricts and I believe facilitates the continued and progressive use of form. But I also think that what you're saying is right, I do agree with you in as much as it is within the realm of the other subjects where the work needs to take place.

NB: It can certainly make more interesting films than are being made today, yes absolutely 100 per cent.

CM: Not just more interesting, more politically relevant and ones which engage with the areas you're talking about but still engage with representation in cinema.

NB: Yes absolutely, but one has to be very prudent to say the least about the illusions one has for the political efficacy or social efficacy of any such films, because 90 per cent of any such films are going to be addressing themselves to the already converted, as we know and I think this is a fundamental problem and even the idea of introducing radical ideas into TV series, which I'm all for – anyone who has tried to do this I'm completely in sympathy with. At the same time I think we've reached the stage where it going to be you know, a conversation piece for certain journals. In 1980 there was a series on American television called *Centenary* – do you know about this?

CM: No.

NB: It's absolutely amazing; I saw bits of it in Minneapolis. It was a history of the United States from the point of view of Howard Zinn[9] basically. It was filmed in a little town in the Rockies or somewhere. It was the history of capitalism, it was just incredible from beginning to end. Okay, it came and it went and has never showed again and there it is. Whatever the form, there was an adequate form to what it was talking about and obviously what it was talking about was totally mind-blowing in the American context. But it was part of the whole flow of information we get.

CM: Of course it came and it went, you wanted it to stick, but it's got to go as soon as it comes.

NB: What I mean is it made no impact of any kind, hardly anyone noticed it.

CM: You noticed.

NB: A woman did the work on the impact, it was brought in by a scholar who had done research on it and clearly this discourse was inaudible, precisely because of the American context and there is no, how should I say, political relay, the only way consciousness raising makes any impact is in struggle. It's in strikes, it's in struggle, whatever the form it may take. And obviously film can have eventually some kind of role in this; one could perhaps say that something like *The Day After* (1983), that TV thing on American television about the consequences of an atomic war, I think that probably did, because it was made at a time when there was a rather strong campaign around these questions in America. It took place in this general movement if you like, why not. But there's the question of the form that was used. It's interesting, I wrote an article somewhere – I think I wrote a letter to *Time Out* because somebody had trashed it and I said you don't understand, this thing is important and somebody else wrote 'who is this liberal wimp Noel Burch who dares to defend this piece of vulgar trash?', well because we were still in a period where people thought that things had to be artistically innovative to be politically impacting.

CM: These are two different issues Noel, one at the barricades – no problem with that, vitally important to be there and at that moment with that conjuncture there will be radical ideology and aesthetics again, I have no doubt about that. However, while not at the barricades, where we spend most of our lives, I suggest there is still an area of work to be done, which in a sense because it's not a question of elitism or populism, it's perhaps, I don't know, scientific research or whatever you want to call it, but therefore surely must be done and if we do not understand mass consciousness then that work is vital.

NB: I'm quite sure that's true, whether it can be done with actual films or visual products possibly, but I do say that the experiments or experiences I have observed or encountered in this respect have not been terribly convincing. But okay why not, certainly I have no problem about, for example, how today history is often taught using films. Well why not, that's obviously one approach, certainly to the history of mentalities and so on, in fact it's almost essential to use films if one wants to understand really what was going on in peoples minds in the 1930s.

CM: I seem to recall, I think it was you who wrote an article on the difference between the avant-garde and the vanguard (1976: 52–63) and you certainly defined a difference between the two and described what happened to the vanguard. So why shouldn't those two things, both practically and intellectually, exist simultaneously and be a proposition towards a new vanguard?

NB: Why shouldn't they, obviously not. I mean they exist anyway, I suppose they must exist or they can exist. Although you said at one point in your presentation that France was ahead, that's absolutely untrue. The whole question of avant-garde practice as political practice was an entirely British thing and it became somewhat an American thing later on, but it was never here in France, except obviously with Godard, but he was practically alone you understand. I'm serious about this people here who made and still make films today of an explicitly political content are totally allergic to avant-gardism.

CM: What about to Duchamp and to Leger?

NB: We're talking about other periods; I'm talking about the 1970s. Duchamp went to America and Leger was not making political films. He was a communist painter and his painting later on became indeed committed art, but that's another period. The whole question of avant-gardism of the 1920s is a completely different matter in my opinion. I'm talking about the 1970s and an attempt to repeat all that in this funny way. I had a point I wanted to make there.

CM: It wasn't the French...

NB: Absolutely not and I think that even today, even more so today, I know quite a few people slugging away in the shadows producing little documentary films, often quite interesting and informative and useful and often with somehow innovative forms I suppose, but there has never been this idea among those people, and the only person who keeps doing that is Godard – who keeps producing these films which become more and obscure and totally incomprehensible I find, I've stopped watching them frankly. Okay, but he's a sort of a voice from the past, highly respected and all that. But it was an English thing essentially and I must say sometimes I wonder why, I've often tried to work that out. I had a certain role perhaps in that brief period I was in England at the RCA and so on, but obviously it was an ongoing thing – Screen and all that, which I had nothing to do with at all, I didn't understand a word of that at the time. So there was this British thing and okay it's interesting, but

I think that here it was actually never the case and the documentarists, there are still many and they're all political in some way or another, a lot of them are in any case, they are concerned with readable films, the problem was never raised in those terms and the whole problematics of *Cinétique*[10] and all that washed over that world without leaving a trace you see.

CM: I don't think it's an issue of readability and non-readability. The main point is to do with the accessibility point at which the people that you are talking about have indeed real access to that knowledge, because that knowledge cannot simply be given to them – because of the space they already inhabit.

NB: Okay I agree. This is obviously true but the problem is again this cannot be broken down with the tools which are at the disposal of the filmmaker. The filmmaker is dealing with a given, which is intangible, in my opinion absolutely intangible and the idea of trying to come up against it, somehow attempting to deal with it fertilely, to modify a perception of the world let us say, which is implicit in that one we were just talking about. This is I think an undertaking that is absolutely doomed to failure. I guess that in a way is the bottom line. This is a glass wall if you like, there's nothing to do about it, absolutely nothing. One cannot do anything about it, one can obviously hope to modify the context and by modifying the context, which is what we mean when we speak of revolution, whatever form that may take. Once you've done that then indeed I assume - it's my assumption, that possibly will reappear questions such as those that were raised by the Russians in the 1920s, because for me there remains a kind of exemplarily moment of rethinking representation and as I say perhaps Cuba in the 1960s, I don't know much about it, but otherwise no, it's a bloody waste of time. We can hope that individuals can seek out individual solutions and maybe do innovative work in terms of the fact that they've studied the things that they wanted to study in the ideal film school. But this innovative work will be immediately sucked into the mass, or else it will never be seen. One or the other and that's it.

CM: If one continued along that dystopic view, or even a utopian one that, as you say is still about struggle, then come near to some form of radical social change taking place, filmmakers might be unable to produce another ideological context.

NB: You mean your students' grandchildren!

CM: It could be a real problem, this is why I disagree with you – it's a minor but major disagreement. My position is that one has to actually continue that representational struggle because at the same time as working towards a reformed context in society, a social context, then if the work wasn't continuing to be done on a formal or representational basis, there is no way at that moment that anyone is going to come along and be another Eisenstein or a Vertov. It's too late, that's what's too late from my side of the fence because we are so sucked into a representational belief system that we will not know how to react in that situation. Therefore one has to continuously redefine.

NB: I certainly would agree with that, I just do feel that I think its pie-in-sky this assumption that the cake that one aspires to is just around the corner, I think that in a way, what is the expression – one has to teach people to live in a dangerous world, hostile to any kind of progressive ideas. Which is why we sort of withdraw into little communities and so on, which is obviously what we're seeing all the time, is that it's a kind of mode of survival and it's perfectly understandable, it drives me mad, it infuriates me. But unfortunately all I know how to react with is anger. Oh, one can always hope that the ten students one is teaching this year will somehow or other receive the good word and go out and spread it. I guess one ought to be quite tolerant of the aspirations of most of the young – to just get on with it you know. Well, I'm not very tolerant of that and it's one of the reasons I had to get out of teaching, I was glad to get out of teaching because it's difficult to be telling people come on, you're just barking up the wrong tree. What can you do, again it's a context. There are certain moments – one can look at Chávez in Venezuela and so on and say it's possible to resist up to a point maybe and that gives one some small bit of hope, but its very remote.

CM: On that point I totally agree with you and it was three years ago when I said I can't teach undergraduate students anymore, because I'm not prepared to teach people who don't want to be taught and they shouldn't have been on this course in the first place.

NB: That's exactly the case. I don't know, I got into that actually. I structured my teaching in such a way, I had an amazingly privileged situation which was that I was teaching three undergraduate courses and one graduate seminar each week, all to the same students so they would sometimes be in the same classroom and we'd change classes, but they wouldn't change rooms. I also managed to get it to be all year round; they put us on a semester system to be in tune with Europe but I and other teachers just said fuck that and we divided the course into an arbitrary two parts. So for a year I had these students for ten hours a week, plus I had them next year for another few hours in a Masters class, and this was like brainwashing, because it was all the same; it was all gender in various ways, gender in the silent German cinema, gender and orientalism in French and American cinema and gender in six great Hollywood authors, this was all I taught. At Christmas time they had to write this exam and nobody had understood anything, there was nothing, it was really terrifying. But by Spring the penny had dropped and I had the most amazing papers. It's very rare that anyone can do that, it was because I was this honcho so I was able to impose this thing, nobody said anything, they just let me off. It's very permissive here in the University, if you have tenure – and you have tenure as soon as you're appointed to a full-time post – you do what you want, it's not like anything at all in England.

CM: I'm in Wales.

NB: I know, but it's all the same isn't it – you have these controls, but here there's nothing like that. So I just did this brainwashing, it took a couple of years and then it began to tick and I had only two people in my Masters class in the first couple of years and suddenly I began having twenty or thirty and it was very moving actually and they got into the thing and began doing really extraordinary work, which I showed to my friend Geneviève Sellier who teaches at the University of Caen which is a very middle-class university and she said Jesus if I had papers half this quality I'd be happy. She was going to get appointed at Lille after I left but she's a very strong woman and that doesn't go down well at places like that... So anyhow, these were undergraduates, they'd already had a year of bullshit from people talking about the history of the lap dissolve or whatever and so it took a while to get rid of that, but once you got rid of that, they were really available. I wasn't the only teacher there but on the whole they had me and I was the only one they cared about because the others were mediocre.

CM: I've been fortunate to be able to have, on a smaller basis, a similar relationship with filmmaking practice students, whose work I think has been, you know some of it has been very fine, they've been able to produce in the same way that the essays you're talking about, in a sense the films are the essays – very few and far between, not very many of them, but now I'm excited because I'm trying to put this film school together, which as I said only has a maximum of twenty students per year in it and who will be able to work within the context of the subject of the film they are making – for example, at the University there are Schools of Criminology, Law, Business

Studies – all as Schools in their own right. The idea is that the two tutors of each doctoral student should represent the form and content of each film, one to be a film professor, the other – if they're interested in say crime film, I want the other tutor to be a criminologist, not a film historian, so one can work with Criminology and Filmmaking or Law and Filmmaking or Business Studies and Filmmaking for producers.

NB: Absolutely, that I think is 100 per cent spot on.

Paris, October 2003

BIBLIOGRAPHY

Burch, N. (1973) *Theory of Film Practice*. London: Martin Secker and Warburg.
_____ (1976) 'Avant-garde or Vanguard', *Afterimage*, 6, Summer, 52–63.
_____ (1990) *Life to Those Shadows*. Berkeley and Los Angeles: University of California Press.
_____ (2007) *De la Beauté des Latrines*. Paris: Éditions l'Harmattan.
Burch, N and G. Sellier (1996) *La Drôle de Guerre des Sexes du Cinéma Français: 1930–1956*. Paris: Editions Nathan.
Coquillat, M. (1982) *La Poétique du Mâle*. Paris: Gallimard.
Eagleton, T. (1990) *The Ideology of the Aesthetic*. Oxford: Blackwell.
_____ (1996) *The Illusions of Postmodernism*. Oxford: Blackwell.
_____ (2003) *After Theory*. London: Allen Lane Penguin.
Fielder, L. (1960) *Love and Death in the American Novel*. New York: Criterion.
Gubar, S. and S. Gilbert (1979) *The Madwoman in the Attic: The Woman Writer and the 19th-Century Literary Imagination*. New Haven: Yale University Press.
_____ (1988) *The War of the Words*, Volume I of *No Man's Land: The Place of the Woman Writer in the Twentieth Century*. Haven: Yale University Press.
_____ (1989) *Sexchanges*, Volume II of *No Man's Land: The Place of the Woman Writer in the Twentieth Century*. New Haven: Yale University Press.
_____ (1994) *Letters from the Front*, Volume III of *No Man's Land: The Place of the Woman Writer in the Twentieth Century*. New Haven: Yale University Press.
Hammett, J. (1997) 'The Ideological Impediment: Feminism and Film Theory', *Cinema Journal*, Winter, 36, 2, 85–99.
Lasch, C. (1979) *The Culture of Narcissism*. New York: Norton.
Mannoni, O, (1969) *Clefs pour l'imaginaire ou l'Autre Scène* (Keys to the Imagination or the Other Stage). Paris: Seuil.
McClary, S. (1992) *Georges Bizet: Carmen*. Cambridge: Cambridge Opera Handbooks.
Modleski, T. (1988) *The Women Who Knew Too Much: Hitchcock and Feminist Theory*. New York: Methuen.
Monbiot, G. (2003) *The Age of Consent*. London: Flamingo.

New York Times available at http://www.nytimes.com/. (Accessed: 12 April 2010).

Sartre, J. P. (1981) *The Family Idiot: Gustave Flaubert, 1821–1857.* Chicago: University of Chicago Press.

Sekula, A. (1999) *Fish Story* [Photographs]. Seattle: Henry Art Gallery.

Sellier, G. (2005) *La Nouvelle Vague: Un Cinéma au Masculin Singulier.* Paris: CNRS.

Sollers, P. (1984) *Femmes.* Paris: France Loisirs.

Truthout available at http://www,truthout.org/. (Accessed: 12 April 2010).

USA Today available at http://www.usatoday.com/. (Accessed: 12 April 2010).

Zinn, H. (1980) *A People's History of the United States.* New York: Harper Collins.

FILMOGRAPHY

Bowling for Columbine (2002) Directed by Michael Moore [DVD]. Amazon: Warner Home Video.

Buffy the Vampire Slayer (1997-2003) [DVD]. Amazon: WB Television Network.

Correction Please: or How We Got into Pictures (1979) Directed by Noel Burch [Film]. London: Concord Films.

Cuba: Entre Chien et Louve (*Cuba: Mothers and Machos*, 1997) Directed by Noel Burch and Michele Larue [Beta SP]. Paris: Kanpai Distribution.

Day After, The (1983) Directed by Nicholas Meyer [DVD]. Amazon: MGM.

Festen (1998) Directed by Thomas Vinterberg [DVD]. Amazon: Universal Studios.

Gummo (1997) Directed by Harmony Korine [DVD]. Amazon: New Line Home Video.

Idiots, The (1998) Directed by Lars von Trier [DVD]. Amazon: Zentropa.

JUSTINE, by the Marquis de Sade (1976) Directed by Stewart Mackinnon [DVD]. London: Film Work Group.

Le Fils (*The Son*, 2002) Directed by Jean-Pierre and Luc Dardenne [DVD]. Amazon: New Yorker Video.

Mars Attacks (1996) Directed by Tim Burton [DVD]. Amazon: Warner Home Video.

Nurse Betty (2000) Directed by Neil LaBute [DVD]. Amazon: Columbia/Tristar Home.

Passion of Joan of Arc, The (1928) Directed by Carl Dreyer [DVD]. Amazon: Criterion Collection.

Pi (1998) Directed by Darren Aronofsky [DVD]. Amazon: Artisan.

Riddles of the Sphinx (1997) Direceted by Laura Mulvey and Peter Wollen [DVD]. London: Mulvey.

Scary Movie (2000) Directed by Keenen Ivory Wayans [DVD]. Amazon:

Scream (1996) Directed by Wes Craven [DVD]. Amazon: Dimension.

Sentimental Journey: Refuzniks USA (1994) Directed by Noel Burch [Video]. Paris: Doc & Co.

Signs and Wonders (2000) Directed by Jonathan Nossiter [DVD]. Amazon: Strand Releasing Home Video.

Starship Troopers (1997) Directed by Paul Verhoven [DVD]. Amazon: Columbia/Tristar Home Video.

Taxi Driver (1976) Directed by Martin Scorsese [DVD]. Amazon: Columbia/Tristar Home Video.

Taxi Parisien (2002) produced by Jacques Bidou [Video]. Paris: FR3.

Ten (*10*, 2002) Directed by Abbas Kiarostami [DVD]. Amazon: Zeitgeist Films.

There's Something About Mary (1998) Directed by Bobby and Peter Farrelly [DVD]. Amazon: 20th Century Fox.

Une Part du Ciel (2002) Directed by Bénédicte Liénard [DVD]. Amazon: Seven7.

Vendredi Soir (*Friday Night*, 2002) Directed by Claire Denis [DVD]. Amazon: Tartan Video.

Very Bad Things (1998) Directed by Peter Berg [DVD]. Amazon: Bridge Entertainment.

Year of the Bodyguard (1981) Directed by Noel Burch [Video]. London: Channel Four.

NOTES

1   Institut des Hautes Études Cinématographiques

2   École Nationale Supérieure des Métiers de l'Image et du Son. FEMIS stands for Fondation Européenne pour les Métiers de l'Image et du Son

3   ARTE (Association Relative à la Télévision Européenne) is a European Franco-German TV channel dedicated to culture and the arts.

4   The French regulation that protects and encourages indigenous culture against international competing commercial interests. For more information see http://www.understandfrance.org/France/FrenchMovies.html#ancre1228089 (accessed 10 August 2008).

5   'Woman Is the Future of Man' (Louis Aragon in the poem 'Le fou d'Elsa' (1963). It became a famous expression through the French singer Jean Ferrat's song of the same title).

6   Rachilde was the *nom de plume* of Marguerite Vallette-Eymery (1860–1953), considered to be a pioneer of anti-realist drama and a participant in the Decadent movement (associated with such writers as Charles Baudelaire and Oscar Wilde), regarded by some as a transition between Romanticism and Modernism.

7   'Desire in Narrative' in *Alice Doesn't: Feminism, Semiotics, Cinema* (1984).

8   The Film Academy was active between 2003 and 2007 and was the film theory and practice base for innovative doctoral work. However, the university could not maintain the Academy on PhD work alone and it developed some interesting Masters programmes including the MA in Film Producing and Business Management, a collaboration between the Film Academy and the Business School at the University of Glamorgan. In 2007 the Academy merged with the new Cardiff School of Creative and Cultural Industries.

9   An American historian, political scientist, activist and playwright, best known as author of *A People's History of the United States* (1980).

10 The main 1970s French film magazine to propose a modernist counter-cinema.

INDEX